"*Where*
Mormonism
Meets Biblical
Christianity
Face to Face"

"Where Mormonism *Meets* Biblical Christianity *Face to Face"*

An 'A to Z' doctrinal
comparative between
Mormonism and
biblical Christianity

Shawn Aaron McCraney

New York ▪ 2011

Published by Alathea Press, New York, NY.
First edition, December 2011.

2015 2014 2013 2012 2011 6 5 4 3 2 1

To order books or inquire about group sales, contact the distributor:

Alathea Ministries, Inc.
4760 Highland Drive #515
Salt Lake City, UT 84117

Library of Congress Cataloging-in-Publication Data
McCraney, Shawn Aaron, 1961-
Includes some biographical references.
Where Mormonism Meets Biblical Christianity
Face to Face/Shawn Aaron McCraney
LCCN:
ISBN 978-0-615-56963-5
1. Mormonism 2. Christianity 3. Jesus Christp
McCraney. Shawn Aaron. IV Title.

Printed in the United States of America

Contents

Acknowledgments

In late 2005 I was invited to host a live, call-in television program out of what we called "the Mecca of Mormonism," Salt Lake City, Utah. On Tuesday night, March 7th of 2006, this simple invitation became a frightening reality. At exactly 8pm mountain standard time, a camera man pointed at me and clearing my throat I feebly stated, *"Welcome to Heart of the Matter. I'm Shawn McCraney."* We thank the living God of heaven and earth for the harvest of souls this simple invitation has produced over the years. The following are the topical, alphabetical teachings from the programs we aired in 2010.

I would more than prove myself an idiot if I didn't take a moment and thank all the many people involved in not only getting *"Heart of the Matter"* out on the television airwaves, but in keeping it alive and going over the years. Without them, their support, and their contributions large and small, we would not have been able to produce this book or the hundreds of hours of recorded television information comparing Mormonism with Biblical Christianity. So, thank you …

Dr. Charles Stanley; Cynthia and Dennis; Venessa; Michelle and Denny Ermel; Pat Oppenshaw; Connie and Spence Whitney; Kevin and Kelly Kennington; Marcus Maher; Micah Bailey (and sons); Calvary Chapel of Costa Mesa, California, (most notably Pastor Chuck Smith, Pastor Brian Broderson, and my personal mentor Carl Westerlund); Micah Coleman (who went to live with the Lord); the legendary pioneer to the LDS, Sandra Tanner; Andy Casper, my dear friend Roger (and Julisa) Workman; Jed; Pastor Travis Mitchell; Pastor Scott McKinney; the

Roberts family, including Jeremy, Aimee, Emma, Calvin, and Sophia (you are the best); Dennis and Jeannie Glassburn; Lucy and Corey Eakins; Dave and Nancy Bontempo; Margaret and Katherine; Kevin Bradford; Dave and Janet (and family); Millie the streetwalker and Dave, Brandon and Kara (and their handsome son Eli); Glenn and Kathy; Nathan Doubleday; Stan Felder; Jamie and Laura S.; Lauran B.; the entire Derrick and Denita Webster family, including Blake, Tiff, and Joycelyn; Brandi, Krystal, Chance, and Kelsie – (you've been lifesavers); Merle Hodel; Kathy-Maggie; Linda Cassidy; Kasey and Mark; Mary Ellen and Janet; Nancy Allen and Ken; Robert Verdin; Reed, Ken and Dave; Anthony; the Dave and Julie Nelson family; Natalie Murdock; Rich and Ellen Broggi (Thank you! Thank you!); Russ East; Rusty and Barb; Steve and Venessa (love you guys); Jeff and Joan Shreeve; Marinetta (one of the greatest women to ever walk the face of the earth); my dear friend Walt; Tony Wolf and his skills; and any and all who have supported Alathea Ministries through prayer, insights, or financial contributions. We also thank those of you who have shared "Heart of the Matter" with friends, family, co-workers or other LDS family and friends; to Andrew, our dear and selfless friend out of Norway who got us out all over YouTube by his own time, volition, and dime; to my wonderful daughters, Mallory, Cassidy, and Delaney who, for years, accommodated my absence and gave up much of their lives to see the program air live each week; for Lazer Floyd, my first and only grandchild (to date) and the light and joy he brings to my aging heart; to Niklas, his talented and devoted Pappa; to Mary Marguerite, the wife of my youth who, beyond anyone's comprehension, sacrificed her all so this work could move forward; and to my Lord, Savior, and King, Jesus Christ, for saving a wretch like me – and then giving me a voice and chance to share His love and glorious gift of salvation with others.

All glory and honor to God Almighty.

Why should those who are not of our faith be so opposed to us? They say we have a false doctrine. But is it false? Have they proved it to be so? We invite a comparison of the principles we believe in with those taught by Jesus Christ and His disciples.

–LDS Apostle Anthon H. Lund,
LDS Conference Report,
April 1905, page 14

Introduction

From almost the onset of Mormonism, the faith has disclaimed, renounced, and even vilified Christianity. Back in a day when great Christian men like D.L. Moody were alive and teaching God's word here on earth, LDS Church President John Taylor said (*Journal of Discourses* 13:225):

> What does the Christian world know about God? Nothing; yet these very men assume the right and power to tell others what they shall not believe in. Why so far as the things of God are concerned, they are the veriest of fools; they know neither God nor the things of God

And yet today, one of Mormonism's most persistent claims in print, over airwaves, and online is, "*We're Christians, too.*"

How can we tell? What makes a person or group Christian? Is it in the name they use? Couldn't be. Even Jesus said (Matthew 7:21), *"Not all that say Lord, Lord will enter the Kingdom of Heaven."* Can we identify Christians by the good works they do? Impossible. There are far too many organizations on earth that don't even believe in the divinity of Jesus Christ that do many, many wonderful good works; so works alone certainly can't be the deciding factor. Hmmmmm?

Maybe we could say that a Christian is someone who agrees with, and attempts to follow, the Christian manual known as the Bible. Hey, that's getting closer to a working definition, isn't it?

A true Christian is someone who reads and trusts what the Christian manual says.

I like this definition. Oh, sure, we can argue the fine points about what the Christian manual says. There will certainly be differences so long as there are two thinking people walking around on this earth. But to the whole of Christianity these differences are not deal breakers. Why? Because the core issues – "Who Jesus is" (God); "How was He born?" (of a virgin); "How did He live?" (perfectly); "How did He die?" (on the cross); "Was He resurrected?" (yes); "How are we saved?" (by grace through faith); and, "Is His Word trustworthy?" (yes) – are all agreed upon by those who truly can lay claim to the title Christian.

So that is what this book is about: comparing and contrasting the manual embraced and endorsed by genuine Christians (the Bible) with what the members of the Mormon Church claim and support (a whole lot more).

When you're through reading, maybe you can say whether Mormonism is Christian or not.

To the reader:

The contents of this book are extracts from a year of weekly television programs where we compared and contrasted Mormonism with Biblical Christianity. I have purposely edited them minimally for readability. As a result, each reading may take a little more effort on your part to try and understand the angle I took to illustrate the conflicts and differences between the two sides relating to the topic at hand. I offer no apology for this approach but instead am presenting what I consider my true heart and mind on the topics discussed.

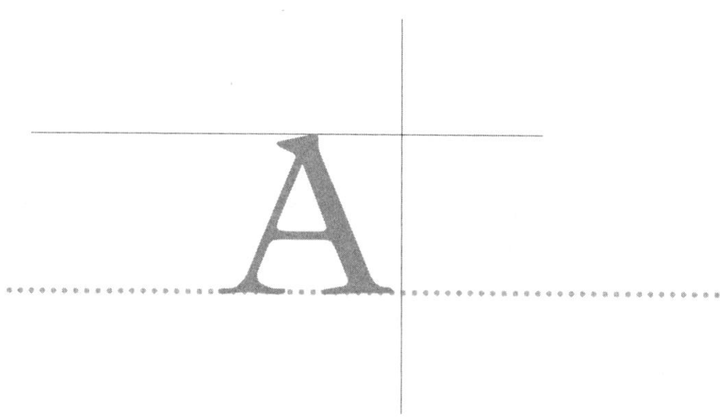

"If the LDS teaching on the Fall is correct, you know, about it being a 'good thing and requisite for God's plan of salvation to be put into effect,' I don't understand why Satan chose to tempt them to fall in the first place. It would have been more to his diabolical purposes to have just left them alone."

Adam & Eve

Interestingly enough, the Bible doesn't really say all that much about Adam and Eve. There are maybe 30 verses that speak of them directly and another twenty or so that speak of them inferentially.

What do we, as Bible-believing Christians, say about Adam and Eve? We say what the Word says:

> Genesis 2:7. *And the LORD God formed man of the dust of the ground, and breathed into his nostrils the breath of life; and man became a living soul.*

This Spirit that God breathed into Adam kick-started all human life that descended physically out of our first parents. Then

God took the Man and put him in a garden called Eden, a location somewhere near Iraq in the middle east.

> Genesis 2:16. *And the Jehovah Elohim commanded* ***the man****, saying, Of every tree of the garden thou mayest freely eat: But of the tree of the knowledge of good and evil, thou shalt not eat of it: for in the day that thou eatest thereof thou shalt surely die.*

Then…

> Genesis 2:18. *the Jehovah Elohim said, It is not good that the man should be alone; I will make him an help meet for him.*

God then brought the animals he had created to Adam and Adam had the full mental capacity to name them all.

Then…

> Genesis 2:21. *And the LORD God caused a deep sleep to fall upon Adam, and he slept: and he took one of his ribs, and closed up the flesh instead thereof; And the rib, which the LORD God had taken from man, made he a woman, and brought her unto the man. And Adam said, This is now bone of my bones, and flesh of my flesh: she shall be called Woman, because she was taken out of Man. Therefore shall a man leave his father and his mother, and shall cleave unto his wife: and they shall be one flesh. And they were both naked, the man and his wife, and were not ashamed.*

That is the Biblical account, friends, of the origins of Adam and Eve. A simple and beautiful way. God's way. Without suffering, death, pain, and evil. The Bible states the plan for the continuance of the human race:

> Genesis 2:24. *Therefore shall a man leave his father and his mother, and shall cleave unto his wife: and they shall be one flesh.*

Adam understood that there in the garden, they could exist with God in their presence; they could procreate and live forever in a state that we would today describe as heaven.

This was God's offering to humanity.

Being the good and holy God that He is, and not a despot, God was not going to force Adam and Eve to love and honor Him. If they wanted to, they could disobey Him and go their own way, by their own thinking, and their own ideas. So God also placed a tree in the garden that gave Adam and Eve the opportunity to reject God's gifts and presence. And He told Adam:

> Genesis 2:17, 18. *Of every tree of the garden thou mayest freely eat: But of the tree of the knowledge of good and evil, thou shalt not eat of it …*

That was a direct command from God to Adam. Now the first seven verses of Genesis chapter three tell us what our first parents did with the choice God gave them: they followed Satan and his enticements and disobeyed God and His command. Beginning at verse one, Genesis chapter 3 says,

> Genesis 3:1. *Now the serpent was more subtle than any beast of the field which the Jehovah Elohim had made. And he [the serpent] said unto the woman, Yea, hath God said, Ye shall not eat of every tree of the garden? And the woman said unto the serpent, We may eat of the fruit of the trees of the garden: But of the fruit of the tree which is in the midst of the garden, God hath said, Ye shall not eat of it, neither shall ye touch it, lest ye die. And the serpent said unto the woman, Ye shall not surely die: For God doth know that in the day ye eat thereof, then your eyes shall be opened, and ye shall be as gods, knowing good and evil.*
>
> *And when [...and when...and when] the woman saw that the tree was good for food, and that it was pleasant to the eyes, and a tree to be desired to make one wise, she took of the fruit thereof, and did eat, and gave also unto her husband with her; and he did eat. And the eyes of them both were opened, and they knew that they were naked [they were ashamed]; and they sewed fig leaves together, and made themselves aprons [created the first man-made religion].*

These passages frankly and simply show that at the heart of Eve was the decision to take matters into her own hands, to discount all that God said and done for them, to listen to Satan and trust His promises, and to, in the end, believe that she knew better than God Himself; that she and Adam could benefit from the food of the tree, because it was easy on the eyes, and could make them wise (to the ways of the world) – and so she took it and ate it.

The tension was between God's will and ways and plans – and the blessings thereof – and Satan's will and ways and plans – and the cursings and counterfeit blessings thereof.

Get it?

And by disobeying God, Eve and Adam chose the latter.

Were they rewarded? In a sense, yes. They received the things of this world that they sought. But these things brought with them a terrible, horrible, dreadful result: a fall. And the paradise God gave was lost.

Now, was God pleased with Adam and Eve's choice to disregard His commands?

Genesis three beginning at verse eight:

> Genesis 3:8-13. *And they* [Adam and Eve] *heard the voice of the LORD God walking in the garden in the cool of the day: and Adam and his wife **hid** themselves from the presence of the Jehovah Elohim amongst the trees of the garden. And Jehovah Elohim called unto Adam, and said unto him, Where art thou? And he said, I heard thy voice in the garden, and I **was afraid**, because I was naked* [ashamed]*; and I hid myself. And he said, Who told thee that thou wast naked? Hast thou eaten of the tree, whereof I commanded thee that thou shouldest not eat? And the man* [passing the buck], *said, The woman whom thou gavest to be with me, she gave me of the tree, and I did eat. And the LORD God said unto the woman,*

> ***What is this that thou hast done?*** *And the woman said, The serpent* ***beguiled*** *me, and I did eat.*

And then what did God do because of their actions?

He *cursed them* and *cast them out* of His presence, out of the garden, and into an existence of pain, sorrow, and death. And the title deed to this earth was handed over to Satan, who entices all offspring of Adam and Even with the very same things with which he enticed Eve. As the Apostle John wrote, "*with the lust of the flesh, the lust of the eyes, and the pride of life* (1 John 2:16);" and then he rewards them with horrific pain, sorrow, and death.

Listen, every time a child or woman is raped, mutilated, or beaten; every time cancer and AIDS and disease takes the life of someone we love; whenever there is a war; or whenever healthy people are paralyzed or maimed; it is the DIRECT RESULT OF ADAM AND EVE'S CHOICE.

I cannot comprehend a God who would ***want*** His creations to experience such horrors – but this is the very thing Mormonism teaches relative to Adam and Eve and the Fall.

Now, let me pause here and say something important:

I love and respect all people as my earthly brothers and sisters; LDS people included. So when I go after their beliefs, I am not – AM NOT – attacking them. I am convicted by the unequivocal Christian demand to love all people – all. And I generally do. However, even in this pluralistic and relativistic age of *respect everyone's religious beliefs* where it is not at all popular to criticize people and their faith, Mormonism claims to be not only Christian, they also claim to be the only TRUE Christian faith on earth. Because of that claim, their doctrines are worthy of all scrutiny and criticism relative to what the Bible teaches.

In the story of Adam and Eve, Mormonism blatantly reveals

a horribly TWISTED perspective. I'm not even going to talk about Brigham Young's teachings that Adam was God himself and that Eve was one of his many wives. You can discover those teachings yourself by going to www.utlm.org. But what do the LDS teach about our first parents and their role in what we commonly call the Fall?

I am going to break their twisted Christianity ("twistianity") down into several large categories, which all defy what the Bible, and Biblical Christians, know to be true.

First, Latter-day Saints teach that Adam was actually Michael, an archangel, before becoming the earth's first man. I don't need to provide proofs for this teaching as it is foundational to the religion. However, Paul makes Adam's origins clear when he writes:

> 1 Corinthians 15:47. *The first man* [Adam] *is of the earth, earthy: the second man is the Lord from heaven.*

Second, Latter-day Saint doctrine says that Adam, as Michael the archangel, played a significant role in creating the earth. Again, a huge departure from the Biblical view that Adam was created by God from the dust of the earth and given life by His breath. (It is also a significant departure from the sound Biblical teaching that angels and men are of a different order from one another. But this is for another day.)

Third, Latter-Day Saints teach that the title, *Ancient of Days*, used in Daniel chapter seven is a reference to Adam! This is founded in a direct revelation Joseph Smith claims to have had in 1838 which is included in Doctrine and Covenants 116:1 and supported by Smith who said (*History of the Church* 3:386):

> *Daniel, in his seventh chapter speaks of the Ancient of Days; he means the oldest man, our father Adam, Michael ...*

This is one of the laughable and lamentable mistakes of Joseph Smith because the Bible is clear that this revelation refers to deity; namely, and uniquely, first to the Father, and then the Son – not Adam.

Fourth, LDS doctrine teaches that Adam and Eve were presented by God with two opposing commands: to *"multiply and replenish the earth* (Genesis 1:28)," AND to not "*eat of the tree of knowledge of good and evil* (Genesis 2:17)," the idea being that Adam and Eve were incapable of *multiplying and replenishing the earth,* without first having a *knowledge of good and evil* – or the knowledge on how to reproduce.

All of this is built on man-made pre-supposition and a kind of strange notion that God is a God of tricks and games. It assumes that Adam and Eve could not have learned to multiply; or, if they had had questions on how, that they couldn't have asked God how to go about it.

This brings us to a fifth difference between Mormonism and Biblical Christianity relative to our first parents. In the LDS temple film, it is Eve who actually understands that there is a conflict between the commands that God has given them, and she makes what the LDS consider a *noble* decision to break one command (to *not eat the fruit*) in order to be obedient to the greater command (which was to *multiply and replenish the earth*).

Part of what allowed Eve to see the need to break one command in order to be obedient to the other presents us with the sixth LDS twist on Adam and Eve, which states that they were fully aware of the whole LDS plan of salvation from beginning to the end. In fact, Mormonism teaches that all of the Old Testament prophets were fully aware of the LDS gospel plan from the beginning of time.

This is in plain conflict with Biblical teachings which state that God revealed his ways progressively. Speaking of the gospel of Jesus Christ, Paul writes that it was

> Romans 16:25-26. … *a mystery which was kept secret since the world began, but now is made manifest …*

And then in a letter to the Ephesians, referring again to the gospel of Jesus Christ, Paul writes that…

> Ephesians 3:5. …*in other ages it was not made known unto the sons of men, as it is now revealed unto his holy apostles and prophets by the Spirit.*

Back to Eve and Adam's fall being noble: the seventh twist. Christianity teaches that God's creation, called humanity, started when God breathed into the nostrils of Adam and he became a living soul. Mormonism teaches something wholly different but very present in Greek mythology: that all human beings existed as spirit beings in a pre-mortal existence; that Adam and Eve were the first to come to earth and obtain bodies; and that they had the obligation to start bringing these spirit children down to earth through procreation.

But according to Mormon doctrine, *they wouldn't know how to procreate until they ate of the tree of knowledge of good and evil!* So in ORDER to get God's true plan going, they had to eat the fruit – the fruit that God Himself commanded them not to eat. And then, when they did, He punished them for their disobedience to His will.

LDS scripture testifies of this twisted position over and over again.

In the Book of Mormon, it reads:

> 2 Nephi 2:25. *Adam fell that men might be, and men are that they might have joy.*

LDS Prophet Joseph Fielding Smith said (*Conference Report*, October 1967, page 122):

> Let us thank the Lord, when we pray, for Adam. If it had not been for Adam, I would not be here; you would not be here, we would be waiting in the heavens as spirits pleading for somebody ... to pass through a certain condition that brought upon us mortality.

The LDS scripture Pearl of Great Price has the audacity to personally quote Eve as saying:

> Moses 5:11. Were it not for our transgression we never should have had seed, and never should have known good and evil, and the joy of our redemption, and the eternal life which God giveth unto all the obedient.

There is so much convoluted thinking here, I really don't know where to start!

First of all, Eve states, "*If it wasn't for our transgression, we would never have known the joy of our redemption!*"

In other words, she is saying, "I am so glad I sinned so I could then experience Jesus saving me from sin."

Forget about the price He paid for the sin. Forget about the pain HE endured or the crime that sin is against God in the first place. Instead, Joseph Smith has Eve rejoicing in her transgression because she could now rejoice in the solution to it!

Understand, the environment in which Adam and Eve lived in the Garden was akin to the condition we long to return to once this life is through! They lived in heaven, so to speak, with God present, and themselves in a paradise! But here, in the LDS Pearl of Great Price, Eve is saying that it is great that they left heaven in order to then appreciate that they then have the chance to get back into it.

Then Eve continues to say that unless they transgressed, they would not *know the joy of eternal life which God gives to all the obedient.* Do you hear the absolute irrationality of this comment? Joseph Smith has Eve saying that it is only because they disobeyed that they can now understand the joy of eternal life that comes ... *only to those who obey?* I mean, we're talking about twist, twist, twist here, friends. Twisting the good news, twisting the whole of God's Biblical revelation!

Now notice a word that is used to describe Eve's and Adam's actions against God: "*transgression.*" This leads us to the eighth twist: Mormon doctrine claims Adam and Eve did not sin, they, ah, "*transgressed*!" LDS Prophet Joseph Fielding Smith said (*Doctrines of Salvation* 1:115):

> This was a transgression of the law, but not a sin in the strict sense, for it was something that Adam and Eve had to do!

Marion G. Romney, an LDS apostle, stated (*Conference Report*, April 1953, pages 122-126):

> I do not look upon Adam's action as a sin. I think it was a deliberate act of free agency. He chose to do that which had to be done to further the purposes of God.

Herein lies a point-blank contradiction of the Bible, my friends.

What do we know from God's account of Adam and Eve's actions? God told them they could eat of all the trees He had given them EXCEPT one. And of that one, He COMMANDED them not to eat it. If the LDS commend the eating of it, they commend Eve and Adam for following Satan's advice.

And the rewards? All that is in the world! The lust of the flesh, the lust of the eyes and the pride of life.

This is serious "schnit," friends.

The Bible tells us that God did what when Adam and Eve transgressed? Did He commend them or condemn them? What is the fruit of their partaking of the fruit? Goodness, kindness, love? Or evil, darkness, suffering and pain?

How does an actual apostle of Jesus Christ, John the Beloved, define SIN?

> 1 John 3:4. *Whoever commiteth sin transgresseth the law: for sin is the transgression of the Law.*

What else does the Bible say about Adam and Eve? Do we have anyone, anywhere within the text commending them for their choice? Did Isaiah, or Peter, or Paul ever say, "We thank God for Adam and Eve's choice?" Ha!

Clear about the nature of Adam's action, Job asked,

> Job 31:33. *If I covered my transgressions as Adam, by hiding mine iniquity in my bosom...*

Listen to the words Paul used in his letter to the Romans:

> Romans 5:12, 15, 18. *Wherefore, as by one man sin entered into the world, and death by sin; and so death passed upon all men, for that all have sinned...For if through the offence of one many be dead, much more the grace of God, and the gift by grace, which is by one man, Jesus Christ, hath abounded unto many... Therefore as by the offence of one judgment came upon all men to condemnation; even so by the righteousness of one the free gift came upon all men unto justification of life. For as by one man's disobedience many were made sinners, so by the obedience of one [Jesus] shall many be made righteous.*

Now I want you to consider one of the greatest cracks in the LDS ideas of Adam and Eve, their fall, and the notion that they did a good thing by listening to Satan's temptation and disobeying God.

Ready?

If Adam and Eve were supposed to eat the fruit in order to open the door for spirit children to come to earth, ***why would Satan get them to do it***? Wouldn't Satan, who hates everything about God, do everything he could to keep Adam and Eve from eating the fruit INSTEAD of getting them *TO* eat it?

Bottom line, friends, God has NEVER EVER wanted anyone to sin, to suffer, to have pain, to lose children to accidents and murder. The LDS teaching of Adam and Eve and the Fall are about as far from Christianity as you can get. They are not merely twisted, but they are built on a far more sinister premise.

Check it all out yourselves, then ask God to open your eyes.

❋ ❋ ❋

"I dunno, man. I mean, if angels don't have wings like Joseph Smith said, how do they fly? Everything else God has flying around has wings, doesn't it?"

Angels

Angels play a prominent role in the development of Mormonism and are explained and understood in ways that are not Biblical and certainly not embraced by the Christian world. The reason? Joseph, plain as day, authored "another gospel," as spoken of in Galatians 1, even down to the topic of angels.

Why don't we first look to the Word of God – the Bible – and see what it says about Angels. The word Angel, in both the Hebrew and Greek, means a "messenger," and it is used to describe *any agent* God sends forth to execute his purposes. It is used, in Scripture, to describe *ordinary human messengers* (Job 1:14;

1 Samuel 11:3; Luke 7:24, 9:52); for *prophets* (Isaiah 42:19 and Haggai 1:13); for *priests* (Malachi 2:7); and *even human ministers* of the New Testament (Revelation 1:20). The term is also applied to *non-human* impersonal agents like *pestilence* (2 Samuel 24:16-17 and 2 Kings 19:35) and *the wind* (Psalms 104:4).

Now remember, the general title of *angel* does not necessarily denote the heavenly angelic nature in Scripture but often only refers to *the office of a messenger for God.* Even the pre-incarnate LORD Jehovah is described several times in the Old Testament as an "*angel,*" or "*angel of the Lord*" due to His appearing in the office of a divine messenger.

But we are going to focus more on the distinct application of the word *angel* as it relates to heavenly beings whom God uses to do His will in the heavens and on earth. In the Bible, God does not say, *In the beginning I created angels in heaven this way, with these attributes, and this is how you relate with them.* God didn't do this; but Joseph Smith decided he should, which we'll discuss in a minute.

The Bible *does*, however, provide us with ample incidental details about the subject. This is really important because where the Word of God gives us numerous puzzle pieces that come together in a wonderful picture *to those who study it and search*, Joseph Smith provided extra-Biblical information which LDS people assume to be true, just because he said it.

We know from the Bible that heavenly angels have a personal existence. This is plainly implied in such passages as Genesis 16:7, 10, 11; Judges 13:1-21; Matthew 28:2-5; and Hebrews 1:4.

Angels are superior beings and they are very numerous: "*Thousand thousands,*" according to Daniel 7:10. See also Matthew 26:53; Luke 2:13; Hebrews 12:22,23.

They are also spoken of as having different ranks in dignity and power, according to Zechariah 1:9,11; Daniel 10:13, 12:1; 1 Thessalonians 4:16; Jude 1:9; Ephesians 1:21; and Colossians 1:16. We might not be incorrect to liken them to an army, with various ranks and purposes.

Based on Hebrews 1:14 they are spirit; but also seem to be constructed in soul like man, that is, with mind, will, and emotion.

Whenever angels come to speak to man it seems they always appear in human form (Genesis 18:2, 19:1,10; Luke 24:4; Acts 1:10). Imperfection is ascribed to them as creatures and created beings (Job 4:18; Matthew 24:36; and 1 Peter 1:12). Therefore, because they are finite creatures they can fall into temptation. And accordingly we read about *fallen angels*.

Often, in the context of an after-life discussion people will say, "Who wouldn't accept God when they are dead, if they are standing there looking at Him?"

And I always reply, "Look at some of the angels."

To the question of why some angels fell, we are *wholly* ignorant. We do know that, based on Scripture, they *"left their first estate* (Matthew 25:41; Revelation 12:7,9)," and that they are *"reserved unto judgment* (2 Peter 2:4)." Joseph Smith took the Biblical term "first estate" which is applied to heavenly creations like angels, and applied it to humanity, which is a wholly false, corrupt, and unoriginal application of that notion, which originally thrived within Greek mythology.

We know angels never die (Luke 20:36) and they possess superhuman intelligence and power (Mark 13:32; 2 Thessalonians 1:7; Psalms 103:20). We know their strength is great, which could be a result of not being confined to a physical nature (Psalm 103:20; Revelation 5:2, 18:21). We also know their activities are described as "*marvelous* (Isaiah 6:2-6; Matthew 26:53; Revelation 8:13)."

Some *possible* angelic beings are named by their specific category, like seraphs and cherubs, who are winged, or fiery, or that always seem to "*stand*," or that were created to worship at the throne of God, saying, "*HOLY, HOLY, HOLY*" forever.

That's wild, huh?

Matthew 28:2-7 and Revelation 10:1,2 state that their presence on earth is often described as brilliant or magnificent, and they are called "*holy*" and "*elect*" in Luke 9:26 and 1 Timothy 5:21.

When human beings are redeemed by the blood of Jesus Christ, Scripture says they are "*like unto the angels* (Luke 20:36)" so it is quite possible human beings will appear as angels in the afterlife in terms of brilliant glory.

Of course angels are not ever to be worshipped (Colossians 2:18 and Revelation 19:10).

There are no reports of angelic appearances to man until after the call of Abraham. And then from that time onward there are frequent references to their ministry on earth (Genesis 16, 19; Genesis 24:7,40; 28:12; 32:1). They appear and rebuke idolatry (Judges 2:1-4), they called Gideon (Judges 6:11,12), and consecrated Samson (Judges 13:3). In the days of the prophets, from Samuel on down, the angels appear only in their behalf (1 Kings 19:5; 2 Kings 6:17; Zechariah chapters 1-6; and Daniel 4:13, 23; 10:10, 13, 20, 21).

Then Jesus was born.

And here we are introduced to what we call *the ministrations of angels*. It sort of seems like Jesus brought them with Him to earth and they came with their King to do him service while He was here.

In connection to Jesus, angels

- predicted his coming in Matthew 1:20 and Luke 1:26-38.
- ministered to him after He was tempted in the wilderness and while in agony in the garden (Matthew 4:11 and Luke 22:43). They were all around His tomb.
- declared His resurrection and His ascension into Heaven (Matthew 28:2-8; John 20:12,13; Acts 1:10,11).

Since the finished work of Jesus, they are now "*ministering spirits*" to the "*people of God* (Hebrews 1:14; Matthew 18:10; Acts 5:19; 8:26; 10:3; 12:7; 27:23)."

We know that they rejoice over a penitent sinner (Luke 15:10).

They bear the souls of the redeemed to paradise (Luke 16:22) and they will be the ministers of judgment hereafter on the great day (Matthew 13:39, 41, 49; 16:27; 24:31) which seems to mean that it will be angels who grasp the hell-bound and cast them into the pit.

SCARY.

Some people believe, like the premise found in films like "It's a Wonderful Life" that we all have been assigned a specific life-long guardian angel to protect us. This thinking is taken from Hollywood and a couple passages in Scripture like Psalm 34:7 and Matthew 18:10.

And while God certainly does employ the ministry of angels to deliver his people from affliction and danger, there is no basis for the personal angel myth and all it tends to do is tempt humans with idolatry in some form or another.

So there's the Biblical view. In summary, angels are a creation of God, superior to human beings in power, might and ability, who govern the affairs of heaven and earth, and the final state of redeemed humanity is said to be "*like*" them.

Bottom line of angels in Mormonism: they are all human beings in some state of progression or another. The LDS completely discount the Biblical idea that angels are a completely different species from humans, created in heaven for heavenly purposes.

It is illogical to the LDS mind that man is not the end-all of all God created. They seem to forget that God created fleas and microbes and barracudas and grey whales – all beings that will not ever become human.

Oh well.

Regarding the nature of angels, LDS Apostle Parley P. Pratt said in his *Key to the Science of Theology* (page 69):

> Angels are of the same race as men.

In the October 1969 LDS General Conference, Seventy Sterling W. Sill said,

> It is helpful for us to remember that God, angels, spirits and men are all of the same species in different stages of development and in various degrees of righteousness.

And the *Encyclopedia of Mormonism* (1:40), taking its lead from founding prophet Joseph Smith, Jr. on the subject of angels, reads:

> All people, including angels, are the offspring of God. In form angels are like human beings. They do not, of course, have the wings artists symbolically show.

Adding the LDS view of man being the center of everything, the LDS also hold to the notion that angels are inferior to man, whereas the Bible is clear that man is lower than the angels and only through the blood of Jesus will mankind ever hope to reach their glory.

Inferring the inferior eternal state of angels, listen to what Joseph Smith himself wrote would happen to human beings who did not rise to the top of the Mormon celestial kingdom (by practicing polygamy) as found in their *Doctrine and Covenants*:

> D&C 132:16-17. Therefore, when they are out of the world, they neither marry nor are given in marriage; but are appointed angels in heaven, which angels are ministering servants, to minister for those who are worthy of a far more, and an exceeding, and an eternal weight of glory. For these angels did not abide my law; therefore, they cannot be enlarged, but remain separately and singly, without exaltation, in their saved condition, to all eternity; and from henceforth are not gods, but are angels of God forever and ever.

Echoing Doctrine and Covenants 132, LDS President Spencer W. Kimball said (*The Teachings of Spencer W. Kimball*, p. 51):

> Those without eternal marriage may be angels. Now, the angels will be the people who did not go to the temple, who did not have their work done in the temple. And if there are some of us who make no effort to cement these ties, we may be angels for the rest of eternity. But if we do all in our power and seal our wives or husbands to us ... then we may become gods and pass by the angels in heaven. Some might say, 'Well, I'd be satisfied to just become an angel,' but you would not. One never would be satisfied just to be a ministering angel to wait upon other people when he could be the king himself.

As stated, angelic visitations were foundational to the formation of Mormonism. Joseph Smith claimed to have been visited by a half a dozen or more "angels" as the LDS define them: men in some state of their pre-existent or heavenly progression. All of them appeared in glorious white light; all of them brought a message from the throne of an anthropomorphic God.

Now, we can assume one of a couple of possibilities here with Joseph Smith's claims to having these glorious visitors appear to him.

First, he was making it all up. Second, he was telling the truth and he actually did have either all or at least some illuminated visitors. Or third, no visitor ever came but he imagined that they had.

Many critics take up the claim of the first route – that he was making it all up. That there was never any Angel Moroni; Peter, James, and John; John the Baptist; Nephi, etc. This is possible.

Some critics take the third route, believing Joseph was an epileptic or mentally imbalanced and saw visions. Also possible.

But in the context of actual spiritual visitations, I wonder if the second possibility holds the most water: that Joseph Smith was, indeed, actually visited by something claiming to be from heaven.

I think this explanation is most reasonable for the following reasons:

- Joseph Smith's involvement with folk magic
- Joseph's explanation, as found in Doctrine and Covenants, of what to do when you meet a ministering angel
- The Biblical declaration that even Satan can appear as an angel of light

We have done entire programs on the Smith family's involvement in magic and the occult. Joseph Smith Jr. and his father were the most involved. LDS defenders attempt to say Joseph's connection to magic and the occult were merely the activities of a young man. Not so. Magic elements and the occult played a significant part in Joseph Smith's founding and establishing the Mormon faith.

If you don't believe me, go to *www.utlm.org* for first hand information. Or read D. Michael Quinn's *Early Mormonism and the Magic World View.*

The night the "Angel Moroni" visited Joseph Smith was September 21. Joseph had been out seeking buried treasure using the very seer stone he claims to have used to translate the Book of Mormon, and had no luck. Why that night? It was the autumnal equinox, the night when all folk-magic people believed messengers would reveal the secret hiding places of buried gold in the earth. And guess who shows up? The Angel Moroni.

Joseph Smith kept his "peep stone," and his magic parchments, and his Jupiter talisman his whole life. When he was shot dead they found the Jupiter talisman on his body. This is occult stuff, my friends.

Then there is Joseph's revelation, still found in the LDS *Doctrine and Covenants*, section 129, that tells about how to greet these visiting spirits.

Listen:

> D&C 129. Instructions given by Joseph Smith the Prophet, at Nauvoo, Illinois, February 9, 1843, making known three grand keys by which the correct nature of ministering angels and spirits may be distinguished. *THERE* are two kinds of beings in heaven, namely: Angels, who are resurrected personages, having bodies of flesh and bones—For instance, Jesus said: Handle me and see, for a spirit hath not flesh and bones, as ye see me have. Secondly: the spirits of just men made perfect, they who are not resurrected, but inherit the same glory. When a messenger comes saying he has a message from God, offer him your hand and request him to shake hands with you. If he be an angel he will do

> so, and you will feel his hand. If he be the spirit of a just man made perfect he will come in his glory; for that is the only way he can appear—Ask him to shake hands with you, but he will not move, because it is contrary to the order of heaven for a just man to deceive; but he will still deliver his message. If it be the devil as an angel of light, when you ask him to shake hands he will offer you his hand, and you will not feel anything; you may therefore detect him. These are three grand keys whereby you may know whether any administration is from God.

So, here Joseph Smith tells the world, through this "instruction," which Mormons today consider scripture, how to detect a truthful spirit visitor: offer them your hand! He says angels of heaven will shake your hand because they are resurrected beings and you will feel their grip. Then he says the other heavenly being, the spirit of a just man, will not offer you his hand because "*it is contrary to the order of heaven to deceive*" but he will still deliver his message. So you can trust it.

Then, he says, the old demon spirits will, because they are demons, try and trick you, and they will offer their hand, but you won't feel it – and therefore you will know it is a demon!

Unbelievable!

I mean, what stops a demon from delivering his message who also refuses to shake hands?

Finally, the Bible states that Satan himself can appear as an *angel of light.*

> 2 Corinthians 11:14. *And no marvel; for Satan himself is transformed into an angel of light.*

The Book of Mormon, Joseph's early work that often concurs with the Bible, agrees:

> 2 Nephi 9:8-9. The angel who fell from before the presence of

> the Eternal God, and became the devil ... that being who beguiled our first parents, who transformeth himself nigh unto an angel of light.

And Joseph Smith himself admitted that "*ministering angels*" from Satan had appeared in the church as angels of light [Teachings of the Prophet Joseph Smith (*TPJS*), page 214]:

> There have also been ministering angels in the Church which were of Satan appearing as an ANGEL OF LIGHT [emphasis Shawn's].

All this being said, it is really interesting that in the LDS Doctrine and Covenants (1921 version), in the "Explanatory Introduction," page 1, it reads:

> In September, 1823, [which date, remember, was the autumnal equinox, the most important day in folklore occult] and at later times, Joseph Smith received visitations from Moroni, an ANGEL OF LIGHT, who revealed the resting place of the ancient record from which The Book of Mormon was afterward translated.

❋ ❋ ❋

"At the end of the day, what Mormonism is saying about there being a world-wide apostasy is that Jesus failed - and Joseph Smith had to come in and finish the job He started."

Apostasy

Central to the LDS teaching that Mormonism is *"the only true Church on the face of the whole earth"* is their faulty idea that a "restoration" of the primitive church of Jesus Christ *had* to occur because the church Jesus established fell into a COMPLETE, world-wide state of apostasy. Everything the LDS do and believe grows up and out from this false teaching that Mormonism is Jesus' church restored.

The Bible teaches two things quite plainly about apostasy.

First, it teaches that there would be, and will continue to be, a number of ugly but *partial* "*apostasies*" or "*falling aways*" within the body of Christ, the church (Colossians 1:24), throughout its history.

Second, the Bible teaches that the church Jesus established would wholly win against any and all apostasies, and that even "*the gates of hell* (Matthew 16:18)" would not prevail against it – ever.

Christians know that Jesus established His gospel and while it might struggle because of the fallen nature of its human membership, it would continue; Mormons believe Jesus' work was doomed and that a man named Joseph Smith had to come along to restore it.

The topic of apostasy is made all the more difficult due to the LDS claim that a non-existent "priesthood authority" was also lost along with the church Jesus established and that it, too, needed to be restored. This is absolutely counter to what the Bible says about priesthood, especially in the book of Hebrews (4:14-5:10; chapters 7-10). Because of time constraints, however, we are going to talk specifically about "complete world-wide apostasy of the church Jesus established" and discuss the fallacious teaching on priesthood in a following section.

Speaking of this "world-wide apostasy," 8th President of the LDS Church, Heber J. Grant said in his April 1926 Christmas greeting:

> As time passed dissentions occurred in the primitive church. The laws governing the church established by the Redeemer were

> transgressed, the ordinances were changed, the everlasting covenant was broken. Men began to teach for doctrine their own commandments; a form of worship had been established which was called Christianity, but was without the power of God which characterized the primitive church. Spiritual darkness covered the earth and gross darkness the minds of the people.

Tenth LDS President Joseph Fielding Smith, in his book, *Answers to Gospel Questions* (1:97), wrote:

> Religious denominations relied entirely on the dead letter of the Bible for their authority. They closed the heavens against themselves and their interpretations of scripture without divine guidance led them into division, into subdivision, and multiplication of churches, each going its own way blindly and in confusion. The power of the priesthood was lost the true Church of Jesus Christ ceased to exist on the earth. There had been no prophet, no revelation, or divine instruction from the time of the apostles of old until the Lord again opened the heavens and sent holy messengers to restore that which had been taken away.

Twelfth LDS President, Prophet, Seer and Revelator, Spencer W. Kimball said (*Teachings of Spencer W. Kimball*, page 423):

> This is not a continuous church, nor is it one that has been reformed or redeemed. It has been restored after it was lost. It was lost – the gospel with its powers and blessings – sometime after the Savior's crucifixion and the loss of his apostles.

And fifteenth President Gordon B. Hinckley said (*Ensign*, June 2004, p. 3):

> The prophet Joseph Smith was told that the other sects were wrong. These are not my words. Those are the Lord's words. But they are hard for those of other faiths.

Now, Latter-day Saints strongly refute the idea that Joseph Smith merely *reformed* the church, but say that he actually had to *restore* it because it had totally lost its power, priesthoods, and way.

Their own *History of the Church* states (1:XL):

> Nothing less than a complete apostasy from the Christian religion would warrant the establishment of the Church of Jesus Christ of Latter-day Saints ... *there was no possible excuse for the introduction of a new Christian sect.*

When the Mormons claimed that God told Joseph that all the churches were wrong, that all the Christian creeds on earth were an abomination to him, and that all the Christian professors of faith were corrupt, they meant it.

Brigham Young said (*Journal of Discourses* 8:171):

> The Christian world, so called, are heathens as to their knowledge of the salvation of God.

McConkie taught (*Doctrinal New Testament Commentary* 2:113; *Mormon Doctrine*, page 626):

> Mormons have the only pure and perfect Christianity on earth. *All other systems of religion are false.*

The negative beliefs and statements about Christians and Christianity abound in Mormonism – from the pen of its founder to the mouths of sixty thousand-plus full time missionaries to discussions that occur privately in LDS wards around the world.

"Oh, no, we love everyone. We never attack another person's faith."

Yeah, right.

I would be negligent in our examination of "apostasy" if we did not look at some of the pre-existing factors that lead Joseph Smith Jr. to claim that he, in fact, restored the true Church of Jesus back to the earth in 1830. Consider these factors when you try and understand what motivated the man to say and do what he said and did.

Before Joseph Smith Jr. was born in the winter of 1805, the foundation for Mormonism was well established, in part by his paternal grandfather and father. His grandfather, whose name was Asael, was extremely opinionated on the subject of religion, and looked for the day when the primitive Church would be restored back to the earth. Joseph Smith's own father ardently REFUSED – REFUSED - to ever join any religion because he felt they were all wrong and the true one needed to be restored. Additionally, the Smith patriarchs believed two very important things relative to what young Joseph Smith would ultimately propose.

First, they believed that America was chosen by God as a land of liberty and that the true "church of Jesus Christ" would someday be restored on this continent. The Smith patriarchs were not alone in these beliefs. There were a whole bunch of men and women around at the time, who were known as "restorationists" or "primitivists," who, too, were looking for the original church of Jesus Christ to be restored. In all probability the body of Christ was going through an ugly period – as it is wont to do – and these people longed for a more genuine religious approach. I can see this even in this day and age.

This environment is one reason why self-proclaimed "religious revelators" like Ellen G. White, William Taze Russell, Mary Baker Eddie, and Joseph Smith, Jr. all started to sort of pop up around the same time, each claiming a fresh new world view. LDS author Richard L. Bushman, in *Joseph Smith and the Beginnings of Mormonism* (Urbana: University of Illinois Press, 1984, p. 34) stated that early Mormonism was known as a Campbellite sect, a name taken from Joseph Campbell who, well before Smith, also sought to restore the primitive church to the earth.

Second, the Smith patriarchs believed, even before Joseph was born, that this Church would be restored through the Smith family itself. George Q. Cannon, LDS Church apostle, writes in his book, *The Life of Joseph Smith the Prophet* (page 32), that Joseph's grandfather Asael said:

> It has been borne in upon my soul that one of my descendants will promulgate a work to revolutionize the world of religious faith.

History proves that from a very young age, Joseph Smith Jr. was taught that

- The primitive religion of Jesus had been taken from the earth (meaning the gates of hell did in fact prevail against what the LORD set up);
- That America was set apart for the "restored gospel" to come forth; and
- That young Joseph would, in fact, be the one who would restore this true religion to earth.

With such soil under his feet, Joseph Smith Jr. was primed for founding a new religion almost from birth. Everything about early Mormonism – the angelic visits, the Book of Mormon, the new revelations, the twists, and its strong attraction to people who were burned by the antics happening in traditional Christian churches – were fruit from the notion that Mormonism was indeed, the "restored Church."

Very quickly Smith sensed the liberty that came with being a "restorationist" and began to take advantage of the trust people had in his visions. In time, he would become more and more aggressive in his assertions of what was actually part of this "restored gospel," culminating in the fact that by the end of his life he thought nothing of secretly taking dozens of wives, of inserting *his own name* into the book of Genesis, and of even having himself ordained "King of the World."

And yet today millions continue to sing, “Praise to the Man.”

LDS missionaries use the Bible to mislead unsuspecting and unlearned people on the idea that the church Jesus established failed and was indeed restored by Smith. There are several key verses they use – out of context, of course. Let’s read them and see what they really mean and say!

> Acts 3:20-21. *And he shall send Jesus Christ, which before was preached unto you: Whom the heaven must receive until the times of restitution of all things, which God hath spoken by the mouth of all his holy prophets since the world began.*

The LDS misrepresent this verse to mean that Jesus will not return to earth until there has been a “*restitution of all things*,” which they say is the LDS gospel and that this was prophesied since the world began.

Wholly incorrect.

Peter was speaking to whom? The “*men of Israel* (verse 12)”; and a CENTRAL message of all Old Testament prophets was about Israel’s restoration (see, Isaiah 40:9-11; Jeremiah 32:42-44; Ezekiel 37; Hosea 11; and Amos 9). This passage has NOTHING to do with a world-wide apostasy or the idea that the church Jesus established could not be trusted. Contextual reading of Scripture reveals it.

> Acts 20:29-31. *For I know this, that after my departing shall grievous wolves enter in among you, not sparing the flock. Also of your own selves shall men arise, speaking perverse things, to draw away disciples after them. Therefore watch, and remember, that by the space of three years I ceased not to warn every one night and day with tears.*

What is the context here? Paul is speaking to the elders in the church at Ephesus (verse 17). And he is warning them about what is headed their way, *in their respective church at Ephesus*,

NOT in the entire world! The pastoral epistles verify that Paul indeed spoke prophetically.

> Galatians 1:8. *I marvel that ye are so soon removed from him that called you into the grace of Christ* ***unto another gospel:*** *Which is not another; but there be some that trouble you, and would pervert the gospel of Christ. But though we, or an angel from heaven, preach any other gospel unto you than that which we have preached unto you, let him be accursed.*

First, what does this passage NOT say? It does NOT say anything about a world-wide apostasy. This is a letter to the Galatian church!

Come on!

And the other gospel referred to, the perversion of the true gospel, referred to what? BRINGING legalism back into the good news which added works to the gospel of grace, something the Judaizers did in response to the freedoms Paul taught that were found in Jesus Christ. According to Acts 15 and 20 these false teachers crept in and began to teach things that took believers away from the gospel of grace.

Many false doctrines have been brought into the hearts of believers over the centuries. But the true church, made up of faithful believers, has never been lost.

One of the BIGGIES the LDS use in Scripture is found in 2 Thessalonians. Speaking of Jesus' immediate return, Paul wrote:

> 2 Thessalonians 2:3. *Let no man deceive you by any means: for that day shall not come, except there come a falling away first, and that man of sin be revealed, the son of perdition …*

Respected LDS apostles and prophets like Ezra Taft Benson have taken passages like this and ridiculously said things like ("I Testify" *Ensign* (Conference Edition), November 1988, p. 86):

> Scripture ended, apostasy spread, and the church that Christ established during his earthly ministry ceased to exist."

It is amazing that intelligent LDS people will read commentary from men like this and because they call themselves apostles, they believe it! This passage is speaking of a very specific period of time, AN END-TIME PROPHECY, when there will be an apostasy, but not of the whole church!

Paul prophetically reassures the people that Jesus will not be returning until

> 2 Thessalonians 2:3. *there come a falling away first, and that man of sin be revealed, the son of perdition ...*

He is saying that Jesus will not come until there comes a falling away first, a specific falling away WHEN the Anti-Christ is revealed, and then Paul describes him in the following verse:

> 2 Thessalonians 2:4. *Who opposeth and exalteth himself above all that is called God, or that is worshipped; so that he as God sitteth in the temple of God, shewing himself that he is God.*

Yes, this passage does refer to apostasy, but it is a SPECIFIC apostasy, at a SPECIFIC time and a SPECIFIC place in history when the anti-Christ reveals himself – nothing before and only one.

Finally, we have 1 Timothy:

> 1 Timothy 4:1-2. *Now the Spirit speaketh expressly, that in the latter times some shall depart from the faith, giving heed to seducing spirits, and doctrines of devils; speaking lies in hypocrisy; having their conscience seared with a hot iron;*

Now, notice that Paul didn't write...*that in latter times* ***all*** *shall depart from the faith*! But instead wrote, *"that in latter times* ***some*** *shall depart from the faith."*

"Some." ***Some!*** Not the entire world!

Perhaps even more importantly is the context of this passage. Here Paul is addressing a specific kind of apostasy, one related to dualistic Gnosticism, which deals with distinction between flesh and spirit. It has nothing to do with a whole church apostasy!

In addition to clarifying the Twists the LDS have done on these simple passages, there are a number of valid, contradictory elements found both within and outside the Bible which completely refute the Mormons' claims of a world-wide apostasy.

First, think about their claim *rationally. Why would Jesus come to earth, teach and train His apostles as first hand witnesses to all He said and did, tell them to go forth unto all the nations, and be martyred for it, only to have it all lost? And why would God allow the church to fall into complete apostasy after His only begotten Son established it, ONLY* then *to completely protect it from wholesale apostasy because Joseph Smith supposedly restored it?*

It's man-made idiocy, I tell you!

Then, what about the fact that God always has a remnant of true believers on earth? In the book *The Blood-Line of the Church*, the author lays out a profound lineage of solid believers through thick and thin, through the Dark Ages, through times of revolt, through governmental influences and doctrinal disputations. God has always had the principle of a *remnant* in His divine work, from Noah and his family and the flood; to grapes on the vine to wheat in the field for the children of Israel; from the Babylon captivity, to the struggling Christians.

What supports this? How about statements from Scripture itself?

Jesus said to Peter,

> Matthew 16:18. *I will build my church and the gates of hell will not prevail against it!*

He said to His followers,

> Matthew 28:20. *Lo, I am with you always, even to the end of the world!*

He promised that where *"two or three are gathered together in my name, there am I in the midst of them* (Matthew 18:20)." Just two or three believers on earth, and He is in the midst? That may be a very weak force, but that is all Jesus said was necessary.

In Ephesians Paul writes:

> Ephesians 3:21. *Unto him be glory in the Church by Christ Jesus* ***throughout the ages****, world without end.*

How could God be glorified "*throughout the ages*" if His church fell into total darkness?

Ephesians 4 describes the church Jesus established GROWING in SPIRITUAL MATURITY, NOT into spiritual degeneracy. Explain this if there was to be a complete apostasy.

The Apostle Peter wrote:

> 1 Peter 1:25. *The word of the Lord endureth forever*

FOREVER! And then he adds, *"and this is the word which by the gospel is preached unto you."*

The Author of Hebrews wrote that:

> Hebrews 12:28. *We [are] receiving a kingdom which* ***cannot be moved*** ...

Sound like a church founded on sand or upon Jesus, the eternal, immovable Rock?

Finally, the book of Revelation describes seven churches of the early church group, which are also pictures of the epochs of time in the body of Christ following Jesus' ascension. What are they and what do they mean?

Jesus Christ Himself says to John the Beloved:

> Revelation 1:11. *I am Alpha and Omega, the first and the last: and, What thou seest, write in a book, and send it unto the seven churches which are in Asia; unto Ephesus, and unto Smyrna, and unto Pergamos, and unto Thyatira, and unto Sardis, and unto Philadelphia, and unto Laodicea.*

And then He goes on to describe these seven churches, which, remember, picture the periods of time the Christian church would pass through but endure until His return. Let me hit on them quickly, which perfectly and prophetically detail the trials the Christian church would endure. The important thing to notice here is *THE CHURCHES NEVER GO AWAY*. Do they have trouble? Sure. But they never, ever disappear.

So here they are in the order Jesus lists them in Revelation.

Ephesus: which means, *full-purposed* and/or desirable. God had a purpose in forming His true church here and, though it would fail, He would complete it. This local church at Ephesus failed because it ceased to love the Lord Jesus Christ more than anything else. Ephesus is a picture of the first few years of church history before the wholesale persecutions of the church began to be severe.

Smyrna: which speaks of bitterness and/or suffering. This church is a picture of the time when the Roman empire persecuted the true church Jesus established. During this time many Christians were thrown to the lions and burned at the stake. The more they suffered for Him, however, the more joyful they appeared in their fellowship with Him and in their witness for Him.

Pergamos: means *mixed marriage.* 2 Corinthians 11:2-3 tells us that God intends His church to be the "*bride of Christ*," but around AD 300 the Roman Emperor Constantine decided that he was going to be a Christian and, stopping the persecutions, he forced everyone in his empire to adopt Christianity. In what seemed like a magnanimous gift, he offered to build the church great cathedrals and to give it a great deal of money. This sounded like a good deal and the church leaders took it. With this came thousands of heathen priests who had no real experience with Jesus and offered no repentance. As a result millions of heathens began to call themselves "Christians." In time, the church itself began to sort of lay back and enjoy its own power and prestige. It was a time when the Lord's church had actually been "married" to the world. As a result many heathen and pagan rites and rituals were adopted by the church without many true Christians realizing what was happening, and real Christianity, founded in faith, love, and regenerated souls who love Jesus Christ, was shrouded in ceremony and untruth.

Thyatira: this name means, *continual sacrifice.* Why? Continual sacrifice was one of the errors the church slipped into after the advent of Pergamos. Hebrews 10:12 tells us one sacrifice (of Jesus) had taken care of it all, but the church of Thyatira thought differently, and sacrifices were continued as if required by God: sacrifices of money, time, duty, self, and family. The church at this time, and its power, was placed in the hand of one man; removed, as it were, from the hand of Jesus Christ, whose authority no man has the right to usurp. This was the beginning of popes.

Sardis: means, *those escaped.* It describes those in the universal church who began protesting against the erroneous teachings that began in Pergamos and continued into the church of Thyatira. These protests started around AD 1500 as attempts to reform the church when the Spirit of God began to take rise in the lives of people and prompt them to resist papal authority.

Buried under this usurped authority were Biblical truths long since forgotten. While those who protested a false and unnecessary clergy had every right to do so, they professed to believe all the Bible taught but unfortunately failed to carry those beliefs out into the day to day living of their lives. For this reason the Lord says to them in Revelation, "*Thou hast a name that thou livest and art dead.*" But remember, this was still His church, and they were still His people.

Philadelphia: the word means, *brotherly love*. Following the years of reformation (Sardis), the Holy Spirit began to revive believers from within. It was a period of great religious upheaval which drew together many people, even in Europe which had been torn apart by religious wars. To the church at Philadelphia, Jesus commends believers saying, "*Thou hast kept My Word and hast not denied My Name* (Revelation 3:8)."

Laodicea: the name means, *the people speak*. It refers to a time when the church will care more about the ideas and words of man than about the Word of God. The city of Laodicea was known for its lukewarm springs which are pleasant to bathe in (externally applied) but sickening to drink (internally taken). It is a picture of His church just prior to His return where some will be hotly devoted and others cold, but most of the Church will be a lukewarm mix, which, according to the Lord, disgusts Him and He will spew them out of His mouth.

David Reed and John Farkas, as quoted in a great book by Ron Rhodes called, *Reasoning from the Scriptures with the Mormons* (page 59), wrote:

> With church history so well preserved, it is possible for us today to trace the development of doctrines and practices over the years. We can follow the course of the debates over Gnosticism, Arianism, Sabellianism and so on. Yet the mountains of manu-

> scripts dating back nearly two thousand years, nowhere do we find evidence that the church originally thought anything resembling the "restored gospel" of Mormonism ... if it were true that the church founded by Jesus Christ originally taught such LDS doctrines as the Plurality of Gods, men becoming Gods, celestial marriage, and God the Father having once been a man, and if it were true that those doctrines were later set aside in favor of what is now considered orthodox Christianity there would certainly be some evidence of this...but no such evidence is available.

Listen, do we trust what Scripture calls "*His finished work*" or not? Is He the author and *finisher* of our faith (Hebrews 12:2) – or is Joseph Smith? Was more gospel needed? More additions? How come Jesus didn't speak of the temple endowment? How come Jesus didn't tell us about celestial marriage?

My friends, there was NO world-wide apostasy. The gospel that Jesus Christ gave to the world was never lost. Believers, true and faithful believers, have kept it alive and going since the ascension. This is one of the great miracles of Christianity.

And the myths of Joseph Smith were introduced to bring Smith power, glory, and gold.

❋ ❋ ❋

> "I mean, aside from all the Biblical proofs that speak against modern-day apostles I wanna know why all the Mormon apostles are men of such great educational and/or temporal accomplishment? Holy cow, Peter was a lowly fisherman, Matthew a hated tax-collector. And it wasn't like there weren't accomplished men around in Jesus day He could have picked from either. So why the disparity?"

Apostles

Years ago I was invited by a good friend to have lunch in the

LDS Church headquarters cafeteria. We got our food and then sat at a table and began to eat and talk. Suddenly the noisy cafeteria, starting from behind me, began to subtly get quiet.

My friend kept talking, and then noticing the growing silence looked up, and there, walking across the floor was a man named Dallin Oaks, a man the LDS believe is as much of an "apostle" of the Lord Jesus Christ as was Peter, James, and/or John.

My friend got all exited and said in a very low whisper, *"Do you see him? Do you see him?"*

"Who?" I replied.

And he motioned with his eyes over my shoulder. "*Elder Oaks!*"

I turned and looked and watched as he contemplatively passed through a sea of silent, humbled admirers.

"Hey," I said to my friend, "I'm gonna go talk to him."

My friend who works in the church office building grabbed my wrist. *"No!"* he said, *"don't. We're not allowed. Only if he speaks to us first."*

"You're kidding, right?" I replied.

"Shawn?" he said sort of exasperated, *"he is an apostle! An apostle of Jesus Christ!"*

"Which is exactly why I want to talk to him," I said. But the look on my friend's face pleaded against my determination. And so I sat down...left only to dream of what I could have said.

An apostle of the Lord Jesus Christ? Really?

While I served my full-time mission for the LDS church, one of my favorite lines to prove the truth of Mormonism was the ...

ahem ... FACT that Mormonism was the only church on earth that claimed twelve apostles – and that this made Mormonism just like the original church Jesus started! I mean, this was the thinking. And without knowing the Bible, the thinking makes some sense. In *The Seventeen Points of the True Church,* a pamphlet that promotes Mormonism as the Only True Church on earth, it reads, "The True Church must have a foundation of Prophets and Apostles."

The premise of this statement was taken right out of the Bible; *taken* from it, but completely twisted when we examine the contextual understanding of apostles in Scripture. Let me explain.

In Ephesians chapter 2, which is in the New Testament of the Bible, it says that the redeemed are members of God's household, built upon the foundation of apostles and prophets, Jesus Christ being the chief cornerstone. I think it's important to consider the context of the passage. Speaking to the believers who were once sinful Gentiles, Paul writes:

> Ephesians 2:11-20. *Therefore remember that you, once Gentiles in the flesh--who are called Uncircumcision by what is called the Circumcision made in the flesh by hands-- that at that time you were without Christ, being aliens from the commonwealth of Israel and strangers from the covenants of promise, having no hope and without God in the world.* ***But now*** *in Christ Jesus you who once were far off have been brought near by the blood of Christ. For He Himself is our peace, who has made both one, and has broken down the middle wall of separation, having abolished in His flesh the enmity, that is, the law of commandments contained in ordinances, so as to create in Himself one new man from the two, thus making peace, and that He might reconcile them both to God in one body through the cross, thereby putting to death the enmity.*
>
> *And He came and preached peace to you who were afar off and to those who were near. For through Him we both have access by one Spirit to the Father. Now, there-fore, you are no longer strang-*

ers and foreigners, but fellow citizens with the saints and members of the household of God, having been built on the foundation of the apostles and prophets, Jesus Christ Himself being the chief cornerstone, in whom the whole building, being joined together, grows into a holy temple in the Lord, in whom you also are being built together for a dwelling place of God in the Spirit.

Is the Gospel of Jesus Christ built upon a foundation of apostles and prophets?

Certainly!

Read the Old Testament and the gospels! This is the foundation laid! Now if you were to build a house, you would start with a foundation, and once it was laid and cured, you would begin to build your house upon it, right? How often would you go back and re-pour the foundation? NEVER, if it was poured right the first time. How many times does the foundation of a household have to be laid? Once. It is the foundation!

The building *upon* the foundation is forever growing. You might redecorate or remodel. You might paint or add aluminum siding to the building, but the *foundation* remains in place – unless it is faulty and cracked. Did Jesus lay a faulty foundation? No; He built upon the foundation He Himself laid. And He laid it with

apostles and prophets, with Jesus Himself serving as the chief cornerstone! That is solid.

But there's more. We KNOW that once the foundation was laid, it was laid permanently – *once and forever* – and we know this by looking at the Greek. The word used here is the participle "*epoikodo methentes,*" which, in proper syntax is translated "*having **been** built.*"

Not "continuing now that it was laid." Not "being restored." But *"having been built!"*

It's an *aorist passive participle*, referring to a *past action* and in this specific case, it is *an action that has been fully completed!* It's been done!

My friends, the LDS church's system constantly uproots and demolishes the early Christian foundation, which Jesus laid permanently, by replacing it over and over again (now listen to this description closely) with *unqualified* men.

"What do you mean, 'unqualified men? How could you say such a thing, you mean, mean man?"

"*Why,*" the LDS proudly state, *"our apostles are the most qualified men on earth! They are judges, and surgeons, and prominent lifelong faithful members of the church! Educated! Articulate, and astute in the ways of the world!"*

In the first place, the qualifications of these LDS men who call themselves apostles are NOT anything like the qualifications of the apostles the Lord Jesus chose. He could have chosen learned successful men of His day – authorities, religious leaders, scholars, and businessmen. But NOOOOOOO.

Who did Jesus chose for His apostles when He was on earth? Common fishermen. Hated tax collectors. I would LOVE to see a fisherman sit down around the table with the so-called apostles of the LDS church today.

Can you imagine the disconnect?

"D' Arrrrgh, matey. 'Ow you doin' over there, 'Olland? You gonna eat that toast and jelly Boyd-y-buddy or nibble on it, ya panty-waist?" (Well I guess fishermen aren't pirates but you know what I mean.)

Anyway, it was not the apostles' worldly stature or successful lives that qualified them as true apostles. Besides their humility and desire to follow Jesus, it was a number of other factors.

Paul writes:

> Corinthians 9:1. *Am I not an apostle? am I not free? have I not seen Jesus Christ our Lord?*

There is the first qualifier of being an apostle: being a firsthand eye-witness of Jesus.

When the apostles sought to replace Judas with someone to continue on as a personal witness, which thing was prophesied to occur, and is in part why they did it, they looked for an individual who had:

> Acts 1:21, 22. ... *companied with us all the time that the Lord Jesus went in and out among us, beginning from the baptism of John, unto that same day that he was taken up from us, must one be ordained to be a witness with us of his resurrection.*

So Jesus established His Church upon apostles who, as Luke said, "*have seen Him,*" as *"He went in and out;"* and as Peter said, were "*witnesses of His resurrection.*" (See John 15:27; Acts 1:21, 22; 1 Corinthians 9:1; Acts 22:14, 15.)

So the first *BIBLICAL* rule for being an apostle is...

1. Apostles must be first-hand witnesses of Jesus Christ.

Additionally,

2. Each of the apostles of the Lord received their call to that office by *Christ*._

Luke 6:13. *And when it was day, he called unto him his disciples: and of them he chose twelve, whom also he named apostles*

In the calling of Paul, the same was true:

Galatians 1:1. *Paul, an apostle, (not of men, neither by man, but by Jesus Christ, and God the Father, who raised him from the dead;)*

3. Apostles must be infallibly inspired._

1 Thessalonians 2:13. *For this cause also thank we God without ceasing, because, when ye received the word of God which ye heard of us, ye received it not as the word of men, but as it is in truth, the word of God, which effectually worketh also in you that believe.*

You see, it was essential that these apostles were infallibly inspired. As such, they secured against all error in their public teaching, whether by word or writing. This is why Jesus gave them in-person training when he established His church. No passed down office from men to other men who are qualified in the ways of the world!

The final Biblically established qualification for an apostle was,

4. The power of working miracles._

Listen to what the word says about the apostles after Jesus ascended into heaven:

Mark 16:19. *So then after the Lord had spoken unto them, he was received up into heaven, and sat on the right hand of God. And they went forth, and preached every where, the Lord working with them, and confirming the word with signs following.*

> Acts 5:12. *And by the hands of the apostles were many signs and wonders wrought among the people*

Luke said of Paul:

> Acts 19:11. *And God wrought special miracles by the hands of Paul: so that from his body were brought unto the sick handkerchiefs or aprons, and the diseases departed from them, and the evil spirits went out of them.*

Speaking of Peter, Luke also wrote:

> Acts 5:15. *Insomuch that they brought forth the sick into the streets, and laid them on beds and couches, that at the least the shadow of Peter passing by might overshadow some of them.*

As a result of *all* of these factors, and within the context of Scripture, the true apostles of the early church could not any more have had successors than there needed to be a successor to Jesus Himself! They are the only authoritative teachers of the Christian doctrines. The office of an apostle ceased with its first holders.

So, in light of all this, I want to know a few things about the Mormon apostles.

Ready?

1. Of the 100 or so self-proclaimed LDS apostles since Joseph restored the church to earth, have ANY of them admitted being eyewitnesses of Jesus Christ and His resurrection? And in reality, the truer question is HAVE ALL OF THEM LAID CLAIM TO SEEING JESUS PERSONALLY?
2. Have each and every one of the them received their call to that apostolic office *by Christ Himself?*
3. Have all the LDS apostles' professions been infallible as to the whole of the Word?

4. What miracles have been done from the hands of these businessmen-become-apostles?

I think it is important to realize that the *word* apostle and the *office of* apostle have two very different applications. Apostle, the word, just means a person sent, or a messenger. This word is even used twice as a descriptive designation of Jesus Christ, who was "*sent of the Father* (Hebrews 3:1 and John 20:21)." It is, however, generally used as designating the body of disciples to whom He entrusted the organization of His church and the dissemination of his gospel, "*the twelve*," as they are called, who held the OFFICE of apostle (Matthew 10:1-5; Mark 3:14; 6:7; Luke 6:13; 9:1).

Twice in the New Testament (2 Corinthians 8:23 and Philippians 2:25) the word "messenger" is used; *but it is the same Greek word as "apostle."*

Now remember – and this is important – as first-hand witnesses of the Lord Jesus and His resurrection, none of the apostles ever hesitated in proclaiming their special witness: *We have seen Him … He lives … I testify of this!* And they all – except John the beloved – were martyred for their very verbal and vocal testimony of what they witnessed with their own eyes!

Now how many LDS apostles stand and state that they have "seen" the resurrected Jesus with their own eyes? This is an essential for filling the office of an apostle! No; they walk about looking holy and unapproachable, allowing this inferential guessing game to exist amidst their followers. Make me a fool, Holland, Oaks, Packer: tell the world that Jesus came to you, showed Himself, and called you personally to your office. Don't play nuance games with us. Don't wink and say "we really know."

Tell us plainly that you have seen Jesus Christ.

Or, *perhaps even more importantly,* if you haven't seen Him, would you please admit this?

Please.

Because if you haven't seen Him with your eyes (He still has His Body, you know) you have been deceiving millions of people with your charade.

But not being an actual eyewitness is only one reason the LDS apostles are not true apostles. Now the LDS defenders use the fact that Judas Iscariot was replaced by Matthias as evidence that Jesus' church must always have a perpetual quorum of twelve apostles. Joseph claimed to have restored Jesus' original church back to earth and the LDS have had a revolving quorum of twelve men who have referred to themselves as actual apostles of Jesus Christ. The first "apostles" within Mormonism were not called of Jesus personally, nor did they claim to witness Him in body, but their supposed calling came about by way of a revelation to the three witnesses of the Book of Mormon who then chose the first "replacement twelve apostles" of the LDS restoration. And they weren't called until five years after Joseph formed the church.

One of the FIRST things Jesus did in establishing His church was call His apostles.

Think my friends!

And what did Paul say:

> 1 Corinthians 4:9. *For I think that God hath set forth us the apostles last, as it were appointed to death: for we are made a spectacle unto the world, and to angels, and to men.*

It is clear from this passage that the office of apostle was a one-time situation (that they were last) and that they were "*appointed unto death*" (meaning they would die for the cause) and that they would be made a spectacle before the world, and angels, and men, through this sacrifice, to launch the church Jesus established out into the world FOREVER! Does this in any way match the way an LDS apostle is seen today? As a "*spectacle unto the world...appointed to death*?"

Instead of allowing Jesus true apostles to stand last, bearing their witness by their blood, Mormon apostles try and continue on! Instead of being appointed unto death, they are protected by limousines, body guards, and luxury! Instead of being a spectacle, they are revered! People stand when they enter the room!

Then there are the simple numbers to consider.

If LDS apostles are the same as the apostles Jesus chose, explain why, in the book of Revelation (21:14), it states that the wall around God's heavenly city is supported by "*twelve foundations, and in them the names of the twelve apostles of the lamb*."

Wooops!

Hey, Holland, is your name on one of those pillars? How about you Eyring? Think your pillar is right between Peter and James? Even the foundation of heaven – not just the church of Jesus but the foundation of heaven! – is built upon *twelve* pillars named after the *twelve* apostles of the Lamb!

Now, the LDS argue, *if there are "only twelve apostles," why did the first apostles get together and call Matthias to replace Judas when he killed himself*? First, and as I already mentioned, to fulfill prophecy. Peter states this when they called the replacement man Matthias. Second, they had a mission to fulfill – to "kick-start" the gospel so to speak – and God initiated twelve men – representing the twelve tribes – to do the work. Once it was kick-started, the work was done. The apostolic witnessing was done – and they sealed their witness in blood. Additionally, the apostles, under impetuous Peter's lead, called Matthias after limiting the candidates to just two men. All of this occurred by their own will and prior to the arrival of the holy spirit – which Jesus had told them to wait upon. From the text we see that God had another idea – Paul – who He called later on. I base this not on anything more than the fact that we never hear from Matthias again. But Paul?

Finally, there is no continuing office of apostle as Paul gave Timothy no qualifications for the position, as he does for a bishop, deacon, elder, etc. (1 Timothy 3).

Are you beginning to see the mockery of Mormonism's continuing "revolving door" of apostles? Can you see what an insult these men are to the twelve who gave their everything to see people come to the cause of Christ? Rather than GAIN everything?

My friends, the twelve of Jesus ate the dust of the earth. They were mistreated, they suffered, and they gave their all – even their very lives – to share Jesus with the world. In the narrow sense (as the *office of apostle*) they were hand chosen by Jesus Christ, were witnesses of Him, and performed great miracles in His name.

The LDS apostles meet none of these conditions for apostleship.

Now, I mentioned that there is a wider sense of the word, apostle, and it means "one sent." There were many ones sent in the Word who were known as "apostles" like Barnabas, Andronicus, Junia, etc. They did not fill the office of apostle as far as we know. But if they were first hand witnesses called of Jesus, they could have.

Finally, in relation to apostles, why do you suppose no Bible-believing, Bible studying, truth-seeking Christian church, with all the denominations established over the years, has ever instituted twelve apostles? The world's greatest scholars who understand Biblical exegesis and interpretation have never said, "We need twelve apostles! We need twelve apostles!"

Why?

Because they know what being an apostle means, what their purposes were, and the narrow and broad context in which the word is used in the Bible today and how ludicrous it is having more than twelve in light of the Bible.

In conclusion my friends, I think it interesting that the New Testament does speak, however, of false apostles. Paul describes them:

> 2 Corinthians 11:13. *For such are false apostles, deceitful workers, transforming themselves into the apostles of Christ.*

So ask yourself something:

Where on earth is there a Church that has deceitful men who appear to have been *"transformed into apostles of the Lord Jesus Christ?"*

I can only think of one.

❋ ❋ ❋

> "Yes, yes, yes, the LDS believe in the atonement of Jesus Christ. This is true. But even the devils believe. The question is 'how do they believe in His atonement?' In other words, what does the fact that He shed His blood actually mean and translate to in their hearts and minds? I would suggest that the answer to this question is significantly different when it comes out of the mouth of a Bible-believing Christian."

Atonement

If you have ever had a conversation of any length with a Latter-day Saint, especially the true believing LDS, it does not take long before you will hear them use the word – often gravely

– "a*tonement.*" In their testimony meetings it usually comes out like this:

> I want to bear my testimony. I know this church is true. I know Joseph Smith was a prophet and that we are guided by a living prophet today. I am grateful for the atonement which makes it possible for me to live with my heavenly Father again.

The atonement.

What is it? What does it mean? Where did it come from? Why is it here? Where is it going?

In Mormonism, the first use of the word atonement can, ironically enough, be found in the Book of Mormon.

> 2 Nephi 9:26. *For the atonement* ***satisfies the demands of his justice*** *upon all those who...*[and it goes on to detail some doctrine].

I say ironically because the word *atonement* is an invented word! In the sixteenth century, Bible scholar and translator William Tyndale recognized that there was not a direct English translation of the Biblical Hebraic concept of deific satisfaction. So he took two words "at" and "onement" and put them together to reflect the dual aspect of Christ's sacrifice: the remission of sin and reconciliation of man to God. Tyndale's concept overcomes the limitations of the word "reconciliation" while incorporating aspects of propitiation and forgiveness.

The LDS mock Christians for using the word Trinity while they more laughably believe a sixteenth century man-made term was somehow translated from ancient golden plates into their Book of Mormon.

Whatever.

The word atonement is only found once in the King James version of the New Testament – in Romans 5:11 – and it was changed to "reconciliation" in later translations. But the word is frequently used in the Old Testament and was used to refer to when something *made satisfaction* for sin. Moses said,

> Exodus 32:30. *You have committed a great sin. So now I will go up to the LORD; perhaps I can make atonement for your sin.*

Thus, when atonement was done in the Old Testament, an act was done which would bring temporary satisfaction for sin which would reconcile the sinful individual (or nation) to God.

It was only by the shed blood of Jesus that permanent satisfaction can be had.

For the children of Israel, under the Law, the shed blood of animals made this temporary propitiation, and the people's righteous living by faith, ordinances, and works was requisite to show their love for God and man. By the "atonement of Christ" Christians generally mean all the work He did which expiates sin once and forever. When speaking of Christ's saving work, the word *satisfaction*, which is a word theologians of the Reformation used, is preferable to the word *atonement*, for Christ satisfied all demands of God – ALL – in behalf of sinners. To Christians, Christ's work consisted of suffering *and* (listen closely) ***and*** obedience! And because this work was vicarious, meaning it was not merely for our benefit but was in our very stead, He was our full and total substitute.

Because our sin and guilt was fully expiated (or covered) by the punishment which our Savior and King bore, God is rendered propitious, which simply means God's unconditional love and mercy is now made consistent with the eternal demands of His justice. By virtue of CHRIST'S work – obedience, righteousness, suffering, and death – our alienation from God ceases and reconciliation is brought about for good. And this reconciliation is mutual, meaning it is not only that of sinners toward God but it is also and pre-eminently that of God toward sinners!

It must also be constantly kept in mind that the atonement or reconciliation or satisfaction is not the cause of God's love toward guilty men and women but it is the consequence of His love toward us. Remember,

> John 3:16. *For God so loved the world that He gave His only begotten Son, that whoever believes in Him should not perish but have everlasting life.*

Christians know from the Bible that because Jesus came, lived perfectly and lovingly, obediently fulfilling the Law and the Prophets, and then suffered and died, full and complete forgiveness for all sin past, present, and future is had through grace by faith … and faith alone.

We joyfully read:

> Romans 5:1. *Therefore being justified by faith, we have peace with God through our Lord Jesus Christ.*

John 3:15 reminds us that *"whosoever* ***believeth in him*** *should not perish, but have eternal life."* Additionally, the Bible is clear that we are not only cleared and cleaned of all sin by our faith, we are also made righteous through His eternal reconciliation.

Listen carefully to what Romans 5 lays out for us, starting with verse six:

> Romans 5:6. *For when we were still without strength, in due time Christ died for the ungodly. For scarcely for a righteous man will one die; yet perhaps for a good man someone would even dare to die. But God demonstrates His own love toward us, in that while we were still sinners, Christ died for us.*

We learn here that God demonstrated His love for us by having His Son die for us WHILE we were sinners. The blood was not shed because we were righteous or would repent, but while we were sinful.

That's you and me.

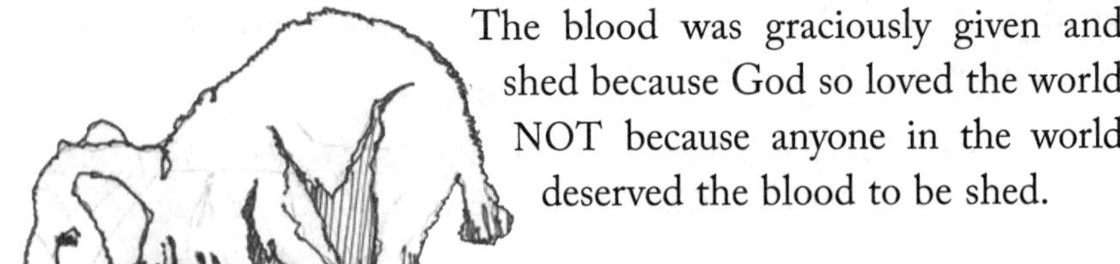

The blood was graciously given and shed because God so loved the world NOT because anyone in the world deserved the blood to be shed.

Got that?

Then in verse nine it reads (now listen closely):

> Romans 5:9. *Much more then, having now been justified by His blood, we shall be saved from wrath through Him.* ***For if when we were enemies we were reconciled to God through the death of His Son …***

[Meaning, if we were reconciled to God through the death of Jesus – meaning we are cleaned from sin by His death …] … *much more, having been reconciled, we shall be saved by His life.*

Meaning, we are imputed with His righteousness earned by HIS life – and not our own. This is very, very, very important, my friends in the LDS / Christian dialogue about atonement.

Why?

Because the LDS take Jesus' life, suffering, and death, and twist it up, then give it only partial significance and import – the rest is up to YOU. And this not only amounts to another gospel, it amounts to a burden and a lack of peace.

Let me give an example before I back it up with some support.

To Christians, Jesus' atonement could, in a very limited manner, be seen in the following illustration:

> We are all of us living in a village that is ruled by a benevolent and caring King. This beautiful King has provided a special servant to the small village who takes care of every need the people of the village might encounter. He brings them milk, food, heals them by the powers with which the King has invested him, and makes all things right and good. Everything the servant does is free to the people of the kingdom by virtue of the King's love and grace; but what enables the servant to show up and serve is a villager's belief – belief that the servant really will appear and that he will do as the King has promised. Nothing more.
>
> Now the villagers are broken up into two parties. One party believes that all they need to do is believe the King's promises and the servant will appear – and He does! They experience it constantly in their lives. But the other group of villagers doesn't think that believing the king is enough. So they send gifts to the King's castle, and dress really nicely, and post pictures of the King outside their homes, thinking they must do something to earn the King's favor, which, they believe, causes him to send the servant to their homes.
>
> Interestingly, the servant comes to all the homes of the village. He comes most abundantly to those who do nothing but believe and trust. These find themselves free to live and love others because of the unconditional love shown them by the King and not by their own efforts. The other villagers, because they do believe the servant does in fact exist, also have Him appear; but they are burdened with the false notion that they must do all sorts of things to keep the King happy so that the servant will continue to show up on their behalf.

This story illustrates the difference between the LDS understanding of atonement and the Christian knowledge of it. Christians believe in the servant wholly. They trust the King's written promises that the servant is there for them NOT because they deserve it, but because the King loves them and they trust his love and promises. The LDS believe that the servant will only appear and do work for them IF they do their part, if they throw in their efforts, if they merit the King's love.

Listen to what self-described LDS Apostle James E. Faust said about atonement as quoted in a 2001 November *Ensign* article ("The Atonement: Our Greatest Hope"):

> Our salvation depends on believing and accepting the Atonement. Such acceptance requires a continual effort to understand it more fully. The Atonement advances our mortal course of learning by making it possible for our natures to become perfect. All of us have sinned and need to repent to fully pay our part of the debt. When we sincerely repent, the Savior's magnificent Atonement pays the rest of that debt.

It is really important to know that, to the LDS, what Jesus did with His life and through His death does two things:

First, it gives all – everybody – the unconditional free gift, the unmerited gift, of physical immortality. To the Mormons, where Adam introduced physical death to the world, Jesus overcame it for everyone, and this part of the atonement amounts to all human beings being resurrected whether they believe in God or not. That is part A of the LDS interpretation of atonement: resurrection. Often, when a Mormon says they believe that people are saved by grace, what they really mean is by God's pure grace all people are saved from eternal physical death.

Part B of the LDS atonement is that Jesus' death and resurrection gives everyone "the opportunity" to become exalted, or in Christian parlance, to live with God. This comes by our work, our righteousness, our obedience, and our receiving all the required LDS ordinances.

Self-described Apostle Russell M. Nelson wrote in an *Ensign* article dated Feb 2003 ("Divine Love"):

> Thanks to the Atonement, the gift of immortality is unconditional. The greater gift of eternal life, however, is conditional. In order to qualify, one must deny oneself of ungodliness and honor the ordinances and covenants of the temple.

Where the Bible is emphatically clear that we are saved by our faith through grace alone (Ephesians 2:8-9); that there is nothing we can add to grace otherwise it would cease to be grace (Romans 11:6); and that if salvation is by grace it cannot be by ANYTHING else (Galatians 2:16); the LDS beliefs firmly deny such Biblical teachings.

Well-respected LDS apostle of old James E. Talmage said (*The Articles of Faith*, page 432):

> The sectarian dogma of justification by faith alone has exercised an influence for evil.

When a Latter-day Saint says that the atonement of Jesus Christ makes it possible for any and all of us to "live with God," that is an immediate confession, that they believe the wholly false notion that men are not saved by grace through faith alone but by grace through faith AND works – that it is the works they do that allows God to *apply the atonement* to their lives.

Another distinction between the LDS and the Bible-believing Christian is the way the atonement of Jesus Christ is applied to those who believe. To Christians, once a person comes to a saving faith, they are saved past, present, and future for the entire life of sin. This brings a peace to then follow God's commands out of gratitude, love, and a desire to improve that comes from the unconditional presence of His Holy Spirit. To the LDS, it is a much different matter because the atonement is sort of seen as being a powerful disinfectant that rests inside a locked first aid kit. If and when sin is committed, the sinful Latter-day Saint must prove their repentant attitude and do their part to cleanse the wound before they are given the combination to the lock on the first aid kit by God or their bishop. AFTER they are found worthy to apply the atonement to the sin-wound, they are given the combination and allowed to apply it – never before. This is wholly inconsistent with Jesus' work on earth and on the cross, for when He cried, "*It is finished!* (John 19:30)," the work was done. And when we receive the offering of His life by faith, the antiseptic is eternally applied.

My friends, one of the greatest religious lies ever printed and believed in the annals of false Christianity is the LDS Third Article of Faith, which reads:

> *We believe that through the Atonement of Christ, all mankind may be saved, by obedience to the laws and ordinances of the Gospel.*

How can I make such a brash statement? By reading the Word:

> Romans 3:20-28. *Therefore by the deeds of the law no flesh will be justified in His sight, for by the law is the knowledge of sin. But now the righteousness of God apart from the law is revealed, being witnessed by the Law and the Prophets, even the righteousness of God, through faith in Jesus Christ, to all and on all who believe. For there is no difference; for all have sinned and fall short of the glory of God, being justified freely by His grace through the redemption that is in Christ Jesus, whom God set forth as a propitiation by His blood, through faith, to demonstrate His righteousness, because in His forbearance God had passed over the sins that were previously committed, to demonstrate at the present time His righteousness, that He might be just and the justifier of the one who has faith in Jesus. Where is boasting then? It is excluded. By what law? Of works? No, but by the law of faith. Therefore we conclude that a man is justified by faith apart from the deeds of the law.*

"If water baptism were necessary for salvation God would have had a font sitting there next to the cross. Water baptism no more makes a person a Christian than circumcision makes a man a Jew."

Baptism

Baptism in water.

It's actually one of the more difficult topics we will discuss because what the Bible says has been very misunderstood by many people of many denominations and it takes an in-depth study of the Word to get to the heart of it all. Because many Christian denominations differ on the matter, the Christian/Mormon debate is further complicated.

Generally speaking, there are *two* main views regarding water baptism in the vast arena of doctrinal opinions.

The first states a person must be baptized to enter heaven.

The second states it is not essential to salvation.

Where the Anglicans, Apostolic Brethren, Christadelphians, Jehovah's Witnesses, Oneness Pentecostals, Revivalists, Roman Catholics, and a number of other faiths join the LDS belief that it is required for salvation, Baptists, Disciples of Christ, Anabaptists, Lutherans, Methodists, Wesleyans, Pentecostals, Presbyterians, Seventh-day Adventists, and the broad category of non-denominational born-again Christians say it is not.

One thing is certain: it is ignorant for anyone to take a single verse from the Bible to prove his pet position. Controversial as it may be, let me share my personal take on the debate before we examine the Biblical perspective: If someone thinks getting water baptized is a requirement to getting into heaven, they better do it. And if someone claims to want to follow the set-up of the early Christian church, they would want to embrace it joyfully. But, if someone misses the opportunity to be water baptized in this life it is irrelevant to their standing with God in the hereafter.

Now, what *does* water baptism mean to the Christian? Is it necessary for salvation? Why was Jesus baptized?

I want to try and plainly lay out the Biblical view of water baptism. Taken exegetically and contextually, the purpose and meaning of water baptism is quite clear once all things are considered.

So let's start by talking about John "*Le Baptiste*!"

What was that guy up to? A number of things.

First, John the Baptist was sent to prepare a way for the House of Israel to meet its King. God said:

> Malachi 3:1. *Behold, I will send my messenger, and* ***he shall prepare the way before me.***

And John came calling the Kingdom of Israel to repent and to prepare themselves to accept their King. His was a "Baptism of

Repentance" and he was preparing the Jews of Israel to repent for their failure under the system of the Law and to receive their King with their hearts and minds. And what method did John the Baptist use to prepare them? Water baptism!

Why water baptism?

Remember who he was dealing with – the Jews: a group of people who had a thousand years of washings (*mikvehs*) and cleansings which were primary in their rituals and rites of symbolic cleansing.

Symbolic cleansing of what? SIN! The water washing was symbolic of the cleansing of sin by the washing of the Holy Spirit.

> Ezekiel 36:25-27. *Then I will sprinkle clean water on you, and you shall be clean; I will cleanse you from all your filthiness and from all your idols. I will give you a new heart and put a new spirit within you; I will take the heart of stone out of your flesh and give you a heart of flesh. I will put My Spirit within you and cause you to walk in My statutes, and you will keep My judgments and do them.*

All the water and washings were emblematic of the washing away of sin by the presence of the Holy Spirit. But the Holy Spirit, Who does the cleansing in substance (not in symbolism, like the Jewish rituals), was not given by John, but by Jesus. Remember what John said to the Jews?

> Matthew 3:11. *I indeed baptize you with water unto repentance: but he that cometh after me is mightier than I, whose shoes I am not worthy to bear: he shall baptize you with the Holy Ghost, and with fire.*

This was the whole event for which John was preparing the Kingdom of Israel: the baptism of the Holy Spirit, and this came by Jesus.

Now these cleansing rituals of water with which the nation of Israel was so familiar were especially binding on their priests.

You see, at first, before the Law of Moses was given, every man was his own priest, and presented his own sacrifices before God (Genesis 4:3-7). Later on the office of priest devolved onto the head of the family, as in the cases of Noah (Genesis 8:20); Abraham (Genesis 12:7; 13:4); Isaac (Genesis 26:25); Jacob (Genesis 31:54); and Job (Job 1:5).

Then, with the Law of Moses given, God designated only men from the tribe of Levi to be His priests, specifically only those who came through Levi's son, Aaron. But all of these priesthood appellations were only temporarily in place and looked to the time when the true High Priest would come, Who was without sin; and shed His own perfect blood instead of the blood of animals, entered into God's presence once and for all with His eternal offering (Hebrews 10:10-14).

So when John the Baptist began his prophetic mission to prepare the way for the King, he was calling all of Israel to repent and prepare themselves for the King's coming and there was no more symbolic method to prepare the people than an act tied to the water and washing rites of purification: baptism. Add the fact that when a Gentile converted to being a Jew they, too, were immersed in water and we have a solid picture of John's baptism unto repentance and why he did it.

Now understand, this specific water baptism that John performed has *nothing* to do with us who have faith in Jesus and have become the recipients of His Grace. It was a completely different baptism and had a completely different purpose than baptism has for us.

The Bible speaks of all sorts of baptisms. Some are wet, some are dry, some are moist. There are baptisms of spirit, baptisms unto suffering, baptisms of trials.

So why *was* Jesus baptized by John the Baptist?

Mormonism makes it seem like Jesus was baptized to show the world that they had to be baptized, too, as a means to be righteous and to join a church. This is such a simplistic manipulation of the event! Remember, John's baptism was NOT a Christian baptism. Nor were the water baptisms Jesus' disciples did while He was alive! Those were "baptisms unto repentance" for the house of Israel.

Listen closely.

There was no "Christianity" when Jesus was alive, no body of Christ was established: His body was still here on earth! There was no Christian baptism until after the death, resurrection, and ascension of Christ, as the New Testament economy did not even exist until then. John's baptism bound its subjects to repentance relative to the Law and the Messiah, and not to the faith of Christ and being buried with Him. To support this, remember that John's baptism was not administered in the name of the Father, Son and Holy Spirit. It was a water baptism unto repentance, AND (and this IS very IMPORTANT) those whom John baptized were re-baptized by Paul later on! (see Acts 18:24; 19:7 for support of this).

Are you starting to get the Biblical picture of the baptism John the Baptist performed and that the purposes behind it are not tied to why we are baptized today?

Now there are a number of very important reasons why Jesus was baptized but obviously, it was not for a remission of sin or an act of repentance. Let me ask you a question, what was the initiatory ordinance of the <u>Mosaic</u> dispensation? It was the old "snippy-snippy:" circumcision. (Ouch!) And just as Christ was submitted to circumcision, which was the initiatory ordinance of the Mosaic dispensation, it was necessary that he should submit to the initiatory ordinance of the dispensation of grace and truth – water baptism! *Christ was circumcised, and observed all the other ordinances of the law of Moses, not with a view to his own justification, but to fulfil the dispensation committed to him by God.*

Sometimes, when people ask, *"Why was Jesus baptized?"* I ask, *"Why was He circumcised? Was circumcision mandatory to salvation for the Jews or to Jesus?"*

No.

"So then, to Jesus, is baptism mandatory for Christians today?"

No.

Circumcision is *best* understood as an ordinance of "identity" which, in and of itself, had no power or ability to actually make a person part of the house of Israel. A pagan could go out and circumcise himself and it would not make him pleasing to God; rather, it was the heart and faith. In the Christian economy the rite of water baptism ought to be seen in the same light: as a means to identify ourselves as His, as Christians. The problem is organized religions have taken the beauty and power of baptism and applied and *used it* to their own benefit, NOT to the benefit of the believer and his or her life of faith. They act as if baptism actually cleanses sin, or that it makes a person a member of the Body of Christ. And through this perfunctory approach to it, it is stripped of its pure purpose. I mean, the LDS baptize children when they are eight years of age and make the intended purpose of it perfunctory.

Now, Jesus was also baptized for other necessary and important reasons. The book of Hebrews tells us plainly that Jesus is our final and last high priest, and will be this high priest for us forever and ever. And as every high priest was initiated into his office by washing and anointing, so was Christ: by being baptized (washed) and anointed (by the Holy Spirit), Who descended upon Christ in the form of a dove. By this, therefore, He fulfilled the righteous ordinance of his initiation into the office of High Priest, and thus was prepared to make a full and final atonement once and for all for the sins of mankind.

It was in this respect that Jesus "fulfilled all righteousness" by being baptized or washed by water.

In another respect, Jesus was baptized by water as a means to fulfill prophecy. Jesus not only let John the Baptist baptize Him to put an end to the Mosaic dispensation and to initiate the beginning of the Christian dispensation of grace, He at the same time affirmed the purpose of John the Baptist's ministry as it was prophetically recorded in Malachi. Remember what it said?

> Malachi 3:1. *Behold, I will send my messenger, and he shall prepare the way before me:*

And then in the Gospel of John we read the fulfillment of the Malachi reference when John the Beloved tells us the story of the meeting of Jesus and John the Baptist.

Listen!

> John 1:29. *The next day John seeth Jesus coming unto him, and saith, Behold the Lamb of God, which taketh away the sin of the world. This is he of whom I said, After me cometh a man which is preferred before me: for he was before me. And I knew him not: but that he should be made manifest to Israel, therefore am I come baptizing with water. And John bare record, saying, I saw the Spirit descending from heaven like a dove, and it abode upon him. And I knew him not: but he that sent me to baptize with water, the same said unto me, Upon whom thou shalt see the Spirit descending, and remaining on him, the same is he which baptizeth with the Holy Ghost. And I saw, and bare record that this is the Son of God.*

When John baptized the Lord, God – the One Who sent John

out to baptize – had told Him that He "*Upon whom thou shalt see the Spirit descending, and remaining on him, the same is he which baptizeth with the Holy Ghost* (John 1:33)." In other words, God told John the Baptist to look for the sign of the Holy Ghost descending upon a Person and when he saw it he would have the sign and know who the Messiah was.

And what would that Messiah do? Baptize with the Holy Spirit, which is what spiritual rebirth is, and which is what we have to experience if we ever want to see the Kingdom of Heaven (John 3:3).

Bottom-line, Jesus being baptized has nothing to do with baptism being mandatory for YOUR salvation, as the LDS attempt to imply. In Mormonism, baptism is not only requisite to enter the celestial kingdom, it is tantamount to being born again. (I am not going to cover this aspect of the LDS view of baptism because I will cover that when we discuss being born again in another section.) Nevertheless, to the LDS, official water baptism, which can ONLY come by the LDS priesthood holder, and receiving the gift of the Holy Ghost, which also can only come through the hands of an LDS priesthood holder, are what being born again means to a Mormon.

So then, what of water baptism in the Christian dispensation?

The words "baptize" and "baptism" are simply Greek words transferred into English. This was done by the translators of the Scriptures and no literal translation can really express all that is implied in the Greek terms. The modes of baptism – you know, dipping, sprinkling, immersing – can in *no way* be determined from the Greek word rendered "baptize." *Baptizo* means both to dip a thing into an element or liquid, and to put an element or liquid over or on it. It was an industrial term for dying a fabric, which truly relates to the important overall concept of "identification." The word has a wide latitude of meaning as it is applied even in the Septuagint to sprinklings, washings, pourings, and dippings.

In the New Testament there is not one single well-authenticated instance of the occurrence of the word where it necessarily means immersion, and none of the instances of baptism recorded in the book of Acts (Acts 2:38-41; 8:26-39; 9:17,18; 22:12-16; 10:44-48; 16:32-34) favors the notion that it was by dipping or immersing, although it seems immersion was most probable. Remember, the gospel and its elements are designed for all people over the whole world, and we cannot become so dogmatic or religiously institutionalized as to believe there is only one way to administer something that is symbolic in the first place. A person who loves Jesus in the Arctic or the Sudan will seek identification in whatever way is available – and God honors their faithful attempt.

Mormonism would have you believe otherwise. Because it wants to come between you and God.

Baptism and the Lord's Supper are the two symbolic ordinances of the New Testament which serve to remind and identify us with Him. The supper represents the work of Christ, and baptism the work of the Spirit. We take communion because we believe and *have been* saved by His blood, not *to* believe or *be* saved by His blood. We are baptized because we believe and *have been* saved by His blood, not *to* believe or *be* saved by His blood. To the Christian, water baptism is an outward, public pronouncement of an inward faith, symbolic that we are willing to be buried with Christ (thus turning our back on the former things of our life) and being raised with Him unto a new life. It is *the* public profession of our faith.

Perhaps one of the best verses that illustrate this order of saving faith before the public profession of water baptism is found in the second chapter of Acts. Ironically, it is also a verse that makes the subject of baptism so controversial.

Peter stands up before a crowd of Jews on the day of Pentecost. They believe his message surrounding Christ, and Peter cries:

> Acts 2:38. *Repent, and be baptized every one of you in the name of Jesus Christ* **for** *the remission of sins . . . .*

Now these Jews, who came from all over, *believed* what Peter was preaching: that Jesus, Whom they crucified, is indeed their Messiah (Acts 2:23, 36). As a result of their faith (Acts 2:37 says, *"when they heard [Peter's preaching], they were pricked in their heart …"),* Peter then says, *Now change your minds on all you have carried with you regarding the Messiah, and be baptized for the remission of sins ...*

The key to a proper understanding of this verse is the Greek. *"Repent and be baptized every one or you in the name of Jesus Christ FOR the remission of sins..."* In the Greek, "for" is "*eis*," a preposition that can indicate *causality* (like "in order to get" something) OR as a *resultant preposition* (as in "the result of" or "because of" something). So let's read this verse in the causal preposition sense:

> Repent and be baptized every one or you in the name of Jesus Christ IN ORDER TO GET the remission of sins...

Now let's read it with the preposition being resultant.

> Repent and be baptized every one of you in the name of Jesus Christ BECAUSE YOU HAVE RECEIVED the remission of sins...

Guess what? In Acts 2:38, the preposition sense is RESULTANT! And it clearly states that they were to embrace water baptism BECAUSE they had received the remission of sin!

Praise God!

Baptism is not some act we take to get us into heaven. It is a sacrament, like taking communion, which serves as a gift from God to man. Religions want you to believe you must have their respective baptism and you must take their communion to enter heaven.

Not so.

You must believe on Him whom God sent to save us from sin. Baptism follows them that believe.

I love the Lord's gift of baptism. And I think it is certainly a command of God for every Christian saved by grace who is in a place to undertake it. With it comes a power and a peace that is other worldly, one I never expected prior to my own public descent unto His death.

I challenge all Latter-day Saints, if they really love Jesus, to get baptized as a public profession of faith and a willingness to follow Jesus and Jesus alone - NOT A CHURCH. What have you to fear? Certainly not the Lord. He will delight in your coming to Him in this way, the way of faith.

And let me tell you, you'll experience Him in ways that defy R-E-L-I-G-I-O-N.

* * *

"Joseph Smith's older brother Alvin died without being baptized. A Christian pastor told his family that because of this he was in hell. Herein lies the genesis of the LDS practice of baptism for the dead. Revealed, so to speak, to Joseph so he could comfort his parents and family."

Baptism for the Dead

In the last section we discussed Baptism, and talked about how within Mormonism it is doctrinal to believe it is necessary for salvation.

Because the LDS believe baptism is required to enter heaven, Joseph had to sort of figure out what happens to people who die without having ever had a chance to hear the Mormon gospel and receive the LDS baptism that is requisite to enter the celestial kingdom. The problem of people who die without water baptism was not only a hot topic among interested Christians living around the Smiths in the early 1800s; it was a very important topic to Joseph Smith personally. Joseph had an older brother named Alvin, whom the entire family looked to as a leader in the home. Well, Alvin got very sick and died – without ever having received water baptism.

Enter one ignorant and insensitive Christian preacher who came to the Smith home shortly after Alvin passed and announced that Alvin was in hell because he lacked the water rite. Needless to say, the preacher's errant opinion deeply hurt Joseph's mother and, in my opinion, served to inflame young Joseph against all creedal Christianity.

Hard to blame him.

I suggest that young Joseph, smart as a whip, said to himself, "This makes no sense to me at all. There must be some other solution." Then later, as Joseph was wont to do, he provided a solution – a ritual called baptism for the dead – which, unlike some of his other ideas, he could support through a single Bible reference.

This is how it works: Faithful LDS believers qualify to go to LDS temples. Inside they perform vicarious LDS works and ordinances for those who have passed on to the spirit world. This is why they do genealogy – to find the names of people and relatives in whose names these ordinances can be done. The works done in the temple for dead people include what are called the "endowment," "washings and anointing," "sealings," "priesthood ordinations," and "baptisms," or "baptisms for the dead," which is the first rite performed in the name of a deceased person.

So let me give you an example of how it works. Let's say there was a man named Jacobus Fountainbleau who lived in Paris France and died in 1752. Someone alive today, in doing her genealogy, discovers all the necessary information on the life and death of Jacobus Fountainbleau. This living person would submit Jacobus' name to an LDS temple for all the required works of salvation to be done on his behalf. The first thing to be done for Jacobus is baptism.

And in the LDS church, while any adult can do baptisms for the dead, the youth – ages 12 and up – are allowed and encouraged to step in and get baptized on behalf of them. This is one of the only things youth get to do in LDS temples. So, for example's sake, one day after school, an LDS ward takes its youth to the temple to do baptisms for the dead. They change into white clothes and go down to the basement of the temple where they will find a baptismal font, usually a large Jacuzzi-like tub that rests on twelve graven oxen. One by one a youth will step into the waters and get baptized on behalf of a number of dead people, including Jacobus Fountainbleu. And then others, over the course of time, will actually go through and do the rest of those rites and rituals for Jacobus in the LDS temple.

Where Christians trust that the thief on the cross went directly to paradise without water baptism, the LDS reconcile the LORD's words to the thief – that *today you will be with me in paradise* (Luke 23:43) – with the idea that the thief had to wait for all these rites and rituals to be done on his behalf before he could actually enter into heaven.

How important is this so-called *"work for the dead"* to the LDS?

Where Jesus said, *"Let the dead bury their dead* (Matthew 8:22; Luke 9:60)," Joseph Smith Jr. said (*TPJS*, page 356):

> The *GREATEST* responsibility in this world that God has placed upon us is to seek after our dead.

In a world where many people struggle just to help, serve, and love the living, the LDS have the added responsibility of saving everyone who has EVER died!

And the yoke is not easy nor the burden light.

Listen to another more ominous teaching from Mormonism's founding prophet, Joseph Smith, relative to baptism for the dead (*TPJS*, page 356):

> This doctrine presents in a clear light the wisdom and mercy of God in preparing an ordinance for the salvation of the dead, being baptized by proxy, their names recorded in heaven and they judged according to the deeds done in the body. This doctrine was the burden of the scriptures. Those saints who neglect it on behalf of their deceased relatives do it at the peril of their own salvation.

So this is the situation: Latter-day Saints are told that they must do and receive a number of things for their own person in order to be accepted of God. That list is LONG. But it doesn't end there. Joseph Smith himself said that the MOST important work for a Mormon is the work they do for the dead – which, if neglected – places their very salvation in peril!

And what is required for a member to do the work for their dead?

More requirements, including the payment of a full tithe, which has been determined to be 10% of a member's gross income.

And Jesus said,

> Matthew 11:28. *Come unto me and I will give you rest.*

Rest.

Peace. Rest. Ease. Joy.

Now, when LDS missionaries knock on an investigator's door and share the message of Mormonism, they have a really nice method of justifying and supporting their practice of baptism for the dead: a single, solitary reference to it found in 1 Corinthians chapter 15 and verse 29. The method is effective as the missionaries will first teach about the unique LDS practice of baptism for the dead, and then they will say, "Mr. Investigator, will you please turn to first Corinthians 15:29 and read it?

And opening the Bible, the investigator reads, wholly out of context, a question Paul asks the people of Corinth:

> 1 Corinthians 15:29. *Else what shall they do which are baptized for the dead, if the dead rise not at all? why are they then baptized for the dead?*

With the missionaries having first planted a pretext in the mind that the LDS are the ONLY ones who do and teach this unique concept, and then to actually open the Bible and read a passage out of the New Testament that refers to it specifically, many investigators of Mormonism are at least minimally intrigued – if not completely convinced - that baptism for the dead makes sense and is of God.

At the Salt Lake City LDS Headquarters Visitors Center there is a plaque titled "Baptism for the Dead." It reads:

> To give everyone the opportunity for baptism, the Savior established a sacred ordinance which the apostle Paul referred to as 'baptism for the dead.' Although this ordinance was lost for cen-

> turies after the death of the original apostles, it has been restored in our time by the Savior himself...

Did "*the Savior himself*" establish this "*sacred ordinance*" as the LDS claim? Let's take a look at the historical/Biblical supports of this practice. The next several pages are taken from the article, "Did Jesus Establish Baptism for the Dead?" (Luke Wilson, www.inplainsite.org):

> 1 Corinthians 15:29 reads, "*Else what shall they do which are baptized for the dead, if the dead rise not at all? why are they then baptized for the dead?*" The first thing to notice about this verse is that baptism for the dead is only *mentioned*, it is not actually *taught.* Given the scanty nature of the evidence, it is especially important to follow sound principles of scriptural interpretation in seeking to understand this verse. Two basic principles relevant to this task are:
>
> 1. Do not read a verse in isolation, but carefully consider it in its *context*; and
> 2. Use clear, unambiguous scriptural passages to interpret what is obscure or less clear, not the other way around.
>
> A superficial reading of 1 Corinthians 15:29 in isolation from its context may suggest support for baptism for the dead. However, a careful study of the verse in its context and in the light of other relevant Biblical passages, shows that this support is anything but obvious. Following the principles described above, we should ask several diagnostic questions:
>
> 1. Is there anything earlier in 1 Corinthians (i.e., the broader context) that throws light on the mention of baptism for the dead in 15:29?
> 2. What is the theme and line of argument in the verses leading up to Paul's mention of the rite (i.e., the immediate context)?
> 3. How does its mention in verse 29 fit into this line of argument?

4. What about the teaching on baptism in other epistles of Paul and elsewhere in the New Testament (Biblical theology): is the view that the apostle is here giving approval to baptism for the dead consistent with other Biblical teaching, and with that of Jesus and the other New Testament writers?

Questions such as these will help us arrive at an accurate interpretation of verse 29, and avoid the pitfall of reading into it our own preconceived ideas.

The broader context. There are three other references to baptism in 1 Corinthians: 1:14-17, 10:2, and 12:13. In 1:14-17 Paul raises the subject of baptism in the context of expressing his concern about contention and party factions among the Christians at Corinth:

> 1 Corinthians 1:14-17. *I thank God that I baptized none of you, but Crispus and Gaius; Lest any should say that I baptized in my own name. And I baptized also the household of Stephanas: besides, I know not whether I baptized any other. For* ***Christ sent***

> ***me not to baptize, but to preach the gospel:*** *not with wisdom of words, lest the cross of Christ should be made of none effect.*

By his words, "*Christ sent me not to baptize, but to preach the gospel,*" Paul is reminding the Corinthians that it is the message of Christ's death for our sins (received in heartfelt faith) that can regenerate and transform the inner person, *not* the external rite of baptism, important though it is as an outward sign of faith and obedience. The fact that the Corinthian Christians needed this reminder indicates that they over-rated the importance of baptism, and that the apostle felt the need to steer them back to a correct, balanced understanding of its significance.

Then in 10:2, the apostle uses the word "*baptized*" in describing the Israelites' crossing of the Red Sea:

> (1 Corinthians 10:2) … *all were baptized unto Moses in the cloud and in the sea.*

Though this is a figurative use of the term, Paul uses it to build on his earlier reminder of the priority of faith and inner regeneration over baptism (1:14-17). To the Corinthians with their inflated view of baptism, he makes the point that though all the Israelites who came out of Egypt were figuratively "baptized," they were not all thereby insured of God's favor:

> (1 Corinthians 10:5) *But with many of them God was not well pleased: for they were overthrown in the wilderness.*

Finally, in 12:13, Paul mentions baptism as an argument for Christian unity:

> (1 Corinthians 12:13) *For by one Spirit are we all baptized into one body.*

Here again, it is not the rite of baptism itself that is critical, but the reality of union with Christ which baptism pictures (Romans 6:3-4), wrought not by water but by the Spirit.

The Corinthians' inflated view of baptism holds an important clue to the meaning of 1 Corinthians 15:29. For as we shall see, baptism for the dead is linked by the apostle to an errant group within the Corinthian church, whose false teaching the entire fifteenth chapter of 1 Corinthians – including verse 29 – aims to correct.

The immediate context. The best way to understand any single verse in Scripture is to examine the verses surrounding it. And when we read 1 Corinthians 15:29 in its context, it is clear that resurrection, not baptism, is the single, dominating theme throughout chapter 15.

In verses 1-11, Paul declares that Christ, after he died for our sins, was raised from the dead, a fact amply attested to by "*above 500*" witnesses (verse 6), most of whom he says are still alive as he writes.

Then in verses 12-49 the apostle marshals a series of arguments for the importance and reasonableness of the doctrine of the resurrection of the body. Here, the modern reader needs to keep in mind that the Hebrew-Christian doctrine of the resurrection, which we take for granted, was considered foolishness in ancient Greek culture (and of course Corinth was a Greek city). What is important to see is that Paul's mention of baptism for the dead in verse 29 is one of this series of arguments introduced to serve his purpose of defending the reasonableness of resurrection.

The real question to ask then is, *who is it at Corinth that is practicing baptism for the dead, and do they and the practice have the apostle's approval?*

"Some among you." Paul's blunt rhetorical question in verse 12 expresses the burden of the chapter:

> 1 Corinthians 15:12. *Now if Christ be preached that he rose from the dead,* ***how say some among you that there is no resurrection of the dead?***

An important thing to notice is that the entire series of arguments in verses 13-49 is specifically aimed at refuting these false teachers within the Corinthian congregation *("some among you")* who are openly denying the resurrection. The following outline gives an overview of the passage:

1. If there is no resurrection, Christ is not risen (vv. 13,16); therefore
2. Our preaching is vain, we are yet in our sins (vv. 14,17); therefore
3. We are false witnesses (v. 15); therefore
4. The dead in Christ are perished (v. 18); therefore
5. Christians are of all people most miserable (v. 19).
6. As death came by one man (Adam) upon all who descended from him, so resurrection to life is brought by one man (Christ) to all who belong to Him (vv. 20-22).
7. The order of resurrection: Christ first, then those who are Christ's at His return (vv. 23-28).
8. The false teachers who deny the resurrection are inconsistent when they baptize for the dead, for the practice is based on the hope of resurrection (v. 29).
9. Why suffer abuse for the gospel if there is no resurrection (vv. 30-34)?
10. Resurrection is analogous to a seed, which through death brings forth more abundant life (vv. 35-38).
11. The nature of the resurrection body is different from the mortal body, as the flesh of humans, mammals, and fish are different from each other (v. 39).
12. The resurrection body is of greater glory than the mortal body, as the sun is of greater glory than moon (vv. 40-41).
13. Various contrasts are given between the resurrection body and our mortal bodies (vv. 2-49).

Verse 29 takes the form of another rhetorical question:

(1 Corinthians 15:29) *Else what shall they do which are bap-*

tized for the dead, if the dead rise not at all? why are they then baptized for the dead?

Here the Paul points out the fact that since it is the human body that is baptized, those who perform such a rite in proxy for a deceased person must do so because they have the hope of future resurrection for that person. Thus, the primary function of the verse is as yet another argument in support of resurrection.

Did Paul endorse the practice? The fact that Paul's mention of baptism for the dead is not an endorsement is signaled by the impersonal manner in which he refers to the practitioners: *"Else what shall **they** do which are baptized for the dead, if the dead rise not at all? Why then are **they** baptized for the dead?"* If the rite was a legitimate part of apostolic teaching, we might have expected the apostle to say "what shall *you* do..." or "what shall *we* do..."

It is clear from Romans 9:1-3 and 10:1-4 that Paul was acutely conscious that many among his own Jewish kinsmen were outside the gospel fold. He speaks of having *"great heaviness and continual sorrow in my heart"* for his Hebrew brethren (Romans 9:2), and declares that *"my heart's desire and prayer to God for Israel is, that they might be saved* (Romans 10:1)." Certainly there would have been some from the apostle's own extended family who had gone to their graves unbaptized. *If Paul taught baptism for the dead, it is inexplicable that he would exclude himself from those who practiced the rite*, as he surely does when he writes, "*what shall **they** do which are baptized for the dead...*"

Notice, too, that in verses 30-32 the apostle immediately contrasts the fringe group practicing baptism for the dead with himself and the broader Christian community: *"And why stand **we** in jeopardy every hour...what advantageth it me if the dead rise not."* Indeed, the impersonal "*they*" contrasts markedly with Paul's practice throughout 1 Corinthians 15, where he consistently addresses his readers as *"you"* (vv. 1, 2, 3, 11, 12, 14, 17, 31, 34, 36, 51, 58, or, (including himself) *"we"* or *"us"* (vv. 3, 15, 19, 30, 32, 49, 51, 52).

Who are "they"? If we ask who the "they" in verse 29 refers to, the context clearly points us back to verse 12. It is those within the Corinthian congregation who are denying the resurrection, and whom the entire passage is written to refute. Then the biting aspect of Paul's argument becomes clear: *These false teachers are inconsistent; they deny the resurrection, yet engage in a practice – baptism for the dead – which is based on the hope of resurrection.*

This is exactly the understanding of the text held by the early Christian writer Tertullian. Writing about A.D. 180, he makes this comment on 1 Corinthians 15:29:

> His [Paul's] only aim in alluding to it was that he might all the more firmly insist upon the resurrection of the body, in proportion as they who were vainly baptized for the dead resorted to the practice from their belief of such a resurrection"

Ironically, the *Encyclopedia of Mormonism* (1:97) espouses this same interpretation of the verse:

> ... Paul clearly refers to a distinct group within the Church, a group that he accuses of inconsistency between ritual and doctrine.

Thus, far from endorsing baptism for the dead, Paul associates it with a group whom he has already identified as being in deep spiritual error.

Why didn't Paul refute the practice? But would the apostle Paul use a practice of which he disapproved (baptism for the dead) to support something he wanted to affirm (resurrection)? On thoughtful study, this objection proves to have much less basis than first meets the eye. There are at least four grounds for answering *yes* to this question, and for explaining why the apostle does not stop to refute the practice of baptism for the dead.

First, Paul has already associated the rite with false teachers. So in this sense, it has no positive standing and needed no special refutation.

Second, history has amply vindicated the apostle Paul's inspired judgment. The practice of baptism for the dead, in fact, never became widespread, which even the *Encyclopedia of Mormonism* acknowledges, as noted earlier. Only a few isolated sects have practiced it, including the heretical Marcionite sect in the second century, and the Ephrata Society, a Christian occult group in Pennsylvania in the 1700s. These two groups have little in common with each other, and even less with Mormon teaching, so the claim that baptism for the dead was part of original Christianity that was lost lacks any historical or logical basis.

Third, Paul's statement at the beginning of 1 Corinthians, noted earlier – *Christ sent me not to baptize but to preach the gospel* (1:16) – is a reminder that baptism does not have the same indispensable importance that faith in Christ has. This is an indirect slap at the logic of baptism for the dead, which implies that baptism is indispensable for resurrection to eternal life.

Fourth, Paul does elsewhere use something with which he disagrees to make a theological point. In 1 Corinthians 8:10, the apostle refers to eating meat in an idol's temple without showing it to be wrong in itself; however, that he believed it is wrong is clear from what he says later in 1 Corinthians 10:21ff.

Although the Book of Mormon is described as containing "*the fullness of the everlasting gospel* (*Doctrine and Covenants* 27:5)," and although baptism for the dead is a central teaching of the LDS gospel, the Book of Mormon contains no reference whatsoever to the practice, either direct or indirect. This can easily be verified by checking under "Baptism for the Dead" in the LDS Church's *Topical Guide to the Scriptures* or the Index to the Triple Combination – the only references given there are from four sections of the *Doctrine and Covenants* (124,127,128,138). This point can also be verified by looking in the Index provided at the back of the Book of Mormon; it has no entry for baptism for the dead. Thus, there is no evidence that the people described in the Book of Mormon practiced, or knew of, baptism for the dead. This being the case, either the Book of Mormon does not contain the fullness of the gospel or baptism for the dead is not part of the fullness thereof.

❋ ❋ ❋

"Since the beginning of time, there has been a war against God's revealed word. Today, that war continues. People demean it, mock it, hate it, alter it, abuse it, misquote it, change it completely, or deny its authenticity. They say it cannot be trusted, that it was written by men, that it is mis-translated, and they ignorantly liken the translating process to party games like, 'telephone.' But God Himself said, 'Heaven and earth shall pass away, but my Word shall never pass away.' In this we can trust."

The Bible

The Lord said unto Moses:

Exodus 17:14. ***Write*** *this for a memorial in a book, and rehearse it in the ears of Joshua.*

The Lord told Isaiah:

Isaiah 30:8. *Now go,* ***write it*** *before them in a table, and* ***note it in a book****, that it may be for the time to come for ever and ever.*

Jeremiah wrote:

Jeremiah 30:2. *Thus speaketh the LORD God of Israel, saying,* ***Write thee*** *all the words that I have spoken unto thee in a book.*

Habakkuk reports:

Habakkuk 2:2. *And the LORD answered me, and said,* ***Write*** *the vision, and make it plain upon tables, that he may run that readeth it.*

Paul wrote:

> 1 Corinthians 14:37. *If any man think himself to be a prophet, or spiritual, let him acknowledge that the things that* ***I write*** *unto you are the commandments of the Lord.*

John the Beloved wrote:

> 1 John 2:13. ***I write*** *unto you, fathers, because ye have known him that is from the beginning.* ***I write*** *unto you, young men, because ye have overcome the wicked one.* ***I write*** *unto you, little children, because ye have known the Father.*

Peter wrote:

> 1 Peter 1:25. *But the* ***word of the Lord*** *endureth for ever. And this is the word which by the gospel is preached unto you.*

Peter called Paul's writings "scripture:"

> 2 Peter 3:15, 16. … *the longsuffering of our Lord is salvation; even as our beloved brother Paul also according to the wisdom given unto him hath written unto you; As also in all his epistles, speaking in them of these things; in which are some things hard to be understood, which they that are unlearned and unstable wrest, as they do also the other Scriptures...*

Jesus Himself told John,

> Revelation 1:11. *I am Alpha and Omega, the first and the last: and, What thou seest, write in a book, and send it unto the seven churches which are in Asia.*

I have a question: Why did God tell all of these men, all the way back 4000 or so years, to write?

Why does Jesus say,

> Matthew 24:35. *Heaven and earth shall pass away, but my words shall not pass away.*

Why did the Psalmist (138:2) write that God *magnifies* ***His Word*** *above His own name?*

When Jesus was tempted by Satan in the wilderness (Matthew 4), His constant response was, *"It it written ..."*

How can God expect people to *"keep My commandments"* if the record of His commandments are not reliable?

Is the God who created everything from nothing, who measures the heavens with the span of his hand, who controls all things, powerful enough to preserve the words He commanded men to write to this day and age unscathed? These are just a few – of the hundreds – of questions I have regarding the certainty of God's holy word known as the Bible.

There seem to be a couple of central themes enemies of Christianity go after when it comes to attacking the faith. The first is when they go after the deity, person, and story of Jesus; but in close second – which we are going to talk about tonight – is the reliability *and exclusivity* of the Bible as God's Holy Word. We have long maintained that if someone can remove a person's trust in the Bible as reliable and/or get them to believe that other writings are just as valid (if not more), then he can get anyone to believe anything he wants. It happens all the time.

One remarkable fact about the Bible is that in and of itself it has no "owner" here on earth. Have you ever thought of that? In and of itself, within its covers, it has everything necessary to lead any person to salvation, and to then serve as a guide to their Christian walk. The same cannot be said of other proprietary religious books like *Dianetics*, *A Course in Miracles, The Koran,* and/or The Book of Mormon. And yet so many people who are willing to place their faith and trust in books like these insist on labeling the Bible as faulty, fiction, or the manipulation of men, which naturally opens them up to embracing all sorts of myths and fables.

In this past month alone I have personally broken bread with two very intelligent men, both of whom completely and fully reject the Bible as reliable and trustworthy and/or as God's inspired word to man, but who both, fully, completely, and without even knowing each other, are certain that alien life-forces are not only here on earth right now, but assign the creation of heaven, earth, and humanity into these alien hands as well! Reject the trustworthiness of the Bible and you can get searching men and women to embrace almost anything. One man who understood this premise very well was one Joseph Smith, Jr.

Back in 1827 through 1829 Joseph had been telling people in his wooded community that he was visited by an angel (on the eve of the Autumnal equinox, no less) who revealed to him that there were some buried golden plates hidden in a hill near his home. Over the course of around seven years Joseph had been promising to bring forth this new book once he had translated it. He assured many that this was going to be a new book of ancient scripture.

Once the book known as the Book of Mormon was published, a reader could open it up and within thirty pages begin reading built-in attacks on the Bible. In the beginning of the Book of Mormon it says (of the Bible):

> 1 Nephi 13:38. Wherefore thou seest that after the book [meaning the Bible] hath gone forth through the hands of the great and abominable church [meaning the Catholics] that there are MANY PLAIN AND PRECIOUS THINGS TAKEN AWAY FROM THE BOOK which is the book of the Lamb of God.

In other words, the Bible cannot be trusted.

Not too many pages later, the Book of Mormon presents a built-in justification for its own existence relative to the Bible, by stating:

> 2 Nephi 29:6. Wherefore, because you have a Bible ye need not suppose that it contains all my words; neither need ye suppose that I have not caused more to be written.

So right in the founding writings of Mormonism we discover the two-pronged method of attacking God's Word:

> First, state that "it cannot be trusted," and second, "that there are other writings that can." This method is used by scientologists, Christian Scientists, Jehovah's Witnesses, Muslims, and almost every single religious group centered on the ideas and thoughts of man instead of what men of God were told to write.

As time passed, Joseph Smith continued to subtly demean the reliability of the Bible. In an LDS Article of Faith, he said:

> We believe the Bible to be the Word of God as far as it is translated correctly.

Unfortunately, the way and method that the LDS determine if a Biblical verse has been "translated correctly" or not is not through scholarship or the study of the ancient language but WHETHER or not the Bible passage in question supports Mormon doctrine!

I'm not kidding.

Founding prophet Joseph Smith is quoted (*TPJS*, page 310) also as saying:

> There are many things in the Bible which do not, as they now stand, accord with the revelations of the Holy Ghost to me.

From this little collection of subtle statements, Joseph Smith, while alive, released a giant dismissive snowball, which began to roll from the Latter-day Saints against the ability to trust God's Holy Word.

Late LDS Apostle – APOSTLE! – Orson Pratt said (*Divine Authenticity of the Book of Mormon* 3:47):

> Who, in his right mind, could, for one moment, suppose the Bible in its present form to be a perfect guide? Who knows that even one verse of the Bible has escaped pollution?

APOSTLE Bruce McConkie (**APOSTLE!**) wrote that (*The Millennial Messiah*, page 161):

> Satan guided his servants in taking many plain and precious things, and many covenants of the Lord, from the Bible, SO THAT MEN WOULD STUMBLE AND FALL AND LOSE THEIR SOULS!

In 1991, Brigham Young University … *ahem* … Professor, Robert Matthews, wrote ("What the Book of Mormon Tells Us," *Doctrines of the Book of Mormon: The 1991 Sperry Symposium*, pages 95-96) :

> Soon after the New Testament was written there were persons among the Gentiles who systematically, with wicked motives and evil intent, removed portions of the sacred Word, and took from the Bible much very important doctrinal information.

So even though the LDS include the Bible in the four books they call Scripture, the bottom line reality is the Bible, within Mormonism proper, is:

1. Considered unreliable, especially compared to the BOM;
2. Considered corrupt to some degree or another;
3. Is NOT taught but is truly only reviewed in a sense, highlighting areas that support LDS thought and teachings; and

4. Is inferior to other LDS scripture and to modern-day revelation.

I suggest to you, here and now, that the SINGLE most damaging doctrine, teaching, and attitude in Mormonism today is NOT their strange and esoteric teachings, NOT their history, NOT their temple rites and rituals. These things are all the result of the single most damaging doctrine Joseph ever introduced to these people, which is that the Bible cannot be trusted and the Bible is not enough.

I'd like to take a few minutes and sort of lay out the best I can a set of thoughts for you to consider, thoughts we hope will lend to your seeing the Bible as the authentic, singular, reliable wonder from God that it is.

First, I think it is important to review how the Bible actually came to be. Now there are excellent and far more exhaustive books available on this subject – especially stuff from Norman Geisler (e.g., *From God to Us: How We Got Our Bible*) – so this is just a thumbnail sketch.

Anyway, some religious romantics like to believe that true and real messages from God ought to come in singular events; you know, like a revelation sent down to us via heavenly fax. It is appealing to our flesh to think holy writings come to us in a fantastic and *singular* fashion. Natural men and women are far more inclined to receive books like the Book of Mormon – which supposedly came from buried treasure – and/or books like the Koran – produced by a single individual like Mohammed – than to receive a book that took more than 1500 years to produce and compile into one volume. But that is part of the miracle. God has historically shown that His ways are not ours. He works over time, through real, historical, actual ways, and from real, historical, actual people and places. The Bible was written over a great span of time, through different human beings, who had different life-styles, purposes, languages, backgrounds, insights, and countries of origin.

Many of them did not know each other, which made collusion impossible.

What we now call *"THE"* Bible actually consists of sixty-six different books, written by forty-plus different human writers, who lived on at least three different continents, and spoke in at least three different languages, writing over the course of no less than a period of one thousand five hundred years.

That is powerful, magnificent, *real* stuff.

And then within this compiled book of writings there are not only NO contradictions (with the exception of a couple of dates and numbers) but the separate writings actually interweave and support each other! However, I've got to say that the original manuscripts were wholly inerrant.

It is singularly the most amazing book on earth.

Now ask yourself again, "Why did Moses write?" So we could only consider it untrustworthy later on down the road? Why did God have prophets record their revelations? So believers could read it and wonder whether it was from Him or not? So we could question every word? So we could doubt it? So we could think God is ***incapable*** of bringing us His Word over time? Consider this.

In Matthew chapter four, Jesus had just finished fasting forty days in the wilderness and was hungry. Fittingly, Satan came to tempt Him with three specific temptations. Each of Satan's offers to Jesus was met with rejection. Each of these rejections was prefaced by Jesus saying, *"It is written..."* To what was Jesus referring when he said, *"It is written?"* The Old Testament!

And how could Jesus trust such ancient writings *that were just as old to Him as some of the New Testament writings are to us?* And, and, and *why* didn't Satan ever question Jesus about the reliability of what he was quoting? Why didn't Satan say, "It is written? Ha! Jesus! Are you me telling me you trust those ancient writings? Ha! That foolish book wasn't translated correctly."

Not even Satan made such an accusation.

Second, and without going into great detail because of time, Old Testament scribes and scholars were exacting, tedious, and relentless in transcribing accurately the Word of God. If a mistake was made, the whole parchment or scroll was destroyed and tossed away *immediately*. Older manuscripts – and this is important – were burned as newer ones were completed, NOT because of changes, but because of wear and tear, and to make sure only the MOST correct parchments were in use.

Then around 285 B.C. *seventy* Jewish scholars came to Alexandria and under the direction of the Ptolemies translated the Old Testament (what the Jews call the *TANAKH*) from Hebrew and into Koine Greek. The resulting translation is called the Septuagint, referring to the seventy scholars who worked on it. The Septuagint provides us with a tremendous bridge between the Hebrew and Greek worlds. By New Testament times, it was the most widely used edition of the Old Testament.

The existence of the Septuagint essentially solidified the existence of the Old Testament books 285 years before Jesus was even born!

So that is the Old Testament.

The terms *Old Testament* and *New Testament* originated with the prophet Jeremiah (Jeremiah 31:31). The word "testament" means *covenant*; Jesus, being the long awaited Messiah, made the *New Covenant* with God's people. The *Old Covenant* contains, amidst history and poetry, many prophecies pointing to Jesus. The New Covenant, amidst parables and historical events, provides the fulfillment of these Old Covenant prophecies.

Third, one of the MAJOR factors in proving the Bible valid and reliable is its sound and unfailing prophetic nature. Hundreds of prophecies have come true and those that remain will come true in the time appropriated by God. No prophecy that was supposed to have come to pass has ever failed to come to pass. Go online and type in "fulfilled Bible prophecies of the Messiah" and you can get an entire list.

Now the Gospels of the New Testament – Matthew, Mark, Luke, and John – are actually a continuation of the Old Testament. They speak of Jesus coming to earth, His ministry among God's chosen people, and *their* rejection of Him. Jesus came to show them that He was the ONLY way because He was the only one righteous. His words made all men and women sinners. His words condemn each of us, with the intent of resigning us to the fact that we NEED Him.

The actual New Testament doesn't really begin until Chapter Two of the book of Acts (which is the Day of Pentecost). And after the Day of Pentecost, those firsthand witnesses of the Lord Jesus and those closely associated with them wrote letters and revelations as inspired by the Holy Spirit to help govern and guide His new body, the church. Before these writings were ever collected and included in what we now call the New Testament, they were considered inspired. These men were called to write BECAUSE they were first hand witnesses, and what they wrote was considered Scripture JUST like the Old Testament!

Remember, Peter equates Paul's letters to Scripture, saying:

> 2 Peter 3:15,16. … *even as our beloved brother Paul also according to the wisdom given unto him hath written unto you; as also in all his epistles, speaking in them of these things; in which are some things hard to be understood, which they that are unlearned and unstable wrest, as they do also the other scriptures, unto their own destruction.*

Once the last apostle, John the Beloved, passed away, the first hand witnesses of Jesus, having written and recorded both the fulfillment of Jesus and the directives to His church, were gone; both the Old Covenant and the New were fulfilled. The Holy Spirit continued to inspire and grow the Church in miraculous and wonderful ways.

Nothing more in terms of writing is needed as the Word from Genesis to Revelation wholly completes it all with the Old Testament foretelling of His coming, the gospels testifying that He came, the epistles directing the new Church and Revelation completing all end-time prophecy. What else need be said?

It's not that God has stopped speaking to men and women today. Of course He speaks to us – by His Spirit and His Word. But CANONICAL writings are another matter. Any inspiration to us must be supported by Scripture in order to be His.

The word *canon*, in classical Greek, is properly understood as a straight rod, "a rule" in the widest sense –

- "The rule of the church,"
- "The rule of faith,"
- "The rule of truth."

When the canon or "rule of truth" is complete, what is the need for more, especially, ESPECIALLY when purported additions are in OPPOSITION to the proven, existing, historically accurate texts given by God?

So the New Testament texts were written by virtue of the Holy Spirit working on the Lord's first hand witnesses.

Fourth, there were several factors early Christian leaders took into consideration when it came to including or excluding candidates for New Testament writings in "the rule of truth" or canon.

Here are the major considerations:

- The book had to have a history of being included in Christian worship.
- The book had to have a connection to an apostle or first-hand witness of Christ.
- The book had to evidence power in the lives of believers.
- The book had to maintain a "consistency of doctrine."

Let me give you an example of this.

In the Gnostic *Gospel of Thomas*, Jesus is quoted as saying:

> *Lucky is the lion that the human will eat, so that the lion will become human. And foul is human that the lion will eat, and the lion still will become human.*

Doesn't sound like consistent doctrine relative to the rest of God's word, does it? So it was excluded. To continue:

- The book also had to ratify Christian virtue and spiritual values.
- All books had to be in harmony/unity, regardless of prose or style.

Quoting again from verse 14 in the Gnostic *Gospel of Thomas*:

> *If you fast, you bring sin upon yourselves, and if you pray, you will be condemned, and if you give to charity, you will harm your spirits.*

Obviously, this clap-trap is outside the "harmony and unity" of the other inspired books, so it was excluded.

Tertullian, one of the very early church fathers, states that by 150 A.D., the church in Rome had compiled a list of New Testament books that matches what we would call the Bible today. This was *ONE HUNDRED AND FIFTY* years before Councils at Nicea took place.

The Muratonian Canon, a fragment dating from 170 A.D., lists the same New Testament books that we have in the Protestant Bible today.

Fifth, if we take all the writings of the early Church Fathers …

Clement of Rome
Irenaeus
Justin Martyr
Polycarp
Ignatius
Hippolytus
Origen
Cyprian
Tertullian
and Clement of Alexandria

all but eleven verses of our PRESENT NEW TESTAMENT can be reconstructed and compiled through their writings alone.

In other words, the entire New Testament text, with the exception of eleven verses, is quoted in the early church writers' writings. This is not constructed or prefabricated stuff, as critics would like you to believe, my friends.

Finally, the individual books of the Bible did not derive their *authority* and *authenticity* as being of God *because* they were selected to be included in the Bible. This is the idea the LDS attempt to convey at times. Each of the books in the Word are from God and simply sat waiting to be gathered and included in His holy Book, just like what was done in the Old Testament.

The purpose of the Bible is to point people to Jesus, the salvation He offers, and the Christian walk He prescribes. **To state or imply that the Bible is polluted, fallible, or unreliable, is to create doubt in the minds of anyone who has considered or embraced such a position or will ever do so.**

So getting back to the point, what is the result of Joseph Smith and those who followed him saying that the Bible is not to be completely trusted? **Every time a Latter-day Saint reads the Bible, they discount it in their heart if not their mind.** Every time they read a passage that causes them to think, they put it in the "not correctly translated" bin. **Every time the Word causes them to wonder about their own faith, they think of corrupted texts, evil copyists, and the uninspired philosophies of men.**

And what is the result? **A bastardized view of Jesus, of the salvations He offers, and of the Christian Walk He prescribes.**

It is high time for Latter-day Saints – especially if they want to be considered Christian – to take their QUADS (or four-in-one books of "scripture") and rip three of those books out, toss them in the garbage, and search the only book of the four that was written by God Himself: the Bible.

Jesus said,

> Mark 13:31. *HEAVEN AND EARTH WILL PASS AWAY BUT MY WORD WILL NOT PASS AWAY*

The "not" pass away – in Greek, "*ou me*" – is a double negative which strengthens the statement to its utmost, meaning, "it will *never-ever, not ever, in no way ever, impossible for it to ever, cannot ever* pass away."

Mormons say otherwise.

❋ ❋ ❋

Golden plates, placed under the earth on a hill not far from the home of a family who spent much of their time searching for buried gold with magic stones? Really? I mean, really?"

The Book of Mormon

I am not going to discuss the problems with the Book of Mormon itself, its plagiarisms, origins, and anachronisms; these were all covered in Show 18 in 2006 and Shows 12-20 in 2007.

Tonight we are going to examine the Biblical references the LDS will use in their efforts to prove that the Bible spoke of the Book of Mormon's existence. This is important because if the Bible really does support the coming forth of the Book of Mormon then we ought to all RUN – I mean RUN - into the arms of Mormonism and join up.

But why haven't the majority of Christian pastors, scholars, commentators, linguists, and historians discovered these verses in the Bible which the LDS say prove the Book of Mormon true? Because the scholars KNOW what these proof-texts the LDS use from the Bible actually mean. And you will too, if you listen tonight.

Specifically, we are going to look at four Bible references the LDS use to prove that the Bible foretold of the Book of Mormon.

- Isaiah 29:1-4
- Isaiah 29:11-12
- Ezekiel 37:16-17
- 2 Corinthians 13:1-2

So, get your Bibles out, mark these verses, take some notes on what these passages are really all about.

Alright, let's go to the first Bible passage the LDS say speaks of the Book of Mormon: Isaiah 29:1-4.

Apostle (APOSTLE!) Russell M. Nelson said in General Conference, October 2007:

> How do scriptures of the Restoration clarify the Bible? Many examples exist. I will cite but a few, beginning with the Old Testament. Isaiah wrote:

[Then APOSTLE Nelson quotes, only in part, Isaiah 29:1-4:]

> *Thou shalt...speak out of the ground, and thy speech shall be low out of the dust, and thy voice shall be, as of one that hath a familiar spirit, out of the ground, and thy speech shall whisper out of the dust.*

[Of these passages APOSTLE Nelson then states:]

> Could any words be more descriptive of the Book of Mormon, coming, as it did, "out of the ground" to whisper "out of the dust' to people of our day?

And all I have to say is, "You have got to be kidding me, Apostle Nelson!"

Let's take this text Nelson uses and examine it soundly.

First and foremost, we cannot forget that the Old Testament was written to and for the children of Israel. It is their history, their covenant with God, and it applies to them – NOT MORMONS, dang it!

Just look at Isaiah 29:1-4 in its entirety, and with clear eyes:

> Verse 1. *Woe to Ariel, to Ariel, the city where David dwelt! add ye year to year; let them kill sacrifices.*

Who or what is Ariel?

It is the city where *who* dwelt, according to the passage? David!

And what city was that? Jerusalem – the City of David. The city of Peace.

Did David ever dwell on the American continent? Did David ever dwell in, say, Missouri? No. Isaiah here called Jerusalem "*Ariel*" which in all probability means, "hearth of God" and it was only in Ariel where God's hearth existed – that is, the altar where sacrifices were offered. This is also the place where Isaiah is saying the judgment of God would soon fall.

And fall it did.

What Isaiah was saying here is Jerusalem, although presently offering sacrifices, would soon become itself like an altar where sacrifices were burned. He was telling them the city itself was going to be razed!

This prophecy was fulfilled when God used Sennacherib, ruler of the Assyrians in 701 BC to attack Jerusalem (or Ariel) with such bloodshed and fire that it seemed like the city was itself an altar. In verses 2 and 3, God warns them through Isaiah that, although they offer sacrifices,

> Yet I will distress Ariel, and there shall be heaviness and sorrow: and it shall be unto me as Ariel. *And I will camp against thee round about, and will lay siege against thee with a mount, and I will raise forts against thee.*

As a result of this devastating attack AUTHORED by God, Jerusalem would be figuratively "brought down to the ground" so effectively that it would be as though they were buried.

This context brings us to verse four which is so popular with the LDS and their misapplication:

> Verse 4. And thou [meaning Jerusalem] shalt be brought down, and shalt speak out of the ground, and thy speech shall be low out of the dust, and thy voice shall be, as of one that hath a familiar spirit, out of the ground, and thy speech shall whisper out of the dust.

Bible scholar Albert Barnes, in his *Commentary of the Old Testament* says of this passage:

> The sense here is that Jerusalem, which was accustomed to priding itself on its strength, would be greatly humbled and subdued. It's loud and lofty tone would be changed. It would use the suppressed language of fear and alarm as if it spoke from the dust, (sounding like the voice. of those who pretended to converse with the dead – hence the phrase "as of one that hath a familiar spirit."

Nowhere in Scripture is the term "familiar spirit" good – it always refers to evil sorceries.

The LDS take that term and try and say that the Book of Mormon, which came out of the ground near Joseph Smith's house, speaks as though it came from the dust of the earth, and that it would have a "familiar spirit" to the Bible. This is utter non-sense!

Now, what is really important to understanding these passages that Apostle Nelson so embarrassingly assigned as proving the Book of Mormon is to look in the preceding chapter, chapter 28 of Isaiah, verse 15.

Here it gives us the reason and context of Isaiah 29:1-4. You see, the nation of Israel made some sort of pact with darkness and they believed that this pact would protect them from what Isaiah 29 describes.

Listen!

> Isaiah 28:14. *Wherefore hear the word of the LORD, ye scornful men, that rule this people which is in Jerusalem. Because ye have said, We have made a covenant with death, and with hell are we at*

> *agreement; when the overflowing scourge shall pass through, it shall not come unto us: for we have made lies our refuge, and under falsehood have we hid ourselves.*

From these verses we have a clear understanding of what Isaiah was saying in chapter 29 and why. The Israelites had made a covenant with death and with hell and thought that the overflowing scourge would not affect them.

Isaiah 29:1-4 tells us otherwise.

God let the overflowing scourge fall upon them so furiously in 701 BC at the hands of the Assyrians that they were decimated to the earth, and their once proud voice was made like that of one from the dust, or how the voice of a "familiar spirit" would sound speaking out from the grave.

This passage HAS NOTHING *AT ALL*, to do with the Book of Mormon...even though a man who calls himself an "apostle" says it does. He is misleading at best, lying at worst.

Okay, then in the same chapter of Isaiah, we come to another passage the LDS use to say that the Book of Mormon is mentioned in the Bible.

It's in Isaiah 29:11-12, which reads:

> *And the vision of all is become unto you as the words of a book that is sealed, which men deliver to one that is learned, saying, Read this, I pray thee: and he saith, I cannot; for it is sealed: And the book is delivered to him that is not learned, saying, Read this, I pray thee: and he saith, I am not learned.*

So here is how the LDS use this passage.

When Martin Harris was helping Joseph with the transcribing

of the Book of Mormon, Harris took some handwritten characters from the golden plates (which Joseph Smith had supplied him) and he went to one Charles Anthon, a professor at Columbia University.

Though Professor Anthon denies Harris's retelling of what happened between them, Harris reported the following, which the LDS embrace (*Joseph Smith History* 1:64,65):

> I went to the city of New York, and presented the characters which had been translated, with the translation thereof, to Professor Charles Anthon, a gentleman celebrated for his literary attainments. Professor Anthon stated that the translation was correct, more so than any he had before seen translated from the Egyptian. I then showed him those which were not yet translated, and he said that they were Egyptian, Chaldaic, Assyriac, and Arabic; and he said they were true characters. He gave me a certificate, certifying to the people of Palmyra that they were true characters, and that the translation of such of them as had been translated was also correct. I took the certificate and put it into my pocket, and was just leaving the house, when Mr. Anthon called me back, and asked me how the young man found out that there were gold plates in the place where he found them. I answered that an angel of God had revealed it unto him.
>
> He then said to me, "Let me see that certificate," I accordingly took it out of my pocket and gave it to him, when he took it and tore it to pieces, saying, that there was no such thing now as ministering of angels, and that if I would bring the plates to him, he would translate them. I informed him that part of the plates were sealed, and that I was forbidden to bring them. He replied, **"I cannot read a sealed book."** I left him and went to Dr. Mitchell, who sanctioned what Professor Anthon had said respecting both the characters and the translation [emphasis Shawn's].

There are several problems with the LDS use of these verses in Isaiah to support the history of the coming forth of the Book of Mormon.

Read the first line of the passage. What does it say?

> And the vision of all is become unto you as the words of a book that is sealed …

What Isaiah was saying it that the visions to Israel were not discernable to them any longer – that these visions had *become unto them as the words of a book that is sealed,* meaning, the visions were not going to be understood because they were ***as*** a sealed book! Isaiah was not in any way speaking of the exchange between Martin Harris and Professor Anthon at Columbia University!

Did you hear what I just said and sense the absolute comedy of the claim? Isaiah was not in *any way* speaking of a conversation between Martin Harris and Professor Anthon at Columbia University!

I mean, come on!

And yet another LDS "APOSTLE," LeGrand Richards, said of these passages (*A Marvelous Work and a Wonder*, page 50):

> Professor Anthon did not realize that he was literally fulfilling prophecy of Isaiah.

My Lord, how twisted can the twisting be!?

Then, just sit down and examine the story Harris told about his meeting with Professor Anthon and then re-read the passages in question. According to Harris, Professor Anthon said the TRANSLATION of the BOOK was ***correct*** but the Isaiah passage states that the learned ***could NOT*** translate the vision.

Next, the Isaiah passage has the visions going ***first to the learned*** and ***then*** to the unlearned – of which neither could comprehend it. But in LDS history, a BOOK first went to the ***unlearned***

(Joseph Smith) and then to the ***learned*** (Professor Anthon) only to have the unlearned translate it – which occurrence the Isaiah passage never suggests! I mean, all the Isaiah account tells us is that visions will be presented to the learned and they will say, "I can't read a sealed book." It says nothing about a translation coming forth.

Re-read these passages and THINK, damn it, THINK!

Okay, next we come to one of the all-time favorite Biblical passages the LDS use to support the Book of Mormon: the great *Stick of Joseph* twist taken from chapter 37 of Ezekiel.

In October 1982, *APOSTLE(!)* Boyd K. Packer said in an LDS General Conference ("Scriptures," *Ensign*, November 1982):

> The stick or record of Judah – the Old Testament and the New Testament – and the stick or record of Ephraim – the Book of Mormon, which is another testament of Jesus Christ – are now woven together in such a way that as you pour over one you are drawn to the other; as you learn from one you are enlightened by the other. They are indeed one in our hands. Ezekiel's prophecy now stands fulfilled.

For a man who calls himself an "apostle," to make such a claim is as ridiculous as my claiming a yellow moon proves it is made of cheddar cheese. I'm not kidding!

So from what passage in Ezekiel does APOSTLE Boyd Packer support this claim?

> Ezekiel 37:15-17. *The word of the LORD came again unto me, saying, Moreover, thou son of man, take thee one stick, and write upon it, For Judah, and for the children of Israel his companions: then take another stick, and write upon it, For Joseph, the stick of Ephraim, and for all the house of Israel his companions: and join them one to another into one stick; and they shall become one in thine hand.*

Taking these passages, LDS missionaries will sit down with unsuspecting investigators and say something like this:

> Mr. and Mrs. Investigator, ancient prophets would take leather or papyrus and lay it flat, and attach long sticks to the end of them. Then they would write scriptures upon them and use the sticks to roll them up into a scroll. So what these passages are saying is that God told Ezekiel to take one "stick" (or scroll of papyrus. and write upon it for Judah, and for the children of Israel his companions – this stick would represent the Bible, Mr. Investigator ... [and the missionary holds up the Bible in one hand] ... And then the Lord tells Ezekiel to take another stick, and write upon it, For Joseph, the stick of Ephraim, and for all the house of Israel his companions and this stick or scroll is the Book of Mormon ... [and the missionary holds up the Book of Mormon in the other hand] ... And then the Lord tells Ezekiel to join them together into one stick; and they shall become one in thine hand.

And then the missionary takes the Bible and the BOM and puts them together in his or her one hand. To the unsuspecting investigator this story seems reasonable, and they buy into the presentation. But what IS Ezekiel 37:15-17 really talking about? ALL A PERSON HAS TO DO IS TO KEEP READING PAST WHERE THE MISSIONARIES HAVE TOLD THEM TO READ!

It's this scary thing called *CONTEXT*.

In so doing, we learn clearly what Scripture says the two sticks represent.

So let's continue to re-read the passages "APOSTLE" Boyd Packer used to justify the Book of Mormon and then let's read beyond verse seventeen in order to understand its true context.

Okay, first of all, God was having Ezekiel create an object lesson using some props. God had many of His prophets use props as symbols to ancient Israel.

According to Bible expositor Charles H. Dyer here is the setting of these verses (*The Old Testament Explorer: Discovering the Essence, Background, and Meaning of Every Book in the Old Testament*, p. 213):

> After Solomon died, the nation of Israel split asunder, in 931 BC. The Southern Kingdom was known as Judah because Judah was its larger tribe and because the country was ruled by a king of that tribe (1 Kings 12:22). The Northern Kingdom was called Israel, or sometimes Ephraim (as in Hosea 5:3, 5, 11 -14. because Ephraim was the strongest and most influential tribe and/or because the first king of Israel, Jeraboam I, was an Ephramite (1 Kings 11:26).

These kingdoms were separately taken into captivity with Israel being taken by Assyria in 722 BC and Judah taken into the Babylonian exile in 605, 597, and 586 BC. These passages clearly depict one nation (represented by a stick for Judah, the Southern Kingdom) and the other nation (represented by a stick for Ephraim, the Northern Kingdom) to be taken into the prophet Ezekiel's hands then joined together.

How can I say this?

Let's read the passages again:

> Ezekiel 37:15-25. *The word of the* LORD *came again unto me, saying, Moreover, thou son of man, take thee one stick, and write upon it, For Judah, and for the children of Israel his companions: then take another stick, and write upon it, For Joseph, the stick of Ephraim, and for all the house of Israel his companions: And join them one to another into one stick; and they shall become one in thine hand. And when the children of thy people shall speak unto thee, saying, Wilt thou not shew us what thou meanest by these? Say unto them, Thus saith the Lord* GOD; *Behold, I will take the stick of Joseph, which is in the hand of Ephraim, and the tribes of Israel his fellows, and will put them with him, even with the stick of Judah, and make them*

one stick, and they shall be one in mine hand. And the sticks whereon thou writest shall be in thine hand before their eyes. And say unto them, Thus saith the Lord GOD; Behold, I will take the children of Israel from among the heathen, whither they be gone, and will gather them on every side, and bring them into their own land: And I will make them one nation in the land upon the mountains of Israel; and one king shall be king to them all: and they shall be no more two nations, neither shall they be divided into two kingdoms any more at all: Neither shall they defile themselves any more with their idols, nor with their detestable things, nor with any of their transgressions: but I will save them out of all their dwelling places, wherein they have sinned, and will cleanse them: so shall they be my people, and I will be their God. And David my servant shall be king over them; and they all shall have one shepherd: they shall also walk in my judgments, and observe my statutes, and do them. And they shall dwell in the land that I have given unto Jacob my servant, wherein your fathers have dwelt; and they shall dwell therein, even they, and their children, and their children's children for ever: and my servant David shall be their prince for ever.

Finally, in reference to the sticks, the missionary's descriptions are pure fiction. If Ezekiel was talking about actual scrolls that were written upon, he would have used the perfectly good Hebrew word for scroll – "*siprah.*" Instead he used a completely different word for wood, tree, branch, or stick – "*es.*"

The Lord told Ezekiel to actually write on two sticks the names Judah and Joseph to represent the Northern and Southern nations, and to then bring them into one hand to illustrate their coming back together.

The Book of Mormon has NOTHING to do with this.

Finally, the LDS missionaries will often use 2 Corinthians 13:1-2 to show the need for their Book of Mormon.

In 2 Corinthians, Paul references Jewish law located in Deuteronomy 17:6, which says

> 2 Corinthians 13:1. *In the mouth of two or three witnesses shall every word be established.*

LDS Missionaries will pull this passage out and say:

> See, Mr. Investigator, the Bible alone is not enough. It needs another witness. And that, boys and girls, is the Book of Mormon.

First of all, the Bible has *dozens* and *dozens* of witnesses as it is a compilation of inspired writings from many men.

Secondly, Paul is warning the people of Corinth that if they continue in sin, they would be officially confronted using the laws of Jewish legislation, and by the mouth of two or three witnesses they would be found guilty. Again, NOTHING to do with the Book of Mormon.

Folks, the way the LDS "apostles" say the Bible supports the Book of Mormon is akin to Mark David Chapman believing *The Catcher in the Rye* told him to shoot Reagan – the words are there but they say NOTHING of the sort.

Read and think for yourselves.

❋ ❋ ❋

> "Show me a Mormon who has been regenerated by the Holy Spirit and I will show you a Mormon who is on his way out the chapel doors."

Born Again I: Justification

In our ministry, there is NO MORE important topic than a clear Biblical understanding of our subject tonight: spiritual rebirth or being born again.

Our first book was called: *Born-Again Mormon.*

The first website we ever created was www.bornagainmormon.com.

The central focus of the ministry was, and remains to this very day, our desire for Latter-day Saints to experience spiritual rebirth – and to then let the Lord guide them in their decisions about family, life, and church membership.

In my heart – and from what I can deduce from Scripture – I recognize that there is not a more important moment in the life of any and every human being. This being the case, it would stand to reason that Satan would spend quite a bit of time creating counterfeits to genuine spiritual rebirth and/or changing the true definition of spiritual rebirth.

After Jesus' telling a man named Nicodemus that a person MUST be born again and that the spirit behind it blows and goes where it wants to go without our being able to direct or originate it (John 3:8), Joseph Smith stepped in and said that (*TPJS*, page 162):

> Being born-again comes by the Spirit of God through ordinances.

Where Jesus' description – and the rest of the Word – supports rebirth as a supernatural act of God through His wind-like Holy Spirit, Joseph Smith reeled the whole experience back into the four walls of a religious institution and claimed it occurs through LDS ordinances.

Summarizing Joseph Smith's original teachings, tenth President of the LDS church, Joseph Fielding Smith, said (*Doctrines of Salvation* 2:223):

> Through baptism and confirmation [people] are born-again and thus come back into spiritual life and through their continued

> obedience to the end, they shall be made partakers of the blessings of eternal life in the celestial kingdom of God.

To give this LDS counterfeit greater clarity, allow me to restate their teachings in my own words, and then we will explore the topic biblically. Latter-day Saints first teach that we are all born literal spirit children of a Heavenly Father. By coming from a pre-existent state as His spirit children we enter into bodies of flesh and face temptations – and the LDS teach that we all sin. In order to overcome sin, Mormonism teaches that a person must enter into a covenant relationship with Jesus Christ. This happens when the person accepts the ordinance of the LDS water baptism, and then they receive the gift of the Holy Ghost which comes ONLY by the laying on of hands by a LDS male priesthood holder. In receiving these LDS ordinances, they believe they have "taken on the name of Christ" which is to them synonymous with being born again.

This is what I would call a perfunctory and institutionalized rebirth brought about by LDS ordinances. To remain worthy of that rebirth they must repent when they sin, or as they say, "*fall short of the mark.*" This repenting culminates in faithfully and repetitively renewing the covenants they made at water baptism by taking the LDS sacrament of broken bread and water every week. Do you see that cycle, which includes the need to remain faithful to Mormonism in order to remain saved?

To Latter-day Saints spiritual rebirth does NOT occur when God sends His Spirit to dwell in a believer, but when a person receives LDS ordinances. The LDS approach effectively avoids a recognition of our broken and helpless state before God, which helps fallen man to receive Jesus as Lord and King.

As a result, most Latter-day Saints wander about not ever having experienced true, regenerative spiritual rebirth; instead they find themselves chained to a hamster wheel of striving, achieving, measuring up, and accomplishing personal sanctification by their own efforts.

In the realm of Mormon / Christian debate, spiritual rebirth is either tied to ordinances, as the LDS claim OR it is an event received outside the administration of men.

Let's take a look at the Bible and compare and contrast how it describes spiritual rebirth.

The first thing to consider is the idea of birth itself. Ask yourself: how many times is a person born and how long does the actual birth take? There is a divine reason Jesus likened spiritual regeneration to birth and not to a life-long, repetitive action like "swimming over an endless ocean" or rolling a stone up a mountain over and over again like Sisyphus.

Physical birth - and spiritual rebirth – are singular events. Once a woman enters the birth process, it ends in delivery. She does not spend her life in labor.

Once God moves in, the regeneration, the change, the rebirth is done.

This is the Jesus moment which is completely missing from the LDS experience.

This is the Romans 10:9 moment:

> *That if thou shalt confess with thy mouth the Lord Jesus, and shalt believe in thine heart that God hath raised him from the dead, thou shalt be saved.*

In this moment, we are justified before God by the blood of Jesus Christ. *Justification* means our sins have been forgiven. And because our sins have been forgiven PAST, PRESENT, and FUTURE, and our person has been permanently cleansed from sin by the shed blood of the Lord Jesus Christ, the Holy Spirit moves in and an individual is born-again.

And he or she becomes the recipient of a new heart, or what God promised through the prophet Ezekiel, saying:

> Ezekiel 36:26. *A new heart also will I give you, and a new spirit will I put within you: and I will take away the stony heart out of your flesh, and I will give you an heart of flesh.*

This new heart filled by His Holy Spirit is indicative that the believer has been justified by God.

Justification is the opposite of condemnation.

The term might be considered a legal term and is the judicial act of God, by which He pardons all the sins of those who receive Christ, and accounts, accepts, and treats them as righteous in the eye of His law – meaning the person has, by Christ, conformed to all of the demands of God's law. In addition to this pardon of sin, justification declares that all the claims of the law have been permanently satisfied.

It is the action of a judge.

The law is not relaxed or set aside, but is declared to be fulfilled in the strictest sense; and so the person justified is declared to be entitled to all the advantages and rewards arising from perfect obedience to the law – by Christ – while we were still in sin!

Romans five lays it all out very nicely.

Chapter four ends by telling us the righteousness of Christ is imputed to those who believe. And then chapter five continues:

> Romans 5:1-9. *Therefore, having been justified by faith, we have peace with God through our Lord Jesus Christ, through whom also we have access by faith into this grace in which we stand, and re-*

> *joice in hope of the glory of God. And not only that, but we also glory in tribulations, knowing that tribulation produces perseverance; and perseverance, character; and character, hope. Now hope does not disappoint, because the love of God has been poured out in our hearts by the Holy Spirit who was given to us. For when we were still without strength, in due time Christ died for the ungodly. For scarcely for a righteous man will one die; yet perhaps for a good man someone would even dare to die. But God demonstrates His own love toward us, in that while we were still sinners, Christ died for us. Much more then, having now been justified by His blood, we shall be saved from wrath through Him.*

To any Bible-believing Christian, these verses describe a simple message: ***While we were sinners Jesus died for us.***

By believing in Him, God pours His Holy Spirit into us, and we know we are saved from wrath. And this knowledge produces peace – rest in Him.

Freedom from worry, wrath, and the wrangling of man.

Now, what causes this rebirth to occur?

Is it our being worthy? Our efforts? Do we call the Holy Spirit down when we are good and ready? Jesus makes that all perfectly clear:

> John 3:8. *The wind blows where it wishes, and you hear the sound of it, but cannot tell where it comes from and where it goes. So is everyone who is born of the Spirit.*

Where John came to baptize with water, Jesus came to baptize with the Spirit, meaning, by and through ***His*** shed blood, all who believe are able to have NEW LIFE in Him – brought about and given according to God's ways and will, and not man's. Not by ordinances, but by broken hearts calling out to God in humble faith – and waiting for Him to send "*the Wind.*"

The Bible is full of stories and illustrations not only of this new-life-giving Spirit, but how it works. As a beautiful picture of God's power to regenerate new life, we turn to the book of Ezekiel, chapter 37 (verses 1-14).

Hear God's Word:

> Ezekiel 37:1-14. *The hand of the* LORD *came upon me and brought me out in the Spirit of the LORD, and set me down in the midst of the valley; and it was full of bones. Then He caused me to pass by them all around, and behold, there were very many in the open valley; and indeed they were very dry. And He said to me, Son of man, can these bones live? So I answered, O Lord GOD, You know. Again He said to me, Prophesy to these bones, and say to them, 'O dry bones, hear the word of the LORD! Thus says the Lord GOD to these bones: Surely I will cause breath to enter into you, and you shall live. I will put sinews on you and bring flesh upon you, cover you with skin and put breath in you; and you shall live. Then you shall know that I am the LORD.' So I prophesied as I was commanded; and as I prophesied, there was a noise, and suddenly a rattling; and the bones came together, bone to bone. Indeed, as I looked, the sinews and the flesh came upon them, and the skin covered them over; but there was no breath in them. Also He said to me, Prophesy to the breath, prophesy, son of man, and say to the breath, 'Thus says the Lord GOD: Come from the four winds, O breath, and breathe on these slain, that they may live.' So I prophesied as He commanded me, and breath came into them, and they lived, and stood upon their feet, an exceedingly great army. Then He said to me, Son of man, these bones are the whole house of Israel. They indeed say, 'Our bones are dry, our hope is lost, and we ourselves are cut off!' Therefore prophesy and say to them, 'Thus says the Lord GOD: Behold, O My people, I will open your graves and cause you to come up from your graves, and bring you into the land of Israel. Then you shall know that I am the LORD, when I have opened your graves, O My people, and brought you up from your graves. I will put My Spirit in you, and you shall live, and I will place you in your own land. Then you shall know that I, the LORD, have spoken it and performed it,' says the LORD.*

In the New Testament, we have other stories that paint a similar and vital picture: that we are dead, and it is ONLY when God so designs to send His Spirit that we receive new life.

Recall the story of Mary, Martha and Lazarus:

> John 11:1-44. *Now a certain man was sick, named Lazarus, of Bethany, the town of Mary and her sister Martha. (It was that Mary which anointed the Lord with ointment, and wiped his feet with her hair, whose brother Lazarus was sick.. Therefore his sisters sent unto him, saying, Lord, behold, he whom thou lovest is sick. When Jesus heard that, he said, This sickness is not unto death, but for the glory of God, that the Son of God might be glorified thereby. Now Jesus loved Martha, and her sister, and Lazarus. When he had heard therefore that he was sick, he abode two days still in the same place where he was. Then after that saith he to his disciples, Let us go into Judaea again. His disciples say unto him, Master, the Jews of late sought to stone thee; and goest thou thither again? Jesus answered, Are there not twelve hours in the day? If any man walk in the day, he stumbleth not, because he seeth the light of this world. But if a man walk in the night, he stumbleth, because there is no light in him. These things said he: and after that he saith unto them, Our friend Lazarus sleepeth; but I go, that I may awake him out of sleep. Then said his disciples, Lord, if he sleep, he shall do well. Howbeit Jesus spake of his death: but they thought that he had spoken of taking of rest in sleep. Then said Jesus unto them plainly, Lazarus is dead. And I am glad for your sakes that I was not there, to the intent ye may believe; nevertheless let us go unto him. Then said Thomas, which is called Didymus, unto his fellow disciples, Let us also go, that we may die with him. Then when Jesus came, he found that he had lain in the grave four days already. Now Bethany was nigh unto Jerusalem, about fifteen furlongs off: And many of the Jews came to Martha and Mary, to comfort them concerning their brother. Then Martha, as soon as she heard that Jesus was coming, went and met him: but Mary sat still in the house. Then said Martha unto Jesus, Lord, if thou hadst been here, my brother had not died. But I know, that even now, whatsoever thou wilt ask*

of God, God will give it thee. Jesus saith unto her, Thy brother shall rise again. Martha saith unto him, I know that he shall rise again in the resurrection at the last day. Jesus said unto her, I am the resurrection, and the life: he that believeth in me, though he were dead, yet shall he live: And whosoever liveth and believeth in me shall never die. Believest thou this? She saith unto him, Yea, Lord: I believe that thou art the Christ, the Son of God, which should come into the world. And when she had so said, she went her way, and called Mary her sister secretly, saying, The Master is come, and calleth for thee. As soon as she heard that, she arose quickly, and came unto him. Now Jesus was not yet come into the town, but was in that place where Martha met him. The Jews then which were with her in the house, and comforted her, when they saw Mary, that she rose up hastily and went out, followed her, saying, She goeth unto the grave to weep there. Then when Mary was come where Jesus was, and saw him, she fell down at his feet, saying unto him, Lord, if thou hadst been here, my brother had not died. When Jesus therefore saw her weeping, and the Jews also weeping which came with her, he groaned in the spirit, and was troubled. And said, Where have ye laid him? They said unto him, Lord, come and see. Jesus wept. Then said the Jews, Behold how he loved him! And some of them said, Could not this man, which opened the eyes of the blind, have caused that even this man should not have died? Jesus therefore again groaning in himself cometh to the grave. It was a cave, and a stone lay upon it. Jesus said, Take ye away the stone. Martha, the sister of him that was dead, saith unto him, Lord, by this time he stinketh: for he hath been dead four days. Jesus saith unto her, Said I not unto thee, that, if thou wouldest believe, thou shouldest see the glory of God? Then they took away the stone from the place where the dead was laid. And Jesus lifted up his eyes, and said, Father, I thank thee that thou hast heard me. And I knew that thou hearest me always: but because of the people which stand by I said it, that they may believe that thou hast sent me. And when he thus had spoken, he cried with a loud voice, Lazarus, come forth. And he that was dead came forth, bound hand and foot with graveclothes: and his face was bound about with a napkin. Jesus saith unto them, Loose him, and let him go.

Just like Lazarus was dead and stinking, we are also dead in our sins and just like Lazarus, we need the supernatural power of God to raise us out of our tombs of sin and death!

Where the LDS say we are all "*children of God,*" John the Beloved, who knew Jesus so intimately – lived and walked with Him – says otherwise.

Listen!

> John 1:12-13. *But as many as received Him, to them He gave the right to become children of God, to those who believe in His name: who were born, not of blood, nor of the will of the flesh, nor of the will of man, but of God.*

My friends, we are born spiritually dead. Yes, created in God's image (three in one) but dead in spirit because of Adam's fall. Jesus said we *must* be born-again.

This occurs when we stop, look, and see ourselves in desperate need of a redeemer. We ask God to forgive us, change us, live in our hearts, and we wait on Him and Him alone

- To be saved.
- To have a new heart placed within us.
- To be born-again.

Mormonism would LOVE to have everyone believe a counterfeit to this simple message. They would love to make you think you have to go through them and their institution to be right with God. And that it is ONLY through them that a person can be with God for eternity.

This is a lie.

You can be with God, and God can and will be with you – living inside of you, permanently, right now.

How?

Go to Him. Pour out your heart. Ask Him to reveal Himself to you. Believe in His promises, in His Son and in His shed blood.

Then in faith wait for Him to open your eyes to His truth.

He will.

And one day, you will with great AMAZEMENT and absolute peace and hope, raise your hands, and praise Him and His name.

Romans chapter 5 speaks all about justification in verses 1-9.

Then verse 10 says something really important.

Let me close with these words from Romans. Paul says,

> Romans 5:10. *For if when we were enemies we were reconciled to God through the death of His Son, much more, having been reconciled, we shall be saved by His life.*

⁂

> "Justification (or the 'Jesus experience') is an immediate event, whether it is recognized by the participant at the time or not. Sanctification comes in two parts; the first is sanctification by imputation. This is when the righteousness of our Lord is imputed to us by virtue of our belief in Him. The second part of sanctification is the method God uses in the lives of believers who are allowed to tarry in this fallen world."

Born Again II: Sanctification

Last time we left off having discussed one part of spiritual rebirth – JUSTIFICATION - from both the LDS and the Biblical perspective.

We ended with a verse which says:

> Romans 5:10. *For if when we were enemies [or when we were sinners] we were reconciled to God through the death of His Son, much more, having been reconciled, we shall be saved by His life.*

What exactly does this verse mean?

The verse actually describes all the effects of true salvation, which includes our being justified by grace through faith in the shed blood of Jesus (or, as it says, "*through the death of His Son*") AND it also it speaks of our being, *"saved by His life."*

I think most of us have some understanding of what it means to be *justified* by His blood.

As we said last week, justification is the opposite of condemnation, and it is basically a legal term which announces once and for all that we have been rendered innocent of breaking any of God's commands or laws, due to our faith in the finished work of His Son.

And nothing more.

You see, we live in a world where people are paraded as heroes because they tell the truth when it is tough, or return a lost wallet full of money, or keep their virginity until after marriage. In God's economy, these are plain and simple expectations of all people; not worthy of reward, but simply expected. When someone claims, "Well, I've lived a good life." God could say, "Well, you should have lived a good life." It's a basic expectation. Why should there be a reward for doing what everyone should do in the first place?

So, in a sense, this is what justification means for us. The shed blood of Jesus takes our failure to meet God's basic expectations (HIS LAW) and removes the condemnation *completely.*

And through this justification we are essentially made a blank slate by His shed blood. A big blank *tabula rasa*. Certainly our crimes on the books are cleared. There are no charges against us.

But we are NOT made holy in this state, just freed of all negative charges.

Holiness implies more than just a clean slate, it implies righteous attributes, actions, and attitudes. The word Holiness is synonymous with the word sanctify or sanctification. Now, if all that Jesus did was to *justify* those who believe on His name, then the end result would be that at our death we would go to God cleared of all charges, yet without possessing any righteousness or holiness.

But God desires all to bear holy fruit.

So how does the Christian, who confesses Christ and dies, like the thief on the cross, or those who are babes in Christ, ever really have any merit of their own?

The answer: through the merits of Jesus.

Enter the second part, if you will, of being born-again: immediate *positional sanctification.*

If all Jesus did in terms of our salvation was to come and justify us or remove all charges from our slate, then I suppose He could have dropped down from heaven, whipped up the body of a fully grown man, been crucified, and the debt would have been paid.

But God also gives every believer what is called *positional sanctification*, meaning His righteousness is imputed to those who believe in His atoning death on the cross.

Therefore, when a person believes on His name, they are not

only justified of their sins – not condemned – but they are also sanctified: made righteous and holy, through His life!

Is this amazing or what?

This aspect of sanctification is why Christians believe in deathbed repentance and know that the thief on the cross was not only cleared of His failures regarding God's law but was actually made righteous and holy before God THROUGH the righteous life Jesus actually lived!

Speaking of our being sanctified by faith in the Lord, 1 Corinthians 1:30 says that Jesus Christ

> ...became for us wisdom from God--and [became for us] righteousness and sanctification and redemption--that, as it is written, He who glories, let him glory in the LORD.

Christ Jesus became for us wisdom, righteousness, sanctification, and redemption.

WHY?

So that when anyone would glory, they would – or ought to – *"glory in the Lord."*

A believer does not ever glory in his own righteousness, not in his own purity or preparation. But in Him!

When a person understands that Jesus not only erased his crimes against God's law but that He also makes them righteous and holy before God, all the elements of human pride are stripped away, and the person is left to GLORY ONLY IN THE LORD. With regard to this aspect of sanctification, Mormonism and Christianity are worlds apart. In Mormonism there is no imputed righteousness that immediately comes from the life of Christ to those who believe. Why?

Because to the LDS, righteousness, holiness, sanctification, and personal merit begins and ends in *them,* by their *own* works of righteousness. Where Christians know that they are holy and righteous and worthy ONLY in and through Him, Latter-day Saints are certain that they are establishing their own righteousness before God.

In Romans chapter 10 there are a series of passages that, in my opinion, clearly describe this errant LDS view, which truly presents another gospel.

In it, Paul is speaking to the Jews – whom He dearly loves. And He says:

> Romans 10:1. *Brethren, my heart's desire and prayer to God for Israel is that they may be saved. For I bear them witness that they have a zeal for God, but not according to knowledge. For they being ignorant of God's righteousness, and seeking to establish their own righteousness, have not submitted to the righteousness of God. For Christ is the end of the law for righteousness to everyone who believes.*

Speaking of Christ's work, the author of Hebrews says:

> Hebrews 10:10. *By the which will we are sanctified through the offering of the body of Jesus Christ once for all.*

Every Bible-believing Christian understands that once a person receives Jesus, they are saved by grace through faith, having been both immediately JUSTIFIED *and* immediately SANCTIFIED in God's eyes.

The peace and truth in this assurance cannot be bought or found in any other form as it literally frees a person from fears, worries, and concerns about someday having to face the wrath of a holy God; it brings them wholly and securely to His throne by the righteous blood and life of their new King. Here, God becomes our "Papa," our Dad, our personal Father. Then and only then can people say, without hesitation, that they have been *born again* (1 Peter 1:23), that they are then *new creatures in Christ* (Galatians 6:15), and that *old things have passed away and all things have become new* (2 Corinthians 5:17).

Within Mormonism, there exists perhaps one of the ugliest admixtures or twists of Scripture relative to this subject. These sick, man-made doctrines ensure that most Latter-day Saints will never experience true rebirth but are instead trapped into a life of servitude to the LDS church itself. We know from last week's program that Mormonism first teaches that spiritual rebirth ***only*** comes about by receiving *their* ordinances of water baptism and what they call *their* "gift of the Holy Ghost."

Brigham Young said (*Discourses of Brigham Young*, page 152):

> Every ordinance, every commandment and requirement is necessary for the salvation of the human family.

But the demands necessary for salvation do not end here. They then take the grace wrought by faith and remove it even further from the hearts of their members by teaching that holiness (or sanctification) comes only by the works and efforts of the individual and that it is NOT imputed to a believer by faith in Christ alone.

Wilford Woodruff, 4th President of the Church said (*Discourses of Wilford Woodruff*, page 23):

> If I ever obtain a "full salvation," it will be by my keeping the laws of God.

Joseph F. Smith, 6th President of the LDS church, added to this insanity by saying in the April General Conference of 1915:

> *I do not believe that a man is saved in this life by believing, or pro-*

> *fessing to believe on the Lord Jesus Christ, but that He must endure to the end and keep the commandments that are given.*

Since these early years it seems that the animus these leaders have held for the Biblical doctrine of salvation by grace through faith alone has increased.

Where the Bible plainly says:

> Romans 10:9. *That if thou shalt confess with thy mouth the Lord Jesus, and shalt believe in thine heart that God hath raised him from the dead, thou shalt be saved.*

And where it says:

> Ephesians 2:8. *For by grace are ye saved through faith; and that not of yourselves: it is the gift of God: not of works, lest any man should boast.*

Tenth President of the LDS church, Joseph Fielding Smith, said (*The Restoration of All Things*, page 192):

> One of the most pernicious doctrines ever advocated by man, is the doctrine of "justification by faith alone," which has entered into the hearts of millions since the days of the so-called reformation.

When I was a teenager, 12th ... *ahem* ... prophet of Mormonism, Spencer W. Kimball, wrote this in his piece of literary filth, *The Miracle of Forgiveness* (pages 206-207):

> One of the most fallacious doctrines originated by Satan and propounded by man is that man is saved alone by the grace of God; that belief in Jesus Christ alone is all that is needed for salvation.

Where Kimball said that the doctrine of faith alone saves a person is a *doctrine of Satan*, the Bible says:

> Galatians 2:16. *knowing that a man is not justified by the works of the law but by faith in Jesus Christ, even we have believed in Christ Jesus, that we might be justified by faith in Christ and not by the works of the law; for by the works of the law no flesh shall be justified.*

Now, I would be remiss if I did not speak of another aspect of sanctification, which many people just do not understand, LDS and Christian alike. When the thief on the cross believed, he was justified and sanctified fully and completely by His faith. And the shed blood and righteousness of Jesus fully took away his condemnation AND made Him holy.

And the thief died perfect before God.

But what if, after his dialogue with Jesus on the cross – *just what if,* okay – the Roman soldiers suddenly took him down, treated his wounds, and then he went on to live another forty or fifty years of life?

Here is where another aspect of Christian sanctification comes into play. Some people from Vermont call it "progressive sanctification. Once a person has been justified and sanctified by the shed blood of Jesus and the Holy Spirit moves into their heart permanently, He begins to change that person from within.

Now sometimes people experience rebirth and they are immediately able to toss away much of the world, becoming actual new creatures in their flesh in a very short period of time. We all hear stories of alcoholics who receive Jesus and never take another drink and criminals who are saved and immediately turn from a life of crime.

To this, we all praise God, right?

But we also know that having been reborn, many others are literally "babes in Christ," and babies make a lot of mistakes and messes when they are learning to walk.

What the thief would do we are not sure. Maybe he would for a season return to a life of crime. Or maybe he would make a 180 about face and become an immediate missionary for Christ; we don't know.

But what we do know is that the thief is saved.

This knowledge would immediately or over the course of time free the thief in his heart and mind from the bondage he experienced from a life of sin and uncertainty. In time, God would begin to have the one-time thief producing fruit.

How do we know this?

Because he has been born again! He has a new heart, a new spirit within him. He is a new creature. And the Holy Spirit (God) within him will forever prompt and push and challenge him to release his fleshly will, and turn it all over to God.

This progressive sanctification is the making holy of what was once defiled and sinful within a person. It is a progressive work of divine grace upon the soul who has been wholly saved by the love of Christ. These believers are gradually changed from their corrupted natures, and they will be REWARDED in the eternities for the fruit of the Spirit produced in their Christian walk.

This second part of sanctification we'll call "living sanctification." Faith is instrumental in securing wholesale justification and imputed righteousness because it insures our union with Christ (Galatians 2:20), and brings us into living contact with the truth through the indwelling of the Holy Spirit. Living sanctification occurs in the lives of those who both believe and are permitted by God to continue living on this earth.

Notice something very important:

Living sanctification is the *RESULT* of spiritual rebirth, and not the opposite. In other words, living a good life does NOT produce or merit spiritual rebirth, but spiritual rebirth produces a desire to sanctify our lives to the Lord.

It is our brokenness, not our worthiness, that opens the door to spiritual rebirth.

Notice it was a thief on a cross and not a king in a carriage who was saved. We do not try and perfect ourselves IN ORDER to be born-again or in order to be worthy of Jesus' shed blood and/or the presence of the Holy Spirit within us.

And yet this is but another twist the LDS suggest to their overburdened members: that they must be worthy and righteous by their own efforts in order to have the Holy Spirit with them and that this Holy Spirit's presence is highly conditional on the continuation of the individual's personal worthiness. What a burden!

What a load of man-made twistianity.

Listen, we do *NOT* cause the Holy Spirit to leave by our failings. The Holy Spirit stays in spite of our failings! To help us through. To lead and guide and comfort and transform us.

Amen!

Doesn't this view support both the sacred and important work of Jesus and the love God has for all?

Now achieving perfect living sanctification is not attainable in this life. (1 Kings 8:46; Proverbs 20:9; Ecclesiastes 7:20; James 3:2; 1 John 1:8). But this does not mean we abandon our faith! Instead it ought to mean we cling to our faith more tightly, realizing that we have NO HOPE but our hope in Him.

This is where God's chastening and pruning comes into play as believers are subject to the constant chastisement of their Father's loving hand. In this we find true meaning and sound context for good lives lived.

Second Timothy says it all really well. Speaking of God, Paul says:

> 2 Timothy 1:9. *[He] hath saved us, and called us with an holy calling, not according to our works, but according to his own purpose and grace, which was given us in Christ Jesus before the world began.*

Mormons today attempt to teach that being saved and/or born again - justified and sanctified – is a combined one-two punch of grace and works.

This is a Biblical impossibility.

Paul makes this plain:

> Romans 11:6. *And if by grace, then is it no more of works: otherwise grace is no more grace. But if it be of works, then is it no more grace: otherwise work is no more work.*

Now, having heard this plain reasoning from God's word, let's hear what "Apostle" Bruce R. McConkie said (just listen to this utterly binding double-speak); *Doctrinal New Testament Commentary*, 3:256:

> Salvation is free, but it must also be purchased; and the price is obedience to the laws and ordinances of the [LDS] gospel.

In a futile and utopian effort to free the proletariat from the bondage of the ruling classes, Karl Marx wrote in the last chapter of his *Manifesto of the Communist Party* (page 32):

> The Communists disdain to conceal their views and aims. They

> openly declare that their ends can be attained only by the forcible overthrow of all existing social conditions. Let the ruling classes tremble at a Communistic revolution. The proletarians have nothing to lose but their chains. They have a world to win.

I would like to borrow his theme but alter his words and address the LDS leadership today:

> The Christians disdain to conceal their views and aims. *They openly declare that their ends can be attained only by the forcible overthrow of all existing religious conditions. Let the ruling brethren tremble at this internal Christian revolution. The believers have nothing to lose but their chains. And heaven to win.*

"To the Latter-day Saints, Cain is not only like 'Nessy' to the Scots, he is also responsible for the skin tone of black people. I'm not kidding, these guys have answers for everything, and some of them are not very nice."

Cain

With the exception of a few references to him, the Bible says little about Cain.

I mean, he is part of the story of the first murder and the punishment that follows. There isn't a reason that more needs to be said, unless a person or group is in the business of making myths and mountains out of scriptural mole-hills.

Enter the Latter-day Saints, more specifically, Joseph Smith Jr., its founder, who, as he did in the case of Kolob, Zelph, Mahonri Moriancumer, and a host of other unprovable exaggerations, made up a very insensitive and destructive myth about Cain.

Most of this information can be found in Joseph Smith's translation of the Bible, known as the *Inspired Version*. Get ahold of one of these *Inspired Versions* and open it up and compare it to, say, a King James version. It will amaze you what the man did to the Bible in terms of adding to it without any apparent concern for committing blasphemy.

These extra verses which Joseph produced straight out of his head, tell us that Cain, son of Adam and Eve, came under the influence of Satan, whom he *"loved...more than God* (Moses 5:18)," and that he thereafter became the founder of a *"secret combination* (i.e., secret society; Moses 5:51)," whose purpose included to *"murder and get gain* (Moses 5:31; cf. 5:49-51)."

The emphasis Joseph Smith put on "secret societies" was a direct result of the secret Masonic societies, which Joseph detested at one point and which flourished over most of settled early America.

Joseph's translation says that when Eve bore Cain, she rejoiced in the prospect of a child who would accept his parents' teaching concerning the true Son (Moses 5:7-8). She said, *"I have gotten a man from the Lord; wherefore he may not reject his words."* But later we read:

> Moses 5:16. But behold, Cain hearkened not, saying: Who is the Lord that I should know him?.

Joseph informs us in his retranslation of the Bible that it was Satan who commanded Cain to make an offering to the Lord. And once Cain followed Satan's instruction, his offering was rejected.

Joseph Smith tells us,

> Moses 5:21 Now Satan knew this, and it pleased him.

Smith tells us that earlier instructions from an angel to Adam and Eve had emphasized that animal sacrifice *"is a similitude of the sacrifice of the Only Begotten of the Father.... Wherefore, thou shalt do all that thou doest in the name of the Son* (Moses 5:7-8)."

Therefore, according to Smith, Cain already knew what was acceptable to God – animal sacrifice – but he refused to follow counsel (*TPJS*, pages 58, 169).

Because Cain had possession of a body – and Satan doesn't – Joseph also lets us know, "[Cain] *would rule over him* [Satan]*; for from this time forth* [Cain] *shalt be the father of his* [Satan's] *lies; thou shalt be called Perdition; for thou wast also before the world. And it shall be said in time to come—That these abominations were had from Cain; for he rejected the greater counsel which was had from God* (Moses 5:23-25; cf. *TPJS*, page 190)."

Cain also tells us why he killed Abel as Joseph writes:

> Moses 5:35-38. And Cain said unto the Lord: Satan tempted me because of my brother's flocks. And I was wroth also; for his offering thou didst accept and not mine.

Joseph then tells us that Satan had convinced Cain that by committing murder he would acquire both power and wealth. To support this, Joseph actually ties Cain to Masonic rhetoric, which originated in the late 1600's in England or France, and actually has Cain say of himself:

> Moses 5:31. Truly I am Mahan, the master of this great secret, that I may murder and get gain.

Mormons believe that this became the foundation of secret "combinations" instituted by Cain in collusion with Satan and perpetuated by Cain's descendant Lamech, as well as other secret combinations found on earth today (Moses 5:47-52)!

Even in the Book of Mormon, the theme of secret combinations is frequent and recurring. Referring to Cain, Book of Mormon character Moroni said that he does not *"write the manner of their oaths and combinations,"* for it had been made known unto him *"that they are had among all people* (Ether 8:20)." Then he says:

> Ether 8:25 ... whoso buildeth [a secret combination] seeketh to overthrow the freedom of all lands, nations, and countries; and it bringeth to pass the destruction of all people, for it is built up by the devil, who is the father of all lies; even that same liar...who caused man [Cain] to commit murder from the beginning.

But the scathing fictional and mythical blame for all things evil upon Cain does not end with his authoring dreaded "secret combinations." The LDS have long pinned black skin as the mark God placed upon him for murdering Abel. And this black skin is what black people today – African Americans – bear as his, CAIN'S, descendents.

Again, another example of Joseph producing a myth to explain everything.

You know, God is pretty simple in his love and beauty and creative skill. To him, black is beautiful. So are brown and white and gray and yellow and red. These attributes God gave cannot be altered, any more than a Zebra's stripes are altered because he is naughty.

Listen to what God says in Jeremiah 13:23:

> *Can the Ethiopian change his skin, or the leopard his spots?*

This is the simple, beautiful, open way of God. Black skin came as a result of God and His creative providence.

But needing to answer everything so as to be the sole authority on earth – on everything – Joseph was willing to speak for God, call it scripture, and sway millions toward some very ugly thinking. Listen to the results, for example, of Joseph's teaching that Cain was cursed with a black skin.

LDS prophet Joseph Fielding Smith said (*The Way to Perfection*, page 101):

> Not only was Cain called upon to suffer, but because of his wickedness he became the father of an inferior race.

Brigham Young taught (*Journal of Discourses* 7:290):

> Some classes of the human family that are black, uncouth, uncomely, disagreeable and low in their habits, wild, and seemingly deprived of nearly all the blessings of the intelligence that is generally bestowed upon mankind ...[Young connects these people to Cain by using Joseph's scriptures regarding the teaching; he then continued] ...the Lord put a mark upon him, which is the flat nose and black skin.

When I was a youth, LDS Apostle – APOSTLE! – Mark E. Petersen said the following, in all seriousness, from a pulpit at BYU ("Race Problems – as they affect the church," page 15):

> Think of the Negro, CURSED AS TO THE PRIESTHOOD ... This Negro, who, in the pre-existence lived the type of life which justified the Lord in sending him to the earth in the lineage of Cain with a BLACK SKIN, and possibly being born in darkest Africa—if that Negro is willing when he hears the gospel to accept it, he may have many of the blessings of the gospel. IN SPITE OF ALL HE DID IN THE PRE-EXISTENT LIFE, the Lord is willing, if the Negro accepts the gospel with real, sincere faith, and is really converted, to give him the blessings of baptism and the gift of the Holy Ghost. If that Negro is faithful all his days, he can and will enter the celestial kingdom. He will

go there *AS A SERVANT,* but he will get celestial glory [all emphases Shawn’s].

All because a man thought he had the right to change, alter, and add to the Word of God.

❋ ❋ ❋

“What most LDS people do not understand is that when Joseph Smith supposedly asked God ‘which church is true?’ it was a problematic question from the start. The Bible plainly states that the church is made up of individual believers, not an institution housed in brick and mortar.”

The Church

When it comes to our topic for tonight, *church*, there are a few angles people can take. I can think of five.

The **first** is that all churches, or in this case, all religions, are good and true and correct. It is said that we all worship the same God, and so we ought to all receive everyone’s message equally.

I refute this position based on simple logic alone since contradictory teachings cannot all be considered true. And since most religions do in fact contradict one another, they cannot all be true – unless of course, God is contradictory, but then THAT would be nonsensical, too.

The **second** thought says that no churches or religions are true. They all have error and they all fail and they all are the product of human imagination. In the way human beings define church and religion, I would greatly agree with this position. Any and every religious institution has problems and errors; so to call any one "true" is ridiculous and causes people to place their trust and focus in or on the wrong thing.

The **third** position says that there is one single true church or religion on the face of the earth. It has buildings, and leaders, and doctrines, practices, rites, and rituals that are stamped "of God."

This is what Catholicism, Mormonism, Jehovah's Witnesses, etc. teach and would have you believe.

The **fourth** position says that some religions have some truth, others have other truths, they all have good, they all help humanity reach God, and in the end, it will all work out – so don't worry, be happy. While I think it is true that most earthly religious institutions teach some truth, this is not the yardstick by which to tell whether they are true or not.

The **fifth** attitude, which I wholly embrace, redefines church altogether. So where we might use the term "church" to describe where we physically join up with a group of like-minded believers, the true church on earth is not defined by race, memberships, or cement and mortar, but by people who are united in faith, belief, and allegiance the world over.

In the debate between Mormonism and true Biblical Christianity, Mormonism would have the world believe that there is one true Church on the face of the earth, established by Jesus Christ, defined by priests, authority, brick and mortar, membership rolls, and tithing receipts. Bible-believing Christians the world over KNOW that God's true church is constructed of believing people, NO MATTER where they attend weekly religious meetings. The differences between the two perspectives results in a wholly different "type" (if you will) of person.

One creates a person whose allegiance is to a religious institution while the other creates a person who relies solely upon their relationship with God.

One creates a rigidity of motion, restricting the religious expressions of a people while the other allows God to work with people outside of the box.

One creates uniformity, sort of like McDonald's, where a church meeting in Guam tastes exactly like a church meeting in Massachusetts. The other shares in a universal reception of the Bible, but allows for all sorts of divergent expressions to exist.

So let's take a minute and talk about what the LDS say is the *Church of Jesus Christ* – and what this teaching amounts to in their members - and then what the Bible says the *church* is, and how this is generally manifested in its believers.

In order to really understand the LDS position on what the "True Church" is, we have to go back to Joseph Smith's story. Joseph Smith claims to have been confused about what church or religious institution he should join when he was but a young teenager, and so in search of an answer, went to a grove of trees and asked God which church is true (*Joseph Smith History* 1:18):

> ... which of all the sects is right...Which [should I] join?

"God," responding to the errant question, told him to (*Joseph Smith History* 1:19):

> ... join none of them, for they were all wrong...all their creeds were an abomination in his sight; that those professors were all corrupt ...

Unlike what the Bible plainly states, "God" did not say to Joseph there in the grove, *"Joseph, my church is built of believers who know me by faith."*

But instead Joseph says He affirmed the LDS idea that there

was an institutionalized religion that was established by Jesus Christ and that Joseph Smith himself was supposed to restore it to the earth. Thereby, yet another false, non-Biblical premise was introduced by Joseph that said that Christ's church is a brick and mortar institution with an associated priesthood authority.

The inherent problems associated with this completely man-made position are nothing short of staggering.

Where Mormonism claims that so-called "Biblical Christianity" is proven a failure by the fact that it lacks uniformity and unity, and deals with its fair share of financial and moral failures, Mormonism fails to see how its successes in uniformity, conformity, and financial successes feed off the souls of a people trapped by spiritual and religious bondage and death.

In Mormonism, the thinking has been done.

In Mormonism, the spirit does not work outside the confines of accepted culture.

In Mormonism, the "Church," the religious institution, the *brethren* – men – are everything.

In November of 1857, Apostle Heber C. Kimball said (*Journal of Discourses* 6:32):

> If you are told by your leaders to do a thing, do it. None of your business if it is right or wrong.

In 1995 late LDS prophet Gordon B. Hinckley said, in a speech at Rick's College ("Hold to the Church," October 29, 1995):

> Hold to the Church. Do not ever lose sight of the fact that the Church must ever remain preeminent in your lives if you are going to be happy as the years pass. Never let yourselves be found in the position of fighting the Church of Jesus Christ of Latter-

> Day Saints. You cling to it and be faithful to it. You uphold and sustain it. You teach its doctrines and live by it. And I do not hesitate to say that your lives will be richer and happier because of that.

Let me read how a Christian would say these very same words but with the Biblical and therefore the Christian emphasis:

> Hold to the Lord. Do not ever lose sight of the fact that the Lord is faithful to you whether you are faithful to Him or not. If you want to experience His joy as the years pass, hang on to Him. Never let yourselves be found in the position of fighting Him and His love for you. You cling to Him and be faithful to believing Him. Let Him uphold and sustain you. You teach His doctrines and live by Him. And I do not hesitate to say that your lives will be full of joy and love because of it.

Within Mormonism, everything – and I mean everything – is the Church.

Let's take a look at a video clip of a speech the President of BYU Hawaii gave a number of years back. Take a minute, go on-line, and type in the address bar:

> http://www.youtube.com/watch?v-JThMzwjTRaM

Just listen not only to what this LDS man supports, but his justification for supporting it. How strongly does the LDS Church place the superiority and importance of itself and its leaders on Mormon members?

Listen up:

LDS prophet Harold B. Lee said (*Teachings of the Living Prophets Student Manual*, page 32):

> Your safety and ours depends upon whether or not we follow the ones whom the Lord has placed to preside over his church. He

> knows whom he wants to preside over this church, and he will make no mistake. The Lord doesn't do things by accident...Let's keep our eye on the President of the Church.

Eternal safety and salvation is explained as being inextricably tied not only to membership in the Church and following the brethren in the church, it is tied to doing everything the Church requires!

LDS apostle Bruce R. McConkie said (*Doctrinal New Testament Commentary* 3:256):

> Salvation comes by obedience to the whole law of the whole gospel. [meaning, the whole of what Mormonism says; McConkie goes on, and quotes Joseph Smith as saying] Any person who is exalted to the highest mansion has to abide a celestial law [which, according to Mormonism, is only found in the LDS church] and the whole law too.

The previous words from Joseph Smith caused LDS apostle McConkie to conclude:

> Thus, a man may be damned for a single sin!

This anti-Biblical message is enough to make a Christian die of hyper-nausea.

Spencer W. Kimball, supposed prophet of the LDS church during my youth, said of the Mormon priesthood which is ONLY available through the Mormon Church (*The Teachings of Spencer W. Kimball*, page 51):

> Men require priesthood for exaltation. No man will ever reach godhood who does not hold the [LDS] priesthood. You have to be a member of the higher priesthood – an elder, seventy, or high priest – and today is the day to get it and magnify it.

Apostle McConkie also tied salvation to the LDS temple, which is also ONLY available to members of the LDS church. Said he in his book, *The Mortal Messiah: From Bethlehem to Calvary* (1:99):

> With temples men can be exalted; without them there is NO exaltation [emphasis Shawn's].

Brigham Young taught that salvation is available only to people who have a spouse by their eternal side – and of course, a spouse can only be at our side if the spouse is sealed to us in the LDS temple, which belongs to the LDS Church.

Young said, as quoted in Spencer Kimball's blasphemous work, *The Miracle of Forgiveness* (page 245):

> If a man wishes to be saved, he cannot be saved without a woman by his side.

LDS leaders have even gone so far as to tie salvation to accepting the LDS Church and the founder of this faith, Joseph Smith, by saying (Brigham Young, *Journal of Discourses* 4:298):

> I wish we had more Elders to go and preach just such sermons by the power of God, that is, "I know that Joseph Smith is a Prophet of God, that this is the Gospel of salvation, and if you do not believe it you will be damned, every one of you."

Joseph Smith himself said, as found in the *History of the Church* (6:408-409):

> I have more to boast of than ever any man had. I am the only man that has ever been able to keep a whole CHURCH together since the days of Adam. A large majority of the whole have stood by me. Neither Paul, John, Peter nor JESUS ever did it. I boast that no man ever did such a work as I.

And upon this man's very person, this religious institution called

Mormonism claims it is the *ONLY* true church on the face of the earth!

❋ ❋ ❋

"The lack of crosses in LDS culture and architecture is indicative of their lack of understanding of who Jesus is, what He did, and how these things actually translate to the lives of people who call themselves Christian. The lack of the cross symbol is not just an issue of culture or preference, it is a central theme to a religion which claims His name but does not know Him."

The Cross

Tonight we come to one of the most obvious external differences that exists between Bible-teaching churches and the LDS Church: the presence or the absence of the cross.

Interestingly enough, when most Latter-day Saints are asked if they are Christian they ardently confirm that they are. And yet on almost every doctrinal point, Mormon doctrine differs in some way or another with Biblical Christian doctrine or practice.

The views on the cross are no exception.

Now while I believe that there is a great difference between the official doctrines of Mormonism and the heart-felt beliefs that many Latter-day Saints privately maintain, when it comes to how most of the LDS general population views the cross, I think I am safe in saying that most faithful members of the Mormon church miss the meaning of it completely. In fact, in some ways I think the basic differences in the way Mormons and Christians see the cross perfectly pictures how vastly different Mormonism is from Biblical Christianity.

We live in a world of symbols. Some are internationally recognized and others only locally significant. Symbols evoke deeply felt emotions within human beings. They encapsulate epochs of time and moments in history; they articulate in a single icon what entire libraries often fail to describe. Icons and symbols serve to remind people of their allegiance to a cause or group and can be pregnant with deep multi-faceted meaning. I am always taken back when I watch Olympic champions shed tears of allegiance as they look upon their country's flag from the award stand.

God knows human beings relate to icons and symbols. He made us this way. And before the foundation of the world, He knew the import of the cross.

Think of the Star of David, or a peace sign, or even the "golden arches." All of them speak to specific groups, with certain agendas, and bearing a particular philosophy in some area or aspect of life. To Christians, the cross is symbolically central to the single most important thing in their existence. But there exists a few common misunderstandings that occur when it comes to this universal symbol, which Mormonism rejects.

First, it is not a man-made icon, like the swastika or the black and white Yin and Yang, but is found in Scripture itself.

We remember that when Jesus was crucified, the Jews, not wanting Him to hang there overnight because of the onset of Passover, asked the Roman soldiers to break His legs so He would die before sunset. But when they got to Him He was already dead so, in fulfillment of prophecy, there was no need to break any bone in His body. Well, another Old Testament picture was fulfilled here in Christ.

Looking all the way back to the book of Deuteronomy, Moses foretold the very circumstance of Jesus' crucifixion ON A WOODEN CROSS when he wrote:

> Deuteronomy 21:23. *His body shall not remain all night upon the tree, but thou shalt in any wise bury him that day; (for he that is hanged is accursed of God;) …*

Generally speaking, in Scripture, the cross represents two very different but interconnected things.

First, it is most often seen as an instrument of death and torture.

This is the cross's *material* meaning. Often, this understanding of the cross is where it all begins and ends in the minds of many people, especially with the Mormons. They see it only as the barbaric fixture upon which Jesus suffered the brutality of physical death. In a very simplistic way, Mel Gibson's film, "The Passion of the Christ," could be seen by some as a cinematic representation of the cross as an instrument of physical death.

While on my full time LDS mission, people would ask, *"How come you guys don't have crosses in or on your churches?"* I had been taught in the MTC to say something to the effect of, *"Well, suppose someone you loved very much was murdered by a buck knife. How would you like it if people stuck replicas of bloody buck knives all over the place in memory of him?"*

This is an example of seeing or representing the cross in a very limited way – only as an instrument of death. As an unregenerate non-believer, and therefore before I was capable of understanding the Bible with spiritual eyes, I thought this response was so clever and witty. It made sense to me logically because I had an intellectual understanding of His death and sacrifice but no personal, Biblical understanding of what His time on the cross REALLY meant for me spiritually.

When I was born-again, and remained LDS by the way for another four years, I almost immediately developed a new understanding and love for the symbol of the cross. This understanding wasn't taught to me nor did I have to think about it or choose to love or resonate to it. I just did.

What changed? How did I go from viewing the cross only as an instrument of death, which was *humanistically repulsive* and *intellectually insipid* to me, to viewing it as an object of honor and eternal appreciation? I went from seeing the cross as ONLY an instrument of death to understanding what I call, the "Doctrine of the Cross."

Biblically, the cross of Christ is represented in three distinct ways: *materially*, *metaphorically*, and *metonymically*.

We have covered the first way: the *material* cross.

The material cross of Christ is the object he physically died upon.

It is believed that the LORD was crucified on a "*tau*" (from the Greek letter for "T"), which is also known as the St. Anthony's cross. This cross has no top to it (like the Latin cross has) but instead looks like a capital "T." The Latin cross is the lower case "t" often depicted in religious art and jewelry, like the stuff I have hanging about my neck. The material cross is very important to the Church of Rome but it does not hold a place of importance to most Protestant believers around the world. To the Catholics, the material cross is often accompanied by a figure of Jesus attached to it. This icon is known as a crucifix. A cross without Jesus is not a crucifix, it is just a cross. Yes, we do embrace, honor and revere his physical suffering and know that we cannot comprehend it. But the material cross is only part of the cross's import.

The *metaphorical* cross of Christ also plays an important part in Biblical Christianity. It represents afflictions. According to Scripture, it is metaphorically assigned to all believers. So important is the metaphorical cross to God that Jesus said,

> Luke 9:23. *If any man will come after me, let him deny himself, and take up his cross daily, and follow me.*

So important is the metaphorical cross in the lives of believers that Paul wrote:

> Romans 6:6. … *our old man is crucified with him, that the body of sin might be destroyed, that henceforth we should not serve sin.*

We see from this passage (and others like it) that the cross is far more than just the instrument of death that the Romans used to kill the physical body of Jesus. It also has metaphorical application to all who choose to follow him. With this metaphorical significance, the Holy Spirit utilizes this God-given icon to remind every Christian that we, too, ought to be crucified with our King and to take up our cross and walk with Him.

The LDS are so myopically focused on the "instrument of death" aspect of the cross that they errantly and ignorantly say some of the most demeaning things about it. Consider what noted science-fiction writer and LDS thinker, Orson Scott Card, wrote about the cross, which was published in the official Mormon periodical *Meridian Magazine* (non-subscribers may view a full reprint at The Ornery American Website, http://www.ornery.org/essays/warwatch/2004-02-29-1.html):

> **I don't believe that the manner of Jesus' death had anything to do with either the atonement or the resurrection.** That's why we Mormons don't use the symbol of the cross on our churches — to us, crucifixion was merely the method that the Romans used to execute those of whom they wanted to make a public example. **Had the death been by lethal injection, the effect on our salvation would have been the same.** I believe that Christ's real

> suffering was the anguish he felt as he bore the horror of complete spiritual separation from God — taking upon himself to an infinite degree the torment that is the natural spiritual consequence of sin. The remorse and despair we feel (or will feel to varying degrees) because of our disobedience to or rejection of God, he felt so utterly that we cannot imagine it. In this context, **what was done to his body was almost a distraction.** Many people have borne as much [all emphases Shawn's].

We can't blame Card for his ignorance. He only mimics the twisted thinking he has been taught by his LDS leaders over the years.

One of these twists is the LDS notion that the garden of Gethsemane was the "true place of the atonement of Jesus" and not the cross.

BYU Professor Robert J. Matthews wrote in his book *A Bible, A Bible* (p. 282):

> It was in Gethsemane, on the slopes of the Mt. of Olives, that Jesus made His perfect atonement by the shedding blood – more so than on the cross.

Nowhere in the Bible is the garden of Gethsemane noted as a place of shame or atonement or as the place where the suffering for sin took place. And the fact that Jesus sweat "***as it were great*** *drops of blood*" in the garden while contemplating what He was about to endure is only recorded by Luke (22:44). (The meaning of the phrase, "*as it were*" is, "*as IF it were really so;*" or "*in a manner of speaking,*" which means Luke might have been using a figure of speech.)

This is simply another form of Mormon twistianity. Accept enough of them and before you know it, you are on the opposite side of the Good News.

LDS Prophet Gordon B. Hinckley added to the LDS distancing of itself from the cross when he wrote in the April 2005 edition of the LDS magazine, the *Ensign* (page 3):

> [For the LDS,] the cross is the symbol of the dying Christ, while our message is a declaration of a Living Christ.

This is another major twist away from the Biblical exegesis of what Jesus did. All of these LDS twists take the single most important view of the cross – *what it fully represents to human kind spiritually* - and reduces it to a common and meaningless form of Roman capital punishment.

So we have the material meaning of the cross.

And we have the metaphorical meaning of the cross.

Let's talk about the third way the Bible presents the importance of the cross: *metonymically.*

This way is COMPLETELY lost on the LDS – and it is perhaps the most important.

Metonymy is a figure of speech in which one word or phrase is substituted for another with which it is closely associated. For example when we say *Washington* we are metonymically using Washington D.C. to represent *the whole of the United States government.* Or when we say *the power of the sword* we are using the sword metonymically for *military power.*

This view of the cross is perhaps the MOST important as the cross of Christ is used metonymically for the gospel, the doctrine of the gospel, and of what He did upon the cross to bring about the Good News for us. In this case, the cross is metonymical for everything the Good News represents: it's the work of Christ for man, the shed blood, the hope, the miracle, our justification, and our sanctification ... it is emblematic of our very eternal life. And the Bible tells us so.

In my opinion, all references to the cross are important, but this metonymical association really touches on the present-day significance of the cross to born again Christians.

It is also this most important aspect of the cross that the LDS miss entirely!

Under the guise of restoring the early church back to the earth, Joseph Smith took full theological license to twist a number of core Biblical Christian beliefs and to label these twists as part of this restoration. Such twists have helped to remove the metaphorical and metonymical applications of the cross from the Mormon mind, leaving it only to be errantly identified as a Roman instrument of death.

And what have they been willing to replace it with? Graven images of mythical angels and phallic spires pointing to deification of man.

Listen very carefully to the metonymical sense of these verses.

Paul wrote:

> 1 Corinthians 1:17-18. *For Christ sent me not to baptize, but to preach the gospel: not with wisdom of words, lest the cross of Christ should be made of none effect. For the preaching of the cross is to them that perish foolishness; but unto us which are saved it is the power of God.*

The cross is metonymically THE POWER of GOD!

And the LDS refuse it?

In Galatians 5:11 Paul refers to *"the offence of the cross."* How can the cross be "*an offence*" to someone? Ask the LDS! Here is a perfectly clear picture of what their *"other gospel"* (Galatians 1:8) has created! They are offended by the cross!

Is the cross an offence to you or is it a symbol of joy, peace, and God's great love? How you view the cross is very dependent on whether you have been spiritually reborn or not and whether you truly understand Jesus. Those who have NOT been born again by God will almost always view the cross in errant terms, even as an offence.

In Galatians 6:12, Paul speaks metonymically of *"suffer*[ing] *persecution* ***for the cross of Christ.***" Then he continues:

> Galatians 6:14. *But God forbid that I should glory, save in the cross of our Lord Jesus Christ, by whom the world is crucified unto me, and I unto the world.*

You notice Paul says nothing about glorying in the garden, that he glories in nothing other than the cross of our Lord Jesus Christ. He doesn't say he glories in temple ordinances or rites, in church membership or baptisms, or in his righteous walk as a follower of Christ – no. He says he glories ONLY *"in the cross of our Lord Jesus Christ."*

Again in Ephesians 2:16, the cross is used metonymically as the thing that unifies sinful man to Holy God, saying, "*that he might reconcile both* [Jew and Gentile] *unto God in one body* ***by the cross,*** *having slain the enmity thereby*:" By his bloody death on the cross we are reconciled into one body through the expiation of sin. By slaying the hatred ("*enmity*") between all peoples *on the cross*, Jesus annulled the Jewish ceremonial law!

How about a few more?

Speaking of Jesus, Paul again writes:

> Philippians 2:8. *And being found in fashion as a man, he humbled himself, and became obedient unto death, even the death of the cross.*

Why is this important?

Because the death on the cross was a public and humiliating death. It was planned and highly purposeful in the mind of God from before the world began. Fashioned as man, Jesus allowed himself to come all the way down to the most despised death of all, a condemned criminal on an accursed cross.

This is important stuff, my friends, because Jesus didn't suffer for the sickness and sins of the world in private. Or by lethal injection.

God the Father had Him out in the public eye, suffering for the sins of the world for all to see in the MOST humiliating of circumstances – purposefully.

And the LDS discount this! They have the audacity to challenge its meaning and purpose in the eternal economy of God and the sacrifice of His only Son.

Unreal!

Look at this passage from Hebrews:

> Hebrews 12:2. *Looking unto Jesus the author and finisher of our faith; who for the joy that was set before him endured the cross, despising the shame, and is set down at the right hand of the throne of God.*

Shamed and brought to the lowest of low. Hung on a tree publicly. With common criminals. Spit on, mistreated, shamed, and ridiculed publicly. For what?

For you and me.

And on top of it all, here is where all of God's wrath was placed.

What greater ploy could there be than to get people – well-meaning people – to take their eyes off *the very place where they were each reconciled to Him*! And to have them look up at golden angels or spires that inspire the proud hearts of men!

The LDS claim the blood in the garden! Unreal!

Read:

> Colossians 1:20. *And, having made peace through the blood of his cross, by him to reconcile all things unto himself; by him, I say, whether they be things in earth, or things in heaven.*

And, having *"made peace through ..."* what? The blood of the garden? The gospel of a golden angel? No! Never!

"The blood of his cross!"

He made our peace **through the cross!** He endured shame **on the cross!** He reconciled us **by the cross!** He fulfilled the Law **on the cross!** Ordinances were nailed **to the cross!**

Now listen to this. Listen.

> Colossians 2:14. *Blotting out the handwriting of ordinances that*

> *was against us, which was contrary to us, and took it out of the way, nailing it to his cross;*

When Christ was nailed to the cross, our obligation to fulfill ordinances was done away with, forever, releasing us, freeing us, giving us peace. Are you getting the picture here? What happened on that cross fulfilled, atoned, connected, and completed what God had intended from the beginning!

I pray that Latter-day Saints everywhere will demand the cross in their chapels. I pray they will add a cross-bar to those chapel spires out of respect, adoration, and worship of Jesus Christ. I pray they will tear down those golden images from the tops of their temples and rend every temple veil in the name of Him who already did the job with His life, taken – *given* – on the cross.

"To the LDS, David is more of a type who illustrates that there are some sins God will not forgive – and I'm not talking about the blasphemy against the Holy Spirit."

King David

As we have said many times over the years, one of the distinctive aspects of Joseph Smith's Mormonism is that he supplied supposedly "inspired" information on a number of topics, many of which make Mormonism distinct from all other churches and religions, especially since most of the information he provided was unverifiable. At least, it was at the time.

Remember, Joseph claimed to know where the American Indians came from. He said that there were men on the moon and described how they dressed (like Quakers!). He actually proclaimed that he had translated writings of father Abraham from a common Egyptian funeral text. Through an imaginative interpretation and application of a single vague Biblical reference about baptism for the dead, an entire ritual superstructure was built which today keeps millions of people pre-occupied for a good part of their lives with a made-up ritual for the dead.

Our topic tonight? King David's sin.

The point or problem? Mormonism claims, by virtue of Joseph Smith's "revelations," that David is in spirit prison to this very day and will not ever go to their celestial kingdom because of his sins.

Jews, and Bible-believing Christians say much differently.

So while it may seem like, *"well, what's the big deal about what happened to David?"* what the LDS teach has great implications on the Good News.

Now to show the import this king has and had with the Jews, and to the establishment of Christianity, let me talk for a minute about David. It is significant to know that the Bible mentions his proper name, "David," 969 times.

"Abraham?" Mentioned 230 times.

Even the name "Jesus?" Twenty-six times fewer than David at 943!

This, of course, is not to say that David was anything in comparison to Jesus, but he *was* a picture of the Messiah and David's impact on Judeo/Christian life is profound. The most oft quoted Old Testament passage found in the New Testament was uttered by David; it is, in fact, the most oft quoted Old Testament passage by Jesus Himself (Psalm 110:1): "*The LORD said unto my Lord, Sit thou at my right hand, until I make thine enemies thy footstool.*" Quoted eighteen times, by Jesus: Matt. 22:44, 26:64, Mark 12:36, 14:62, 16:19, Luke 20:42-43, 22:69, Apostles: Acts 2:34-35, Rom. 8:34, 1 Cor. 15:25, Eph. 1:20, Col. 3:1, Heb.1:3, 13, 8:1, 10:12-13, 12:2*)*

David's name means "beloved."

Speaking to a sorcerer in Acts 13, Paul clearly illustrated the type of man David was, saying,

> Acts 13:22, 23. [God] *raised up unto them David to be their king; to whom also he gave testimony, and said, I have found David the son of Jesse, a man after mine own heart, which shall fulfil all my will. Of this man's seed hath God according to his promise raised unto Israel a Savior, Jesus.*

David was the eighth and youngest son of Jesse, a citizen ***of Bethlehem***. As to his personal appearance, we know that he was red-haired and had a fair face (1 Samuel 16:12; 17:42). As a very young man he tended his father's sheep on the uplands of Judah.

David – a shepherd of sheep, born in Bethlehem.

Out in the fields he seems to have perfected playing what is called the shepherd's flute and out there on the vast plains of nature he seemed to have learned lessons of governance and courage. According to 1 Samuel 17, his first recorded exploits were violent encounters with the wild beasts that sought to attack his sheep. With his own unaided hand he killed a lion and then a bear, beating them to death in open conflict with his club (1 Samuel 17:34,35).

Now while David was out with his flocks the prophet Samuel paid an unexpected visit to ***Bethlehem***, having been guided there by divine direction (1 Samuel 16:1-13). Once there, the prophet offered up sacrifice, and then called the elders of Israel and Jesse's family to the sacrificial meal. Among all who appeared before him Samuel failed to discover the one he sought. Eventually David was sent for, and the prophet Samuel immediately recognized him as the chosen one of God to succeed Saul, who was the people's first choice for king.

Accordingly, and in anticipation of His future kingship, Samuel poured anointing oil on David's young head and David went back to shepherding. According to 1 Samuel 16:13-14, *"the Spirit of the LORD came upon David from that day forward,"* and *"the Spirit of the LORD departed from Saul."* We never read of the Spirit of the Lord departing from David, in spite of his failures, throughout the rest of his life. In fact, after many of his failures occurred, he continued to write Holy Scripture.

As a young man David played the harp for Saul, and when he was about twenty years old he killed Goliath of Gath, who defied the armies of Israel. The result was a great victory to the Israelites, who pursued the Philistines and then defeated them. David's popularity from this kill made Saul jealous. (1 Samuel 18:6-16). So much so that Saul tried a number of ways to kill him. But David stayed true to the King and continued to prosper.

In the end, David by necessity became a fugitive to escape from the vengeance of Saul and, while a vagabond, experienced a whole host of wild adventures. But all the while David remained loyal to King Saul and proved himself a truly heroic warrior on behalf of Israel. When Saul was killed in battle, David was made King of Israel at thirty years of age and reigned from the place of Hebron (2 Samuel 5:4).

His throne was hotly contested many times, yet David always prevailed.

When He was anointed king over all of Israel, he sought out a new seat of government, one more suitable than Hebron. He discovered a Jebusite fortress on the hill of Zion. David conquered the Jebusites, and made this site the capital of Israel (2 Samuel 5:6-9). This City of David, Zion (2 Samuel5:7) is today known as Jerusalem.

David now resolved to bring up the ark of the covenant to this new capital and ultimately he was successful, placing it in a new tent which David had made specifically for this purpose (2 Samuel 6:1-19).

And then, according to 1 Chronicles 16:1-43, David carefully set in order all the rituals of divine worship at Jerusalem, with Abiathar being the high priest (1 Chronicles 15:11). Because of David's heart for God a new religious era began for Israel. Because of his military conquests an enormous area of land was under his righteous and fair sway (2 Samuel 8:3-13; 10:1-19). At the height of his glory, when he was ruling over a vast empire, and his capital was enriched with the spoils of many lands, David fell into temptation and sin and his character was marred with the sin of adultery (2 Samuel 11:2-27).

It is of great interest that while David's immense military conquests are recorded in only a few verses, the sad story of his fall is given in great detail, making it a story fit for the ages as a great warning. Unfortunately this crime of adultery with Bathsheba, and the attempt to conceal it, led to another sin. And David was then also guilty of murder. God sent Nathan the prophet to David (2 Samuel 7:1-17; 12:1-23) to bring home the crimes to the conscience of the guilty monarch.

And David became a true penitent.

Being a man after God's own heart, David bewailed his sins before God in bitterness. The thirty-second and fifty-first Psalms reveal the deep struggles of his soul, and...and...and his certain spiritual *recovery* and restoration.

Bathsheba became his wife after David had her husband killed and, according to the word of the Nathan the prophet, their first born son died. But it is also noteworthy how God restores and fixes the fallen – and uses our sin for good in the end – if we let him. For it was this very relationship with Bathsheba that produced a second son, whom David named Solomon, who ultimately succeeded him on the throne and fostered the seed through which the Messiah would come. This is the lineage that Jesus claimed when introducing Himself in Revelation 22:16: "*I Jesus…am the root and the offspring of David, and the bright and morning star.*"

Life was both peaceful and, as a result of his sin, troubling for David, especially with regard to his own family. So where he continued to lead, and amass tremendous amounts of wealth and power, he also faced an extreme amount of personal pain, betrayal, and discomfort as an individual.

After a reign of forty years and six months (2 Samuel 5:5; 1 Chronicles 3:4), David died (around B.C. 1015) at the age of seventy years, *"and was buried in the city of David* (1 Kings 2:10)."

His tomb is still pointed out on Mount Zion.

David, in his prophetical and in his regal character, was a great type or picture of the Messiah. The book of Psalms commonly bears the title of the *"Psalms of David,"* because he was the largest contributor to the collection (totaling about eighty of them) and many of them post the Bathsheba affair.

With the exception of his failures as a human being, David lived in harmony with both the priesthood and the prophets, which was a sure sign that the spirit of his government had been completely loyal to the higher aims of God. The nation had not ever been oppressed by him, but had been left in the freedom of its ancient liberties. According to 2 Samuel 8:15, and as far as his power went, he had striven to act justly toward all.

Any Jew and most Bible-believing Christians know, and patiently understand, that his weak indulgence of his sons and his own personal sins had been bitterly atoned for and were certainly forgotten by God. The writer of Hebrews includes David in his Faith Hall of Fame (Hebrews 11).

Jesus repeatedly associates His very existence to David; but the MORMONS say, "so what!" David is in hell and will remain there because of his sins, one of which is unforgiveable! And here, again, Joseph Smith's Mormonism, runs roughshod over the beautiful gospel of grace and truth. While the Bible offers the repentant sinner forgiveness for any sin, including murder, Mormonism maintains a murderer cannot achieve eternal life. And they use David as an example.

Joseph Smith states:

> Doctrine and Covenants 42:18. Thou shalt not kill; and he that kills shall not have forgiveness in this world, nor in the world to come.

It also says in another section (Doctrine and Covenants 132) that those who have been married "by the new and everlasting covenant" will be forgiven of any sin except murder "wherein they shed ***innocent blood*** (verses 19 & 26)." This LDS teaching on murder has led the Mormons to conclude that, when King David arranged to have Uriah killed (2 Samuel 11:15-17), he committed an unpardonable sin which would keep him from exaltation.

Joseph Smith taught that *"no murderer hath eternal life* (*TPJS*, page 188)."

But Jesus said:

> Matthew 12:31. *All manner of sin and blasphemy shall be forgiven unto men: but the blasphemy against the Holy Ghost shall not be forgiven unto men.*

So what to, did Joseph do with this? He simply redefined *"blasphemy against the Holy Ghost,"* saying:

> Doctrine and Covenants 132:27. The blasphemy against the Holy Ghost, which shall not be forgiven in the world nor out of the world, is in that ye commit murder wherein ye shed innocent blood, and assent unto my death, after ye have received my new and everlasting covenant, saith the Lord God; and he that abideth not this law can in nowise enter into my glory, but shall be damned, saith the Lord.

In two other places Joseph Smith reiterated this stance.

In *Teachings of the Prophet Joseph Smith*, page 339, he said:

> A murderer, for instance, one that sheds innocent blood, cannot have forgiveness. David sought repentance at the hand of God carefully through tears for the murder of Uriah, but he could only get it through hell: he got a promise that his soul should not be left in hell.

And then, as recorded in *Discourses of the Prophet Joseph Smith*, page 221, he added:

> Remission of sins by baptism was not to be preached to murderers. All the priests of Christendom might pray for a murderer on the scaffold forever, but could not avail so much as a gnat towards their forgiveness. There is no forgiveness for murderers.

Applying this to David, Joseph went on, and taking the Bible completely out of context, said (*TPJS*, page 188):

> Now, we read that many bodies of the Saints arose at Christ's resurrection...but it seems that David did not. *Why? Because he had been a murderer.*

So let me first explain what the Bible actually said about David – in context – and then finish up by showing you the slippery slope Joseph introduced by claiming murder cannot be forgiven.

In Acts chapter 2 we have the day of Pentecost, fifty days after the Lord's ascension, when the Holy Spirit descended upon the apostles. Gathered there were three thousand-plus Jews, listening to Peter's sermon. To these Jews, David was a very important figure. It is not by any mistake, first of all, that they were gathered in the very city David conquered and that carried his name: the City of Peace, the City of David, Jerusalem. Neither is it accidental that Peter in his preaching would use David and his words to help the Jews see their need for the only true Messiah.

In the Jewish writings, Rabbi Jose wrote (Hieros. Chagig. fol. 78):

> David died at Pentecost, and all Israel bewailed him, and offered their sacrifices the day following.

So here is what is happening in Acts chapter 2. In an effort to convince the Jews that Jesus was the one to look to and no other, Peter quotes Old Testament Scripture. He tells them that they have crucified the Messiah. Then Peter brings David's words into the sermon and he quotes David, who was speaking prophetically of the Messiah. And the doctrine David introduced was that the *Messiah* must rise from the dead.

In the New Testament, Peter quotes David's words taken from Psalm 16:8-10:

> Acts 2:25-28. *For David speaketh concerning him* [Jesus of Nazareth, verse 22], *I foresaw the Lord always before my face, for he is on my right hand, that I should not be moved: Therefore did my heart rejoice, and my tongue was glad; moreover also my flesh shall rest in hope: Because thou wilt not leave my soul in hell, neither wilt thou suffer thine Holy One to see corruption. Thou hast made known to me the ways of life; thou shalt make me full of joy with thy countenance.*

What is so revealing is that these words are NOT about David at all – Peter demonstrates by his use of them in his sermon at Pentecost that these words had been a prophetic utterance about the coming Messiah. But as we saw earlier, Joseph Smith, the so-called prophet of the LDS faith, said that David received a promise that his soul would not be left in hell as a result of his committing murder. Peter shows us that this Psalm was not about David at all – it couldn't have been: David wrote this Psalm *before* he sinned with Bathsheba!

In another place in the Bible, Paul clearly points out when teaching another group of Jews that David's words in Psalm 16 had nothing to do with Him but with the Messiah!

> Acts 13:36-37. *For David, after he had served his own generation by the will of God, fell on sleep, and was laid unto his fathers, and saw corruption: but he, whom God raised again, saw no corruption.*

Going back to Peter at the day of Pentecost, he continues speaking to the Jews, who loved David, saying,

> Acts 2:29-31. *Men and brethren, let me speak freely to you of the patriarch David, that he is both dead and buried, and his tomb is with us to this day. Therefore, being a prophet, and knowing that God had sworn with an oath to him that of the fruit of his body, according to the flesh, He would raise up the Christ to sit on his throne, he, foreseeing this, spoke concerning the resurrection of the Christ, that His soul was not left in Hades, nor did His flesh see corruption. This Jesus God has raised up, of which we are all witnesses.*

Joseph Smith said point blank that David was given a promise that his soul would not be left in hell nor see corruption; but it is clear this was a prophetic promise made about Jesus.

Got all that?

Now, this teaching about David is throughout Mormonism.

When I was a kid and a teenager and was asked who my favorite Old Testament prophet was, I would always say, David, and I never really understood why this response was always met with crickets. I learned why later.

But think about this. Joseph and Mormonism thereafter said David's sin of murder was unforgiveable. But David only set it up – he didn't actually shed the blood! He was just a conspirator.

Why is this important? Because Paul, who calls himself "*chief of sinners*" (1 Timothy 1:15) did the very same thing – many times over. He did it in the case of stoning Stephen, complicit and guarding the coats of those doing the killing and he shut many Christians up in prison, it says in Acts 26:10, who were put to death by his word. Paul describes himself, saying,

> Acts 22:4. *And I persecuted this way unto the death, binding and delivering into prisons both men and women.*

Is this not as complicit of murder as David? Is Paul in hell, too?

Besides being absolutely wrong on the Biblical status of David, Mormonism creates several other problems with their stance that the blood of Jesus cannot atone for all sin. First, they, once again, limit God's ability and willingness to forgive all sin, which tacitly demeans the shed blood of the Lord. I want anyone out there – anyone and everyone – the men in prisons – Mark Hoffman, the Lafferty Brothers – *anyone* out there at the Point of the Mountain, to know that Jesus' blood paid for all sin – all. Don't let this pernicious lie based in human conformity keep you in chains.

Secondly, this stance places sin in a hierarchy relative to God. Sin certainly can be placed in a hierarchy relative to earthly laws and human living, but to God, all of it is filth and it all only has one solution: Jesus.

Finally, one of the supports Mormons use to justify their belief that sin cannot be forgiven is this erroneous idea that in order to truly be forgiven for sin, a person must truly repent. And to truly repent, a person must follow and complete all the LDS steps of repentance. To omit a step negates any and all repentance.

These are the steps:

STEP 1. Recognize you have sinned.

STEP 2. Feel sorrow for your sin.

STEP 3. Confess your sin to God and your ecclesiastical authority if it is serious.

STEP 4. Ask forgiveness from God and those you hurt.

STEP 5. Make restitution for your crime. If you stole something, you must replace its value.

and finally,

STEP 6. Forsake your sin forever.

If a Latter-day Saint does not complete all of these requirements for a sin, repentance has not been done and forgiveness cannot be given by God. This is one reason why murder cannot be forgiven to the LDS – because step five cannot be completed. How can you make restitution for the taking of another life? You can't. So the LDS say, it's bye-bye fathead. You have not repented.

Enter one big slippery slope.

LDS Prophet Spencer W Kimball said (*Teachings of Spencer W. Kimball*, page 85):

> Perhaps one reason murder is unforgivable is that having taken a life, the murderer cannot restore it. Restitution in full is not possible. Also, [he adds] having robbed one of virtue, it is impossible to give it back.

So Mormon doctrine emphatically states that murder cannot ever be forgiven because a person can't make restitution. And then guys like Kimball allude to the idea that having sex is in a similar vein. And people needing to be liberated, and set free by the blood of Christ, are doomed to trying to make restitution for their crimes for the rest of their lives!

But aren't most sins irretrievable and unrestitutionable (if that's even a word)?

How do you make restitution for an abortion?

How about for gossip, embarrassing someone?

How do I make restitution for teaching people as an LDS missionary that Mormonism is true and encouraging them to join, altering their lives forever, only to now know is it a lie?

Let me end with the whole point of the LDS doctrinal response to David's sin: It is all a lie, and it leads to a premise that traps good, searching souls who could eternally be freed from the burden of sin by the blood of Jesus.

No matter what you have done in your life – and I want to say this, too – no matter what failures you will have in your life in the future, all of it – all of it was paid for on the cross by the Lord.

All of it.

Let me end with a verse of great hope found in Isaiah, who wrote about Jesus and His mission:

> Isaiah 61:1-3. *The Spirit of the Lord GOD is upon me; because the LORD hath anointed me to preach good tidings unto the meek; he hath sent me to bind up the brokenhearted, to proclaim liberty to the captives, and the opening of the prison to them that are bound; To*

proclaim the acceptable year of the LORD, and the day of vengeance of our God; to comfort all that mourn; To appoint unto them that mourn in Zion, to give unto them beauty for ashes, the oil of joy for mourning, the garment of praise for the spirit of heaviness; that they might be called trees of righteousness, the planting of the LORD, that he might be glorified.

❋ ❋ ❋

"Interestingly, the LDS actually permit divorce where Jesus and Paul give us an emphatic no on the topic (in most cases). The subject actually helps illustrate that participation and/or membership in the LDS church is more important in Mormonism than observing biblical truths. You would never hear a Mormon leader state that those who divorce without cause are adulterers."

Divorce

Tough topic tonight, kids. I mean rough and tough – to deliver properly and to hear rightly. As with any tough topic, some people are going to get rather incensed with me while others are going to find great relief.

So what are we comparing and contrasting between Mormonism and Biblical Christianity?

"Da-da-da-divorce."

What makes this topic so difficult is that I am obligated, by virtue of what the Big Manual says contextually, to speak the truth about it even if it hurts.

Like the subject of homosexuality, the Biblical truth regarding divorce is plain. BUT, as in the case of homosexuality, the great hope for the matter is plain as well – and it is NOT what most people think it is.

Perhaps the best single summary about divorce came from the mouth of Jesus himself. The Pharisees came to Jesus and, in an effort to trap Him, asked:

> Mark 10:2. *Is it lawful for a man to put away his wife?*

Now, there was a great debate among the Jews dating way back about what they called the "*putting away*" of a wife. One opinion came from the school of Hillel and it said that a man might divorce his wife for any offence, or any dislike he might have of her.

She burns the toast? DIVORCE!

She gives him the mean old sea hag face? DIVORCE!

And the woman was left dangling out there in society because of the whim of the man.

The other major opinion came from the school of Shammai. It maintained that divorce was unlawful, except in case of adultery. But again, even this option was pretty much up to the man and his accusations and so women got the brunt of the deal.

So being asked His thoughts, the Pharisees hoped to get Jesus to commit to either the Hillel or Shammai party, which would serve to bifurcate His ministry and influence among the Jews. Well Jesus, the Master Teacher, replied:

> Mark 10:3. *What did Moses command you?*

Instead of immediately answering and implicating Himself, He refers them back to a source they both respected: Moses. In response to His question, *What did Moses command you?*, they replied,

> Mark 10:4. *Moses suffered to write a bill of divorcement, and to put her away.*

Was this true? Yes it was. You see, here was the situation. Moses was leading millions of people out of bondage and into the promised land. This was an enormous endeavor and yet amidst this mass exodus and all that it entailed, Moses was being faced with one of the single most emotional issues in human existence: the dissolution of a marriage. So instead of letting some very misogynistic men just walk away from their wives, literally leaving them without any hope of a future, Moses, because of the hardness of their hearts, had their husbands write a *"bill of divorcement,"* which allowed the women to prove that they had been freed from the contract of marriage to the man.

Jesus said:

> Mark 10:5. *For the hardness of your heart he wrote you this precept. But from the beginning of the creation God made them male and female. For this cause shall a man leave his father and mother, and cleave to his wife* [that literally means to be glued to her]*; and they twain shall be one flesh: so then they are no more two, but one flesh.*

In Matthew's account (19:8), Jesus says to the Pharisees, *"Moses because of the hardness of your hearts suffered you to put away your wives, BUT FROM THE BEGINNING IT WAS NOT SO."*

So what does Jesus mean, *"from the beginning?"*

In order to contextually understand divorce and what Jesus said about it, we have to go back to this beginning He was speaking about: Adam and Eve.

Now ask yourself, "Where did Adam come from?" From the dust of the earth, right? Then where did Eve come from? From Adam's own body. Eve was taken from Adam. So they were wholly one and the same. And who made them one? God – because He created them, two from one, and then commanded the two parts to remain one flesh for life. Now listen closely: was there anything on earth that could take Adam and Eve and tear them apart or make them NOT one? Anything?

Nothing.

If Adam and Eve "got divorced" would the divorce change the fact that Eve was taken from Adam's side and that they were literally of one flesh? Not in the least.

From the beginning, Eve came from Adam and they were one, and nothing could ever separate them.

This is how Jesus was able to say that *Moses may have granted you all a bill of divorce, but from the beginning it was not so.* Meaning, from the beginning God made the unity of a couple absolutely permanent and impossible to separate.

And this is the model for the marital union today.

In this model we find an extremely limited expression of sexual intimacy. It should only occur between those who consummate their marriage to each other. The exclusiveness of Adam and Eve to each other is a type for the total exclusiveness a man and woman are to have with each other in marriage. God takes marital fidelity very seriously.

It does not matter what men or women think on the subject today when it comes to what God wants. His ideal of marriage was pictured in the beginning with the sacred creation of Adam and Eve, a union literally created by God Himself of two people from one source.

This is why Jesus added:

> Mark 10:9. *What therefore God hath joined together, let not man put asunder.*

Got all that?

Well, the disciples, having heard Jesus say this, were quite befuddled. And once they were away from the eyes and ears of the Pharisees, it says (verse 10), "*And in the house his disciples asked him again of the same matter.*"

Now what Jesus tells them fits perfectly with the way God set up and sees male and female marital relationships from the beginning. How?

> Mark 10:11-12. *And he saith unto them, Whosoever shall put away his wife, and marry another, committeth adultery against her. And if a woman shall put away her husband, and be married to another, she committeth adultery.*

What did Jesus mean?

Exactly what He said.

If a couple marries, and they divorce each other and join with another in marriage, Jesus calls them adulterers.

When a man and a woman come together in marriage and consummate it, they are one in God's eyes, just like Adam and Eve were one from God's hands.

Man can attempt to separate the couple, we can call it divorce, but to God, the first couple is one, just as Adam and Eve were one from the beginning.

And what God has put together let no man put asunder.

Now some will say, "*Well, God didn't put **my** marriage together.*"

Again, even if the couple didn't believe in God when they married it doesn't alter the fact that God sees them as one, and the same rules apply to them as if they were believers. John the Baptist was beheaded because he fearlessly told a non-Jewish governor that his marriage was illegal and improper. John the Baptist fearlessly confirmed to a non-believer that even he was subject to God's ways.

Okay, so those are some of the hard Biblical facts about marriage and divorce.

If you are married and consummate that marriage, you have become one in God's eyes and are not permitted to be divorced. I know this is hard to hear, but nobody is in any position to alter the facts.

When people come up to me and say, "Shawn, I was married, got divorced because we didn't get along, and then I got remarried. Does this mean I am an adulterer in God's eyes?"

And I say with all frankness and love, "Yes. In His eyes you are an adulterer." And then they freak out. And I usually lose another friend or supporter, unless I can convince them to hang around and hear the rest of the story found in the Good News.

So, how do the LDS differ in their perspective of divorce? In two distinct ways. First, if a spouse becomes an enemy to the church, Mormon leadership almost always counsels divorce. I know this from firsthand experience.

Secondly, in Mormonism, where divorce is more and more becoming a huge reality, the brethren today would never tell their faithful members who remarry after a divorce that they are adulterers. It's just too harsh. It doesn't bring the spirit. And so they ignore and alter the facts that Jesus Himself plainly stated. They haven't always done this, but they do it today.

And as long as people are supportive and believing in the Church, Biblical truths will usually take a back seat in order to not offend or grieve the spirit. But I have to be fair. In our day and age, the Christian body is not much better, and many pastors the world over condone divorce and remarriage as a means to keep people happy and to keep the pews full.

Now, let me turn to the hopeful facts regarding divorce because with the true and living God there is always hope in the face of this fallen world.

First of all, while Jesus said to the Pharisees that *"divorce was not so from the beginning,"* neither was any sin from the beginning, or lust, or anger, or selfishness, or any of the things that make marriage difficult today. So while we must be faithful to describe and understand God's perspective on how things are supposed to be – from the beginning – we may also note that we live in a fallen, messy world, one where Jesus came and did for us what we could not do for ourselves.

Now, there are some very rigid types of people out there who maintain a "stay married at all costs" position. And they seem to relish in castigating people who have been divorced.

These types usually cite a passage in Malachi 2 where it says God hates divorce ("*putting away*," verse 16). But they never seem to get as frothy over people who have a

- Proud look (Proverbs 6:17); or
- A lying tongue (Proverbs 6:17); or
- Hands that shed innocent blood (Proverbs 6:17); or
- Hearts that devise wicked imaginations (Proverbs 6:18); or
- Feet that be swift in running to mischief (Proverbs 6:18); or

- With false witnesses that speaketh lies (Proverbs 6:19); or
- People who sow discord among the brethren (Proverbs 6:19),

all of which, Scripture tells us, God hates, too.

The point is, God hates the condition of this fallen world and that is why He sent His Son: to save us from sin.

What is *really* interesting to me is that when Jesus addressed divorce He seemed to level the playing field and finally bring justice to a people-group who have for a long time been badly mistreated: women. Let me explain.

Jesus gave one reason for how a person could divorce a spouse and remarry another and NOT be an adulterer. When Jesus is teaching the disciples in the Sermon on the Mount, He says:

> Matthew 5:31-32. *It hath been said, Whosoever shall put away his wife, let him give her a writing of divorcement: But I say unto you, That whosoever shall put away his wife, saving for the cause of fornication, causeth her to commit adultery: and whosoever shall marry her that is divorced committeth adultery.*

Jesus here reiterates the fact that anyone who remarries after an unlawful divorce becomes an adulterer. However, He gives an exception for a marriage to be lawfully destroyed without it ending in the offended spouse being an adulterer if remarried. He says, "*saving for the cause of fornication.*"

Now this is really important, my friends. Listen: a married man or woman cannot – *cannot* – commit *fornication* by having sexual relations with a person other than a spouse. A married man or woman can only commit *adultery* through such an act. But Jesus uses two very different Greek words here when explaining the only justification for divorce.

The Greek word for adultery is "*moichao.*"

Now ask yourself, why doesn't Jesus say that, *"Whosoever shall put away his wife, saving for the cause of adultery, causeth her to commit adultery: and whosoever shall marry her that is divorced committeth adultery."*

But instead says that *"Whosoever shall put away his wife, saving for the cause of fornication ..."*

What is the Greek word for fornication used here? *Porneia!*

And while we all know we get the word pornography from *porneia*, it means, *"any and all sexual immorality or deviancy."*

What Jesus says here is that the only justifiable grounds, not only for divorce, but for the offended spouse to move on and remarry with God's full approbation, is when the other spouse is involved in *"any and all sexual immorality or deviancy"* committed outside the purview of marriage. It doesn't mean you should or have to divorce, but it is the grounds for a lawful divorce in God's eyes.

So we have some facts to consider.

ONE: God demands total sexual fidelity in marriage.
TWO: If there is not sexual fidelity, it is grounds for divorce.
THREE: And this sexual infidelity Jesus speaks about is porneia, which means any sexual deviation.

Now, looking at marriages today, who do you suppose is now in the seat to put away a spouse?

The wife!

You see, women have for centuries been the ones to have been "put away" for no justifiable reason, and now Jesus steps in here and says the marital union is sacred, and God expects every married couple to remain together.

But, Jesus says, if this union is broken by any sexual deviation or perversion from either side, the marriage *can* end, and the offended parties would not be considered adulterers in God's eyes if and when he or she remarries.

Finally, I'd like to speak to those people who have divorced for reasons other than "*porneia*" in their marriage, and are, by definition, seen as adulterers if they remarry, according to the Bible. If you find this title bothering you, check your pride at the door and praise God for His grace. Didn't the blood of Jesus spill over any and all who believe on Him?

Yes it did, overall, because all have fallen short of the glory of God.

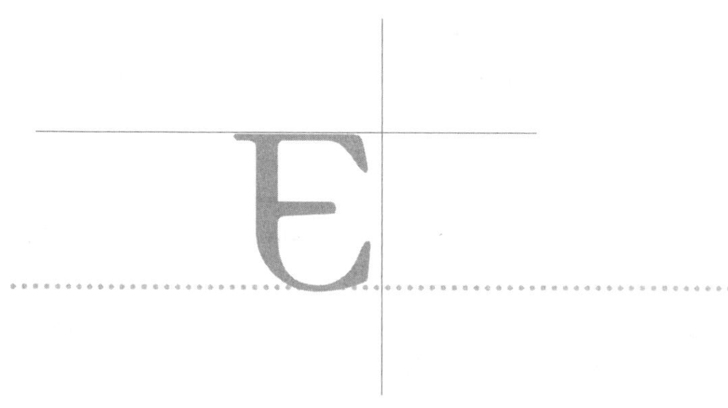

"Poor John the Baptist. The LDS speak of him, teach of him, and use him to explain all sorts of things ... except the truth."

Elijah / John the Baptist

While our topic – Elijah – is fairly straight forward, the LDS have put a twist on it that is frankly mind-boggling.

In the last book of the Old Testament, we read:

> Malachi 4:5-6. *Behold, I will send you Elijah the prophet before the coming of the great and dreadful day of the* LORD*: and he shall turn the heart of the fathers to the children, and the heart of the children to their fathers, lest I come and smite the earth with a curse.*

What does this mean and then what do the LDS twist it to mean?

First of all, Elijah was a tremendous prophet of the Old Testament. In fact, no prophet is more frequently referred to in the New Testament. There are a number of things to consider about this powerful prophet, including the fact that John the Baptist would come in the spirit of Elijah to prepare the way of the Lord. Let's consider some things these great men of the Lord had in common.

First of all, they were outwardly quite similar. Elijah lived close to the wild wilderness, including a long retirement in the dry and barren desert. Suddenly, Elijah, like John the Baptist, entered his ministry with an abrupt and startling beginning.

Elijah and John the Baptist even wore similar clothing as 2 Kings 1:8 says of Elijah, *"He was an hairy man, and girt with a girdle of leather about his loins."* And Luke 3:2 says of John the Baptist, *"And the same John had his raiment of camel's hair, and a leathern girdle about his loins; and his meat was locusts and wild honey."*

This picture was also fulfilled in the way both Elijah and John the Baptist were stern and powerful in their reproofs, which they, without hesitation, aimed at anyone who stood in the way of their message, including powerful men of politics. In other words, John the Baptist, in the spirit and power of Elijah – who was austere in his manner of life and in his zeal for the truth and renunciation of the world – would come and prepare the way for the Lord.

It is not an accident that John the Baptist would be asked repeatedly over the course of his ministry if he was Elias, which is just the Greek way of saying Elijah (Matthew 11:13,14; 16:14; 17:10; Mark 9:11; 15:35; Luke 9:7,8; John 1:21). So, under the inspiration of the Holy Spirit, Malachi offered this prophetic utterance as an indication of what would preceed the Messiah's coming, and here the Old Testament concludes.

Now, this coming of Elijah was so prominent in the Jewish mind that anytime someone popped up that was powerful or wearing a leather girdle, they wondered if he was the promised prophet. So anxious were they for his reappearance that at their marriage feasts they always set a chair and knife and fork for him, whom they supposed might be invisibly present. But we have already seen that John the Baptist, who was the forerunner of our Lord, was the person designated.

In another chapter of Malachi, it was also foretold that this messenger would come to "prepare the way for the Lord." It reads:

> Malachi 3:1. *Behold, I will send my messenger, and he shall prepare the way before me: and the Lord, whom ye seek, shall suddenly come to his temple, even the messenger of the covenant, whom ye delight in: behold, he shall come, saith the LORD of hosts.*

Then of course, when John the Baptist began his ministry, Mark described him as

> Mark 1:3. *the voice of one crying in the wilderness, Prepare ye the way of the Lord, make his paths straight.*

Scripture interprets Scripture, folks, and we know from the New Testament writers the exact meaning of these Malachi prophecies.

Turn with me, if you will, to Luke, chapter 1 and start reading at verse 13. Here, an angel appears to a faithful Jew named Zacharias, to tell him and his barren and aged wife Elizabeth that their lives were about to change. Well, Zacharias was quite afraid, and the angel said to him:

> Luke 1:13-17. *Fear not, Zacharias: for thy prayer is heard; and thy wife Elisabeth shall bear thee a son, and thou shalt call his name John. And thou shalt have joy and gladness; and many shall rejoice at his birth. For he shall be great in the sight of the Lord, and shall drink neither wine nor strong drink; and he shall be filled with the*

> *Holy Ghost, even from his mother's womb. And many of the children of Israel shall he turn to the Lord their God. And he shall go before him in the spirit and power of Elias, to turn the hearts of the fathers to the children, and the disobedient to the wisdom of the just; to make ready a people prepared for the Lord.*

Luke took the Malachi prophecy and applied it directly to the child John, called the Baptist. What does it mean that John, in the Spirit of Elijah, would, *"turn the heart of the* ***fathers*** *to the* ***children****, and the heart of the* ***children*** *to their* ***fathers****, lest I come and smite the earth with a curse* (Malachi 4:6)?

There are a number of potential meanings, all of which are quite viable. First, and in the bigger picture, gross ignorance had taken place in the hearts of the Jewish people and they were certainly in need of a passionate, fearless instructor. John could be seen as such. From the plenitude of God's Spirit that dwelt upon him and his continual self-denial, to his ardent zeal to make Christ known and his fidelity and courage to rebuke the powers that be, a reformation was effected among the people, reviving among them the spirit of the patriarchs, and preparing their hearts to receive the Lord Jesus. With this very expressive figure of speech, it is my opinion that Abraham, Isaac, and Jacob, and the rest of the patriarchs, are represented as having their alienated hearts turned to their children of unbelief and disobedience and, because of John's work, bring them to repentance.

Secondly, in the time of John the Baptist, the Jews were divided into a number of different sects. They were violently opposed to each other and pursued this opposition with great animosity. I am certain that this opposition found its way into families and divided parents and children from each other. John came that he might allay these animosities and produce better feelings. By directing them all to one Master, the Messiah, he would divert their attention from the causes of their difference and bring them to union. He would restore peace to their families, and reconcile those parents and children who had chosen different sects.

Finally, had the Jews turned to God, and received the Messiah at the preaching of John the Baptist and that of Christ and his apostles, the awful results would not have been executed upon them in 70 A.D.

These passages in Malachi present to Christians some remarkable predictions:

1. The advent of John Baptist who would come in the spirit and authority of Elijah.
2. The manifestation of Christ in the flesh.

These three prophecies were announced nearly four hundred years before their occurrence and the New Testament makes it very clear what they meant.

Then along comes Joseph Smith and his Mormonism in 1820. And what does he say Malachi 4:5-6 means? Mormon temple work. Doing vicarious temple work for people who have passed on so that they can accept it after this life is over and be exalted.

In nearly ANY LDS manual on temple work, you will find them using these passages from Malachi and telling their members that this prophecy was fulfilled, not through John the Baptist coming to turn the hearts of the fathers to the children but through none other than Joseph Smith!

James Talmage, whose book, *Jesus the Christ* is mandatory reading for most LDS missionaries, wrote on page 354 (2006 edition):

> Malachi's prediction, that before "the great and dreadful day of the Lord" Elijah the Prophet would be sent to earth to "turn the heart of the fathers to the children and the heart of the children to their fathers," did NOT reach fulfillment in the mission of John the Baptist, not in that of any other "Elias;" its complete realization was inaugurated on the third day of April, 1836 when Elijah appeared in the temple at Kirtland Ohio, and committed [the keys of authority vested in himself] to ...Joseph Smith and Oliver Cowdery [emphasis Shawn's].

Why?

Because Joseph, with the so-called spirit of Elijah, would introduce vicarious temple rites that would supposedly turn the hearts of the fathers to their children (and vice versa) by doing Mormon temple work for those who had died.

I am not kidding.

Twistianity at its best, folks. And another example of where the simple, beautiful, prophetic meaning of God's word is tweaked and applied to a counterfeit faith.

Run...like hell.

"When it comes to Mormonism, faith in what? is more of the question than deciding what faith actually is."

Faith

Our topic tonight is faith.

It's not a simple one, especially as it relates to the Mormon/ Christian comparative. The reason for this is because faith comes in many forms and purities which make defining and understanding it more difficult than most other topics. I would suggest that perhaps one of the best ways to understand the general, overarching topic of faith is to look at it like we would look at types of water.

God has provided the world with the very essential element of water. We could look at the formula of H2O and liken it to faith because H2O is found in so many different ways – different purities, if you will.

Walk into any supermarket today and you will find rows of bottled water all claiming to be superior or different in one way or another. Additionally, we have natural spring water, ocean water, geyser water, distilled water, tap water, pond water, and at the top of the heap what Jesus called, "*Living water* (John 4:10; 7:38)."

So it is with faith.

Like water, faith is a general term which presents itself in a number of different forms and purities. General faith is available to all human beings and is used by all in some extent or another. Like the essential element of water, faith is foundational to the sustenance and growth of human life. It is by faith that we take our first steps, try to shoot a basket, attend college – believing the acts will benefit our lives and someday prove successful. It is by faith that athletes train, architects draw, people get married and save money.

Intellectual and economic progress would be impossible without faith. Why would anyone get into a plane to visit a country they haven't seen before if it weren't for general faith that such a place existed? Who would go to sleep not having a foundational faith that they will wake in the morning to a new day? I have never seen my brain, but by faith I trust that it will allow me to solve problems and examine information now and in the future. So life on earth is sustained by faith, even for the atheists who ignorantly and arrogantly mock its very name.

However, like water, some faith is good and some faith is bad. And, like water, some faith is capable of sustaining life and some faith is very limited in its ability to do any good for us at all. For this reason, and in this context of our discussion between Mormonism and Christianity, I am going to take the general category of faith and break it into two specific categories: "Bad or Dead Faith" and "Good or Living Faith."

Now, just for tonight, allow me the luxury of taking any and all faith that does NOT save a person's soul and place it in the "Bad or Dead Faith" bin.

I am doing this so that we can better understand "Good or Living Faith."

Obviously, having faith that tells us we can reach our goals in business is not bad in and of itself – any more than tap water is bad in and of itself – but this type of faith is not lasting. Therefore, tonight, I am placing it in the Bad Faith category.

Thomas Browne said:

> To believe only possibilities is not faith, but merely philosophy.

It is on this basis that I am placing any and all faith that exists outside of faith in God in the Bad Faith file.

One of the problems we face when it comes to understanding Good or Living Faith is that it is as different from general faith as pond water is from the living water Jesus offered the woman at the well (John 4:5-14). Human life is filled with purveyors and promoters of this faith that never lasts and is, therefore, by comparison to faith that lasts, bad. For evidences just listen in on any Monday morning sales rally, any positive mental attitude seminar, or to almost any motivational speaker or guru. They are all promoting water, but it is the type of water where you will thirst again.

Hence, again – and just for tonight – I am going to put all faith that cannot be defined as living or lasting faith into the Bad Faith file.

So what is the **best definition** of Good Faith? Of faith that bears eternal fruit and consequences?

(Ready?)

Taking God at His Word.

When God says, *"In the beginning, God..."* and you decide in your mind AND heart to assent to this, to believe this, and to embrace and incorporate it into your existence, you are taking God at His word, and are in possession of Good Faith – lasting faith – living faith.

Good and Living Faith is an assenting of the mind AND the heart; often, I have discovered, it is nothing more than a personal choice to believe and take God at His Word.

Somebody once said:

> Faith is not a sense, nor sight, nor reason, but taking God at His Word.

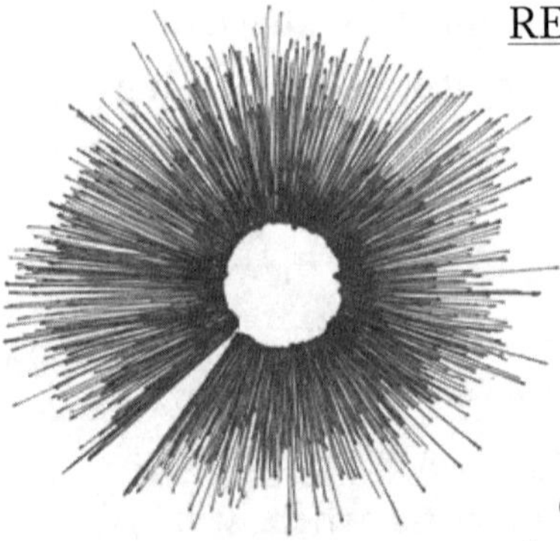

REMEMBER THIS DEFINITION!

I am blessed to meet so many people and many of them do not really understand the properties of Good Faith. Many of them get confused and think that faith is this "magical state of mind" wherein the individual does not really have to think or make a choice, but that God steps in and sort of places a "spell" over their minds and hearts and they automatically and easily accept and believe. And while this may describe one aspect of Good Faith – saving faith, which we will discuss in a minute – this often is not the case in other areas where Good Faith operates.

What is more the reality when it comes to possessing good faith is that even in the face of doubt, difficulty, and sometimes against all logic, people of faith choose to take God at His Word. And this pleases Him. In fact, it is impossible to please Him without this faith. Remember,

> Hebrews 11:6. *But without faith it is impossible to please him: for he that cometh to God must believe that he is, and that he is a rewarder of them that diligently seek him.*

Now, under the general category of Good Faith, we might create some sub-categories. The first category under Good Faith we will call "saving faith." Here is the first place where the Mormons and Christians differ as Christians take God at His Word and Latter-day Saints do not.

What does the Bible say about saving faith?

Well, first it says it comes by taking God at His Word about His Son.

> John 1:1-2. *In the beginning was the Word, and the Word was with God, and the Word was God. All things were made by Him and without Him was not anything made that was made.*

Later, in verse 14 it tells us about this "*Word,*" saying, "*And the Word was made flesh, and dwelt among us.*"

This is *Yeshua*, Jesus. All things – all things – were made by Him. He is God.

Jesus Himself said:

> John 14:6. *I am the way, the truth, and the life: no man cometh unto the Father, but by me.*

So, do you take God at His Word?

The LDS do not. They say that while Jesus came to earth and

made salvation possible, He alone is not the way. There are additional paths and requirements necessary to come to the Father.

Secondly, God says definitively that faith and faith *alone* on His Son is enough to be saved eternally from sin, death and hell.

Speaking to a gathering of Jews, Paul said:

> Acts 13:38-39. *Be it known unto you therefore, men and brethren, that through this man [Jesus] is preached unto you the forgiveness of sins: And by him all that believe are justified from all things, from which ye could not be justified by the law of Moses.*

Paul also wrote:

> Galatians 2:16. *Knowing that a man is not justified by the works of the law, but by the faith of Jesus Christ, even we have believed in Jesus Christ, that we might be justified by the faith of Christ, and not by the works of the law: for by the works of the law shall no flesh be justified.*

This living, saving *"faith of Christ"* is the sole means of salvation. It is a free gift of God. It is not received meritoriously, meaning it is not received by our works, but instrumentally, meaning God holds out to us His Son and desires all to grasp hold of Him. Those who actually do have simply decided to *take God at His Word.*

Such saving faith cannot be forced. It is not a struggle to maintain. It is not earned by squinting and praying really, really hard. It is more a giving up, a relinquishment of the will, and waving of the white flag and simply receiving God's solution, His Son. How? That's right: by taking Him at His Word that He is who He says He is and that faith in Him is sufficient.

Now the LDS state plainly that saving faith is not given or offered by God freely, but is earned. Mormon President Joseph F. Smith was quoted as saying (*Teachings of the Presidents of the Church: Joseph F. Smith*, page 53):

> It is said that faith is a gift of God, and so it is; but faith does not come without works; faith does not come without obedience to the commandments of God.

Where Christians believe saving faith is offered to all unmeritoriously and without any qualifications other than a humble willingness to receive it, Mormons tell us faith is earned through obedience to the commandments of God!

In the LDS Bible Dictionary under the topic of faith, it states:

> … strong faith is developed by obedience to the gospel of Jesus Christ [meaning Mormonism]; in other words, faith comes by righteousness.

Where Jesus says, come as you are, come unto me all ye that are heavy laden (with sin, with trials, with ugliness) and I will give you rest, Mormonism teaches that you must clean yourself up to be worthy of faith, to earn faith, and to possess saving faith.

What is really interesting about the unique LDS stance that faith comes by "righteousness" and "obedience," is that when we look at the men and women listed in Hebrews chapter 11 which is often called, the "Faith Hall of Fame," we find some interesting people listed who, in terms of their personal righteousness, would be considered faith*less* by LDS standards today.

I mean, the Bible hails Noah as an icon of faith. But didn't he get drunk? Noah couldn't get a temple recommend from the LDS and here in Hebrews 11 he is listed as one of the most faithful in the Bible!

Sarah, Abraham's wife is listed. Didn't she go all evil on Hagar and kick her and her son Ishmael out into the desert to die? Yes she did. But she believed God.

Who else is listed as being a beacon of faith there in Hebrews? Oh, that's right ...

Comparatively (and humanistically) speaking Jacob was a sneaky little punk and Esau his brother was more of a real man. But Jacob was a man of faith, who took God at His Word!

Moses? He failed in His duties as a husband, he killed a man in anger. But what a man of faith! What a man who took God at His word!

And then there's old Rahab? I mean the writer of Hebrews refers to her as "*Rahab the harlot*!" The harlot! But she is mentioned here as a female icon of faith!

Hebrews (11:34) mentions Gideon and Barak, of whom Scripture states that, *"out of weakness they were made strong."* They were NOT strong men except strong by FAITH!

The writer adds Samson, who possessed great weakness toward women. But he is listed as a man of faith!

David is listed! An adulterer and a murderer, but a man after God's own heart – a man who took God at His Word. A man of faith.

You see the LDS have it all wrong when it comes to faith and its origins.

Faith is NOT produced by righteousness and obedience, but ultimately, righteousness and obedience follow those who possess faith.

Get it?

It's like the question, "Are you happy because you are good or are you good because you are happy?"

The LDS operate from the premise, *We are happy because we are good.*

Christians operate from the premise, *We are good because we are happy – in Christ.*

Get the difference?

The LDS say, *I have faith because I have been obedient and righteous.*

The Christian says, *I am obediet and righteous because I have faith.*

So that is "saving faith."

It opens the door of heaven to all who embrace it, it comes without a price but to humbly acquiesce ourselves to God.

Saving faith opens the door to new life. And in this new life, as new creatures in Christ, we begin to operate for another type of Good Faith – what we'll call "living faith." Where saving faith is immediate, living faith is processional. It grows and brings with it some amazing factors to the true Christian life.

Let's discuss these factors.

First, there is new vision: seeing the world from God's perspective and not man's.

C.S. Lewis wrote,

> I believe in Christ like I believe in the sun, not just because I see it, but because by it I can see everything else.

Lewis's quote explains why people who experience true faith become "Jesus freaks," so to speak. It is because everything they see now relates to Him. When lived by and through Him, life is completely altered.

Helen Keller summarized this sight with some beautiful prose (from her book, *Midstream: My Later Life*), saying:

> Dark as my path may seem to others, I carry a magic light in my heart. Faith, the spiritual strong searchlight illuminates the way, and although sinister doubts lurk in the shadow, I walk unafraid toward the Enchanted Wood where the foliage is always green, where joy abides, where nightingales nest and sing and where life and death are one in the presence of the Lord.

In addition to a new, fresh and living sight, this living faith, if allowed to thrive, can serve to help reduce, if not eliminate fear, tension, and the anxieties of life.

Someone profound once said, *"To me, faith means not worrying."* How can there be worry if our faith is placed in the hands of the living God? Here again, Mormon faith fails. To them, all assurances are placed squarely on the shoulders of the individual, not on Jesus, which tacitly makes life tenuous, and often amounts, in the end, to stress, fear, and worry.

This is one of the burdens we hope to alleviate from the backs of millions of LDS believers: the burden of not being assured in Christ's shed blood. Of not knowing that you are absolutely lovely and accepted by God because of your faith in Him – and nothing more.

Mahatma Gandhi said, *"You cannot have faith and tension at the same time."* In the realm of Good Faith, fears, worries, and tensions are all placed – NOT in our own hands, NOT in a positive mental attitude and NOT in our works and righteousness – but in the hands of the living God and His righteousness.

This is part of what separates Good Faith from Bad: *where* the actual faith itself is aimed and placed.

This brings us to another divergence of faith that exists between the LDS and the Biblical Christian. Bible-believing Christians ought to place all of their faith and hope in Jesus Christ – on and in God – and to trust Him at His Word. But the LDS are commanded to place their faith in a variety of other man-made institutions, especially in what they call "the Church" itself.

This is why they made face cards that uphold and promote mere men of lust, flesh, and blood.

When LDS prophet Ezra Taft Benson was alive, Mormon … *ahem* … "Apostle" James Faust said the following about the absolutes in the Mormon faith ("An Untroubled Faith," speech given at BYU, September 28, 1986):

> To have a simple, untroubled faith we must accept some absolutes. They are basic. They are to believe:
>
> 1. That Jesus, the son of the Father, is the Christ and the Savior and Redeemer of the world.
> 2. That Joseph Smith was the instrument through which the gospel was restored in its fullness and completeness.
> 3. That the Book of Mormon is the word of God and, as the Prophet Joseph Smith said, it is the keystone of our religion.
> 4. That Ezra Taft Benson is, as were each of his predecessor Presidents of the Church, a successor in holding the keys and authority restored by Joseph Smith.

LDS faithful are told to place faith and trust in their local leaders, the priesthood, in any and every decision passed down to them from Salt Lake and even in their own feelings. But God says, trust Me and Me alone.

Finally, we come to another factor found in living faith: it leads to doing the works and commandments of God. Just as a glass of cold refreshing water energizes the weary into new life, so will Good Faith energize and move a believer to new life and action. But take note: *it is not faith **and** works, nor is it faith **or** works, but it is faith that works.*

This is the final result and effect of Good Faith, manifesting itself after saving faith has worked its wonders, and once living faith begins to take root. This is yet another place where Mormonism and Biblical Christianity part ways. Remember, to the LDS, personal works, personal righteousness, and personal obedience not only precede faith, they produce it! I would suggest that this is a perfect description of bad faith and it is not good.

In essence, the rub between the LDS and Biblical Christians is from whence and what saving faith originates. Where the Christian cries in desperate faith, "Lord, save me!" the Latter-day Saint expects the Lord to reward them for their efforts and lives lived.

The question stands: Is it faith that fuels obedience or is it obedience that fuels faith?

Christianity emphatically states that it is by faith in Jesus and Jesus alone that they are saved and it is by faith in Jesus alone that they walk. Latter-day Saints state that because they are obedient they are blessed with faith – and more faith.

The first (Christian) premise places the onus upon faith in Jesus alone while the second (LDS) premise puts it squarely on the back of the Mormon member.

❋ ❋ ❋

"All anyone has to do to see the spirit behind Mormonism today is to look at its beginnings. It's not a matter of Joseph Smith messing up a bit and dabbling in the occult or magic. He carried these practices throughout his life – even to the point that he had actual magic parchments on his person when he died. And the church today? From the seed comes the tree, from the tree comes the fruit, from the fruit comes more seeds, and on, and on, and on."

Familiar Spirits / Magic

Last week we ended the show with an LDS caller from Provo named Debbie. In essence she was perplexed on how believing in something like Mormonism could produce feelings of love and peace if it is so wrong. She then went on to relate a personal story of a trial she faced 20-plus years ago and how God told her that she needed to read His word. She said she then picked up a Book of Mormon and this resulted in a great spiritual confirmation which changed her and blessed her life with feelings of love and peace.

"Again," she wanted to know, *"how is this possible if Mormonism is so wrong?"*

We ran out of time at this point in the show and I promised that I would provide my response tonight.

Now answering this question is not as easy as it might seem. To me the question is like meeting a homeless man who is dressed in rags, has no job, is missing most of his teeth, has a broken foot, and is covered in lice and thinking that handing him a new pair of Kenneth Cole shoes is going to somehow solve his problems. There is a lot of clean-up work that needs to be done first before the shoes – or an answer to Debbie's question - are going to be of any benefit. What is wonderful about the question, however, is it perfectly dovetails in with our alphabetically chosen subject for tonight – "Familiar Spirits."

To restate, what Debbie wanted to know is how Mormonism could be wrong if she, being a believing Mormon, has experienced healing, love, and goodness by and through embracing it. Especially after reading the Book of Mormon.

So let's examine her question and claim.

The first thing to consider is *God loves and blesses all of His human creations*. He "*sendeth rain on the just and on the unjust* (Matthew 5:45)." Atheists enjoy good health as much as Christians. Sometimes more. Since the coming and death of Christ -Who paid for all sin past, present, and future – all of us find ourselves living today in a dispensation of God's grace. And every second we spend living on this spinning globe, He is calling to each of us, all of us, always. Some choose paths of rebellion against Him ***and are blessed*** with the peace the world gives. Some choose paths of mediocrity relative to Him and are blessed with material abundance. Behind every blossoming flower He is saying, "See Me." With every murder, every death, every bit of suffering, He is reaching out and crying, "Hear Me."

No matter what the course a person takes, I believe God desires all to come to Him and will use the pleasures, the pain, the lies, and the truth to lead all willing people to see and hear Him while somehow remaining true to the unseen principles of free will and choice. This is the first principle to understand. God blesses the just and the unjust.

Keeping this in mind, we might also add that the world is divided into two and ONLY two sides. One is of God, and the other is of everything else. And the "everything else" encompasses a broad, broad spectrum. This realm existing *outside* of God's will can include what human beings might label as good; it also includes what we call bad. In other words, people and groups can represent, feel and do a lot of good stuff and it may in the end prove to be outside of God's will.

So we have discussed two facts:

- God loves, blesses, and calls to *all* of us constantly no matter where we are or where we have been; and
- We are either operating and responding according to His will or we are operating outside of it and are therefore in the will of something else.

Now some people – especially in this day and age – have concluded that "everything is good," meaning, "everything is God." But from a Biblical perspective this is just not so. Bible-believing people could not possibly accept the notion that EVERYTHING is acceptable to God because if this were so, then the words and the life of Jesus were wholly inauthentic. If everything is good to God, then Jesus lied. So I am going to leave this popular ecumenical view right where it belongs – in the trash.

Debbie asked *how could something be so wrong that filled her with love and promise and hope – something that changed her life, even?*

I would turn the question back on her and ask *how does every ardent faithful Muslim make the same claim, Debbie? And how do you respond when they say that the Quran changed their lives?* Debbie, what do we do with the Dalai Lama and his followers who are so full of love and peace? Aren't he and his ways just as viable to God as Jesus was? Because rest assured, Debbie, the Dalai Lama does not receive Jesus at His Word.

What would you say, Debbie, to a stalwart member of the Third Reich, who with renewed hope, and vigor for new life, and love for the Motherland, says, with tears, that the Führer has given him or her new life? What do we say to someone who says that when they read *Mein Kampf*, *The True Believer*, or *The Satanic Bible* that they were filled with new life, love and peace? There are people who walk about apparently teeming with love, Debbie – the hippies of the sixties, the followers of Jim Jones, the Hare Krishnas – whose beliefs and professions are COUNTER to the teachings of Jesus and the Good News He proclaimed. Either we say all roads lead to heaven or we say no roads matter or we claim that there is really only one way. We must determine each claim's value and truth OUTSIDE of our personal and subjective experiences.

Jesus Himself said something really insightful regarding people of light who are full of the dark:

> Matthew 6:22. *The light of the body is the eye: if therefore thine eye be single, thy whole body shall be full of light.*

What did He mean when He said, *"therefore, if thine eye be single?"* He meant fully sold out and committed to Him. That is what He meant. Then He continued:

> Matthew 6:23. *But, if thine eye be evil, thy whole body shall be full of darkness. If therefore the light that is in thee be darkness, how great is that darkness!*

What does Jesus mean, *"If therefore, the light that is in thee be darkness"*? How can a person have *light that is in them* that is actually called *darkness*?

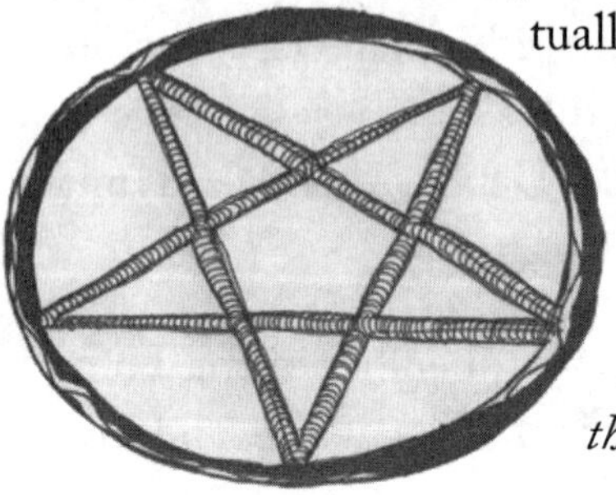

Jesus explained:

> Matthew 7:21. *Not every one that saith unto me, Lord, Lord, shall enter into the kingdom of heaven; but he that doeth the will of my Father which is in heaven.*

> *Many will say to me in that day, Lord, Lord, have we not prophesied in thy name? and in thy name have cast out devils? and in thy name done many wonderful works? And then will I profess unto them, I never knew you: depart from me, ye that work iniquity.*

Could it be, Debbie, that there are spiritual and religious counterfeits out there that actually give the appearance of being true and full of light but are in reality false and dark? Since the beginning, there have existed alternatives – counterfeits, if you will – to God and His will and ways. When Aaron the brother of Moses took his rod or staff and threw it down on the ground and it became a serpent, what happened next? Moses tells us, saying,

> Exodus 7:11-12. *Then Pharaoh also called the wise men and the sorcerers: now the magicians of Egypt, they also did in like manner with their enchantments. For they cast down every man his rod, and they became serpents: but Aaron's rod swallowed up their rods.*

In 2 Corinthians, Paul warns believers in Corinth about deceivers. And just listen to what He says! It has amazing applications to the religion called Mormonism:

> 2 Corinthians 11:13. *For such are false apostles, deceitful workers, transforming themselves into the apostles of Christ. And no marvel; for Satan himself is transformed into an angel of light. Therefore it is no great thing if his ministers also be transformed as the ministers of righteousness; whose end shall be according to their works.*

The context of this passage is made even more complete when we consider what Paul had written just a few verses before, saying:

> 2 Corinthians 11:3. *But I fear, lest by any means, as the serpent beguiled Eve through his subtilty, so your minds should be corrupted from the simplicity that is in Christ.*

Does the Hare Krishna, the Muslim, the Daoist, or follower of the Dalai Lama retain "*the simplicity that is in Christ*"? No. Because they do NOT receive Him at His Word. They add to it, they take from it, or they discount it all together. So even though the many followers of these faiths claim, yes, even appear to possess personal peace and love for man and beast could we say that their minds have been corrupted from the Biblical "simplicity found in Christ?"

Yes.

And can we say the same for Mormonism and its doctrines?

Abso-freaking-lutely.

So the question remains, how was Debbie able to have changed for the better (which I could debate – but don't have the time) by reading the Book of Mormon? Could it be that her getting better is a case of light being darkness, or of a sorcerer's snake, or of another beguiling angel of light doing his work? And if it is, how can we prove it?

First, let me make it clear that God is constantly working on Debbie just like He is constantly working on you and me. He loves her as much as anyone else. And He is still calling to her even though she believes she has found the end-all solution to her spiritual life in Mormonism and its fictional writings. In the meantime, God heals Mormons like He heals Jehovah's Witnesses, like He heals Muslims, and like He heals Buddhists. But because He makes the rain fall on the just and the unjust, we cannot make the mistake of saying God is in favor of Mormonism because a Mormon has been blessed anymore than we can say God approved of Jim Jones because Jim Jones was blessed with a lot of money and land.

Remember, God loves and blesses all.

So how can we tell if Islam, Buddhism, Baptists, Methodists, Mormons, and/or any other faith is on God's side or if it sides with the rest of the fallen world?

There are a number of qualifiers. First, we need to take a look at a group's "*simplicity in Christ.*" Has a respective faith added to the simplicity of Christ, taken from it, or ignored it all together? Do they alter it to fit their desired needs and wants?

Secondly, we ought to look at the fruits they produce, and what the genesis and purpose of that fruit is. Does the fruit that a faith or people produce glorify God and Christ or does it glorify man, a church, or a religious movement? This is another indicator.

Third, how do the beliefs and doctrines of the faith in question measure up to the Word of God? Are they consistent or far afield? It is interesting, but the Bible NEVER tells anyone to pray about whether a doctrinal claim is true. What does it tell us to do? It tells us to take the claim and test the spirit of it against the Word of God.

> 1 John 4:1. *Beloved, believe not every spirit, but try the spirits whether they are of God: because many false prophets are gone out into the world.*

(Back-up verses for this include Jeremiah 29:8; Matthew 24:4-5,24; Acts 20:30; 1 Corinthians 14:29; 1 Thessalonians 5:21; 1 Timothy 4:1; 2 Peter 2:1; 1 John 2:18; 2 John 1:7; and Revelation 2:2.)

If someone comes and makes a claim and the Word stands against the claim, you know it is a dark spirit and to run. It doesn't matter if the claim makes you happier, wealthier, heals you, or makes the thinning hair on your head sprout, it is a dark principality.

Finally, I believe it is important to examine the original seeds of the faith and see from what soil it sprouted. Islam originated with Mohammed and a book he received by revelation. Islam claims this book is the most correct book on the face of the earth. Buddhism originated with the Buddha sitting under the bo tree and contemplating suffering and life. Do his teachings stand up against the Word?

And Mormonism?

When it is really, truly, all said and done, Mormonism originated, prospered, and flourished in a strong environment of occultic influence. It is not by mistake that throughout His Word, God warns both His people of the Old Covenant and His people of the New to be very, very careful of beguiling and deceptive spirits. Where people on God's side are led by Him and His Word, people who fall to the other realm of influence are under strange and powerful forces, seen and unseen.

Paul warns the Galatians that there would come

> Galatians 1:7. *some that trouble you, and would pervert the gospel of Christ.*

And He adds,

> Galatians 1:8. *But though we, or an angel from heaven, preach any other gospel unto you than that which we have preached unto you, let him be accursed.*

Then he repeats the warning for a second time.

Earlier, in 2 Corinthians 11:4, Paul warns believers of those who would come and *"preach another Jesus, whom we have not preached;"* or try to get them to "*receive another spirit, which* [they had] *not received, or another gospel, which* [they had] *not accepted …"* These gospels that preach another Jesus, and seek to get people to receive *"another spirit,"* which comes through *"another gospel,"* all operate, in one way or another, under the direction of spiritual darkness in high places.

Sitting in front of me I have a voluminous book. It was written by D. Michael Quinn, a PhD. from Yale who was LDS at the time of its publication. It's titled *Early Mormonism and the Magic World View*. It explains, in great detail, the early roots of Joseph Smith's family and their involvement in the occult, magic, and the numerous visitations with spirits. By the time you're done reading it you will know the origins of their doctrine and practice.

Before a Mormon tells you that they "know the LDS Church is true," or that they "know Thomas Monson is a living prophet," see if they also know that Joseph Smith's parents and siblings, especially his father, were heavily involved in seeking for buried treasures and for spirits by looking through a magical peepstone. Ask them if they know that Joseph Smith Jr. "translated" their sacred Book of Mormon by putting his favorite stone into a hat – literally – and receiving revelation!

See if they know that second President of the LDS church, Brigham Young said (*Latter-day Millennial Star*, Volume 26, pages 118,119):

> Every man who lived on earth [is] entitled to a seer stone, and should have one.

Ask them if they know that Joseph Smith's sacred seer-stone is still held in the office of the LDS prophet to this day.

Are they aware that divining rods were also used by the founders of Mormonism? That Joseph even has God talk in the Doctrine and Covenants** about Oliver Cowdery's "gift" in using his? That Brigham Young employed the magic of a divining rod to actually locate where the Salt Lake temple should be built?

(**See D&C 8:6-9, which originally read: "You [Oliver] have another gift, which is the gift of working with the rod: behold it has told you things: behold there is no other power save God, that can cause this rod of nature, to work in your hands, for it is the work of God; and therefore whatsoever you shall ask me to tell you by that means, that I will grant unto you, that you shall know;" but which today reads, "Now this is not all thy gift; for you have another gift, which is the gift of Aaron; behold, it has told you many things; Behold, there is no other power, save the power of God, that can cause this gift of Aaron to be with you. Therefore, doubt not, for it is the gift of God; and you shall hold it in your hands, and do marvelous works; and no power shall be able to take it away out of your hands, for it is the work of God. And, therefore, whatsoever you shall ask me to tell you by that means, that will I grant unto you, and you shall have knowledge concerning it.")

Do they know that Joseph Smith carried a Jupiter talisman around with him, which is directly tied to the occult and its powers, and it is believed it was on his person at the time of his death? Do they know that their founding prophet also carried around two separate magic parchments, as did his brother Hyrum. Do they know Brigham Young carried two seer stones and a bloodstone amulet on a chain?

Do they know that the LDS church was founded on a day entrenched in Joseph Smith's personal astrology which includes important ties to Jupiter and the Sun? Did you know that the supposed visit of the angel Moroni was on the night of the autumnal equinox, and it was on this very important occultic night that Joseph says he met and re-met with the same angel of light for years and years to come until the Book of Mormon was completed?

Did you know Joseph Smith actually taught Mormons how to tell the difference between a good angel and a bad one; and that it is done through a ritual of hand-shaking?! And did you know that this very method is still taught in the LDS Doctrine and Covenants today (129:4-9)!

Speaking of today, did you know the LDS relish in telling stories of the dead and departed spirits coming to visit them in their temples, but that the Bible says such spirits are not from God? Did you know that LDS leaders have actually said that the Book of Mormon possesses a "familiar spirit" with that of the Bible? But the Bible itself is emphatic on avoiding any and all contact with any "familiar spirits."

Listen:

> Leviticus 19:31. *Regard not them that have familiar spirits, neither seek after wizards, to be defiled by them: I am the LORD your God.*
>
> Leviticus 20:6. *And the soul that turneth after such as have **familiar spirits**, and after wizards, to go a whoring after them, I will even set my face against that soul, and will cut him off from among his people.*
>
> Deuteronomy 18:11. *Or a charmer, or a consulter with familiar spirits, or a wizard, or a necromancer.*
>
> 2 Kings 23:24. *Moreover the workers with **familiar spirits**, and the wizards, and the images, and the idols, and all the abominations that were spied in the land of Judah and in Jerusalem, did Josiah put away, that he might perform the words of the law which were written in the book that Hilkiah the priest found in the house of the LORD.*
>
> Isaiah 8:19. *And when they shall say unto you, Seek unto them that have **familiar spirits**, and unto wizards that **peep**, and that mutter: should not a people seek unto their God? for the living to the dead?*

My friends, do not be misled for misleaders are everywhere. The Word of God is trustworthy. The words of man, not. Try and test all spirits.

And let the bad ones – even if they do good things – flee.

❋ ❋ ❋

"The 'Families are forever' teaching found in Mormonism is riddled with arrogant pre-suppositional fallacy. I mean, why won't families of believing Christians be together in eternity, too? Heaven is heaven and eternity is eternity. I trust God will have what is best happen during that time and I don't need to do Mormon rites to ensure my family will be there."

Families

Speaking of false Gods, Jehovah says:

Exodus 20:3. *Thou shalt have no other gods before me.*

And reiterates:

Deuteronomy 5:7. *Thou shalt have none other gods before me.*

In almost every warning thereafter in Scripture, God adds to His warning of *having no other gods before Him* the declaration, "*nor serve them.*"

Tonight we are still in the *Fs* of our alphabetical study and we are going to examine family and marriage as it relates and is seen both from the LDS perspective and the Christian.

Now, we all know – all of us – that marriage and the loving family unit is the basic building block of society. We know that they are ordained of God. Christians and Mormons alike strive to build good marriages and loving families.

Families and marriage can both be a great blessing. Fathers and mothers and brothers and sisters are foundational in being a refuge, a resource of peace, and a source of direction and support. But – and this is VERY important to our discussion tonight – marriage and family, while gifts from God, should never be the highest priority any more than our occupations, or avocations, or other God-given blessings should EVER take precedence in our lives.

Notice that in our description of what families may supply, we said *a* refuge, *a* resource of peace, and *a* source of direction and support, NOT ***THE*** refuge, ***THE*** source of peace, or ***THE*** source of direction and support. Why? Because to Christians, Jesus alone is our refuge, peace, and sole source of direction and support: not our marriages, our spouses or our families great and small.

Far too often in the active LDS life, family, marriage and even spouses become gods "before Him." They are the things worshipped, promoted, and adored. And well meaning people by association find themselves serving these "other gods."

Enter cultural Mormonism, which, in my opinion, is a direct product of Mormon doctrine. And when it comes to Mormon doctrine, there are great differences between what the LDS think about marriage and family and what Bible believing Christians think.

Let me explain.

Mormons believe that the single most important decision they can make on earth is the decision of *whom* they marry and *where* they marry them. In the LDS-produced student manual, *Achieving a Celestial Marriage*, it reads (page 4):

> The major crowning point of the law which man must obey is eternal marriage. Therein lies the keys of eternal life ...

LDS President Joseph Fielding Smith said (*Doctrines of Salvation* 2:65):

> Since marriage is ordained of God, and the man is not without the woman, neither the woman without the man in the Lord, THERE CAN BE NO EXALTATION TO THE FULLNESS OF THE BLESSINGS OF THE CELESTIAL KINGDOM OUTSIDE OF THE MARRIAGE RELATIONSHIP [emphasis in original].

Earlier, LDS prophet and President Brigham Young said (cited by Spencer W. Kimball, *Miracle of Forgiveness*, page 245):

> No man can be perfect without the woman, so no woman can be perfect without a man to lead her. I tell you the truth as it is in the bosom of eternity. If he wishes to be SAVED, he cannot be SAVED without a woman by his side [emphasis Shawn's].

Wow. And the Bible says to be saved all we need is faith. Hmmmm.

LDS Apostle Mark E. Peterson taught ("A Commitment to Temple Marriage," speech given at BYU, October 31, 1962):

> We must realize that we can no more have exaltation in the celestial kingdom without temple marriage than we can have membership in the church without baptism.

So why is this eternal marriage element essential to exaltation in Mormonism? It has to do with what that "sealed couple" will do once they have become a celestial couple. They will have eternal, celestial sexual relationships. I don't mean their sexual relationship will be eternal (I don't think) but that it will go on for eternity!

Woooooooo-hoooooooooo!

You see in this way, the LDS believe they can have what they call, "eternal increase," which means an LDS worthy, faithful, sealed-in-the-temple man and his worthy and faithful wife OR wives will be able to continually procreate children eternally, presumably in order to populate the worlds they create.

The founding prophet Joseph Smith himself said (*History of the Church* 5:391):

> Except a man and his wife enter into an everlasting covenant and be married for eternity, while in this probation, by the power and authority of the Holy Priesthood, they will cease to increase when they die; that is, they will not have any children after the resurrection. But those who are married by the power and authority of the priesthood in this life, and continue without committing the sin against the Holy Ghost, will continue to increase and have children in the celestial glory.

Now, regarding marriage, when Jesus Himself was on earth, a

group came to Him known as the Sadducees. Now these guys were a religious bunch who did not believe in angels or the resurrection, but came to Him and tried to set Him up.

They said:

> Luke 20:28-32. *Master, Moses wrote unto us, If any man's brother die, having a wife, and he die without children, that his brother should take his wife, and raise up seed unto his brother. There were therefore seven brethren: and the first took a wife, and died without children. And the second took her to wife, and he died childless. And the third took her; and in like manner the seven also: and they left no children, and died. Last of all the woman died also.*

Then they ask the question:

> Luke 20:33. *Therefore in the resurrection whose wife of them is she? for seven had her to wife?*

Now Jesus is going to teach them plain truth. Remember, they did NOT believe either in the resurrection or in angels. Ready?

> Luke 20:34-36. *And Jesus answering said unto them, The children of this world marry, and are given in marriage: But they which shall be accounted worthy to obtain that world, and the resurrection from the dead, neither marry, nor are given in marriage: Neither can they die any more: for they are equal unto the angels; and are the children of God, being the children of the resurrection.*

In Matthew's account, when the Sadducees approached Jesus, Jesus adds:

> Matthew 22:29-30. *Ye do err, not knowing the scriptures, nor the power of God. For in the resurrection they neither marry, nor are given in marriage, but are as the angels of God in heaven.*

Jesus makes the doctrine of marriage after this life, among other things, perfectly clear to the Sadducees in question.

First, He delineates between His Kingdom and the Kingdom of this world. When Pilate asked Jesus if He was a king, Jesus admitted to being one, and added

> John 18:36. *My kingdom is not of this world.*

So in answering these Sadducees He makes it clear that there are a couple kingdoms: *His* and *that of the world.*

Second, He adds that it is "*the children of this world* [who] *marry and are given in marriage.*" All this means is that while we are in bodies of flesh and blood, as children of this world, we will be having sex and bearing children, and therefore we will marry according to God's law. This is why there is marriage: to sustain the most orderly and functional way to bring in and care for children.

Then Jesus makes it clear what those who follow Him *will* be like, saying:

> Luke 20:35-36. *But they which shall be accounted worthy to obtain* ***that*** *world, and the resurrection from the dead, neither marry, nor are given in marriage: Neither can they die any more: for they are equal unto the angels; and are the children of God, being the children of the resurrection.*

In other words, Jesus makes it clear to these questioning Sadducees three facts:

- One, there is a resurrection.
- Two, there is no marriage in this state; and
- Three, there is such a thing as angels because those who are worthy to obtain His Kingdom will be, Jesus says, "*equal unto*" them.

In Joseph Smith's twistianity, one of the things he did was to sell people on a non-Biblical utopian idea of what heaven was like.

He took earth life and applied it to heaven and took fictional ideas of what heaven is like brought it down to earth. It is fanciful, romantic, and hopeful, but absolutely contrary to the Word of God.

So there is the first difference in the Mormon/Christian comparative when it comes to marriage: the LDS say that a person must not only be married in their temples but that unless they are, they cannot become gods. Biblical Christians agree with Jesus who said that "*the children of **this world** marry and are given in marriage* (Luke 20:34)," but that in heaven, those who are worthy (through faith in His blood) will become "*as the angels* (Matthew 22:30)."

Now ask yourself this – are angels up there having sexual relationships in yonder heavens with each other? It's not even part of their existences in the light, existences that we, as carnal humans, cannot comprehend!

Well, remember, all of this humanistic self-focus on marriage is merely a step in their progression toward godhood because then families begin to play an important role. In the LDS Manual, *Achieving a Celestial Marriage,* it states (page 65):

> Consider this fact: Your marriage is a laboratory for godhood.

This statement echoes the romantic bill of goods Joseph Smith sold the world about being able to create children here and in heaven through the same sexual male/female exchange. And the by-product of this doctrine is the wonderful ideal of families, or more particularly, celestial or Mormon families. Like many romantic, sort-of humanist themes Joseph Smith concocted out of his mind, the LDS have taken the concept of earthly families and romanticized it ad nauseam.

In their proprietary song *Families can be Together Forever*, they sing:

I have a family here on earth.
They are so good to me.
I want to live my life with them
Through all eternity.

Families can be together forever,
Through heavenly fathers plan,
I always want to be with my own family!
And the LORD has shown me how I can.

The LORD has shown me how I can.

This hero worship of the human institution called family can lead to an extreme amount of ugly manipulation. I cannot tell you how many people I meet – and I am talking about good, seeking people – who teeter on the edge of an emotional breakdown because of these families that are *"so good to* [them]." People who have come to know the Truth and the living God, who know Mormonism is built on a lie, who know the teachings of Joseph were contrived, but who are so afraid of disappointing their parents that they cannot break free.

The Lord foresaw the power, yes even the manipulation that families could hold over people, and throughout Scripture reminds all of His children NOT to let their families get in between Him and them.

The Lord said to the children of Israel:

> Deuteronomy 13:6-9. *If thy brother, the son of thy mother, or thy son, or thy daughter, or the wife of thy bosom, or thy friend, which is as thine own soul, entice thee secretly, saying, Let us go and serve other gods, which thou hast not known, thou, nor thy fathers; Thou shalt not consent unto him, nor hearken unto him; neither shall thine eye pity him, neither shalt thou spare, neither shalt thou conceal him: But thou shalt surely kill him; thine hand shall be first*

> *upon him to put him to death, and afterwards the hand of all the people.*

Jesus Himself said:

> Matthew 10:35-37. *I am come to set a man at variance against his father, and the daughter against her mother, and the daughter in law against her mother in law.*
>
> *And a man's foes shall be they of his own household. He that loveth father or mother more than me is not worthy of me: and he that loveth son or daughter more than me is not worthy of me.*

Like in all things, Jesus tells all believers who their real family is when He said:

> Matthew 12:50. *For whosoever shall do the will of my Father which is in heaven, the same is my brother, and sister, and mother.*

Before we move on, let me say that I know there are a LOT of you out there who live, as Henry David Thoreau said, "lives of quiet desperation" because of the family and cultural pressures that are upon you. To you I say:

> Put Jesus first.
>
> Trust in God.

Step out in His Name's sake, remembering what He promised:

> Matthew 19:29. *And every one that hath forsaken houses, or brethren, or sisters, or father, or mother, or wife, or children, or lands, for my name's sake, shall receive an hundredfold, and shall inherit everlasting life.*

Remembering that Jesus Himself, who the LDS say would *never* do anything to break up a family, said that, because of His coming...

Luke 12:53. *The father would be divided against the son, and the son against the father; the mother against the daughter, and the daughter against the mother; the mother in law against her daughter in law, and the daughter in law against her mother in law.*

Luke 14:26. *If any man come to me, and hate not his father, and mother, and wife, and children, and brethren, and sisters, yea, and his own life also, he cannot be my disciple.*

PUT HIM FIRST.

And how about a final redundant thought on the matter? I would like to suggest a couple of things related to families and God. First of all, and this may sound radical, but families can become as much of an idol as anything else in this fallen world. Families are NOT the end all of existence. Jesus, the Author of brotherly love, had much to say about families that are placed out of kilter.

He said,

Matthew 10:35-37. *For I have come to set a man against his father, and the daughter against her mother, and the daughter-in-law against her mother-in-law. And a man's foes shall be those of his own household. He who loves father or mother more than Me is not worthy of Me. And he who loves son or daughter more than Me is not worthy of Me.*

When He was told that His mother and brothers wanted to see and speak to Him, He said:

Matthew 12:48. *Who is My mother? And who are My brothers? And He stretched out His hand toward His disciples and said, Behold, My mother and My brothers! For whoever shall do the will of My Father in Heaven, the same is My brother and sister and mother.*

You want more, you LDS who relentlessly send me emails that paint sickly sweet pictures of Jesus?

When a guy whose father died came up to Jesus and wanted to go and bury his dad before following the Lord, Jesus said to the man, who surely was in the midst of grief:

> Matthew 8:22. *Follow me, and let the dead bury their dead.*

Can you imagine being invited to the funeral of a general authority of the LDS Church and saying the same thing? *"Ahhh, let the dead bury the dead."*

I wish we heard more of this.

Because of Jesus – His gospel, His Truth - He warns us:

> Matthew 10:21. *And brother will deliver up brother to death, and the father his child. And the children shall rise up against their parents and cause them to be put to death.*

The point in this is that the true church of Jesus Christ is made up of individuals. And to be quite frank, such individualism is antithetical to the family unit. Families can actually serve to keep people from a relationship with Jesus because they become a religion in and of themselves.

There was this Chinese sage named Mo Tzu who went about advocating brotherly love and the Confucianists, who worshipped the family unit, hated and condemned him, arguing that the principle of universal love would dissolve family and destroy society.

Heavy stuff, eh?

Brooks Adams, in *The Law of Civilization and Decay: An Essay on History* (page 81), wrote that when St. Bernard preached, "*his influence was so strong that…mothers are said to have hid their sons from him, and wives their husbands, lest he should lure them away.*" In fact, writes Adams, "*He actually broke up so many homes that the abandoned wives formed a nunnery ...*"

This is what Jesus was saying: if you get to a place where the opinions and sway of your family take precedence over Me, you are not worthy of Me.

❋ ❋ ❋

> "I was on a plane the other day and asked an LDS woman where the temple ceremony that Mormons use today came from. She stared at me blankly so I replied, 'I mean, did it come from the temple that was around when Jesus was alive?' She looked relieved and said, 'Yes, that's it. That is exactly where it came from.'"

Freemasonry

Last week we took a call from a kind woman – I think her name was Mary – who stated she was Catholic and then proceeded to tell the viewing audience what she thought Catholicism believes and embraces as truth. Our caller was merely expressing her opinion of what she really believed Catholicism teaches regarding what is "required" to enter heaven. Now, even I could tell she had some of her facts messed up and I know less about Catholicism than I do about trigonometry – meaning very little.

And the calls and emails we've received from our Catholic viewers tell me she did not represent the faith well.

What's the point?

The point is, what does this all mean? Mary, a lifelong Catholic doesn't know her facts about what Catholics say saves you.

Bill, out there in Tooele, doesn't know the facts of Mormonism and what it teaches.

Lucinda, out there in Los Angeles, doesn't know the facts about her faith either.

But Mary, and Bill, and Lucinda all attend divergent religions, which all teach a different body of beliefs! Codified religions would have us believe that we need to possess their special "corner of information" in order to be right with God, but in most cases, with the exception of the clergy, few people on earth really know or understand everything their faith demands.

But Jesus said,

> John 17:3. *And **this** is life eternal, that they might know thee the only true God, and Jesus Christ, whom thou hast sent.*

My daughter Cassidy recently observed that it seems far too many people today are "converted to Christianity rather than to Christ." In a similar vein we could say and not be wrong, that far too many people today are converts to Catholicism, or Mormonism, or any and all the other "*-isms*" and "*-ists*" rather than to Jesus and Jesus alone.

Look, organized religion has its place.

Hooray for you that you're a *this*, or a *that*, or if you attend here or attend there.

But do you *KNOW the True and Living God and His Son Whom He sent?*

Have you, as Paul noted of the believers in Thessalonica, "*turned to God from idols to serve the living and true God*" (1 Thessalonians 1:9), the idols in this conversation being your religion?

This "knowing the only true and living God and Jesus Christ

whom He has sent" is much, much more than having a speculative acquaintance with Him or the stories about His life. It is NOT just attending church, donating money, or even serving at the Memorial Day breakfast. It is KNOWING Him.

KNOWING HIM!

You see, when you know Him, you will be eternally altered in terms of your ideas, opinions, allegiances, and perspectives. And your respective religions, yes, even your respective idols, will take a back seat to your living faith.

Look, unlike other Christian ministries, we do not care at all, where you sit every Sunday week after week, month after month, or year after year. If you choose to feed yourself off the dead teachings of men, be my guest.

What we do care about is that you KNOW the only True and Living God and His Son whom He has sent; because once you do, He will help lead you to where you ought to be sitting every Sunday and every other day of the week for that matter.

There is a very important verse in the book of Galatians that every Christian should constantly consider. Paul is writing to the church at Galatia where the body of believers had re-adopted the Law and mixed it with their faith.

And he asks them:

> Galatians 3:3. *Are ye so foolish? having begun in the Spirit, are ye now made perfect by the flesh?*

In other words, *are you, who have been saved by grace through faith by the Spirit, now going to return to elements of the Law to attempt to be perfected in your flesh?*

We know a few facts about humanity. First, we are typically social animals. We need other people; we like to belong, to be accepted, and to interact. This makes us feel loved and secure. Secondly, we enjoy being part of a group or groups that share similar views, interests, mindsets, and goals. This makes us feel accomplished and progressive. Finally, we like to belong to groups that allow us to advance and we make heroes of those who do rise above.

Finding acceptance by belonging to a group is one thing; belonging to a group that not only accepts you, but is driven by goals and intentions you support is doubly rewarding. Institutions, groups, corporations, religions, and even nations that learn to capitalize on these basic human needs thrive where those who neglect them generally fade and fail.

Unfortunately, these very human needs often lead people to make the mistake of placing their hopes, allegiance, devotion, and trust in the world-group and not on the living God. This is the very thing we were talking about earlier.

Because humans need to belong and be accepted, and because we might lack the faith to face God alone and to trust Him over the group, there exists a very natural inclination for all human beings to organize themselves into collectives, groups, orders, fraternities, corporations, and other entities that will sort of become fathers to the fatherless, husbands to the widows, and brothers and sisters to the brotherless.

Every group or order, from street gangs in Los Angeles to the high brow Skull and Bones society at Yale University, operates from the point of satiating these basic human desires to be accepted, to belong, to find safety in numbers, and to progress up through the ranks to greater glory in the flesh. God Himself implemented such principles in the establishment of the nation of

Israel as a means to strengthen them and keep the pollutions of the pagan world from corrupting His chosen brood.

Nevertheless, since His finished work on the cross and the ascension to His heavenly throne, we can be certain that a personal relationship with Yeshua neutralizes every man made institution, and demands that all earthly institutions, powers, religions, and groups conform to His ways and will – nothing more or less.

Man-made groups will always do one of three things relative to true Christianity and its manual the Bible. It will add to it – you know, expand upon its demands. It will take away from it, and say this isn't important or that isn't really necessary. It will reinterpret it, and assign its own special twist upon it.

Enter Freemasonry, our topic for tonight.

What is Freemasonry, where did it come from, and how has it influenced Mormonism past and present? Let me take you on a very brief historical journey, all of it conceived and contrived by the faithless mind of man. For simplicity's sake, we're going to make our starting point at the time when, out of FEAR that Islam was going to rule the world, men who called themselves Christian began killing Muslims. We know this time as the crusades.

The first crusade began in 1095. Constantinople was under threat of being overtaken by the Turks; since Muslims had overtaken and controlled the holy city of Jerusalem for more than four centuries, the threat had to be taken seriously. The crusade to protect the Byzantine empire from Muslim attack quickly morphed into a crusade to take back the Holy City of Jerusalem – which these "Christian" crusaders did; but they came in and butchered the innocent residents of the city as well, which made them hated by surrounding countries.

By 1119, Christian pilgrims were being slaughtered in their travels near the Holy Land. And something had to be done. Well, a group of nine knights came together and offered to "protect" the Kingdom of Jerusalem. These knights lived under "holy" orders by the rule of Saint Augustine. These warrior-monks won the heart of the Christian ruler of Jerusalem and he let them take up residence on the temple mount where Solomon's temple once stood.

They were known as "The Poor Knights of the Temple of Solomon" or later, for short, the Knights Templar.

I am not going to go into their whole history, but just know they grew wealthy, powerful, and controlling over the years, and as every man-made order, they soon fell. In 1307, the Knights Templar were being led by a man who was known as Grand Master Jacques de Molay, who was burned at the stake, beginning the end of the rule and influence of the Knights.

Enter the Middle Ages.

During these years, builders, architects, and craftsmen gathered to construct Gothic Cathedrals in and around Europe. They were known as Freemasons because, as their name says, they were free to apply their trade as opposed to medieval serfs who were bound to a local noble. On the locations of their job, or on the construction site, these Freemasons who were recognizable by the tool carrying aprons they wore, would set up places to eat, sketch their designs, and even apply their trade. These locations they called "lodges."

No one was allowed in these lodges except those who were initiated in the "mysteries" of the craft. You see, these Freemasons were just as concerned about protecting their craft as writers, musicians, and computer programmers are about their work today. Now, like many myth-makers, the Freemasons liked that their fellowships dated back to the construction of Solomon's temple. It gave them a ready-made history.

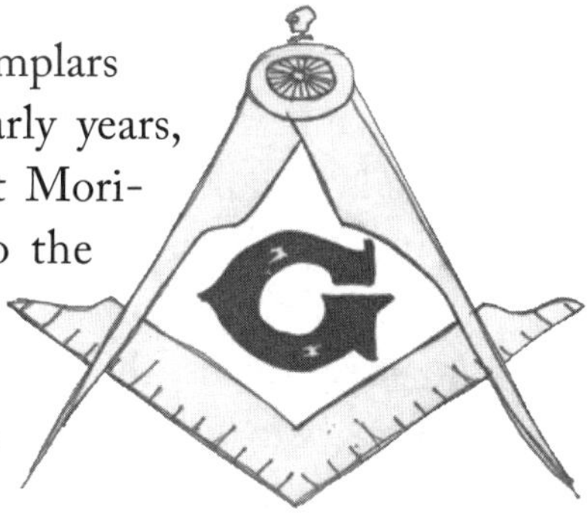

This is where the tie to the Knights Templars comes in because remember, in the early years, they were allowed to reside on Mount Moriah where Solomon built his temple to the True and Living God. And if you don't believe there is a connection between the man-made groups called the Knight Templars and the Freemasons, just ask any Mason today the name of their youth groups. You know what they'll tell you? "Oh, they're called *De Molay's*." And do you remember what the name of the Grand Master of the Knights Templar was who was burned at the stake? That's right, Jacques de Molay. But also KNOW this: Solomon's temple and the activities therein *in no way* resemble or reflect anything done by the Freemasons or by the Mormons who borrowed so heavily from them.

As the guilds and lodges of Freemasons grew, so did their need to have set standards to guard their trade secrets and skills. So they started to participate in special initiations – in special places called temples, no less, in order for the qualified members who pay dues to unite and feel more exceptional, elite, inclusive, and therefore, safe. Because these guilds were composed of men of intelligence and skill, their appeal grew. Once Europe emerged from the Middle Ages, many men of reputation wanted to be admitted.

Where original guilds were getting established somewhere between 1350 and 1450, by 1620, Freemasonry was open to all qualifying men of reputation, whether they were involved in the construction trade or not. By the mid 18th century, Freemasonry became a guild of productive men throughout England, Scotland, and France, who sought to better their lives with a body of rites and rituals.

Remember now, these men used symbols of their trades to remind them of the type of men they longed to remain or become. These symbols included the compass and the square, which were essential to the craft of Middle Ages construction. For example, to Freemasons, the square stood for straightforward virtue; the compass to circumscribe a man’s passions; the plumb line to remind all to “stay upright.” Over time, Freemasonry adopted and incorporated other signs, symbols, lore, and mythology to accompany their secret handshakes, grips, and rituals of advancement within the lodges.

All of these vows and rituals were kept from the curious public, which not only made Freemasonry seem like it had something to hide, it also made it grow. The first American lodge was established in Boston in 1733. By 1752 Benjamin Franklin and George Washington were Freemasons and by the early 1800s, so were most civilized and accomplished men in settled America.

But Masonry made a mistake. It collectively stood behind the strange disappearance of a man named William Morgan who was going to publish all the secret rites and symbols and comings and goings of the Masons. His death and disappearance caused a national outcry and Masonry began to slip into a far less prominent position in America.

Oh, and the widow of William Morgan? What happened to her?

Why, she ended up being one of Joseph Smith’s secret wives.

Enter Joseph Smith and Nauvoo Mormonism.

Now, Joseph Smith's early writings are filled with material that condemns secret societies like the Masons but there are indications that by 1838 his attitude toward secret groups had changed. Once Smith went to Nauvoo, he became a Mason, formed what is known as "The Council of Fifty," and ultimately established the secret temple ceremony that worthy Latter-day Saints participate in today.

Mormon Apostle John A. Widtsoe admitted (*Evidences and Reconciliations*, page 357):

> Many of the Saints were Masons, such as Joseph's brother Hyrum, Heber C. Kimball, Elijah Fordham, Newel K. Whitney, James Adams, and John C. Bennett.

With the permission of the prophet, members of the Church petitioned the Grand Master of Illinois to set up their own lodge in Nauvoo, a town settled by the Mormons. They were granted permission to hold lodge meetings in October, 1841, but it was March 15, 1842 before authority was given to set up an actual lodge and to induct new members. The man they call the prophet of God, *Joseph Smith, became a member of the lodge and there learned all the signs, tokens, grips, and symbols of masonry.* This was prior to his introducing the Mormon temple rituals and rites, which, upon comparison, are proven to be just another plagiarism by Smith.

The following statement is recorded in Joseph Smith's *History of the Church* (4:551), under the date of March 15, 1842:

> In the evening I received the first degree in Free Masonry in the Nauvoo Lodge, assembled in my general business office.

The record for the very next day reads (4:552):

I was with the Masonic Lodge and rose to the sublime degree.

The Mormons who joined the Masonic Lodge, soon found themselves in trouble with other members of the fraternity. You see, Joseph was never content to leave things in their original state or to give credit to the originator. Like Christianity and the Bible, Joseph took what he wanted, made it his own version by twisting it, then called the original sources "corrupt" and his revisions "INSPIRED." This made the Freemasons angry and they ultimately refused to allow the Mormons to continue a Masonic Lodge at Nauvoo. But neither Joseph nor the Mormons cared. Joseph had gotten what he wanted from the whole experience – inspiration, and he soon introduced what Mormons today refer to as the endowment. But Joseph didn't only tie the endowment to living a better life, Joseph tied receiving the endowment to a persons' very salvation! This is the genesis of Mormon temple work.

Did you know that the

- bee hive
- the all seeing eye
- hand-grips
- suns, moons, and stars
- passwords

are emblems of Utah Mormonism today? Many of these symbols are found on the exterior of the Salt Lake City temple. These were all first the products of Freemasonry.

Also employed as icons in Mormonism which Joseph took directly from Freemasonry are

- the compass
- the square
- two triangles forming a six pointed star

  and the phrase,

- "Holiness to the Lord" which the Freemasons took from the Bible.

Speaking of Joseph Smith, LDS author Richard Bushman wrote in one of his more recent books (*Joseph Smith: Rough Stone Rolling*, page 449):

> He had a green thumb for growing ideas from tiny seeds. Masonic rites seem to have been one more provocation.

Joseph Smith's father had joined the Masons when Joseph was just eleven years old. His brother Hyrum joined a few years later. Then in May of 1842, Joseph Smith himself advanced through the Masonic order over a two day period.

Six weeks later, he delivered to those who followed, believed, and trusted him their own "endowment" based on the elements found in Freemasonry. In so doing, Joseph made the progress and advancement of men and women, or the perfection of their flesh, the focus, and he used the symbols of another man-centered group to do it. As a result, Mormonism today, though claiming to be Christian, is not too far from being just another social institution to which people like to belong, because it makes them feel safe, loved, and protected.

Less than a year before he died, Joseph Smith said in an address to the saints (*History of the Church* 5:517):

> Let me be resurrected with the saints whether to heaven or to hell ... what do we care if the society is good?

As we draw toward 2012, when this nation will earnestly look to a political leader to save us from certain social destruction that lies in wait, I fear we, like Joseph Smith and those who follow him, will embrace earthly solutions to our spiritual problems and implement them in the name of God. I fear well meaning Christians will sincerely enter into trade with him who offers institutional hope, promises of peace and an earthly society that seems "good"… at first.

There is not a symbol, a garment, or a hand-shake known to man that will allow her or him to enter the presence of God – only Yeshua my friends, only Yeshua.

Written in 1866 by Malcolm C. Duncan, *Duncan's Ritual of Freemasonry or Guide to the Three Symbolic Degrees of the Ancient York Rite and To the degrees of Mark Master, Past Master, Most Excellent Master, and The Royal Arch* gives the entire rites and rituals of Freemasonry starting back to the early 1700's. I highly recommend a firsthand reading of this little book, front to back, as an introduction not only to the purpose and origin of LDS temples, but to the origin of many LDS things apart from the temple.

Out of respect – and I had no small amount of trouble deciding on how to approach this – but out of respect for those people who really believe God is behind what they do in LDS temples, I will refrain from mentioning things they would feel are too sacred for public disclosure. But listen to some of the other things found as standards in Masonry, recorded around 1717, which I have extracted from *Duncan's Ritual*, available in almost any large bookstore. The page number refers to where I read the common phrase found in Mormonism today.

Phrase or Word from Masonry	page #	LDS connection
"mystic veil which has long been lifted"	preface	*"the veil has been lifted"*
Illustration: Compass and Square	7	temple / garment reference
"*brethren*"	10	common LDS verbiage
"they *put on an apron*"	10	apron an essential part of temple endowment

Phrase or Word from Masonry	page #	LDS connection
"hat, sash, yoke and apron"	12	important temple accoutrements
"*Brethren will be properly clothed and in order*"	12	temple verbiage
"*the Brethren put on their aprons*"	12	temple verbiage
"make the sign"	14	temple instruction
"to *introduce, and clothe* all visiting Brethren; *to receive*"	14	temple verbiage
"*under no less penalty*"	15	temple verbiage
"*The left arm ... forming a square*"	16	temple verbiage
"*drop the left arm* suddenly and with spirit as soon as the *two motions are accomplished*"	16	earlier temple (1989 and before)
"*Holy Bible, square and compass*"	16	temple references
"*Raise the hands (above the head)* and drop ... *repeat three times* ... [saying] '*O Lord ...*'"	18	temple verbiage
"*garments*"	19	temple reference (scripture)
"*whispers the* password ... *in the ear*"	20	temple instruction
"*all rise*"	20	temple directive
"*confirmation* will *make it known by the usual sign (raise the right hand)*"	23	LDS verbiage and LDS practice. "*Please so indicate by the raising of the right hand*"
"*those opposed, by the same sign*"	23	LDS verbiage (see above)
"*found worthy*"	24	LDS verbiage "*has been interviewed and found worthy*"
"three *distinct* knocks"	29	temple verbiage
"*is he worthy?*"	29	LDS verbiage

Phrase or Word from Masonry	page #	LDS connection
"*Let him enter*"	30	temple verbiage
"*should you* attempt to *reveal the* secrets"	30	temple verbiage
"Who comes here? Mr. Parker, *who has* long been in darkness ... *now seek* ... *to receive*"	31	temple verbiage
"*Own free will*"	31	temple verbiage
"I, (state name) of my own free will ... in the *presence of* Almighty *God* ... that I will always hail, ever conceal, and *never reveal*"	34	temple verbiage
"*token*"	35	temple reference
"the Holy Bible is the rule and guide of our Faith and practice; the square, to square our actions; the compass, to *circumscribe* and keep us *within bounds* of all mankind"	36	temple verbiage
"as *the sun rules the day* and *the moon governs the night*"	36	temple verbiage
"By the *signs and tokens*"	37	temple verbiage
"*We are instructed* by *the first* sign to avoid temptation by *proper* restraint of our *passions* ..."	38	temple verbiage
"for *further instruction*"	40	temple verbiage
"as *you are clothed*"	40	temple verbiage
"*Has it a name?*" "*It has.*" "*Will you give it to me?*" "*I did not receive it*"	42	temple verbiage
"*A new name*"	47	temple verbiage
"*deeply impressed upon* the mind"	55	temple verbiage
"never *deviate*"	55	temple verbiage
"*initiated ...*		"(*initiatory*)
"... now wishes to receive *more light* ..."	60	temple verbiage
"*lifting the candidate from his knees* at the altar"	67	temple verbiage

Phrase or Word from Masonry	page #	LDS connection
"when it is conferred"	87	LDS vernacular
"three *loud distinct* knocks"	88	temple verbiage
"*now wishes to receive further light*"	89	temple verbiage
"*that I will not have* illegal carnal *intercourse"*	95	temple verbiage
"looking conductor *in the eye*"	97	temple practice
"Moving off, one says, '*Let us report*'"	111	temple verbiage and stage direction
"All now, *form in a circle* ... the Master makes the signs of 'distress' of a Master Mason, *which is done by raising both hands and arms above the head*"	116-17	temple practice
"gives him the grand Masonic word on the *five points of fellowship*"	120	earlier temple (1990 and earlier)
"orders of the priesthood"	129	LDS theology
"*Adieu*! A heart-warm, fond *adieu*"	145	Book of Mormon, controversy over use
"the veils are now pushed apart to admit the candidate"	235	temple practice
"High Priest"	239	Priesthood office
"... but the true descendants of the twelve Tribes. It is necessary you should be very particular *in tracing your genealogy*"	240	LDS theology and practice
"will most readily pledge *to do all that is required* of them"	267	temple verbiage
"the New Era"	281	an LDS magazine

The woman on the plane said it all came from the temple during Jesus' time. And Joseph Smith said it all came by revelation from God. Really?

"Sometimes people, communities, religions and causes can keep people so busy, they don't have any time to really think about what they are doing, and why."

Genealogy

In the past we have done a lot of talking about the methods men, women and groups use to trap people into their cultic religious web.

There are all types of cults out there but tonight I am speaking primarily of religious cults. I am presently reading an interesting book called *Raven*. It is the definitive book on the Reverend Jim Jones (how anyone could call himself a reverend I don't know – but anyway) the Reverend Jim Jones and his cult called the People's Temple.

Now there are some universal truths or traits that exist within these groups which can be applied to most organizations informed people would consider "cults" or "cult-like." Here are a few of the general categories. Now understand, not all of these traits need be present for a group to be a religious cult, but we might say that the more of them that exist the more proof that the group is a religious cult.

1. **Denial of the Bible**: All cults in one way or another will always deny what God says in His Word as true.

   Christians say the Bible is itself trustworthy and true.

2. **Works Salvation/Legalism**: Religious cults always teach that eternal life depends upon something other than or in addition to faith in the atoning, finished work of Christ on the cross. Rather than relying on the grace of God alone for salvation, the salvation message of the cults always boils down to some required obedience to, or abstention from certain obligations and practices, which might even include obedience to some Old Testament law.

   Christians say that salvation comes by grace through faith on Jesus Christ alone.

3. **In cults there is never an assurance of salvation**: if there was, they would be out of business. The issue of a cult member's salvation is never settled; it is constantly affected by the changing circumstances of life.

   This is because cult "salvation" is always based on the righteousness or actions of the cult member and not on the righteousness of Jesus.

4. **Cults always have a guru-type leader or modern prophet.** He or she is looked to as the infallible interpreter of Scripture because he/she is especially appointed by God.

   Christians know that any man, woman, or child can go directly to God and be saved outside the input of any human being.

5. **Cults often have vacillating and/or ambiguous doctrines.** This means that in order to gain favor with the public, and thereby aid in the recruitment of new members, cult "doctrines" tend to be delivered in degrees. They are often characterized by many false or deceptive claims concerning the cult's true spiritual beliefs (as an example, Mormons are not quick to reveal their belief that God was a man who has now become the God of planet Earth; neither do they discuss Joseph's polygamous activities).

   True Christianity is delivered warts and all, or at least it should be. There is nothing to fear by the facts or the truth.

6. **Cults maintain an extreme exclusivity or a complete denunciation of other competing groups.** The members of each specific organization have been taught that their church, organization, or community, is the only true group and that all other groups are false. The cult explains that it is impossible to please God or live with God without being a member of the specific group.

   Christianity is non-denominational, and freely open to all worshippers of the True and Living God.

7. **Cults almost always lay claim to "special discoveries" and/or "additional revelations."** The fundamental characteristic of Christianity is that it is openly historical and not at all dependent upon "private knowledge" or access to "secret groups or gatherings." But the cults love to claim exclusive revelation which always emanates from visions, dreams, hallucinations, or some other unverifiable and/or self-authenticating form.

   I say unverifiable because where the Bible speaks of real people, from real places, working around real pagan kings, armies, and countries, cult scripture does not.

8. **Next, cults always have and support an altered and defective Christology.** In other words they twist the nature of the Person of Jesus Christ. Cults usually either deny the deity of Christ, or His humanity, or His birth, or His eternality, or the true union of the two natures (Man/God) in one Person.

   To Christians, Jesus is the eternal God incarnate.

9. **Cults also present an errant depiction of the nature of man as either nothing more than an animal or something more like a god or a god to be.**

   To Christians, humanity was created in God's image to have fellowship with God; humanity fell with the world into sin and we are separated from God as fallen beings. The only way to re-establish the fellowship God intended to have with us in the first place is through grace by faith on the blood of His Son.

10. **Cults often use out-of-context Scripture as proof-texts.** They tend to focus on one verse or passage of the Bible to the exclusion of others and without regard for the context in which Scripture is given. Additionally, cults are quite adept at using Christian terminology, all the while pouring out their own meanings into the words.

    Christians take all of the Bible into consideration when seeking truth, not just a single passage.

11. **Cults often teach erroneous doctrines concerning life after death and retribution.** Some of these include: "soul sleep," "annihilationism," "purgatory," "universalism," and "the progression toward godhood." Most cults deny hell or embellish it in some altered manner.

    All of Biblical Christianity understands one simple fact about the eternal state of humanity: if a person is covered by the blood of Jesus, they are saved. If they're not covered, then they aren't saved.

12. **Most cults end up with some sort of entangling organizational structure.** It's like the less truth a movement represents, the more rigid and demanding it is in its organizational entanglements. I mean think about this. There is a Ugandan living in the desert who reads the Bible and believes. This is simple truth – simple, saving truth.

    Then there is the monolithic, multi-national corporate religious conglomerate that has demands, codes, standards for admittance and fellowship which they heap upon their congregants.

    Which is closer to the truth?

13. There is almost always an abuse in finances of any cult; or at least some financial exploitation.

14. **There is often some sort of influence or tie to the group through the pseudo mystical and/or the occult.**

    Biblical Christians would obviously avoid these things entirely.

15. **Cults and cult leaders also thrive off persecution.** It is welcomed, and even glorified in, as "evidence" that they are being persecuted for righteousness' sake.

16. **Cults place their organization and sometimes their leaders right up on the throne of God.** Therefore, if a member decides to leave the group, they are not simply leaving an organization but rather they are leaving "God and His only true organization."

You know we could go on and on as there are a number of other things associated with most religious cults which include:

- Little tolerance for questions or critical inquiry;
- Unreasonable fear about the outside world, such as impending catastrophe, evil conspiracies and persecutions;
- Ecclesiastical abuses;
- Followers feeling they can never be "good enough;"
- Demands that the leaders are always right;
- Warnings about reading outside materials, especially materials that question or reveal the cult;
- Members have their primary identity tied to the cult and not God;
- There are often stilted and programmed-type conversational mannerisms which often clone the group or a specific leader;
- There is often dependency upon cult leaders to solve personal problems, make personal choices, and to even think;
- There can be an increasing isolation from family and old friends unless they demonstrate an interest in the group/leader; and
- Any detrimental fact about the group or its leaders is justified or rationalized away.

All of this being said, I want to focus tonight on just one element frequently found in cults as it relates to this topic: **the tireless, never-ending demand upon the time and energies of its members.**

Within Mormonism there exists an exhaustive and sacred "threefold mission of the Church" (see Ezra Taft Benson, "A Sacred Responsibility," *Ensign*, May 1986): to share the gospel, which is missionary work; to perfect the saints, which means a focus the individual needs to place on his own progress; and to redeem the dead, which is what we are going to talk about generally in this section.

Speaking of work for the dead, the founder of Mormonism, Joseph Smith said as quoted in *History of the Church* (4:425):

> It is no more credible that God should save the dead than that He should raise the dead.

In other words, where Christians are commanded to have faith and to exhibit the works of love as a result of their faith, Mormons must not only perfect themselves and their families by serving in the church AND share the Mormon gospel with others, they are also commanded to save the dead! ALL OF THE DEAD!

Talk about demands on time and energies!

I have a photograph somewhere in my files that depicts a bunch of people roaming through a cemetery trying to get genealogical information off tombstones. Why? Because the LDS take this information, put it in a database, and then do vicarious Mormon temple rites and rituals for and in the names of the deceased so that they can choose to become Mormon as spirits in the afterlife!

How important is this genealogical work? Joseph Smith said (*TPJS*, page 193):

> The greatest responsibility in this world that God has laid upon us is to seek after our dead. Those Saints who neglect it...do it at the peril of their own salvation.

Let me repeat that! *Listen* to the words of the man Joseph Smith and try and see if you could make this statement fit anywhere in the New Testament:

> The greatest responsibility in this world that God has laid upon us is to seek after our dead. Those Saints who neglect it...do it at the peril of their own salvation.

Late President of the LDS Church Gordon B. Hinckley said something absolutely burdensome in the *Church News* of July of 1999 ("Church is Really Doing Well," July 3, 1999). Listen to this:

> Our message is so imperative, when you stop to think that the salvation, the eternal salvation of the world, rests upon the shoulders of this church. When all is said and done, if the world is going to be saved, we have to do it. There is no escaping from that. No other people in the history of the world have received the kind of mandate that we have received. We are responsible for all who have lived upon the earth. That involves our family history and temple work.

Let me just paint a picture here, okay? Brother Billy Bob Jones is a faithful Mormon man. He takes his membership and the things his leaders teach him seriously. He is married to Susie Q. Jones and they have three children. Billy Bob works very hard as a mechanic five days a week and half day Saturday. His wife Susie Q. stays home as instructed by the brethren.

Billy Bob spends the major part of his week at work, but he is also a scout leader for the ward troop, which keeps him very busy on weeknights.

Billy Bob also does his monthly home teaching but not just through a perfunctory visit but because he really cares about the families assigned to him.

He holds family home evening every Monday Night, attends all his Sunday meetings plus ward council.

He tries to split with the missionaries once in a while in the evening so he can share the Mormon gospel, as instructed.

In the meanwhile Billy Bob tries to mow his lawn, pay his bills, and make repairs on his own car and home. But he pays ten percent of his gross income because he wants to be temple worthy, so as to be in a position to see his children wed but also to save the dead – all seven trillion of them.

In addition to all this, plus all the activities that come with being a good father and a good and attentive husband, Brother Billy Bob needs to be cognizant of the fact that the *greatest responsibility in this world that God has laid upon him is to seek after his dead.*

This not only means doing temple work, but genealogy to find the names of the dead!

And Jesus said what?

> Matthew 11:30. *My yoke is easy and my burden is light.*

Well what does the Bible say about Genealogy? It is prevalent in the Old Testament, and even in Matthew and Luke, but then we read passages like these written by the apostle Paul:

> 1 Timothy 1:4. *Neither give heed to fables and endless genealogies, which minister questions, rather than godly edifying which is in faith: so do.*

or

> Titus 3:9. *But avoid foolish questions, and genealogies, and contentions, and strivings about the law; for they are unprofitable and vain.*

Let me give you a few insights as to why.

First of all, genealogy was extremely important to the children of Israel because through it they could determine who could officiate in the temple as priests and high priests and who could not. Bloodlines were extremely important *prior to* the death and resurrection of Christ. But once He came and rose from the dead, the temple veil was rent in two and the priesthoods done away with, Jesus became our final and permanent high priest; genealogy – where you came from or who your ancestors were became meaningless, because the gospel was opened to all.

Ironically, it was opened to all except ... the dead!

Even the Book of Mormon teaches this plainly, that this life is the time to meet God because after it, there is no hope (Alma 34:31-33). But Joseph Smith progressed in his religious claims and dreamed up this post mortem work for the dead *after* writing the Book of Mormon.

Any Bible-believing Christian knows that religiously, there is absolutely no good reason for doing genealogical research. There is no lineal authority or priestly heritage to prove for anyone (as we all come to Christ individually with Him being our only and final High Priest); there are no ordinances requisite for salvation (neither the LDS baptism nor their new and everlasting covenant); and there is nobody who gets to embrace the Mormon rituals once this life is through!

With this all being the case, there must be some other reason why the LDS want their people to do endless genealogies – right??

We'll let me suggest to you what they are.

One: They keep people busy as bees and therefore *NOT* thinking.

Two: Genealogy is directly tied to temple work and temple work requires a 10% of annual income from all as an entrance fee.

So ... you keep people mindlessly busy doing purposeless work, and then they are more willing to pay 10% in order to see that work "completed" in their so-called HOUSE of the LORD. It's a business model, pure and simple.

Finally, I want to read how an LDS defender of the faith responds to the question about why the Bible says to avoid genealogy.

Question: *If genealogies are as important as Latter-day Saints say, why does the New Testament tell Christians to avoid endless genealogies* (1 Timothy 1:4, Titus 3:9)*?*

Answer: *The recording of genealogy is not evil or to be avoided, for if it were, why would genealogical records be included numerous times in the Bible? God surely would never inspire Nehemiah (7:5), Matthew (1:1-16) or Luke (3:23-38) to do something evil!*

Friends, this is a classic example of the kind of slanted scholarship and responses the LDS give to sound inquiry. Unsuspecting souls, who do not know what else to do, believe them.

It is amazing.

Bottom line: Mormon genealogy is just another form of controlling good people who are only seeking to please and find God.

❋ ❋ ❋

"Like baptism for the dead, the whereabouts of Cain, and where the lost ten tribes are likely to be hanging out, Mormonism has no fear in creating yet another myth, this time about the location of the Lord's atonement for sin. The more a group can get us to take our eyes off the cross, the more they can get us to serve them and their empty causes."

Gethsemane

Men and women of pride do not like to belong to the status quo. They like to own and possess the cutting edge, to feel advanced or above what the common rabble dabbles in. They enjoy elitist clubs with limited memberships, owning what is scarce or unavailable, and in the realm of religion, possessing special knowledge or the secrets to eternal life.

Almost from the moment Jesus established His Church here on earth – which, we remind you, is made of believers (not bricks and mortar), a proud group stepped in and sought to take hold of His gospel by claiming to possess some secret insights and knowledge into things not often realized by the "common rabble" of believers.

These groups were known as the *Gnostics*, which is just another word for "knowing," and once again, they made themselves distinct, or … *ahem* … more advanced, by claiming to have possession of some unrevealed secret *gnosis* or knowledge.

Tonight, in our study of Mormon doctrines as compared to the Bible we are going to examine what may seem at first like a minor difference in the Mormon / Christian comparative. But in the end, like a single termite in a giant wooden house, it can lead to the complete erosion of a true understanding of Christ and the cross.

The topic? The LDS view of Christ's atonement occurring in the garden of Gethsemane.

To Bible-believing Christians, Jesus' suffering in the garden of Gethsemane was a preparatory time of prayer and temptation prior to His turning Himself and His will over to both God and sinful man. But to the LDS, the cross was more the place where Jesus simply suffered physical death while the garden of Gethsemane was the place where He actually atoned for sin, which makes it the place of focus, and the cross more of a place of mere acknowledgment. Tonight, we will prove not only that this teaching is false but we hope to expose it for what it is: just another group trying to proudly differentiate themselves from common Christianity.

The problem with the LDS doctrine that the Lord's atonement occurred in the garden of Gethsemane is not only that it is false, but that it negates the real place of atonement: the cross. I imagine that if Satan can ever accomplish getting people to take their eyes off the truths of the gospel and redirect them to something that is false, he has a won a victory.

Nowhere in the Bible is Gethsemane or a garden referred to as a place of atonement. In fact, John the Beloved doesn't even mention the garden experience in any great detail in his account of the Passion of Christ. If it was the place of atonement, I think he would have said more. But late LDS Apostle Bruce R. McConkie wrote in his book, *The Promised Messiah*, page 337:

> Forgiveness is available because Christ the Lord sweat great drops of blood in Gethsemane as he bore the incalculable weight of the sins of all who ever had or ever would repent.

Just so there is no question on the Mormon position regarding Jesus place of atonement, let's turn to Mormon scripture itself. In the Book of Mormon, we read a passage that, speaking of Jesus, states:

> Mosiah 3:7. And lo, he shall suffer temptations, and pain of body, hunger, thirst, and fatigue, even more than man can suffer, except it be unto death; for behold, blood cometh from every pore, so great shall be his anguish for the wickedness and abominations of his people.

Late LDS **Prophet** and President, Ezra Taft Benson said (*Teachings of Ezra Taft Benson*, page 14):

> It was in Gethsemane that Jesus took on Himself the sins of the world, in Gethsemane that His pain was equivalent to the cumula-

> tive burden of all men, in Gethsemane that He descended below all things so that all could repent and come to Him.

Separating themselves even further from Bible-believing Christians the world over, LDS "Apostle" Bruce R. McConkie wrote in his book *The Mortal Messiah* (pages 127-128):

> And as He [Jesus] came out of the Garden, delivering Himself voluntarily into the hands of wicked men, the victory had been won. There remained yet the shame and pain of his arrest, his trial, and his cross. But all of these were overshadowed by the agonies and sufferings in Gethsemane. It was on the cross he "suffered death in the flesh," EVEN AS MANY HAVE SUFFERED AGONIZING DEATHS, but it was in Gethsemane that "he suffered the pains of all men, that all men might repent and come unto him [emphasis Shawn's]."

What would cause McConkie and Benson and many LDS leaders to point to the garden of Gethsemane over the cross as the place of atonement?

Elitist pride.

You have to understand this, and it is going to sting, but Mormons have never liked the Christian focus on the cross. To them, it comes across as so, so backwoodsy and barbaric.

McConkie arrogantly wrote (*Mormon Doctrine*, page 555):

> The sectarian world falsely suppose that the climax of his torture and suffering was on the cross – a view which they keep ever before them by the constant use of the cross as a religious symbol.

This attitude of mocking our love and appreciation for the cross is nothing new to Bible-believing people, however. We recall what Paul wrote:

> 1 Corinthians 1:18. *For the preaching of the cross is to them that*

perish foolishness; but unto us which are saved ***it*** *is the power of God.*

and

1 Corinthians 1:23. *But we preach Christ* ***crucified****, unto the Jews a stumbling block, and unto the Greeks foolishness.*

McConkie must have been a Greek.

Now today's LDS defenders might say that I am quoting from old leaders of the church in using McConkie but even their own *Encyclopedia of Mormonism* (1:85; 3:1090) confirms that Latter-day Saints believe Jesus atoned for the sins of the world in the garden.

In 2004 LDS Apostle M. Russell Ballard said, speaking of Jesus ("The Atonement and the Value of One Soul," *Ensign*, May 2004):

> There in the quiet isolation of the Garden of Gethsemane, He knelt among the gnarled olive trees, and in some incredible way that none of us can comprehend, the Savior took upon Himself the sins of the world.

Having been LDS forty years, I can tell you that these statements, and other statements like them, cause people to miss the cross, to see another Jesus, to discount the meaning of His suffering, and to actually revise the truth of Jesus' atoning work. It is purposeful act of twistianity.

Does it really matter whether His atonement was on the cross or not?

It really does and for several reasons. Foremost, ought not we all want to seek and know truth? In a minute we will show just how much of a lie this teaching is! And if they lie on this singular issue, what else are they lying about? Where one lie is embraced, others are sure to follow.

LISTEN to what Jude implores us; that

> Jude 3. *Ye should earnestly contend for the faith which was once delivered unto the saints.*

Meaning, earnestly defend and present the faith that the apostles of Jesus had ALREADY delivered.

So don't give these guys an inch on their myths because they will take a mile and before you know it you'll have a vacant smile on your face as you're singing, "Praise to the Man"!

Finally, as I said, we are talking about the LORD's suffering for sin. By taking away the full import of this work on our behalf we reduce the importance of His suffering all together. I don't want to do that; do you?

So what are the facts of Gethsemane and how can we defend against this LDS twist while showing those who have believed these lies that the Bible says differently? We are going to give you ten factors to consider about this errant LDS claim relative to the Garden of Gethsemane as the place of atonement for sin.

1. **Jesus shed blood was, for centuries, typified by the children of Israel through animal sacrifice.**

And the animals that were sacrifices had their blood shed by the hands of men. Never did an animal sit somewhere alone and suffer as a picture or type of the atonement to come. This LDS addition of the garden has absolutely no Biblical connection to the animal sacrifices of the Old Covenant, which were a picture of the shedding of the LORD's blood.

2. **It is important to realize the connection of the atonement for sin to the shame of sin.**

There is a reason Jesus was taken to a well traveled spot outside the city. There was a reason He was stripped of His clothing that He was humiliated, shamed, mocked, derided, and publicly denounced. To suffer quietly and relatively alone in the Garden for the sins of the world is *not* a picture of what sin produces. Sin produces shame, embarrassment, public humiliation, and being removed from the presence of those we love - all of these things were elements of His crucifixion and death on the cross and none would have been satisfied by a private suffering in the garden.

For guys who speak and dress like they are so smart, I get frankly amazed at the LDS ignorance.

Hebrews (12:2) tells us that for our sin, Jesus *endured the cross despite its inherent shame.* You know, it is difficult for us to imagine the absolute indignity of suffering death by Roman crucifixion partly because the cross is such an emblem today of our spiritual freedom and salvation. But before Jesus took to that position on that horrible post of terror, only the most vile, heinous, twisted men who were hated by society were hung from them. Anyone - anyone who was crucified, was seen as the lowest of low, a perfect picture of *our* state in sin.

3. **The line that Jesus sweat "as it were great drops of blood," is found only in the gospel of Luke - which does not mean it isn't true; but the way it is written may suggest that His sweat was so profuse that the drops were heavy and large like great drops of blood, rather than smaller, lighter drops that normal sweat looks like.**

I personally believe Jesus could have sweat blood in the garden as His temptation and dread were immense, but the fact that Luke says, "*as it were* great drops of blood" and the fact that only Luke records it makes it more likely that Luke was using a figure of speech. None of the eyewitnesses report Jesus wearing bloody clothing that night, which would have been a noteworthy observation, had He actually bled in that fashion. The LDS teaching that this "sweating great drops" is the way Jesus atoned for sin is highly unlikely.

Now, had all four gospel writers included the blood reference like they do the cross, then maybe they have a point worthy of consideration.

4. **It is also noteworthy that John the Beloved pretty much omits everything about the garden events all together. I would think that if Joseph Smith's Book of Mormon and his Latter-day cronies like "Apostles" McConkie and Ballard were correct, then John who loved and lived with Jesus, would have emphasized more about the importance of the garden too.**
5. **In the gospel of Matthew, Jesus prays three times to the Father that if it be possible, "this cup," meaning His taking on our sin, would pass from Him, but that God's will would be done.**

Once Jesus was outside of the garden facing the temple soldiers, Peter acts rashly by cutting off Malchus' ear. Jesus says to Peter:

> John 18:11. *Put up thy sword into the sheath: the cup which my Father hath given me, shall I not drink it?*

Meaning, Peter, I just overcame the temptation to follow My own will. And now you are stepping in to impede what I was sent to do, which is to drink of the cup my Father gave me to drink! Put away your sword and let's get this thing going.

6. **Additionally, while in the garden, and many times before His passion, Jesus speaks of His "hour" (John 2:4;** 7:30; 8:20; etc.). Once His trial of Gethsemane was OVER, Matthew (and Mark 14:41) reports

> Matthew 26:45. *Then cometh [Jesus] to his disciples, and saith unto them, Sleep on now, and take your rest: behold, the hour is at hand, and the Son of man is betrayed into the hands of sinners.*

His "hour" had not begun – was not "*at hand*" – until *after* Jesus overcame the garden temptation to run and turned Himself into the hands of sinners to do with Him as they would.

9. **In all of the Bible, the suffering for sin is repeatedly equated to the cross but NEVER to the garden of Gethsemane. Check out our show on the cross which we did on April 6, 2010 for more on this.**
10. **While Jesus was in the garden, Luke (22:43) reports that God sent an angel from heaven** to strengthen Him.

However, once Jesus was on the cross, and had taken our sin upon Him, the Father abandoned Him, leaving Him to His own devices, and sending no angels to help. Why? Because Jesus was paying for our sin *on the cross* and NOT in the garden. And this imputed sin caused Jesus for the first time in eternity to be separated from the Holy God.

And how did He respond?

> *He cried, "My God, My God, why hast thou forsaken me? (Mark 15:34."*

He communed openly with the father in the garden and had an angel there to strengthen Him in His time of temptation. It is illogical to think that if God poured out His wrath upon His Son for our sin in the garden, that He would at the same time send an angel to strengthen Him.

Which is, by the way, why no angel was sent to strengthen Him on the cross!

In conclusion, what actually happened in the garden of Gethsemane? What was Jesus doing there? He was preparing to face the most extreme and ultimate suffering imaginable: being separated from His Father on high. So horrible was the task that even Jesus, God in the flesh, asked His Father if there was any other way? *Can this cup pass, Father?*

But being our King and Savior, He added, *"nevertheless, not my will but thine be done* (Luke 22:42)."

Jesus was not above temptation. In fact, Scripture says He suffered and faced all temptation (Hebrews 2:18; 4:15). And Satan was not about to leave our Lord alone when He was about to embark on the only act that would overcome Satan and His powers once and for all. *This* was the trial of the garden: Jesus overcoming the very natural urge or desire to let the cup pass.

Was all of the atonement or payment for the effects of the fall paid for on the cross?

Not according to the Bible.

I would suggest that the second Jesus relinquished Himself into the hands of sinful men, the atonement began. The binding. The slaps out of nowhere. The spitting. The mockery. We know He was scourged; Isaiah tells us *"with His stripes* [of this scourging] *we are healed (Isaiah 53:5)."* Therefore the beatings, the torture, the drudgery, the intolerable fatigue, and all of it culminating in His crucifixion on the cross and death were part of His atonement for our sin.

Doesn't it make you ill when men who call themselves "apostles" take away from His suffering by causing people to focus on things not right or true?

If it doesn't, it should.

❋ ❋ ❋

> "Mormonism has made it seem logical that man should be able to fully comprehend the makeup of God Almighty. Only once I came out from the religion did I realize that if my puny brain can understand Almighty God, He is not a God who deserves to be worshipped and adored."

God: The Trinity

Part 1

The fable of a human pre-existence dovetails naturally into another LDS fable, one of the most pernicious, humanistic, man-centered fables Joseph could have ever devised: that God the Father has a body of flesh and bone.

I want you to just sit back for a moment and think about three basic ideas. I am doing this because I want to plant good seeds of truth in your heart, seeds that will grow and flourish as you examine the fables you have long embraced.

First, I want you to remember a simple phrase Jesus uttered when speaking to the Samaritan woman at the well. Just listen to this phrase.

> John 4:24. *God is a Spirit: and they that worship him must worship him in spirit and in truth.*

Why didn't Jesus say, God has a body of flesh and bones, and they that worship Him must worship Him in Spirit and in Truth? Do you realize what you are doing when you believe a *man* who claims that God is as tangible a being as man, when Jesus Himself said that God is a spirit? Do you understand that you are automatically standing against the entire Word of God by believing this fable?

Why is this so important? Because when you buy into the idea that God the Father has a body of flesh and bone, you will then buy into another fable which says you came from His presence to gain a body …

... Which leads you to another fable that says that with that body, you – YOU – *YOU* must earn your salvation by your efforts, and your determination to do so causes you to miss the whole point of Jesus altogether…

… And then you begin to embrace the deadliest fable of them all – that you can actually become a god *just like* the one you worship – and the simple message of salvation by grace through faith in Him alone is lost. And you might also be chained forever to a system that promises you "*worlds without end*" as long as you commit and dedicate everything to its costly layaway plan.

I agree with Paul when He wrote "*let God be true but every man a liar* (Romans 3:4)."

Do you believe Jesus when He said no man has seen God at any time? Or Joseph who claims to have seen Him in a body of flesh and bone?

Do you believe Jesus when He said God is a Spirit? Or do you believe Joseph who said God has a body of flesh and bone?

Listen, let's be frank here: If you are LDS and you have done ANY independent thinking at all, you know you have been asked to buy into a lot of very sketchy stuff: God appearing in a body; golden plates buried in a hill; ancient papyri written by the hand of Abraham; the secret polygamy of the founders; Mountain Meadows massacre; blacks and the priesthood; and pagan temple rites. I know what has gone through your heads. I've been there. I know you have looked around and wondered. I know you have doubted. And you should doubt! Give yourself the chance to know truth, to know Jesus and to have Him in your life.

The biggest claim to scriptural support that LDS use to show that God has a body of flesh and bone – aside from Joseph saying that he saw Him – is the Bible passage that says,

> Genesis 1:26. *Let us make man in our own image.*

Obviously God must have a body for us to be made in His image, right? We will begin an examination of that claim.

The next thing I want you to consider is why, according to God's Word, Jesus came to earth.

> Isaiah 40:5. *And* ***the glory of the LORD shall be revealed****, and all flesh shall see it together: for the mouth of the LORD hath spoken it.*

> John 1:14. *And the Word* [JESUS] *was made flesh, and dwelt among us, (and* ***we beheld his glory, the glory as of the only begotten of the Father,****) full of grace and truth.*

> Galatians 4:4. *But when the fulness of the time was come, God sent forth his Son, made of a woman,* ***made under the law.***

> Colossians 2:9. *For in him dwelleth* ***all the fulness of the Godhead*** *bodily.*

> 1 Timothy 3:16. *And without controversy great is the mystery of godliness:* ***God was manifest in the flesh,*** *justified in the Spirit, seen of angels, preached unto the Gentiles, believed on in the world, received up into glory.*

You see, Jesus came from a pre-existent life – *as God*, the Creator of all things, and subjected Himself to this world by taking on a body of flesh, and REVEALING TO US the invisible God. Within Him dwells all the fullness of the Godhead bodily (Colossians 2:9). He was God Who took on flesh, and He subjected Himself to the will of the Father, Who, as a Spirit, dwells in places we can only imagine. This Father is not visible by man, for we are taught that:

> John 1:18. ***No man hath seen God*** *at any time; the only begotten Son, which is in the bosom of the Father, he hath declared him.*
>
> John 5:37. *And the Father himself, which hath sent me, hath borne witness of me. Ye have neither heard his voice at any time,* ***nor seen his shape.***

Speaking of God the Father, Paul writes,

> 1 Timothy 1:17. *Now unto the King eternal, immortal,* ***invisible,*** *the only wise God, be honour and glory for ever and ever. Amen.*
>
> 1 Timothy 6:16. [He] ***only*** *hath immortality, dwelling in the light which no man can approach unto;* ***whom no man hath seen, nor can see:*** *to whom be honour and power everlasting.*

Finally, to the third point. The Author of Hebrews writes that,

> Hebrews 12:29. … *our God is a consuming fire.*

With just the *idea* that the writer of Hebrews might be right, I want you to imagine the universe. When we take our last breath, the invisible part of us – our soul and spirit – departs this physical realm. Jesus took His body with Him because He is going to return with that body. And we will someday, as creations, be resurrected into a perfect physical form. But the *invisible* God, the *consuming fire*, is not restricted by a six foot tall, three foot wide, tent. Wake up, my brothers and sisters.

Imagine the universe – unimaginably vast! Billions upon billions of objects floating, orbiting, glowing and dying. Some 200 to 400 billion stars and their planets, and thousands of clusters and nebulae in our beautiful galaxy alone. Then step outside at night and hold your hands up to the dark sky. With your thumbs and pointer fingers make a small circle, like a peep-hole. Within that little area, astronomers say that if you could see into deep space with your naked eyes you would be able to observe some 250 galaxies just like ours – some bigger, some smaller – all in that little area between your fingers and thumbs!

Then make a four by three inch opening and really venture out – out into deep space. There are some quarter of a million galaxies in that small segment of sky! All with billions of stars, planets, and nebulae...

And now, imagine God is sitting over all this immense creation, *upholding all things by the word of His power* (Hebrews 1:3), governing all of this, having created it and managing *all* of it – from a body with armpits, testicles, and a set of lungs that can't be used without the right mixture of oxygen!

Come on.

And yet, those scrubbed and trimmed missionaries continue to hit the streets, selling the message that God was once a man, has a body of flesh and bone, and that you too, can become a God if you join the club.

> Psalms 8:4. *What is man, that thou art mindful of him? and the son of man, that thou visitest him?*

But He does visit us – in *Spirit* and in *Truth.*

The LDS, missionaries especially, refer to a number of Biblical passages to support their claims that God has a body of flesh and bone. We've covered these before on the show. In the end, most of them are known *anthropomorphisms*, figures of speech used in Scripture to explain God and His actions in terms understandable to human beings. If the Bible says that God appeared to Moses (that *the LORD spake unto Moses face to face, as a man speaketh unto his friend*; Exodus 33:11) but other passages state unequivocally that *no man has seen God at any time* (John

1:8; 1 John 4:12); and that *God is invisible* (Colossians 1:15); and that *God is a spirit* (John 4:24); then we must conclude that we are reading too much literal physicality into those passages that speak of God in anthropomorphic terms.

I am going to present to you a Biblical defense of the Christian concept called the Trinity, a teaching that the LDS strongly condemn AND greatly mock as it is found in the Christian faith.

There are several Bible passages Mormons and their missionaries use in an attempt to disprove the reality of the Triune God. We'll highlight the biggies in a moment. Out of all the Christian teachings that the LDS have the hardest time embracing, the Trinity tops the list. There are a number of reasons for this:

First, it has been crammed into their heads that God the Father has a body. This teaching is solely the result of Joseph Smith.

Second, they have been taught that the word Trinity is not in the Bible, that the concept was the result of a council of men in a place called Nicea, and that only the "true" gospel and Church of Mormonism, restored through Joseph Smith, possesses the correct concept of God.

Third, Mormonism's more advanced teachings on the eternality of matter, an eternal regression of Gods, and the idea that God was once a man fortifies around each member a wall of resistance against accepting the Trinity.

However, the number one reason Latter-day Saints can't or won't entertain or embrace the idea of three Persons in one God is because it is *not comprehensible to them*.

This is a very important factor. You see, if the eternal God is not comprehensible to the finite Mormon mind, then the finite Mormon mind will find something that IS comprehensible and make it doctrine. Joseph brought heaven, including even the eternal God, down to earth and supplied us with all the answers.

I don't like the word Trinity and I don't like the term Tri-unity or any other man-made word. I like *God.* But for consistency's sake I'll be using the word Trinity. Before so doing, I want to make a few things clear.

First, in giving you my best defense of the concept of the three-in-one God, I am not going to resort to those cute little man-made illustrations like the "egg-yolk-shell" or the "steam-ice-water" favorites. So please don't call and suggest them. They fail under scrutiny. Besides, God tells us that no one is like Him or equal unto Him (Isaiah 40:25), so to try and compare Him to something with which we are already familiar is just foolish. There is *NO* other being like Him.

Secondly, it is important for you to understand, my LDS friends, that in order to truly apprehend a viable, working knowledge of the Trinity, you have to read the entire Bible WITH regenerated eyes.

> 1 Corinthian 2:14. *But the natural* [unregenerated] ***man receiveth not the things of the Spirit** of God: for they are foolishness unto him:* ***neither can he know them, because they are spiritually discerned.***

Merely reading the Bible alone won't do it. Being born-again alone won't typically do it. You must have and do both, with eyes willing to see and ears willing to hear.

Third, the Bible supports and teaches the doctrine of three Persons in one God. This was not a product of Nicea or of men formulating a doctrine from nothing. Men of God formulated the doctrine using the Bible as their text and they did so to offset heresies (like Arianism) which were cropping up and taking hold on weaker believers.

Fourth, because some Christians explain the Trinity in faulty, unbiblical terms does not mean the Trinity doctrine is faulty. It simply means you are speaking to Christians who do not know or understand the Word.

And this brings me to a final point. Be very careful with feeling victorious because you have a belief in the make-up of God that can be qualified, quantified, and readily explained in humanistic terms. In some areas of life, having all the answers is highly indicative of your having been duped. Groucho Marx once said, “I would never want to belong to a club that would have me as a member.” Similarly, I would never want to worship, trust or rely upon a God whom I could completely comprehend in my little mind.

So on with a case for – and a defense of –the One God, Who is three-in-one, or what Christians refer to as the “Holy Trinity.”

To begin, every one of the three members of the Trinity – Father, Son, Holy Spirit – is called “God” in Scripture.

Speaking of the Father, Jesus stated:

> John 6:27. *...for him hath* ***God the Father*** *sealed.*

Speaking of the Son, Paul wrote that He was:

> 1 Timothy 3:16. ***God*** *... manifest* ***in the flesh.***

In recounting of Ananias lying to the Holy Spirit, Peter said:

> Acts 5:3-4. *Why hath Satan filled thine heart to* ***lie to the Holy Ghost*** *... why hast thou conceived this thing in thine heart? thou hast not lied unto men, but* ***unto God.***

Likewise, the Word describes each as Creator:

- the Father creates, Isaiah 64:8

- the Son creates, John 1:3,
- the Holy Spirit creates, Genesis 1:2;

... each as Omnipresent:

- the Father is everywhere, 1 Kings 8:27,
- the Son is everywhere, Matthew 18:20,
- the Holy Spirit is everywhere, Psalms 139:7-10;

... and each as Omniscient:

- the Father knows all, 1 John 3:20
- the Son knows all, John 16:30
- the Holy Spirit knows all, 1 Corinthians 2:10-11.

The Word also ascribes, to each, the resurrection of Jesus:

- the Son raises Himself, John 10:17-18
- the Father raises Jesus, Ephesians 1:19-20
- the Holy Spirit raises Jesus, Romans 8:11;

... and the indwelling of believers:

- the Father indwells, Ephesians 4:6
- the Son indwells, Ephesians 3:17
- the Holy Spirit indwells, 2 Timothy 1:14.

(Keep in mind that each of the above descriptions is supported by multiple Biblical verses; I'm merely citing one for each in order to be brief.)

Now, understanding the *general names* of God is also important to understanding His nature. When we read "*God,*" the most common name for Deity in the English Old Testament, it is translated from the Hebrew word *Elohim*. Elohim is a noun meaning God and is not necessarily a proper noun (i.e., it can refer to pagan gods as well as to the real God.) It is the plural of *el*: adding an *-im* ending in the Hebrew is like adding an "s" in English. It is NOT God's name, but would be akin to the word captain or general in English.

There is another name in Hebrew which is particularly assigned to God as His special or proper name, the four letters, *YHWH*, sometimes written Yahweh. This name has not been pronounced by the Jews because of the great sacredness of the divine name. Therefore, it has been consistently translated "LORD" (all capital letters) in the English Old Testament. It is believed the pronunciation is "*Yahway*," which has been anglicized to "Jehovah," but this pronunciation is not certain.

This is the NAME OF GOD.

It's referred to as the *tetragrammaton* and is most sacred to the Jews, too sacred to be spoken aloud. It consists of only four consonants without any vowels or vowel markings. Whenever we read the word LORD in the English Old Testament, we are reading the translation of the same word used for GOD'S NAME in Hebrew: YHWH.

Finally, there is the word "Lord" (upper and lower case), which comes from the Hebrew word *adon*. Adon means *one possessed of absolute control*. It denotes a master, as of slaves (Genesis 24:18), or a ruler of his subjects (Genesis 45:8-9), or a husband, as lord of his wife (Genesis 18:12). The plural form of this Hebrew word is *adonai*, and whenever the title *Adonai* has been used for God, it is translated "Lord," referring to one who has absolute control.

The LDS maintain that the name Jehovah is the personal name for Jesus alone and the name Elohim is the personal name for God the Father. However, there are plenty of references, some of which we saw earlier, in the Old and New Testaments which assign traits and characteristics of Elohim to the person Jesus (whom the LDS call Jehovah) and plenty of references where the name Jehovah is assigned to the Father.

There is TOTAL consistency in the Christian application of these names. There are inconsistencies and confusion in the LDS redefinition of these Holy names. I'm NOT going to take the time here tonight, but do a little research for yourself on the names of God.

Part 2

Now, I hope and pray you're still here after all that because now I want to really get to the heart of the matter.

In Deuteronomy 6:4-9, we can still read the great *Shema* (which is Hebrew for "hear") of the Jewish nation: their repeated declaration of Who God is and how He is different from all the gods of the heathen nations, which begins:

> Deuteronomy 6:4. *Hear, O Israel: The LORD our God is one LORD.*

OR, in Hebrew,

> *Shama Yisra'el: Y'hovah, 'elohiym 'echad Y'hovah!*

Hear O Israel: Jehovah, our Elohim, is one Jehovah!

The New Testament reaffirms this when it says:

> 1 Corinthians 8:4. *There is none other God than One.*

When He was asked *Which is the first commandment of all?* Jesus replied by citing the great *Shema*. He said,

> Mark 12:29. *The first of all the commandments is, Hear, O Israel; The Lord our God is one Lord...*

To get a better grasp on this One God, let me take you back to the time before Jesus was born. Did you know that God was not spoken of as Triune Father, Son, and Holy Spirit before the birth of Jesus? Did you know that God, in the Old Testament, would constantly affirm – over and over and over again - that He was God and there was NONE beside, before, or after Him?

Did you know – NOW LISTEN, MY LDS FRIENDS – did you know that out of the entire Old Testament, there are only three verses – THREE – that even refer to God in terms of being a "father," and that only ONE of those verses speaks of Him as God the Father with a capital *F*?! (And wait until you hear the verse that uses Father with a capital *F*.) But let me explain God in Old Testament terms.

In the Old Testament, God is typically described as One God and is *not* differentiated into Father, Son and Holy Spirit. (One God, but certainly plural in nature because in Genesis, God said, "let *us* make man in *our* own image." But never forget, there are plenty of passages that refer to God as One and as only One!) But then, Jesus comes to earth! Now imagine for a minute that Jesus does not call Himself, and neither do His followers call Him, the "Son of God," but instead He calls Himself "God." How much explaining do you suppose He would have had to do every time He prayed?

"So, Jesus, if you're God, duh, who are you praying to? Huh? Huh? Huh?"

So He is called the Son of God. Now this title was a title that made Him *equal to God* (John 5:18), but it also shows Him, having taken on a body of flesh, to be subject to the Father of our spirits. And He represents to us the relationship we can have with the Father of our spirits once we have been born again.

Jesus took upon Himself a body of flesh and blood and condescended below all things; in this state He subjected Himself completely to the will of the Father – the Father who was not generally called or known as *Father* prior to Jesus appearing.

Now listen to the ONLY verse in the Old Testament – a Messianic prophecy – where God is described as the Father with a capital *F*.

LISTEN, all you people who deny the oneness of God!

LISTEN, all you people who say Jesus was not *the* God!

LISTEN, all you people who love to place yourselves next to Jesus!

LISTEN to the words of God through the prophet Isaiah, who was speaking prophetically about the condescension of God:

> Isaiah 9:6. *For unto us a child is born, unto us a son is given: and the government shall be upon his shoulder: and his name shall be called Wonderful, Counsellor,* ***The mighty God, The everlasting Father,*** *The Prince of Peace.*

The Son and the Father, along with the Holy Spirit, are one God. The New Testament is full of supportive passages of the oneness of God which has nothing to do with being "one in purpose."

> 1 John 5:7. *For there are three that bear record in heaven, the Father, the Word, and the Holy Ghost: and these three are one.*

Listen to what Jesus said about Himself:

> John 14:7. *If ye had known me, ye should have known my Father also: and from henceforth ye know him, and have seen him.*

Now the LDS smugly pull several instances from the Bible to support their philosophy that the Father and the Son and the Holy Spirit are not *ONE God*, as God Himself says; but rather are *one in purpose:* two separate gods in physical bodies and one god-to-be in spirit.

The first was brought up to me by the woman on the plane I referred to earlier: when Jesus was baptized by John the Baptist. A voice came from heaven saying (Matthew 3:17; Mark 1:9-11), "*this is my beloved Son in whom I am well pleased,*" and the Holy Spirit descended like a dove.

If we simply look at all the evidence presented, we have no problem understanding that this occurred because God the Son submitted Himself to all things in the flesh, according to the will of the Father, as our example and as a perfect propitiation for sin. He submitted Himself entirely to the will of God the Father and the total influence of God the Holy Spirit:

> John 5:30. *I can of mine own self do nothing: as I hear, I judge: and my judgment is just; because* ***I seek not mine own will, but the will of the Father*** *which hath sent me.*

> Galatians 1:4. [Our Lord Jesus Christ] *gave himself for our sins, that he might deliver us from this present evil world,* ***according to the will of God and our Father***

Where's the issue?

The second example they use occurs when Stephen was being stoned, where Luke writes

> Acts 7:55. *But he* [Stephen], *being full of the Holy Ghost, looked up stedfastly into heaven, and saw the glory of God, and Jesus standing on the right hand of God…*

Oh, this just excites LDS attackers of the Trinity, who are unaware of the blinders over their spiritual eyes!

Read the passage again:

> "But he, being full of the Holy Ghost…"

SO first of all, the Holy Spirit was present within Stephen, who was "*FULL*" – i.e., filled by His Presence ...

> *"...looked up stedfastly into heaven, and saw the glory of God..."*

And he saw the *GLORY* of *GOD*! He didn't see God with a body of flesh and bone, but rather Stephen saw God's Shekinah (in Hebrew, *Sh'cheenah*) glory, blasting infernally into the eternities. Why do I say that? Because the Word has already made it clear that *no man has ever seen God the Father...*

> *"...and Jesus standing on the right hand of God...*

Jesus standing, in His body, at the right hand of God's glory. There is nothing inconsistent in this passage with the construct of the Holy Trinity! Nothing.

Now sometimes the LDS will say "*How was Jesus on God's right hand?*" The "right hand" of God was, and is, a way to say that Jesus has the Father's full power and authority, *NOT* that the glory of God has an actual right hand!

Two more.

In the Lord's intercessory prayer with His apostles, we read Jesus' words:

> John 17:22. *And the glory which thou gavest me I have given them; that they may be one, even as we are one: I in them, and thou in me, that they may be made perfect in one; and that the world may know that thou hast sent me, and hast loved them, as thou hast loved me.*

The missionaries love to say in the face of this passage, "*How could the disciples be one as God and Jesus are one if they were all in different bodies? They couldn't, right? Therefore they must be one in purpose, right? And therefore God and Jesus are one in purpose, not one God!*"

The oneness of God is a oneness of Spirit, a unity of Spirit. God the Father is Spirit. God the Holy Spirit is Spirit. And the

Spirit within the body of Jesus is Spirit, Who also was Spirit before His incarnation. The pre-existent God, the Old Testament God, was one God: three Persons, of one Spirit Essence! Jesus then condescended *for us* and put on a body of flesh, but the Spiritual oneness of God is plainly made manifest here in this passage.

Let me give you one more passage, from the New Testament, which validates all I've said relative to the Trinity, relative to Jesus being God in the flesh, and relative to Mormonism's twist on these Biblical truths. It's almost as though Paul were writing directly to Mormons:

> Colossians 2:8-9. *Beware lest any man spoil you through philosophy and vain deceit, after the tradition of men, after the rudiments of the world, and not after Christ. For in him dwelleth all the fulness of the Godhead bodily.*

Come to the truth, the truth of Christ Jesus, and be set free from the vain deceits of the traditions of a man, my friends.

THEN THERE IS EVEN MORE →

> Deuteronomy 4:35. *Unto thee it was shewed, that thou mightest know that the LORD he is God; there is none else beside him.*

> Isaiah 43:10. ... *before me there was no God formed, neither shall there be after me.*

> Isaiah 44:6. *Thus saith the LORD the King of Israel, and his redeemer the LORD of hosts; I am the first, and I am the last; and beside me there is no God.*

Jesus reaffirmed the truth of the great *Shema*: that the Lord our God is One (Mark 12:29). Paul repeats this truth (1 Corinthians 8:4), as did Jude (1:25), James (2:19), and John the Beloved (1 John 5:20).

Upon this first foundation we MUST stand: there is, there always has been, and there only will be, ONE God. One.

Maybe we could approach this pillar of Truth in some other directions to give it some depth. We have three options regarding God's existence:

- There is NO God.
- There are many gods.
- There is One God.

Which position does the most ancient and reliable book, the Bible, support? And what position tends one toward the greatest allegiance to Deity?

No God certainly flies in the face of the Bible, nature, and existence.

Many gods is a philosophical nightmare for how can a person love, worship, and trust MANY gods? He can't. All that teaching does is muddy the clear waters of a straight shot relationship with the Almighty.

In closing, ask yourself a question relative to the LDS position about God. First, what would be the draw to henotheism, the belief and worship of a single god while accepting the existence or possible existence of other deities? Why would a Latter-day Saint embrace the notion that God has a father, who has a father god, who has a father god? Simply put: PRIDE. Doctrines that make God more understandable are appealing to our flesh. I mean, if I can understand the nature of God, I am someone rather *...ahem...* advanced in my theology, aren't I? *Pride.*

Additionally, henotheism in the context of Mormonism's other teachings on eternal progression allows men and women to believe that they, too, are headed toward godhood. Again, pride.

It's tantalizing, but completely and totally oppositional to the true and living God as defined by Himself, in His Word, the Bible: He is the First and the Last, uncreated, without family, the Alpha, the Omega, the original Source of ALL things.

Latter-day Saints are SO indoctrinated with their distinct idea of "God" being the Father and Jesus *only* being the Son and that they both have physical bodies of flesh and bone that the uniqueness and certainty of Trinitarian doctrine is treated by them as ridiculous.

Part 3

Latter-day Saints have been coached throughout their lifetimes with the teaching that this concept of One God in three Persons is the construct of creedal influence emanating from Nicea. As a result, Mormonism claims that truth needed to be "restored" to the earth, which would include the "true" understanding of God and His make-up.

The late LDS prophet Gordon B. Hinckley claims that Mormonism has "*a perfect knowledge of the nature of God which came through the first vision of the Prophet Joseph* ("First Presidency Message: Inspirational Thoughts," *Ensign*, February 2007)." He also said that, "*when Joseph left the grove that day, he knew more of the nature of God than all the learned ministers of the gospel of all the ages* ("Crown of gospel is upon our heads," LDS *Church News*, June 20, 1998)."

For Gordon B. Hinckley to be right, I would strongly suggest that the Bible is wrong. I would also suggest that the creeds established at Nicea and other places were ecclesiastical in nature and were a Biblical response to heresies which were cropping up like weeds in the church.

An unfortunate result of all this has been a misconstruction of what the Trinity is from both the LDS side and even in some cases, the Christian. And while we covered this topic earlier, let's see if I can do a better job of it this time.

If we go back to one of the Christian definitions of the Trinity, it allows us to see some basic tenets of the doctrine. (Please note: for a more detailed treatment of this topic, see a website called ConcernedChristians.com, from which much of the following is taken. I gratefully acknowledge the use of their excellent presentation.)

Listen:

Within the one Being that is God, there exists eternally three co-equal and co-eternal persons, namely, the Father, the Son, and the Holy Spirit (James White, *The Forgotten Trinity*, page 26).

Or,

In the nature of the one God there are three eternal...persons, and these three are equal (A. H. Strong, *Systematic Theology*, page 144).

The first definition begins, "*Within the one Being that is God...*"

From the Bible, Christians know and trust the idea that there is One God – ONE. *MONOTHEISM*. Do you believe and accept MONOTHEISM? It is the doctrine that there is one God, only One God; that there has only ever been One God; that there will only ever be One God; and that there has never been a God before, during or after this One God. As we discussed, all of Christianity and Judaism agree with the great *Shema*:

> Deuteronomy 6:4. *Hear, O Israel: The LORD our God is One Lord.*

Faithful Jews recite this prayer every single morning.

Now Latter-day Saints maintain that while they agree there is one God *with whom they have to do*, there *are* other Gods out there, including God's father. As we stated previously, this is called *henotheism.*

Are true Christians monotheistic or can a true Biblical Christian be henotheistic?

Latter-day Saints have attempted to say that the great *Shema* allows for henotheism. But in it, the Hebrew word for one is *echad*, referring to "somebody who has no family," and, applied to Yahweh, this means He does not belong to any family of gods. This aspect distinguishes Him from all other gods. Furthermore, the confession that Yahweh is a Single One was directed against the concept of divine families common to many pagan religions. (C. J. Labuschagne, *The Incomparability of Yahweh in the Old Testament*, page 137 as cited in Paul Owens, "Monotheism, Mormonism, and the New testament Witness," *The New Mormon Challenge*, page 274.)

And what does the Bible have to say about there being just one God? Is this point obscurely hinted at in the Word? Or does God make it plainly clear that He is truly the I AM: the First, the Last, the beginning of all things, and the end?

Listen:

> Deuteronomy 4:35. *Unto thee it was shewed, that thou mightest know that the LORD he is God; there is none else beside him.*
>
> Isaiah 43:10. ... *before me there was no God formed, neither shall there be after me.*
>
> Isaiah 44:6. *Thus saith the LORD the King of Israel, and his redeemer the LORD of hosts; I am the first, and I am the last; and beside me there is no God.*

> Isaiah 46:9. *I am God and there is none like me.*

There is ONLY one BEING: GOD.

Within that one Being – God – *there exists eternally three co-equal and co-eternal persons.*

In the his book *The Forgotten Trinity*, James White writes:

> When speaking of the Trinity, we need to realize that we are talking about one what and three who's. The one what is the Being or essence of God; the three who's are the Father, Son and Spirit. We dare not mix up the what's and the who's regarding the Trinity (page 27).

Bible scholar Norman Geisler wrote (*A Philosophical Defense of the Trinity*):

> God is unity of essence with plurality of persons. Each person is different, yet they share a common nature.

Furthermore, each of the persons within the ONE Being that is God is fully divine. White continues:

> Each fully shares the one being that is God. The Father is not 1/3 of God, the Son 1/3 of God, the Spirit 1/3 of God. Each is fully God, coequal with the others, and that eternally (page 27).

Now, the three Persons of God do *function* differently. But this does not make any of them inferior to any other. Here is where the LDS think they get the upper hand. Not understanding the three-in-One nature of God, and somehow coming to believe that Christians believe in the heresy of *modalism* (the non-Biblical, denial of the Trinity which states that God is a single person revealing Himself in three modes, or forms) the LDS will often ask questions like, *"Well, if the Trinity is correct, who did Jesus pray to?"*

The Father, of course.

But back to the idea that, as human beings, we are created in the image of God. Since we have seen clearly the Biblical teaching that *God is invisible* and clearly *we are not,* then being made in the image of God must mean something different than that our bodies are as His. We understand that, we too, are three-in-one beings.

We are body; we are soul; we are spirit.

> 1 Thessalonians 5:23. *And the very God of peace sanctify you wholly; and I pray God your whole* ***spirit*** *and* ***soul*** *and* ***body*** *be preserved blameless unto the coming of our Lord Jesus Christ.*

Now the Son was subject to the Father as He took on flesh and became Man on our behalf JUST AS OUR BODIES should be – *were meant to be, created to be* – subject to our spirits*!*

The LDS would have the world believe that being made in God's image means that we look like God and that the eternal almighty God of the universe, creator of all things, overseer of all things, pulls lint out of His belly button and trims His nose hair, particularly when heavenly mother starts complaining.

Come on.

You cannot reconcile Scripture to support this pagan notion. Pagan doctrines have always taken their gods and put them in human form! Look at the Roman and Greek gods: Zeus, Prometheus, all of them, men and women.

But NOT the God of Abraham, Isaac, and Jacob; ask any faithful Jew. Ask a Rabbi who knows Hebrew and studies the Talmud, "Is God a man? Does He have a body of flesh and bones?" Then sit back and watch the sky light up with scriptural fireworks.

But let's get back to this idea of three in one (and by the way, it is NEVER one in three – that would be the modalism we spoke of above, where some have tried to say that the Father can become the Son and the Son can become the Holy Spirit and One God moves around in three forms. Not so.)

Three in one.

Now the LDS missionaries and the apostles and men they call modern-day prophets have said that it was corrupt Christian creeds that formulated the idea of the Trinity. Christians know creeds are all based on sound exegetical readings. If they weren't, true Christians would *never* have accepted them as reliable.

Grab a pencil and jot these down. Did you know (again, keep in mind that there are multiple Biblical references to support these; I'm citing just one for each) ...

... that the Father, the Son and the Holy Spirit are all described in the Word as being the *Truth* or *True*?

- The Father is True, John 7:28
- The Son is True, Revelation 3:7
- The Holy Spirit is Truth, 1 John 5:6

... that *all three* are called Lord?

- The Father is Lord, Romans 11:3
- The Son is Lord, Luke 2:11
- The Holy Spirit is Lord, 2 Corinthians 3:17

... that *all three* are said to be *Eternal* or to possess *Immortality*? (ETERNALITY – THEY WERE NOT CREATED LIKE YOU AND ME – EVER!)

- The Father is Everlasting, Romans 16:26
- The Son possesses Immortality, 1 Timothy 6:16
- The Spirit is Eternal, Hebrews 9:14

… that *all three* are called Almighty?

- The Father is Almighty, Genesis 17:1
- The Son is Almighty, Revelation 1:8
- The Spirit is Almighty, Job 33:4

… that *all three* are said to have Power?

- The Father has Power, Jeremiah 32:17
- The Son has Power, Hebrews 1:3
- The Spirit has Power, Luke 1:35

… that Holy or Holy One is a title given to all three?

- The Father is the Holy One, Habakkuk 3:3
- The Son is the Holy One, Acts 3:14
- The Holy Spirit is, well, *Holy*, 1 Thessalonians 4:8

Holiness.

There is a reason why Isaiah, when speaking of God, wrote

> Isaiah 6:3. *Holy, holy, holy, is the LORD of hosts: the whole earth is full of his glory.*
>
> Holy Father!
> Holy Son!
> Holy Spirit!

"Holy, Holy, Holy" describes three-in-One – because Isaiah was a committed monotheist!

Prior to His ascension, Jesus said to His disciples,

> Matthew 28:19. *Go ye therefore, and teach all nations, baptizing them in the* **name** *of the Father, and of the Son, and of the Holy Ghost.*

The "*name*" of God – not names, but the name.

If there were three separate gods it would be *names*. There is one God, in three Persons – Father, Son, and Holy Spirit.

As a side but applicable note, consider these interesting points which also lend tremendous support to the apostles' notion of one God in three persons:

> Among the Jews, the doctrinal controversy was always about who *was* the truc Messiah (as opposed to the doctrinal controversy among the Gentiles, which has always been about the true nature of God). The apostles of the Lord, who had the authority to declare this, thought it was therefore proper among the Jews to baptize in the name of Jesus *alone* (Acts 2:38) so that He might be vindicated as the true Messiah and the Jews might accept Him as such – they already acknowledged God the Father and His Holy Spirit! They were therefore identified through John's baptism with the true Messiah – Christ!

But among the Gentiles, they were instructed to baptize *in the name* of the Father, and of the Son, and of the Holy Ghost (Matthew 28:19), so that the Gentile believer might be thereby instructed in the doctrine of the true nature of God!

When the Jews "baptized" (in Hebrew, *mikveh*, ceremonial cleansing) proselytes, they did so in the name of the Eternal God, the Ruler, the Sanctifier, the Creator, the Sustainer – that is, into the profession of God, Whom we know to be the Father.

The Father has revealed Himself in the old covenant; the Son is revealed in the new covenant, by coming in human flesh, by His miracles, doctrine, resurrection and ascension; and the Holy Spirit is revealed since Pentecost by His gifts, His indwelling the hearts of believers, and His miracles. So the doctrine of the ever-blessed Trinity was revealed by degrees to full maturity, until, at Pentecost, the entirety of God was made manifest – and available – to all!

Pretty cool, huh?

The Word also tells us that the Father, Son, and Holy Spirit all have special functions – which naturally leads our little minds to split them up into separate beings. The Father planned salvation, the Son accomplished it on the cross and at His resurrection, and the Holy Spirit applies it to the lives of people who believe, in their hearts, in the Lord Jesus Christ.

There may be situations which make the oneness of God difficult to understand, like when Jesus submits to the will of the Father, and when the Holy Spirit glorifies and testifies of the Son. But, in my limited scope, I see this as no different than my body subjecting itself to my spirit, and my soul pushing my body to go beyond my comfort zone. When we reach that point in our understanding when we can not comprehend the great and Holy God, we should, at that point, do what Thomas did when he saw the wounds in the flesh of our Lord Jesus Christ: worship Him.

> John 20:28. *And Thomas answered and said unto him, My Lord and my God.*

My Lord and my God.

In Greek, *Kyrios mou kai ho Theos mou.*

Literally, My Jehovah and my Elohim.

And Jesus – a resurrected Being – did not correct him.

But don't believe me – really. Listen to what I have to say, but go to God and ask: *Lord, reveal yourself to me. I want to know you. Open my eyes. Open my ears. Open my heart. I want to know you first with my spirit, then with my soul, and someday in my body.*

Part 4

One of the first responses – juvenile responses – you will receive from the LDS defender is that the word Trinity is not in the Bible!

We'll let's first use their logic and apply it to their claims, okay? *New and Everlasting Covenant* isn't in the Bible. *Pre-mortal existence* isn't in the Bible. *Forever families* isn't in the Bible.

Want me to go on?

Look, we all understand codifying words, don't we? We understand and use words to help all minds large and small express and understand concepts that are perhaps too broad or complex to use easily in day to day life.

Get over this one.

The idea, the concept of the Trinity is all over the Bible – all over it. But I have to be honest. You probably won't see it until you possess spiritually regenerated eyes. Ask ANYONE who has come out of Mormonism and into Biblical Christianity and all of them will express how the make-up of God became CLEAR to them once they allowed the Lord to change their hearts.

Another argument the LDS will use to attack the Biblical truth of one God in three Persons is by using statements and situations in the Bible that supposedly prove that the Trinitarian notion is false. There are a few popular ones.

One is when, John reports, Jesus Himself said,

> John 14:28. *The Father is greater than I.*

"*See!!!*" they will say. "*Different people! Jesus wasn't God. He was just His Son.*"

Again, this is the problem with taking any single, specific verse and using it as a proof-text for the entire Bible.

Interestingly, Jesus also claims in John 8:58 that He is "*I Am,*" which caused the Jews to take up stones to stone Him. But for what? Making Himself out to be God!

He also said He was "*equal with God* (John 10:33)"; He received worship from birth in Bethlehem to glorious resurrection (Matthew 2:11; John 20:28); and He told Philip that, having seen Him, he had seen the Father (John 14:8-9).

But aside from all these instances, we still have the greatest foundation of all upon which we stand: there is either one God, or there is no God, or there are many gods. The Bible fully supports One. Therefore, with Jesus being worshipped, being called God, and making Himself equal to God, the Trinity is the ONLY ACCEPTABLE, CONTEXTUAL theology, the only answer to the question, *Who is God?*, that takes *all* the Biblical revelation into account.

Another response, which is similar to the last, is the LDS citing that Jesus prayed to the Father, that the Father spoke to Him out of Heaven, or that the Bible proves His subordination to Him. While these references are all correct, they are not correctly understood. They take into account the "Three-ness" of the God and leave out the "One-ness." When we forget any one of the following Biblical facts regarding God, we run into this type of errant reasoning to which the LDS missionaries and defenders resort:

> There is One God.
> There are Three Persons.
> They are co-equal and co-eternal, but with different roles.

Remove or alter ANY of these Biblical facts from your mind, and you will begin to make inane comments, like, "*Was Jesus praying to Himself?*"

Again,

> There is ONE God.
> There are THREE Persons.

They are EQUAL, but with different roles.

Now, these three "rules of thumb" may lead us to another classic LDS response: "*I don't understand this God. How can I worship something I don't fully understand?*"

My response is, "How can you worship something your little mind can comprehend?"

In reality, this point perfectly illustrates the difference between the true Christian heart and the True LDS. A Biblical Christian's heart would say, "*God is so great, so awesome, so powerful, that I, a sinner, a man of flesh with a 3-pound brain, will never comprehend Him, His Power, or His Love.*" But the LDS heart replies, "*I am so advanced in my righteousness and life choices, so steeped in my possession of the spirit, and by the power of the priesthood that I hold, I am able to fairly easily grasp the nature of God – because when all is said and done, he's just like me! He's just a little farther along in his progression!*"

Get it?

Two more common LDS responses to the Trinity. They say, "*The trinity doesn't make sense.*"

In response to this assertion, C. S. Lewis wrote in *Mere Christianity* (page 165):

> If Christianity was something we were making up, of course we would make it easier. But it is not. We cannot compete, in simplicity, with people who are inventing religions. How could we? We are dealing with fact. Of course anyone can be simple if he has no facts to bother about.

Let me repeat that last line:

> *... anyone can be simple if he has no facts to bother about.*

Simply because the egocentric notion that God was once a man, who has a father, who has a father, who has a father and who sired Jesus as any man would sire a son is easier to accept and understand does NOT mean it is correct! The notion of the Trinity is not irrational, nor is it contradictory. It is unique, as we should expect from a God Who tells us that there is no one *even like Him* (Isaiah 46:5)!

Finally, displaying more sophomoric thinking, some LDS defenders will use the rudimentary elements of arithmetic to prove their multiplicity of Gods. "*Doesn't one God the Father, plus one God the Son, plus one God the Holy Spirit equal THREE Gods? Huhhh huhhh huhhh huuhh?????*"

God is a triune Being (*three-in-one; constituting a trinity in unity)*, not a triplex Being (*threefold)*. He is a single house, more akin to a foundation, walls and a roof rather than three houses connected to each other. One Essence. One Being. One Deity.

Norman Geisler said (*Baker Encyclopedia of Christian Apologetics*, page 732):

> There is no more mathematical problem in conceiving the Trinity than there is in understanding 1 cubed [or 1 x 1 x 1, which equals One].

In the end of it all, let me assure you that as a Christian, you have far more to stand on relative to the Trinity than anything the LDS would say to criticize it. Let me tell you why.

First, as we have shown, the Bible supports the codification completely.

But secondly, Mormonism itself, historically and through the Book of Mormon even today, supports the Trinitarian doctrine. Let me explain. I have long maintained that the Book of Mormon is nothing more than a fictional book which borrowed heavily from themes found in the Bible, from Joseph's own community and country, and from his own family situation. This is what makes it, in and of itself, so benign in nearly every way relative to the Bible. Joseph wrote the book early in his life before his theology began to evolve, when he was using the Bible alone as his template: before the women, the power, the money, the fame, and the wildly imaginative mind took over. As these Joseph-centric traits took over, his ideas and notions of God began to change.

But then he faced a problem: the existing teachings in the Book of Mormon.

In 1837, eight years after the first publication, he went back to the book that he supposedly translated by "the gift and power of God" and changed passages that presented the Father and the Son as one God to a description of them as separate beings. This means – now listen to this – this means that Joseph accepted the idea that the book could be changed.

So much for a pure translation.

But Joseph was growing in popularity and I think he grew tired of trying to correct his mistakes. People seemed to accept him and his writings no matter what they said or how much they contradicted each other. So he only "rewrote" doctrine as far as 1 Nephi (11:16, 18, 21, 32; 13:40). Trouble is, the Book of Mormon retained other doctrinal teachings relative to the One-ness of God that Joseph never took the time to fix. In the end, we see that Joseph's later doctrines and teachings about GOD not only conflict with the Bible, they conflict with what he presented as truth when he compiled the Book of Mormon!

My friends, I am not picking on Joseph Smith exclusively. Many,

many a man has left Biblical truth and gone to the fringes of thought. David Koresh began as a believer. Armstrong was once a solid believer. Jim Jones started as a teacher of truth. We see this time and time again.

But Joseph was shot early in his life. And with his body went his growing postulations. Brigham added a bit to the craziness. A few others set it all in concrete.

And now millions embrace it as truth.

> There is One God.
> He is of three Persons.
> They are co-equal and co-eternal, but with different roles.

We call this the Trinity.

❋ ❋ ❋

> "Many Latter-day Saints today – especially the apologists and missionaries – will actually say with clear expressions, 'Yes, we believe we are saved by grace.' In order to understand what they are really saying, you have to take a minute and have them define what they mean by, 'believe,' by 'saved,' and by 'grace.'"

Grace

When it comes to all the beliefs batted around today, what would you say is the number one core issue, belief, or doctrine that makes a Christian a Christian?

I mean there are a number of very, very important doctrines and theologies Christians stand upon, like the make-up of God, the resurrection, the virgin birth, the veracity of Scripture or the Deity of Christ. But what is the main doctrine that separates

Biblical Christians from the rest of the religious world? I would suggest that it is the Biblical understanding and the personal application of God's GRACE, which is our final "G" topic.

A MAJOR part of the mistake people make when seeking to understand the grace of God through reading the Bible is failing to read the Word contextually. Now I don't just mean the verses before and the verses after but the Word as a whole. Anyone can take a verse and build an entire ERRANT belief system on it alone. I am convinced that in order to help people understand grace we must first expose ourselves to a "Biblical primer" on the context of grace as found in the New Testament.

Once we have this foundation poured (as it were) we will all be better prepared to see and hear most New Testament passages from a proper perspective of the grace of God.

Let's begin with an illustration, okay? Bill Clinton was once the United States President. A Democrat if I am not mistaken. He had his administration, his staff, his cabinet, and his political agenda in place. As president, he "dispensed" his approach to governing the nation. Was he the President of the United States? Yes he was. Did he represent U.S. governance? Yes. Did he do it from the White House or the nation's seat of power? Certainly.

When Clinton left the White House there was a shift in the way things his successor – a Republican, George W. Bush – would dispense his approach to governance. But "Dub-ya," like Clinton, was also the President of the United States who represented U.S. governance and did so from the White House. Through his administration, staff, and cabinet he dispensed his approach to governing the nation.

We saw this same transition of different "dispensations" when Jimmy Carter passed the baton (or the buck) to Ronald Reagan.

Getting to the point, in a much grander way, this is what God did when transitioning from the Old Testament to the New: He governed from the same "throne on high" just like Clinton and Dub-ya governed from the same White House, but God employed completely different administrations when it came to the nation of Israel and the Gentile world. What made the difference between Presidents Clinton and Bush, between Presidents Carter and Regan, was what they were "dispensing" out to the people they governed from the White House.

So it is with the difference between what God in the Old Testament dispensed to the nation of Israel and what God in the New Testament dispenses to the Gentiles. From "dispensing" we get the word, *dispensation*. And tonight I am going to speak about the dispensation of the Law and the dispensation of grace.

Now this word gets really touchy because God has always been full of grace and mercy, and He has progressively built upon previous ages (*administrations*, if you will) to accomplish His will, so in this case there really are no true dispensations. But at the same time, prior to Jesus becoming flesh, God dispensed one form of administration to the Jews, the Law; and then after Jesus came He dispensed an entirely new system called grace.

When Moses went up to Mount Sinai, God dispensed TO THE CHILDREN of ISRAEL the Law, and it was administered in three parts:

The Moral Law – What we call the Ten Commandments

The Ritual Law – How to worship, their priesthood, sacrifices, etc. and

The Civil Law – Rules of interaction among members of the community.

This "Law," for the people of God, was in place for a long time.

It was hard, it was never successful at bringing anyone to God (nor was it intended to save), and it long promised a Messiah. Under it, everything was an exchange: do evil, receive evil; do good, receive good. In the end, the Law served to show the nation of Israel their absolute need for a Messiah.

Now here comes the tricky part.

When the Messiah – Jesus – came to earth, His ministry, while He was alive, was to this House of Israel. To be clear, Jesus' physical ministry was NOT to non-Jews. In fact, Matthew, Mark, Luke, and John are an extension, folks, *AN EXTENSION*, of the Old Testament administration. Jesus' words were to the nation of Israel to convince them that He was their promised Messiah.

Certainly, Jesus came in the flesh and died for the sins of the world; but WHILE He was personally here on earth, His ministry was to His brethren, the Jews, and NOT to us Gentiles. Peter, one of the twelve apostles Jesus chose to carry His message forward into the world, was called to preach to this very same nation, the Jews. So when we read what Peter said and did, it was usually, with only a couple of exceptions, to the Jews and reflected what God expected of *them* upon coming to Christ (see Galatians 2:7-8).

Now, while we all know that the Law was fulfilled at the cross, and the LORD paved the way for the gospel to reach all men by the shedding of His blood, none of the gospels nor even the early chapters in the book of Acts ever has God saying, "You no longer have to go to temple;" or "You are free from having to follow a set list of commandments." Those changes took time. In fact, the word "grace" in the sense of people being saved by it and it alone is not even mentioned until mid-way through the book of Acts. Why? Because a change of administration takes time.

Moses gave the Law and God began building upon that toward an expected end. Then when the children of Israel were settled in the promised land, and they had their temple in place on the mount, the expected Messiah arrived. But what did they do with Him in spite of His miracles and fulfilled prophecy?

They killed Him; they crucified Him.

Changes of administration can be very difficult!

So much were the Jews against Jesus as the Messiah that they continued to reject His apostles through much of the book of Acts, where the earliest years of the Christian faith are detailed. So Peter (and remember he was called to preach to the Jews) and the apostles are filled with the Holy Spirit and draw a crowd in chapter two of Acts because they are seemingly "*drunk,*" not with new wine, but with the Spirit. And this crowd consists of whom?

Jews!

Jews from all over the place, gathered there in Jerusalem to celebrate the feast of Pentecost which was a Jewish feast held fifty days after Passover. So these Jews had come from all around the known world, the Roman empire. And soon three thousand were standing before Peter. (Now remember, the grace administration had not yet taken office, folks. But it was moving in quick.) So here is Peter, still calling to the nation of Israel so that as a covenant people they might believe. And in speaking to them, what does he say? He appeals to their history:

> Acts 3:24. *Yea, and all the prophets from Samuel and those that follow after, as many as have spoken, have likewise foretold of these days. Ye are the children of the prophets, and of the covenant which God made with our fathers, saying unto Abraham, And in thy seed shall all the kindreds of the earth be blessed.*

So right there on that ancient ground of their covenant nation, Peter speaks to them directly, according to the administration of their own dispensation of Law, all the while mixing in the fulfillment of their promised Messiah's arrival. He says:

> Acts 2:36. *Therefore let* ***all the house of Israel*** *know assuredly, that God hath made that same Jesus,* ***whom ye have crucified****, both Lord and Christ.*

Under the Law and all it entailed *morally, ritually, and civilly*, they took their promised Messiah, and when He came, they killed Him.

Now let me introduce to you the president of the next administration, as it were. His name is Paul. If we go to the book of Galatians, Paul is speaking with GENTILES, and listen to the approach he uses:

> Galatians 1:3-4. ***Grace be to you*** *and* ***peace from God*** *the Father, and from our Lord Jesus Christ,* ***who gave himself for our sins****, that he might* ***deliver us from this present evil world****, according to the will of God and our Father.*

Peter is telling the Jews that they are *"the children of the prophets who foretold of the Messiah,"* and then he adds that they are, *"the ones who crucified Him,"* while Paul is telling the Gentiles that *"the Lord Jesus Christ gave Himself for our sins to deliver us out of the present world."* Paul would NEVER say to the Gentile world that they were "*the children of the prophets who foretold of the Messiah!*" Instead He tells them Jesus came to save them from sin.

It was a whole different approach because two different administrations were dispensing two very different themes: one theme is couched in Law and the other is couched in grace.

After Peter dispensed his message, Acts chapter 2, Luke records the Jew's response:

Acts 2:37. *Now when they* [the Jews] *heard this, they were pricked in their heart, and said unto Peter and to the rest of the apostles, Men and brethren, what shall we do?*

Now this is key. LISTEN UP HERE: How did Peter respond to these Jews who were standing on a thousand-plus years of covenantal ground?

Acts 2:38. *Then Peter said unto them, Repent, and be baptized* ***every one of you*** *in the name of Jesus Christ for the remission of sins, and ye shall receive the gift of the Holy Ghost.*

Now, well-meaning people all over take this passage of Peter's and they apply it to their Gentile selves as a directive for what *they* must do in order to be saved. *But this is a misapplication of the word of God and a misunderstanding of grace!*

Peter told *these particular people* that they must, *as a nation*, change their minds [repent] about who Jesus was. They had to repent of killing Him, and then submit to being cleansed for sin [which was so vital to all their rituals under the Law]. That is what they were to do in light of the information they had just heard.

But what did Paul, when he was asked the same question, say to the GENTILES (to whom *he* was called to preach and teach) who had no *idea* about a coming Messiah?

When Paul and Silas were in jail in Philippi (Gentile territory), and a great earthquake caused the jail doors to miraculously open and all their chains to be loosed, the keeper of the prison came to them terrified and asked:

Acts 16:30. *Sirs, what must I do to be saved?*

And what did Paul say?

Remember, Peter told the Jews to *REPENT and BE BAPTIZED* in the name of Jesus Christ for the remission of sins, and they would receive the Holy Spirit. But Paul and Silas said something completely different, as different as Carter was from Reagan.

They said:

> Acts 16:31. ***Believe*** *on the Lord Jesus Christ, and* ***thou shalt be saved***...

Repenting and being baptized was the same clarion call that John the Baptist gave to the Jews when preparing the way for them to receive the Messiah. Peter's message was not much different and neither were directed to GENTILES but to the house of Israel. And repenting of their failure under the Law of Moses and being washed clean in water as an outward symbol was part of their administrational demands! Peter told them to do this in order to receive the gift of the Holy Ghost.

But we have the reverse situation occurring in the case of the Gentiles.

When Peter was having one of his only recorded interactions with some Gentiles in the house of Cornelius, he preached to them, and they spontaneously received the Holy Spirit *without baptism*. Peter then said:

> Acts 10:47. *Can any man forbid water, that these should not be baptized,* ***which have received the Holy Ghost*** *as well as we?*

You see, to the Jews under the Law, the order was:

Repent,
Be baptized,

Receive the Gift of the Holy Ghost.

But to the Gentiles the order was and will always be:

Believe,
Receive the Holy Spirit,
Repent,
Be baptized.

Got that?

Once the good news actually got underway and out to the Gentile nations through Paul, we entered into a new dispensation, a dispensation of utter and total grace. So the book of Acts serves as a very transitional book which allows for "the ebb of the Law" to rescind from earth at the same time allowing for "the flow of grace" to commence.

And in the dispensation of grace, God introduced His new administrator to the world. And his name, Saul, was changed to Paul. Just as Moses went up to Mt. Sinai and received the Law, Paul also went to his own Sinai in Arabia for three full years (Galatians 1:17) receiving his message of the implications of this New Covenant not "*of man but by the revelation of Jesus Christ* (Galatians 1:11-12)."

You see, Peter got the other eleven to pick another apostle by casting lots, whose name was Matthias. But God had another choice for whom He wanted to dispense this new administration of grace. And until Paul was chosen, God kept this administration of grace veiled (Ephesians 3:2-6). When people come to understand that Paul was in charge of dispensing a new administration of grace, and that the Law was completely fulfilled in Christ but still used by Peter with the Jews, the light of what grace means and to whom it is applied will begin to shine as bright as the sun. And so will passages about repenting and being baptized when it comes to understanding the "good news" of grace.

We find in the teachings of Paul, things that are not found anywhere else! But what is important to remember is Paul incorporates all that was said and done before into this new administration. For example, when Paul and Silas visited Berea, the believers there made sure that what he taught was supported by Scripture – which for them was the Old Testament – and they concluded that his message passed the test. Paul was not like some upstart who came along and claimed to have revelations that *added to* what had been already given by the Law, the Prophets, Jesus and His apostles; instead he simply advanced what Jesus had completed on the cross to the Gentile world.

God had been secretly moving this message forward since Adam, and step by step it blossomed more and more fully until it was placed in the hands of Paul; he took it all, by revelation from the risen Lord, and opened up a new dispensation of grace to all non-Jews!

Hard as this will be to hear, Peter didn't even fully understand what Paul was teaching, friends! This is why he wrote that Paul's writings contained

> 2 Peter 3:16. … ***some things hard to be understood,*** *which they that are unlearned and unstable wrest, as they do also the other scriptures, unto their own destruction.*

So, after all this, let me try and make this clear:

DISPENSATIONS

Law	Grace
• YWHW	• YESHUA
• Moses	• Paul

• Visited Sinai (Mountain)	• Visited Sinai (Peninsula)
• LAW introduced	• GRACE introduced
• Children of Israel	• Gentiles

THE EFFECT WHEN JESUS CAME TO EARTH

Israelites	Gentiles
• Repent	• Believe
• Be Baptized	• Holy Spirit
• Holy Spirit	• Repent
• Believe	• Baptized

So, Paul was the apostle to the Gentiles. He even says this very thing:

> Romans 11:13. *For I speak to you Gentiles, inasmuch as **I am the apostle of the Gentiles**, I magnify mine office...*

And going to Gentile nations in personal visits and letters, Paul reveals the gospel of grace that is administered to the Gentiles, and though he preaches and teaches the same Savior that Peter teaches – Jesus Christ – his dispensing to the Gentiles has different demands than the dispensing Peter does to the Jews.

This is not contradictory. It is really no different than a change in administrations.

When people take the messages of Peter and combine them with the messages of Paul, soteriological chaos ensues and they will forever be mixed up about the requirements of salvation.

God began changing administrations the moment Jesus was crucified. And it did not happen overnight. But from Paul, we are able to understand with clarity how God would save all who believed on Him through the death of His Son – by grace and grace alone. The Bible is clear on the subject of salvation by grace and grace alone.

In fact, it is really quite stupid for me to even make the comment, *grace and grace alone* because grace is only grace if it is alone. Change it at all – at all – and it is not grace. The clarity of salvation by grace is increased when a view of it is taken in context, studied as a whole, and understood according to what it says from Genesis all the way through Revelation. Because of time constraints we can't give an exhaustive representation, but we can provide a suitable outline.

Salvation by *grace through faith …*

Exists *logically* by virtue of the good news;

Is presented *exhaustively* in the Word;

Is presented *illustratively* in the Word;

Is taught *specifically* by the apostle to the Gentiles, Paul; and

In the end, anyone and everyone who claims Jesus Christ as their Savior will either

a. fall on the side that says they are saved by grace through faith in Him and Him alone

OR

b. believe that there is some other way: an addition to what Jesus did and who He is; a subtraction from what Jesus did or who He is; or they might even remove Him altogether from being THE key to human salvation.

So let's first look at how the concept of grace exists logically due to the finished work of Jesus Christ.

Simply put, when did Jesus suffer for the sins of the World? Around 2000-plus years ago, right? Did He pay for all the sins of the world? Yes, He did. Did He pay for the sins you committed when you were ten years old? Eighteen? How about the sins you committed yesterday, today, tomorrow?

Since Jesus paid for all sin past, present, and future – wiped the slate clean forever more – we cannot say that it is sin per se that keeps us from entering God's kingdom. The SIN has been paid for. What is the only sin then that condemns us? The sin of disbelief.

And the PAYMENT Jesus paid for sin was something we did not have a hand in – at all. He did it all. So, being covered by the blood of Christ which we did not earn or merit, it is only by His efforts that we are saved.

Now some like to say that having faith in His blood is a "work" on our behalf that saves us. But Scripture differentiates between faith and work. Remember when James (chapter 2) wrote, *"Faith without works is dead"?* Faith is not a work. Standing alone, faith is the ABSENCE of work.

Then let's look at how the Bible – from beginning to end – exhaustively portrays God's grace as ever-present. Who was it that created the heavens and the earth? Was it you, or was it God? Did you have anything to do with it? How did you receive the blessings of life without merit? Who was it that designed our landscapes, our seascapes, our oxygen, our water, our food, our bodies, and all of life? Again – you or God? Were these things, and the benefit you received from them *earned* by you? How did *you* merit your existence? How have *you* merited anything that has been placed before you?

Throughout Scripture, God points out over and over again that He is the source of all things as our sovereign God. He created man and we are beholden to Him. Bad and evil have long been the product of human actions and decisions, but from the start God has done nothing but bless – and relative to the topic of Grace, all of these things He has done without ANY input or merit from you.

This is grace.

Carrying it out a step further, God instituted His Law and not one person could abide it. So even when we were given a *chance* to do something, we failed as a whole. So even in the salvation of humanity, God came down, lived like we could not live, loved like we could not love, died like we could not die, and saved us by His blood, not by ANYTHING you added merited or earned.

Get it?

In the book of Daniel, Daniel prays:

> Daniel 9:18. *O my God ... we* ***do not*** *present our supplications before thee for* ***our*** *righteousnesses, but for* ***thy*** *great mercies.*

Even under the Law the children of Israel were well aware that they were reliant upon the mercy of God and not their own righteousness. This is an excellent beginning definition of grace: *when a person does not receive what he deserves (mercy in place of judgment) but does receive what he doesn't deserve (blessing).*

I want to ask you a very serious question: are you a person who believes you deserve heaven by your own merit? If so, you renounce the doctrine of grace. And I wish you the best of luck with that because you're gonna need it.

OR

Are you a person who believes there is nothing you can do to earn heaven, but that you are going there anyway because of what Jesus did in your place? You then, are a person who embraces the gospel of grace.

Paul tells us Who gives mercy and why:

> Romans 9:15-16. *For God saith to Moses, I will have mercy on*

whom I will have mercy, and I will have compassion on whom I will have compassion. So then it is not of him that willeth, nor of him that runneth, but of God that sheweth mercy.

This theme of God's unearned grace is exhaustively presented throughout Scripture and we readily see that. *When all is said and done, God's will is said...and done.* And we will be the recipients either of His favor or His justice, depending on our faith – or lack of it – on Him who He sent.

The third Biblical support for grace is that it is illustrated throughout almost every story in Scripture. From Noah in the ark to God making the covenant with Abraham while he slept; from the prodigal son to the thief on the cross, the whole thing drips with grace, grace, grace.

Allow me one particular example often overlooked: the story of Lazarus.

Remember, Lazarus was sick when his sisters sought out the Lord to come and heal him. Instead of immediately returning from His journey, Jesus proceeded further away from them, pausing a full three days before returning to Lazarus' location. By this time, good old Lazarus was dead and actually buried in a tomb. When Jesus returned, He was met by Martha who expressed that had Jesus immediately returned, Lazarus would still be living; but now, he was dead, really dead in the Jewish sense, for he had been in the grave three days. Jesus asked to be led to the tomb and then raised Lazarus back to life.

Now the question is, what did Lazarus do to bring himself up from out of the grips of permanent death? Nothing. He merely responded to the call and power of His Lord. All the power to raise Lazarus up from being dead (in sin, as it were) was to come forth when Jesus commanded it. There was no effort Lazarus made while in that dead state, to raise himself.

So it is with salvation by grace and grace alone.

The fourth and final Biblical support for grace is that Grace is *specifically* taught – especially by Paul, the apostle of grace, whom we introduced earlier.

Now, I think it is important to know something about Mormonism at this point. In order for Mormon doctrine to exist in the light of the following Biblical passages, they have to redefine the very definition of salvation.

So when a Christian says, "We are saved by grace through faith," a tricky Latter-day Saint might say, "Oh, agreed! Agreed!" But they mean something entirely different than the Christian when it comes to the definition of *saved.*

We will be doing an entire section on salvation later, but suffice it to say, to a CHRISTIAN, *salvation* or *being saved* means being saved from death and hell and living with God after this life.

Pretty straightforward, isn't it?

LDS President and Prophet Joseph Fielding Smith defined the LDS view of salvation for the Mormon church (*Doctrines of Salvation* 1:134):

> Salvation is twofold: General – that which comes to all men irrespective of belief (in this life. in Christ [i.e., resurrection]– and, Individual – that which man merits through his own acts through life and by obedience to the laws and ordinances of the Mormon gospel.

It is to this concept of *General Salvation* (or physical resurrection) that defenders of the LDS faith use *grace* and *saved* in the same sentence. But when speaking of what gets a person living with God after this life is not grace at all within Mormonism. So, let me restate this to make it clear: Mormon doctrine teaches that all people are resurrected by grace. This is the general free gift to humanity according to the LDS.

But a person may be resurrected to the celestial kingdom or some lesser state depending NOT on grace but on his own *works, obedience*, and *efforts*.

Got that?

So let's hear what the Bible says specifically about salvation by grace and you can see if you agree with the way the Mormons explain it.

Scripture states that grace is free. It is not earned through works.

Speaking of physical AND spiritual death, Paul writes,

> Romans 5:15. *For if through the offence of one* [i.e., Adam] *many be dead, much more the grace of God, and the **gift** by grace, which is by one man, Jesus Christ, hath abounded unto many.*

> Romans 4:4. *Now **to him that worketh is the reward not reckoned of grace**, but of debt.*

Scripture makes clear that grace stands apart from anything and everything else.

Grace plus luck is not grace. Grace plus works is not grace. Grace is grace. Period.

> Romans 11:6. *And if by grace, then is it no more of works: **otherwise grace is no more grace**. But if it be of works, then is it no more grace: otherwise work is no more work.*

Scripture is plain on what justifies us before the Father and makes it clear that there is nothing we can do to add to it.

> Romans 3:24. *Being **justified freely by his grace** through the redemption that is in Christ Jesus:*

Romans 5:2. *By whom also we have* ***access by faith into this grace*** *wherein we stand, and rejoice in hope of the glory of God.*

Ephesians 2:8. *For* ***by grace are ye saved through faith;*** *and that not of yourselves: it is the gift of God:*

Scripture tells us that those who try and use the law to justify themselves before God are fallen from His grace.

Galatians 5:4. ***Christ is become of no effect*** *unto you, whosoever of you are justified by the law;* ***ye are fallen from grace.***

And James 2 reminds us all that if you want to be judged by your living the law, go ahead. But just remember,

James 2:10. *For whosoever shall keep the whole law, and yet offend in one point,* ***he is guilty of all.***

Some people think we need to be "worthy" to *earn* His grace, to do everything possible to have it bestowed upon us.

But Paul writes

Ephesians 2:5. *Even when we were dead in sins, God hath quickened us together with Christ, (by grace ye are saved;)*

Scripture reiterates that grace comes from God unmerited, and not based on our efforts.

In a letter to Timothy, Paul writes that God:

2 Timothy 1:9. … *hath saved us, and called us with an holy calling, not according to our works, but according to his own purpose and grace, which was given us in Christ Jesus before the world began,*

Scripture teaches us that grace is not just forgiveness of sin but it is actually His grace that makes us righteous. Listen!

Romans 5:17. *For if by one man's offence death reigned by one; much*

> *more they which receive abundance of grace and of* ***the gift of righteousness*** *shall reign in life by one, Jesus Christ.*

> Romans 5:21. *That as sin hath reigned unto death, even so might* ***grace reign through righteousness*** *unto eternal life by Jesus Christ our Lord.*

Later Paul reminds us

> Galatians 2:21. . . . *do not frustrate the grace of God: for if righteousness come by the law, then Christ is dead in vain.*

Scripture tells us that grace is the ONLY way for man to achieve righteousness. Listen!

> Galatians 3:21. *Is the law then against the promises of God? God forbid: for if there had been a law given which could have given life, verily righteousness should have been by the law.*

Scripture teaches us that as believers who have received God's grace, we are prone to labor MORE than those who believe they are saved through some other means.

Listen to what Paul says about himself:

> 1 Corinthians 15:10. *But by the grace of God I am what I am: and his grace which was bestowed upon me was not in vain; but I laboured more abundantly than they all: yet not I, but the grace of God which was with me.*

> 2 Corinthians 9:8. *And God is able to make all grace abound toward you; that ye, always having all sufficiency in all things, may abound to every good work:*

At the same time, we know that grace covers all of our failures, past, present, and future, and that because of this, our sin does not overwhelm us. Rather, we are overwhelmed by our faith, our gratitude and our love for God. Paul had some issue of which we are not fully informed where he went to God and what did God say to him?

> 2 Corinthians 12:9. *And he said unto me, My grace is sufficient for thee: for my strength is made perfect in weakness. Most gladly therefore will I rather glory in my infirmities, that the power of Christ may rest upon me.*

Scripture warns us of those who will preach another gospel, one that alters the good news of grace, or adds to it. Listen!

To the Galatians, Paul wrote:

> Galatians 1:6-7. *I marvel that ye are so soon removed from him that called you into the grace of Christ unto another gospel: Which is not another; but there be some that trouble you, and would **pervert** the gospel of Christ.*

Finally, Scripture tells us it is grace that gives us strength.

Knowing we are covered by His life-saving blood, the Writer of Hebrews says:

> Hebrews 4:16. L*et us therefore come boldly unto the throne of grace, that we may obtain mercy, and find grace to **help in time of need.***

In the book of Acts, Luke writes,

> Acts 15:11. *But we believe that through the grace of the Lord Jesus Christ we shall be saved …*

You can listen to *men* who tell you otherwise, or you can trust in what God says, in what Jesus did, and in the power of His life and His shed blood ALONE.

"If you take the time to look, Jesus said very little about the specifics of heaven – what we will do, how we will spend eternity. I think it has to do with living by faith and trusting God with our future. Joseph decided to fill in the blanks."

Heaven

If there is one thing religious visionaries, charlatans and cult leaders love to promote, it's their special vision of what to expect in the afterlife; specifically, what heaven and/or hell – if they admit to their existence – will be like. Where the Bible is unusually silent on such matters, giving very little information, religious con men and women just love to fill in the gaps and tell us what to expect in the afterlife – if we follow them, of course.

Egyptians believed the soul was ferried across the Nile River to the Kingdoms of the Dead and put to work in a field.

The Greeks had their mythological Elysian Fields, rest for the heroic amid a landscape of waving grasses and streams.

Vikings had Valhalla, a special place, of course, for heroic warriors, specially equipped with its own beer hall.

Zoroastrians have the soul going through a long torturous process before reaching its place of rest; and Islam teaches that the soul goes to Jannah at final judgment day but remains in some varying degree of either comfort or misery, depending on the life lived.

Founder of Mormonism, Joseph Smith Jr., imagined his own version of heaven, and the most faithful Latter-day Saints today have it constantly in their crosshairs: the Celestial Kingdom. Mormons state that all human beings first lived in heaven with "heavenly Father," and that we will all return to some semblance of heaven after this mortal experience (with a few exceptions).

Before we talk about Mormonism's views on heaven, let me explain what the Bible says about the place. I will make 3 points.

First of all, we know that not only does the Bible maintain that Jesus came down from heaven, or as He called it, "*from above* (John 8:23)," but that every human being came from the dust of the earth. John the Baptist, speaking of Jesus, said:

> John 3:31. *He that cometh from above is above all: he that is of the earth is earthly, and speaketh of the earth: he that cometh from heaven is above all.*

Speaking of Himself, Jesus said:

> John 3:13. *And no man hath ascended up to heaven, but he that came down from heaven, even the Son of man which is in heaven.*

How anyone who believes they came from heaven after hearing Jesus say this about Himself is beyond me:

> John 8:23. ...*Ye are from beneath; I am from above: ye are of this world; I am not of this world.*

Even Paul differentiated between Jesus coming from heaven and the rest of human kind coming from earth when he said:

> 1 Corinthians 15:47-48. *The first man [Adam] is of the earth, earthy: the second man is the Lord from heaven. As is the earthy, such are they also that are earthy: and as is the heavenly, such are they also that are heavenly.*

These passages, in fact the whole of chapter 15 of 1 Corinthians, merits a closer study, which we will get to in a minute.

Secondly, this is what we know from scripture about heaven. According to Jewish notions, there are three "*heavens*:"

1. The firmament, as in the "*fowls of the heaven*" (Genesis 2:19; 7:3,23; Psalm 8:8, etc.), "*the eagles of heaven*" (Lamentations 4:19) which would be like our atmosphere;
2. The starry heavens (Deuteronomy 17:3; Jeremiah 8:2; Matthew 24:29) which would include things like our galaxy; and
3. The "heaven of heavens," or the "third heaven" (Deuteronomy 10:14; 1 Kings 8:27; Psalms 115:16; 148:4; 2 Corinthians 12:2).

Now the original Hebrew word for "heavens" is "*shamayim*," which is a plural form meaning "heights" or "elevations" (Genesis 1:1; 2:1). So we know that heaven is "above." It is a place.

There are a number of other words in scripture used for heaven. They include:

- *Marom*, which means "high places" or "heights;"
- *Galgal*, literally a "wheel," which is also rendered "*heaven*" in Psalm 77:18 and which Journey incorporated into their great classic rock hit: "Wheel in the sky keeps on turning, don't know where I'll be tomorrow;"
- *Sahaq*, rendered "*sky*" (Deuteronomy 33:26; Job 37:18;

Psalm 18:11), and "clouds" (Job 35:5; 36:28; Psalm 68:34), and refers to our atmospheric heaven or firmament; and

- *Raqiya*, closely connected with and rendered "*firmamentum*" in the Vulgate (Latin Bible) and means "a solid expanse" (Genesis 1:7; Psalm 150:1)

In terms of its spiritual meaning, heaven is a place of the everlasting blessedness of the righteous; the abode of departed spirits.

a. Christ calls it his "*Father's house*" (John 14:2).

b. It is synonymous with "*paradise*" (Luke 23:43; 2 Corinthians 12:4; Revelation 2:7).

And is called…

a. The "*Jerusalem which is above*," "*heavenly Jerusalem*," and "*new Jerusalem*" (Galatians 4:26; Hebrews 12:22; Revelation 3:12, 21:2);

b. The "*kingdom of heaven*," or simply, "*the kingdom*" (Matthew 25:1; James 2:5);

c. The "*everlasting kingdom*" (2 Peter 1:11);

d. The "*eternal inheritance*" that is "*incorruptible*," "*undefiled*," and that "*fadeth not away*" (Hebrews 9:15; 1 Peter 1:4);

e. The "*better country*" (Hebrews 11:14,16).

AND …

a. "*Abraham's bosom*" (Matthew 8:11; Luke 16:22;); and, simply,

b. "*Rest*" (Heb 4:9-11).

Jesus spoke of heaven as a literal reality. It is a place where our spirits go after this life, if the departed meets the requirements for entrance. The "requirements for heaven" have been greatly manipulated by men and women seeking control over others. Some say payment of money is required for heaven, or a life of servile obedience, or membership in one particular religion or another.

Others, like Brigham Young, have said things like (*Journal of Discourses* 11:269),

> It is the word of the Lord ... that if you desire with all your hearts to obtain the blessings which Abraham obtained, ***you will be polygamists*** ... or you will come short of enjoying the salvation and the glory which Abraham has obtained ... if you have in your hearts to say...we will not ... be polygamists ... that man that has that in his heart...will come short of dwelling in the presence of the Father and the Son, in celestial glory. ***The only men who become Gods, even the Sons of God are those who enter into polygamy*** [emphasis Shawn's].

But specifically regarding Heaven, what does the Bible say is required? This is our third point.

Let's make a list of those requirements:

First, humility.

> Matthew 5:3. *Blessed are the poor in spirit: for theirs is the kingdom of heaven.*
>
> Isaiah 57:15. *For thus saith the high and lofty One that inhabiteth eternity, whose name is Holy; I dwell in the high and holy place, with him also that is of a contrite and humble spirit, to revive the spirit of the humble, and to revive the heart of the contrite ones.*

So we know humility is required.

Then we know from the Lord Himself that a person must be born again to even see heaven.

Jesus said to Nicodemus,

> John 3:3. *Except a man be born again, he cannot see the kingdom of God.*

I love this point because upon it hangs everything else.

We know what James, the brother of Jesus, said about those who are "*heirs of the kingdom of heaven*" right? He said:

> James 2:5. *Hath not God chosen* ***the poor of this world rich in faith,*** *and* ***heirs of the kingdom*** *which he hath promised to* ***them that love him?***

So, according to James, a person who is an heir to the kingdom of heaven will be "*poor of this world,*" who are "*RICH IN FAITH*" and who "*LOVE HIM.*"

Scripture also adds that those who have been born again, and who walk by faith and love, will then perform services of love; these will inherit heaven, too.

> Matthew 25:34-36. *Then shall the King say unto them on his right hand, Come, ye blessed of my Father, inherit the kingdom prepared for you from the foundation of the world: For I was an hungered, and ye gave me meat: I was thirsty, and ye gave me drink: I was a stranger, and ye took me in: Naked, and ye clothed me: I was sick, and ye visited me: I was in prison, and ye came unto me.*

Then we know from Acts that trials are a certainty for those who will enter heaven, for when the apostles taught those of the faith they …

> Acts 14:22. *…exhorted them to continue in the faith, and that we must through much tribulation enter into the kingdom of God [or heaven].*

Trials sound a bit scary, but He who is in us is far, far stronger than those against us (1 John 4:4).

And finally, we must hear what the LORD also mandated:

Luke 9:62. *No man, having put his hand to the plough, and looking back, is fit for the kingdom of God.*

So, we endure.

So, speaking directly to inheriting heaven, the Bible says we must:

- Possess humility
- Experience spiritual rebirth
- Be "*poor in the things of this world*" (meaning, not making the things of this world our priorities)
- Be "*rich in faith and love*"
- Clothe and feed the poor; visit the sick and imprisoned
- Endure trials and tribulations
- Once putting our "*hand to the plough*" of God, never looking back

This sounds like a big list, but remember, it is all – even our acts toward the poor and imprisoned – from the heart. It is rooted in our humble attitude of faith and love.

Now you may have noticed that there is nothing said in the Bible about marriage for eternity to reach heaven, paying tithing, obeying a Sabbath day, keeping dietary laws, going to temples, doing home teaching, fulfilling church calls, receiving priesthoods, the new and everlasting covenant or the like.

Just matters of the heart.

And finally, these verses describe the inhabitants of heaven, and some of what they will experience:

2 Corinthians 4:17. [despite their momentary, earthly *"light affliction,"* they may expect] *a far more exceeding and **eternal weight of glory;***

Galatians 1:4. [delivery] ***from this present evil world;***

> Luke 20:36. [they will **not**] *die any more: for they are* ***equal unto the angels****; and are the* ***children of God****, being the* ***children of the resurrection***;
>
> 1 Peter 1:4. *an inheritance incorruptible, and undefiled, and that fadeth not away, reserved in heaven;*
>
> 1 Peter 5:10. *eternal glory by Christ Jesus* … [that will] … *perfect, establish, strengthen,* [and] *settle* [them];
>
> 1 John 3:2. [they] *shall be like him; for* [they] *shall see him as he is;* **and**
>
> 2 Timothy 4:8. *a crown of righteousness* [will be awarded] *unto all them also that love his appearing.*

We know from the Lord that in His Father's house are many mansions (John 14:2); I believe this refers to the abodes found in the universe. We also know that the believer's heaven is not only a state of everlasting blessedness, but also a "*place*," – a location – for as Jesus said, He goes to *prepare a place for* us.

Enter Joseph Smith and his teachings on heaven.

Now, remember, when I speak of heaven as a Christian, I am speaking of heaven: one heaven, all of heaven, and nothing but heaven. To Christians there is heaven and there is hell. Part of Joseph's twistianity was to compartmentalize heaven, with everyone going there no matter what, with "there" being one of three levels:

- The *telestial* kingdom, where non-believers in Jesus, liars, adulterers, murderers go;
- The *terrestrial* kingdom, where good men and women go who believed in Jesus but were blinded by the philosophies of men; and
- The *celestial* kingdom, which is only for the LDS because the entrance "pass" to get into the Celestial Kingdom is baptism by one holding the proper LDS authority.

This celestial kingdom too, contains three levels.

The *Doctrine and Covenants* states:

> D&C 131:1-3. In the celestial glory there are three heavens or degrees*; And ***in order to obtain the highest, a man must enter into this order of the priesthood [meaning the new and everlasting covenant of marriage];*** And if he does not, he cannot obtain it [brackets in original].
>
> (*Note that word *degree*, which originates straight from Masonic folklore.)

So Mormon water baptism gets a person into the celestial kingdom; however, it takes Mormon marriage to get into the highest *level* of the celestial kingdom, which is where faithful LDS people become gods. This highest degree of the celestial kingdom is synonymously known as "*exaltation*" and "*eternal life*"; access to it is only by strict and continual obedience to what LDS doctrine calls "celestial law." Referring to this law, 10th LDS President Joseph Fielding Smith said in his book, *The Way to Perfection* (page 206):

> To enter the celestial and obtain exaltation it is necessary that the whole law be kept.

And this is what you see all around you, folks: Mormon men and women striving to adhere to the whole of the celestial law in order to reach the highest degree of the celestial kingdom and become gods.

Current LDS President Thomas Monson clarified the whole reason and process of entering heaven when he said ("An Invitation to Exaltation," *Ensign*, May 1988; reprinted June 1993):

> It is the celestial glory which we seek. It is in the presence of God we desire to dwell. It is a forever family in which we want membership. ***Such blessings must be earned.***

And where did the term celestial originate? If you were sitting with a pair of LDS missionaries, they would excitedly have you open up your Bible, and turn to 1 Corinthians, chapter 15.

(Now, I want to let you in on a little insight here: if you ever want to take a Latter-day Saint down regarding one of the fallacies of Joseph Smith's teachings, open up to 1 Corinthians chapter 15 – but read the WHOLE thing with him. Call it the "1 Corinthians 15 Challenge." Someday we'll do an entire show on how this works, but just read verse by verse through 1 Corinthians 15:

- Verse 8 refutes apostolic succession;
- Verses 12-32 supposedly discuss "baptism for the dead;" but read contextually, the whole thing teaches about resurrection;
- Verses 46-47 refute the pre-existence; and
- Verses 56-58 refute salvation by works of the law!

But let me finish showing how the LDS will twist 1 Corinthians in order to support Joseph's teachings about the "degrees of heaven."

Throughout the chapter, Paul is teaching the believers in Corinth about death and resurrection. Remember, his teaching is about *RESURRECTION*, not *LEVELS of HEAVEN.* The preface material on this topic takes us to verse 35, where Paul starts to nail it down, stating:

> 1 Corinthians 15:35. *But some man will say, How are the dead raised up? and with what body do they come?*

Paul states that some, who reject resurrection (see verse 12), will ask sarcastically, "How are we resurrected?" He responds with words that, at first glance, may be difficult to understand:

> 1 Corinthians 15:36-38. *Thou fool, that which thou sowest is not*

> *quickened, except it die: And that which thou sowest, thou sowest not that body that shall be, but bare grain, it may chance of wheat, or of some other grain: But God giveth it a body as it hath pleased him, and to every seed his own body.*

He calls the one questioning the doctrine of resurrection a fool! Paul continues, using the idea of a kernel of grain. Once it dies, it comes forth as a very different entity than the kernel itself: it *was* one kernel of grain – round, hard, husky – and is now a green plant. Got that? The seed sown in the ground decays, but gives birth to a new plant. In nature, Paul allegorizes, death leads to a higher life: the actual seed sown does not reappear, but something higher, a complete plant, of the same kind as the seed, springs from it.

Then he points out that there are all **sorts** of flesh that God has created on the earth, but,

> 1 Corinthians 15:39. *All flesh is not the same flesh: but there is one kind of flesh of men, another flesh of beasts, another of fishes, and another of birds.*

He makes a comparison of the differences between the flesh of a dog, and a dolphin, and a bird, and a woman. Okay? This is a model for what he is about to say next and **all of it** is to illustrate the truth about resurrection to those who do not believe in resurrection!

> 1 Corinthians 15:40. *There are also celestial bodies, and bodies terrestrial: but the glory of the celestial is one, and the glory of the terrestrial is another.*

Paul is making a comparison here. He tells us that, just as there are different sorts of flesh here on earth, there are also differences between what earthly creations (the "*terrestrial*") and creations in the heavens, or cosmos, or in space, which he calls the "*celestial.*"

Paul first compares the sorts of flesh on earth – they differ.

Then he compares earthly creations and heavenly – they **also** differ.

Next he compares the differences *between* the heavenly creations - *Listen!*

> 1 Corinthians 15:41. *There is one glory of the sun, and another glory of the moon, and another glory of the stars: for one star* ***differeth*** *from another star in glory.* ***So also is the resurrection of the dead.***

In context we see that Paul is simply telling those who did not understand or did not believe in resurrection *what it is* and *how it would be*. There are earthly bodies, and spiritual bodies; they differ from each other drastically, as drastically as a dead seed to a fresh green plant and as different as the sun is from the stars in light.

Listen to the argument Paul makes to support his premise. Speaking of resurrection, he says

> 1 Corinthians 15:41-49 ***So also is the resurrection of the dead.*** *It is sown in corruption; it is raised in incorruption* [just like the kernel and the plant!]: *It is sown in dishonour; it is raised in glory: it is sown in weakness; it is raised in power: It is sown a* ***natural body;*** *it is raised a* ***spiritual body****. There is a natural body, and there is a spiritual body. And so it is written, The first man Adam was made a living soul; the last Adam was made a quickening spirit. Howbeit* ***that was not first which is spiritual, but that which is natural; and afterward that which is spiritual.*** *The first man is of the earth, earthy: the second man is the Lord from heaven. As is the earthy, such are they also that are earthy: and as is the heavenly, such are they also that are heavenly. And* ***as we have borne the image of the earthy, we shall also bear the image of the heavenly*** [in RESURRECTION!].

Friends, this has NOTHING to do with three heavenly "kingdoms." Paul speaks of the earthly (terrestrial) and of the heavenly (celestial) by way of comparison in order to support the teaching of resurrection. Notice there is ***no*** mention of the Joseph Smith-concocted "telestial" kingdom, which does not fit ***at all*** with what is being taught here.

This gospel the Mormons believe and embrace is "*another gospel*," it is a ***false*** and ***deceptive*** counterfeit, concocted in the mind of a man.

READ 1 Corinthians chapter 15 and ask God to open your eyes to what Paul is saying. Then, ***come to the true and living God*** so you can have what is required for heaven: a humble heart set on Truth.

❋ ❋ ❋

> "Jesus referred to it often. Based on this alone, I believe hell exists as described in His Word. And where the Bible says there are many levels of hell, Joseph instead said there are many levels of heaven. I'll trust the former."

Hell

In the last section we talked about heaven. This time we're headed the other direction, a place that has long been subject to a somewhat errant description: hell.

The word "hell" is derived from the Saxon word "*helan*," which means "to cover" or "conceal;" to be "covered in an invisible place." In Scripture there are three words that describe this covered place:

- "*Sheol*;"
- "*Hades*;" and
- "*Gehenna*."

The Hebrew word *Sheol* occurs 65 times in the Old Testament: 31 times it is rendered "*grave*;" "*hell*" 30 times; and "*pit*" 3 times. Generally speaking, *Sheol* was the place the dead went, and it was composed of two distinct compartments: the prison or hellish part and the Abraham's bosom part. Both good men (Genesis 37:35) and evil men (Numbers 16:30) go there. Jesus describes these two compartments in Luke 16:19-31. In His recounting of the rich man and Lazarus, both men went to *Sheol* or realm of the dead: the rich man to the hellish part where he was "*tormented in this flame*" (verse 24) and Lazarus to Abraham's bosom, a cool place of rest where he "*is comforted*" (verse 25).

The hell part of *Sheol* literally means "*to ask*" or to "*demand*" and describes a type of insatiability, where enough is never enough. Listen to the tone of this passage describing the hellish aspect of *Sheol*:

> Proverbs 30:15-16. *The horseleach* [a blood-sucking, wormlike creature that lives in water] *hath two daughters, crying, Give, give. There are three things that are never satisfied, yea, **four things say not, It is enough: The grave**; and the barren womb; the earth that is not filled with water; and the fire saith not, It is enough.*

Proverbs refers to "*the congregation of the dead*" (Proverbs 21:16), the ultimate end for the man who "*wandereth out of the way of understanding*."

Numbers 16:25-33 calls hell ("*the pit*") the abode of "*wicked men*" that the dead "*go down*" into; Job 24:19 compares the graves of "*those which have sinned*" to the way that "*Drought and heat consume the snow waters*;" and Psalms 9:17 and 31:17 say it is a place for the "*wicked*." Job 11:8 describes *Sheol* as "*deep*;" Job 10:22 describes it as "*dark*" and "*without any order*;" and Job 17:16 adds that it has "*bars*."

But Psalms refers to it also as a temporary place for the good, where they will not be left (16:9-10); from which they will be "*brought up*" (30:3), "*redeemed*" (49:15), and "*delivered*" (86:13).

Okay? Now ...

The Greek word *hades* (found in the New Testament) has the same scope of meaning and significance as *Sheol* of the Old Testament. It is a place where a watch is kept ("*prison*;" 1 Peter 3:19); a place with "*gates*" (Matthew 16:18) and locks requiring "*keys*" (Revelation 1:18); and it is located in the direction of "*down*" (Matthew 11:23; Luke 10:15). Prior to the death and resurrection of Jesus, both the righteous and the wicked were separated in *Sheol* or *hades*, as we've said. *Hades*, as described BY JESUS HIMSELF, is a place of endless and inescapable torment and flaming agony (Luke 16:23-24) .

The third word used for hell word is *Gehenna*.

The word *Gehenna*, the Greek contraction of the Hebrew place *Hinnom* or *Ben-hinnom*, was never used in the time of Christ in any other sense than to denote a place of future punishment. It got its name from a place the Jews called the valley of Hinnom, first mentioned in Joshua 15:8. Now this valley of Hinnom was a deep narrow ravine which separated Mount Zion from a place called the "Hill of Evil Council," a hill south of Jerusalem where tradition says the house of Caiaphas stood. Caiaphas was the high priest and head of the Sanhedrin in Jesus' day and was responsible for the so-called "trial" of Jesus prior to the Jews handing Him over to Pilate (Matthew 26:3, 57). In this valley of Hinnom, the idolatrous Jews burned their children alive as a sacrifice to Molech and Baal in a part of the valley which was called Tophet (2 Kings 23:10; Jeremiah 7:31-32), which means "fire-stove" or a "place of burning."

When the Jews returned from exile, they showed their abhorrence of the locality by making it a place where all the horrible evils of the city took place. Primarily, these things included the burning of human waste, of animals, and of the dead bodies of criminals supposedly because there was a fire there that was constantly burning.

In most of its occurrences in the Greek New Testament, *Gehenna* designates the "place of the lost" and the fearful condition of *Gehenna* is described in various figurative expressions throughout the Word of God. The Jews associated with this valley these two ideas:

1. it was a place of great sufferings; and
2. it was a place of filth and corruption.

Because of this *Gehenna* became a symbol of the abode of the wicked hereafter. Jesus used the word *Gehenna* eleven times in His discourses to describe a future place of punishment (e.g., Matthew 5:22; Matthew 23:33; Luke 12:5) so there must be something to it.

Finally, there is a forth word worth mentioning here that describes hell. It is the Greek word "*abussos*," meaning "abyss" or "extremely deep place." It is usually paired in the Scripture with "*phrear*," a well or pit dug in the earth and is translated "*bottomless pit*" in the New Testament (Revelation chapters 9, 11, 17, and 20), but it is also used alone in Romans 10:7 (the "*deep*") and in Luke 8:31, referring to the prison destined for evil spirits.

It is thought by some students of the Bible that there is a place on earth, some sort of portal or shaft, where demons enter and exit our realm from what is known as the *abussos*. The internet carries all kinds of stories about miners tapping into these portals accidentally and hearing screaming ... but we'll leave all that to George Noory and other purveyors of the bizarre.

Before we proceed, it is important to know that, as with most other subjects, Mormonism has multiple meanings and definitions for hell, most of them completely missing the Biblical mark. In the Encyclopedia of Mormonism it reads (2:585):

Latter-day Scriptures describe at least three senses of hell: (1) that condition of misery which may attend a person in mortality due to disobedience to divine law; (2) the miserable, but temporary, state of disobedient spirits in the spirit world awaiting resurrection; (3) the permanent habitation of the sons of perdition, who suffer the second spiritual death and remain in hell even after the resurrection.

So first, Mormon scripture allows for a person to experience a living hell" – while "*in mortality*" as the result of "*disobedience to divine law.*" I suppose this could happen, but then again it may not.

Secondly, Mormons admit that hell will give up her dead, which they define as the "*miserable, but temporary, state of disobedient spirits in the spirit world awaiting resurrection.*" Listen, Christians would readily agree with the notion of hell giving up her dead, but in a completely different way. The Bible says hell *will* give up her dead, but only when they come before the great "*white throne*" of God to be judged (Revelation 20:11-15). Mormonism states that hell will give up her dead only to let these dead go to a level of heaven! But more on this in a minute.

Finally, Mormonism embraces a "permanent hell, which is similar to the Christian view; but for the LDS, this place omits the burning and is only for what they call "sons of perdition." (Umm, that would be me: sons of perdition deny the LDS holy spirit after receiving "*it*" and sons of perdition deny the Mormon Jesus after the Mormon heavenly father has revealed him; *Doctrine and Covenants* 76:35, 43.)

Now, the Bible teaches some very clear messages about hell. Most of them came from the mouth of Jesus, who talked more about hell than about heaven. MOST of His references are not pleasant or politically correct today. One of the things the Bible makes clear about hell is that it is one of two possible destinations for the departed, with a singular heaven being the other.

> Matthew 25:34. *Then shall the King say unto them on his right hand, Come, ye blessed of my Father, inherit* ***the kingdom prepared for you*** *from the foundation of the world*

And then, in the same narrative, verse 41 states:

> Matthew 25:41. *Then shall he say also unto them on the left hand, Depart from me, ye cursed,* ***into everlasting fire, prepared for the devil and his angels.***

Those on the right? Blessed of the Father to inherit the kingdom prepared for them. Those on the left? Cursed and sent to everlasting fire. Two options.

But Mormonism rejects these Biblical truths out of hand. Apostle Hugh B. Brown stated ("The Church is Christianity Restored," LDS *Conference Report*, April 1965):

> We reject the unscriptural doctrine that there are but two places or states of eternal existence – heaven and hell – and that all men will go to one or the other.

This is really important to understand, my friends, because it actually reveals the LDS rejection of salvation by grace through faith. You see, if a person has been saved by grace through faith, heaven *IS* the destination – *saved* from hell by grace through faith! If a person is not saved, then a singular hell would suffice, right? BUT, if salvation comes by the shed blood of Jesus AND our good works, as the LDS suggest, then a single heaven would not work nor would any sort of hell suffice because, to the LDS, everyone who chose to come to earth has merited some level of heaven.

That would include Hitler, Mussolini, Pol Pot, Charles Manson – you name it, they can claim it: heaven. Of course, as a one-time member who fights against Mormonism and placing *all* my faith in the Lord Jesus Christ, according to them, I will be going to outer darkness.

The second point that the Bible makes clear is that there are varying levels or punishments in hell, based on varying levels of evils done by an individual – just as there are varying degrees or "*crowns*" of reward in heaven – which will be tried by fire. When instructing His disciples to go out in to the world, Jesus said that if a city refuses to receive them,

> Matthew 10:15. *Verily…it shall be* ***more*** *tolerable for the land of Sodom and Gomorrah in the day of judgment, than for that city.*

Speaking in Luke 12:47-48, Jesus says that the disobedient servant, who "*knew his lord's will and prepared not himself, neither did according to his* [master's] *will, shall be beaten with* ***many*** *stripes,*" while the servant who "*knew not* [the master's will], *and did commit things worthy of stripes, shall be beaten with* ***few*** *stripes.*"

And the Author of Hebrews says:

> Hebrews 10:29. *Of how much sorer punishment, suppose ye, shall he be thought worthy, who hath trodden under foot the Son of God, and hath counted the blood of the covenant, wherewith he was sanctified, an unholy thing, and hath done despite unto the Spirit of grace?*

Finally, we're all familiar with what John the Beloved reported in the Revelation, saying:

> Revelation 20:11-15. *And I saw a great white throne, and him that*

sat on it, from whose face the earth and the heaven fled away; and there was found no place for them. And I saw the dead, small and great, stand before God; and the books were opened: and another book was opened, which is the book of life: and ***the dead were judged*** *out of those things which were written in the books,* ***according to their works****. And the sea gave up the dead which were in it; and death and hell delivered up the dead which were in them: and they were judged every man according to their works. And death and hell were cast into the lake of fire. This is the second death. And whosoever was not found written in the book of life was cast into the lake of fire.*

As politically incorrect as it is, hell is described as a place of torture; an eternal exposure to heat, flame, fire, and burning. So many ask, "Why would a loving God create such a place for people?"

The answer? He didn't.

He prepared this place for Satan and his angels. But if men and women want to reject what this loving God offers them – the shed blood of His innocent Son as rescue from this place – then they too, will receive the eternal punishment for such a rejection. Remember folks,

John 3:16. ***God so loved the world,*** *that he gave his only begotten Son, that whosoever* ***believeth*** *in him should not perish, but have everlasting life.*

For God so loved the World!

So let's look at the "*eternal*" description of hell, which Mormons reject. The original languages help refute LDS deception. Jesus said:

Matthew 25:46. *And these shall go away into* ***everlasting*** *punishment: but the righteous into life* ***eternal****.*

In Greek, "And <*kai*> these <*houtos*> shall go away <*aperchomai*> into <*eis*> **everlasting** <***aionios***> punishment <*kolasis*>: but <*de*> the righteous <*dikaios*> into <*eis*> life <*zoe*> **eternal** <***aionios***>." The word for both ***everlasting*** and ***eternal*** are the same: aionios!

It means perpetual (also used of time past and future as well), not transitory, of endless duration: **eternal, forever,** and **everlasting.**

If Jesus tells us that the righteous will go to *zoe aionios* – life eternal – and the evil to *kolasis aionios* – eternal punishment – and the adjectives are one and the same, then we understand that hell is just as eternal as heaven!

Let's look at another passage:

> Revelation 14:11. *And the smoke of their torment ascendeth up forever and ever: and they have no rest day nor night, who worship the beast and his image, and whosoever receiveth the mark of his name.*

In Greek, "And <*kai*> the smoke <*kapnos*> of their <*autos*> torment <*basanismos*> ascendeth up <*anabaino*> for <*eis*> **ever** <***aion***> and **ever** <***aion***>: and <*kai*> they have <*echo*> no <*ou*> rest <*anapausis*> day <*hemera*> nor <*kai*> night <*nux*>, who <*ho*> worship <*proskuneo*> the beast <*therion*> and <*kai*> his <*autos*> image <*eikon*>, and <*kai*> whosoever <*ei tis*> receiveth <*lambano*> the mark <*charagma*> of his <*autos*> name <*onoma*>."

"***For ever and ever***"? It's the same exact Greek word for "everlasting" and for "eternal."

Lutheran Greek Scholar R.C.H. Lenski explains it this way (*The Interpretation of St. John's Revelation*, page 438):

> The strongest [Greek] expression for our "forever" is *eis tous aionan ton aionon*, "for the eons of eons"; many aeons, each of

> vast duration, are multiplied by many more, which we imitate [in English] by "forever and ever." Human language is able to use only temporal terms to express what is altogether beyond time and timeless. The Greek takes its greatest term for time, the eon, pluralizes this, and then multiplies it by its own plural, even using articles which make these eons the definite ones.

Bottom line, folks: hell is eternal, never-ending torment.

Jesus refers three times to a place where "***their** worm dieth not*" (Mark 9:43-48). What is meant by "***their** worm*?" The Lord takes this phrase straight from the book of Isaiah. Listen to what it says:

> Isaiah 66:24. *And they shall go forth, and look upon the carcasses of the men that have transgressed against me: for* ***their worm shall not die****, neither shall their fire be quenched; and they shall be an abhorring unto all flesh.*

"*Their worm*," references the remains of men after writhing in torture for ages and ages.

I know it does not make complete sense; but someday, it will.

Finally, the Bible teaches that hell is not just eternal: it is also painful. The passage from Revelation just cited teaches us something about the pain of hell. Again, it reads:

> Revelation 14:10,11. … *and he shall be tormented with fire and brimstone… And the smoke of their torment ascendeth up for ever and ever: and they have no rest day nor night…*

The Greek word for torment ("*shall be tormented")* is *basanizo*, which means "to vex with grievous pains (of body or mind), to torment (Joseph Henry Thayer, *A Greek-English Lexicon of the New Testament*, page 96)." It has also been defined as "to torture and torment (Bauer, Arndt and Gingrich, *A Greek-English Lexicon of the New Testament and Other Early Literature*, s.v. "basanizo")." It is very apparent, when read in conjunction with other biblical descriptions of hell ("*gnashing of teeth*," Matthew 8:12; "*misery*," Romans 3:16; *unquenched fire*, Isaiah 66:24) that it is in fact, a place of eternal, endless torture and torment.

I joke about a lot of things in life. I take very little in this world very seriously. But as I continue to understand the Word, I do not joke about hell anymore. Jesus came and gave His everything to rescue us from this place. I wholly accept His payment *alone*, to keep us from it.

In contradiction to the Bible, Mormonism has obscured the real hell as the "hell" of not going to the Mormon "Celestial Kingdom," and missing out on the glory of Heaven. These false teachings are VERY palatable to modern man. Hell has been deconstructed in our lives, my friends. But it is a horrible and truly eternal reality.

To make it transitory, or to redefine it as not from a loving God, we are deluding ourselves. When I hear all the humanistic, seemingly logical arguments against hell, like, "*What kind of God would send anyone to hell?*" OR, "*What kind of God would send anyone to a place that burns forever?*"…

I think of Jesus in the garden of Gethsemane.

Here we have a perfect Son coming to the Father, a loving Father, and asking if there is *any* other way to get around what He is about to do. He is not anxious to face the torments, punishment, pain, and agony. Here we have *God in the flesh* asking if there is an alternative to the suffering He is about to endure. He asks, *Is there any other way to let this brutal cup pass*? And what is the answer from the all good, all loving, Father Who *you* think will wink at the sins of those who don't know His Son?

"*No*. No, Jesus, there is no other way."

And He not only allows His own Son to suffer more than anyone else has ever suffered, but it is *His own wrath for our sins that He pours out upon Him*!

Now here you are, Mr. "Jet Set." Mr. "Worldly." Mrs. "*Why, I'm Such a Good Girl.*" Mrs. "*I go to the temple every month faithfully but don't really know much about Jesus.*" Do you think that the God Who allowed His own perfect, beloved Son to suffer and die on the cross is going to just accept you because *you think you're a good person*?? All I can say is – and I promise you – there is a brutish, rotting hell awaiting you.

But there is a simple and Perfect Way of escape: *His name is Jesus.*

And you must be born again to see Him.

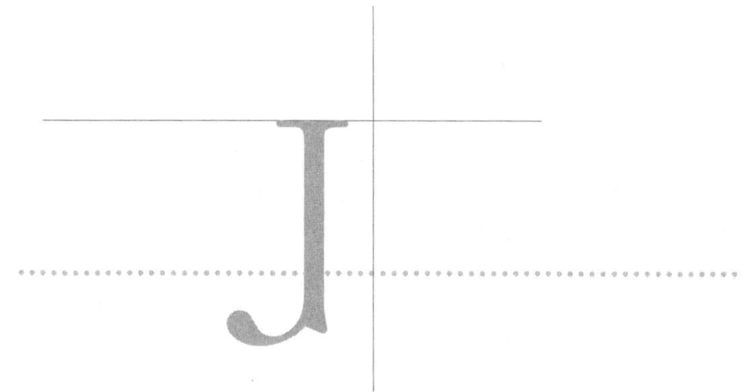

"There are no words available to human kind that can adequately describe what He means to me – and to the rest of the universe."

Jesus

LDS Apostle James E. Faust stated ("The Magnificent Vision Near Palmyra," *Ensign*, May 1984):

> The First Vision [of Joseph Smith] confirms the fact that there are three **separate Gods**: God the Father – Elohim, to whom we address our prayers; Jesus the Christ – Jehovah; and the Holy Ghost – the Comforter, through whose spirit we may know the truth of all things.

Aside from the absolutely heretical and non-Biblical statement (from this man who calls himself an apostle of Jesus Christ) that says the first vision *"confirms the fact that there are three separate Gods,"* James Faust said that God the Father's name is "*Elohim*" and Jesus' name is "*Jehovah.*" Now understand that the LDS literally believe that God's name – like my given name is Shawn – that God's *given name* is Elohim and that Jesus' given name is Jehovah.

Got that?

Every Latter-day Saint who enters one of their temples sees a film. In this film, God the Father is depicted in a body of flesh and bone, and is called by the proper noun "Elohim," and Jesus, also in a body of flesh and bone, is called "Jehovah."

In this section we are going to take a look at these two terms, their meanings, to whom they are applied, and how they reveal the true nature of Jesus.

There are three primary ways that the enemies of Christianity have attacked Jesus Christ since the manger in Bethlehem:

- His identity: Who Jesus is;
- His Word: the literal Words He spoke; and
- His Way: what is meant by the *good news*.

Enemies *question or alter His identity*. Cynics *challenge the reliability of His words.* And false religions *add or take away from His way of salvation.* This has been the case from the beginning. In John's gospel, he reports that Jesus Himself cried out,

> John 12:44. *He that believeth on me, believeth* ***not*** *on me, but on him that sent me. And* ***he that seeth me seeth him that sent me.***

This is very curious speech.

Jesus warned the religious rulers of His day:

> John 8:24. *if ye believe not that* ***I am****, ye shall* ***die in your sins.***

It is not enough to just believe in a personage called Jesus, but it is necessary to believe that this Jesus *was* and *is* the *I Am.* In short, when we are in line with His true identity, we will believe that He is ***I Am,*** and only then can we be assured that we will not die in our sins.

Do YOU believe that Jesus is the I AM?

Moses asked God, Who appeared to him in the burning bush, what he should tell the Israelites God's name is.

> Exodus 3:13. *Behold, when I come unto the children of Israel, and shall say unto them, The God of your fathers hath sent me unto you; and they shall say to me, What is his name? what shall I say unto them?*
>
> Exodus 3:14. *And God said unto Moses, I AM THAT I AM: and he said, Thus shalt thou say unto the children of Israel, I AM hath sent me unto you.*

British theologian Adam Clarke, in his *Commentary on the Whole Bible*, says of this verse:

> These words have been variously understood. The Vulgate translates I am who am. The Septuagint, I am he who exists. The Syriac, the Persic, and the Chaldee preserve the original words without any gloss. The Arabic paraphrases them, The Eternal, who passes not away; which is the same interpretation given by Abul Farajius, who also preserves the original words, and gives the above as their interpretation. The Targum of Jonathan, and the Jerusalem Targum [a "targum" is any of several Aramaic translations or paraphrasings of the Hebrew Scriptures] paraphrase the words thus: "He who spake, and the world was; who spake, and all things existed." As the original words literally signify, I will be what I will be, some have supposed that God simply designed to inform Moses, that what he had been to his fathers Abraham, Isaac, and Jacob, he would be to him and the Israelites; and that he would perform the promises he had made to his fathers, by giving their descendants the promised land. It is difficult to put a meaning on the words; they seem intended to point out the eternity and self-existence of God. Plato, in his Parmenides, where he treats sublimely of the nature of God, says nothing can express his nature; therefore no name can be attributed to him.

Now, there are two Hebrew words we must first consider when it comes to understanding God: Elohim and Jehovah.

Elohim, in Hebrew, is a noun meaning God. It is a general title for God. If I said the following sentences in Hebrew, *elohim* would be used in all three places where the word god is used, and it would be capitalized when appropriate:

- Satan is the god of this world.
- God created the heaven and the earth.
- Ozzy Osbourne is the god of rock.

Okay. Now the personal name of our God – the eternal, the self-existing, the One and only God, the *"I AM"* – is a word we pronounce as *"Jehovah."* Now this name (which is a transliteration of the Hebrew letters *YHWH*, which is probably more correctly pronounced *Yahweh*) is NOT a title, but is a proper noun – a name - His NAME! The King James translators used "the LORD" (all capital letters) when translating YHWH from the Hebrew:

> Isaiah 42:8. *I am YHWH: that is my name: and my glory will I not give to another, neither my praise to graven images.*

It has long been wondered how *YHWH* is pronounced. As we discussed earlier, the Jews never pronounced the sacred name out of reverence and respect for God. Some of the renderings include:

Jehovah
Yehue
Yehveh
Yeve
Jeue
Jao
Iao
Jhueh
Jove

It is also wondered what the name actually means.

Well, God Himself sort of defines His own name in Exodus 34. Moses had shattered the first stone tablets of the law and God called Him up to make others.

> Exodus 34:5, 6, 7. *And the LORD descended in the cloud, and stood with* [Moses] *there, and* ***proclaimed the name of the LORD.*** *And the LORD passed by before him, and proclaimed,* ***YHWH, YHWH Elohim,*** *merciful and gracious, longsuffering, and abundant in goodness and truth, Keeping mercy for thousands, forgiving iniquity and transgression and sin, and that will by no means clear the guilty;*

These words contain the proper interpretation of the venerable and glorious name *JEHOVAH.*

The term YHWH (what we call *Jehovah*) is known by a very large word: the *tetragrammaton.* In almost every case when we read *God* in the Old Testament (a capital *G* with a lower case *od*) it is the Hebrew word Elohim; when we see the word LORD, it is a translation of the Hebrew word *YHWH*, the tetragrammaton.

The next thing we observe is that the terms "God" (*Elohim*) and "the LORD" (*YHWH*) are used INTERCHANGEABLY in the Old Testament. This is *very* important to our present discussion. Take a look at Deuteronomy 4:35:

> Deuteronomy 4:35. *Unto thee it was shewed, that thou mightest know that the LORD <YHWH> he is God <Elohim>; there is none else beside him.*

Jehovah/YHWH is God and there is none else beside him.

> Psalm 100:3. *Know ye that Jehovah he is Elohim: it is he that hath made us, and not we ourselves; we are his people, and the sheep of his pasture.*

> 1 Kings 18:39. *And when all the people saw it, they fell on their*

> *faces: and they said, Jehovah, he is the Elohim; Jehovah, he is the Elohim.*

Note how "the" in "*the* Elohim" is the definite article: *the* ultimate; no other. Jehovah, He is ***THE*** GOD.

> Psalm 97:9. *For thou, Jehovah, art high above all the earth: thou art exalted far above all elohim.*

I wanted to establish this in our minds.

When Jesus says …

> John 12:44-45. *He that believeth on me, believeth not on me,* ***but on him that sent me.*** *And he that seeth me seeth him that sent me.*

… He is expressing who *He* is, *His* identity, and how He is ***one*** with the invisible God.

Yes, Jesus took on flesh. Yes, as a man, he subjected Himself to the will of the Father, Who is Spirit. His purpose was to *show us* the Father, to bring us the Father's will *in person*, in the flesh, to reveal the invisible God to us in living, physical form.

By looking at **Deuteronomy 4:35, Psalm 100:3, 1 Kings 18:39, and Psalm 97:9,** we are able to discover several absolute truths. First, the name Elohim and Jehovah are wholly interchangeable. Jehovah is THE ultimate and only God (or Elohim) and Elohim is the ultimate and only Jehovah. Second, Elohim is a *title*, a noun but not a proper noun. Remember, it can even be a title for Ozzy.

Okay, with all that understanding in place, look again at John chapter 12. Jesus cries out:

> John 12:44-45. *He that believeth on me, believeth not on me,* ***but on him that sent me.*** *And he that seeth me seeth him that sent me.*

It is my hope to spend the next few minutes proving that this babe of Bethlehem, born in a manger, *was* and *is*, wholly, completely, and unquestionably all Elohim, all Yahweh, all GOD. I want to demonstrate from the Scripture that if we were to look upon Jesus, *it is not one whit different* than looking upon God.

So allow me make some "declarations" about God, then back them up by Scripture, proving that these very same passages apply completely to Jesus Christ. In so doing, we will see that the same verses that apply to Jesus apply completely to God.

1. God raises the dead.

John 5:21. *For as the Father raises the dead and gives life to them, even so the Son gives life to whom He will.*

2. Jesus raises the dead.

John 5:21. *For as the Father raises the dead and gives life to them, even so the Son gives life to whom He will.*

3. God is the Word.

John 1:1. *In the beginning was the Word, and the Word was with God, and the* ***Word was God.***

4. Jesus is the Word.

John 1:14. *And* ***the Word became flesh*** *and dwelt among us, and we beheld His glory, the glory as of the only begotten of the Father, full of grace and truth.*

5. God heals all diseases.

Psalm 103:2-3. *Bless the LORD, O my soul, And forget not all His benefits, who forgives all your iniquities, Who heals all your diseases…*

6. Jesus heals all diseases.

Matthew 8:16-17. *When evening had come, they brought to Him many who were demon-possessed. And He cast out the spirits with a word, and healed all who were sick, that it might be fulfilled which was spoken by Isaiah the prophet, saying: He Himself took our infirmities And bore our sicknesses.*

7. God never changes.

Malachi 3:6. *For I am the LORD, I change not;*

8. Jesus never changes.

Hebrews 13:8. *Jesus Christ the same yesterday, and to day, and for ever.*

9. God created the Heavens/Earth by Himself.

Isaiah 44:24. *Thus saith the* LORD, *thy redeemer, and he that formed thee from the womb, I am the* LORD *that maketh all things; that stretcheth forth the heavens alone; that spreadeth abroad the earth* ***by myself;***

Genesis 1:1. *In the beginning* ***God*** *created the heavens and the earth.*

10. Jesus created the Heavens/Earth.

John 1:3. *All things were made through* [Jesus], *and without Him nothing was made that was made.*

Colossians 1:16. *For by him were all things created, that are in heaven, and that are in earth, visible and invisible, whether they be thrones, or dominions, or principalities, or powers: all things were created by him, and for him:*

Hebrews 1:10. [verse 8: Unto the Son, God saith] *Thou, Lord, in the beginning hast laid the foundation of the earth; and the heavens are the works of thine hands:*

11. God is the First and the Last.

Isaiah 41:4. *Who hath wrought and done it, calling the generations from the beginning? I the LORD, the first, and with the last; I am he.*

12. Jesus is the First and the Last.

Revelation 1:17-18. *And when I saw him, I fell at his feet as dead. And he laid his right hand upon me, saying unto me, Fear not; I am the first and the last: I am he that liveth, and was dead; and, behold, I am alive for evermore, Amen; and have the keys of hell and of death.*

13. God forgives sins.

Psalm 103:2-3. *Bless the LORD, O my soul, and forget not all his benefits: who forgiveth all thine iniquities; who healeth all thy diseases;*

Mark 2:5-7. *When Jesus saw their faith, he said unto the sick of the palsy, Son, thy sins be forgiven thee. But there was certain of the scribes sitting there, and reasoning in their hearts, Why doth this man thus speak blasphemies?* ***who can forgive sins but God only?***

14. Jesus forgives sins.

Mark 2:5. *When Jesus saw their faith, he said unto the sick of the palsy, Son, thy sins be forgiven thee.*

15. God is our redeemer.

Isaiah 63:16. … *thou, O LORD, art our father,* ***our redeemer****; thy name is from everlasting.*

16. Jesus is our redeemer.

Titus 2:13,14. *Looking for that blessed hope, and the glorious appearing of the great God and our Savior Jesus Christ; Who gave himself for us, that* ***he might redeem us*** *from all iniquity…*

17. God is one. [One, "Apostle" Faust!]

Deuteronomy 6:4. *Hear, O Israel: The LORD our God is one LORD:*

18. Jesus and God are One.

John 10:30. [verse 25: Jesus answered them] *I and my Father are one.*

John 14:9. *Jesus saith unto him, Have I been so long time with you, and yet hast thou not known me, Philip? he that hath seen me hath seen the Father; and how sayest thou then, Shew us the Father?*

1 John 5:7. *For there are three that bear record in heaven, the Father, the Word, and the Holy Ghost: and* ***these three are one.***

19. God has a son.

Psalm 2:7. *I will declare the decree: the LORD hath said unto me, Thou art my Son; this day have I begotten thee.*

20. Jesus is God's Son.

John 5:18. *Therefore the Jews sought the more to kill him, because he not only had broken the sabbath, but said also that* ***God was his Father, making himself equal with God.***

21. God is *I AM*.

Exodus 3:13-14. *And Moses said unto God, Behold, when I come unto the children of Israel, and shall say unto them,* ***The God*** *of your fathers hath sent me unto you; and they shall say to me, What is his name? what shall I say unto them? And God said unto Moses,* ***I AM THAT I AM****: and he said, Thus shalt thou say unto the children of Israel,* ***I AM*** *hath sent me unto you.*

22. Jesus is *I AM*.

John 8:58. *Jesus said unto them, Verily, verily, I say unto you, Before Abraham was,* ***I AM.***

23. Only God is to be worshipped.

Matthew 4:10. *Then saith Jesus unto him, Get thee hence, Satan: for it is written,* ***Thou shalt worship the Lord thy God, and him only shalt thou serve.***

Exodus 34:14. *For thou shalt worship no other god: for the LORD, whose name is Jealous, is a jealous God:*

23. Jesus is worshipped.

Matthew 9:18. *While he spake these things unto them, behold, there came a certain ruler,* ***and worshipped him****, saying, My daughter is even now dead: but come and lay thy hand upon her, and she shall live.*

Matthew 28:9. *And as they went to tell his disciples, behold, Jesus met them, saying, All hail. And they came and held him by the feet, and* ***worshipped him***

Hebrews 1:6. *And again, when he bringeth in the firstbegotten into the world, he saith, And* ***let all the angels of God worship him.***

24. God is from everlasting.

Psalm 93:1-2. *The LORD reigneth, he is clothed with majesty; the LORD is clothed with strength, wherewith he hath girded himself: the world also is stablished, that it cannot be moved. Thy throne is established of old:* ***thou art from everlasting.***

25. Jesus is from everlasting.

Micah 5:2. *But thou,* ***Bethlehem*** *Ephratah, though thou be little among the thousands of Judah, yet* ***out of thee shall he come forth unto me that is to be ruler in Israel;*** *whose goings forth have been* ***from of old, from everlasting.***

Isaiah 9:6. *For unto us* ***a child is born,*** *unto us a son is given: and the government shall be upon his shoulder: and* ***his name shall be called*** *Wonderful, Counsellor, The mighty God,* ***The everlasting Father,*** *The Prince of Peace.*

26. God does not share His glory.

Isaiah 42:8. *I am the LORD: that is my name: and* ***my glory will I not give to another,*** *neither my praise to graven images.*

27. Jesus is glorified as God.

John 17:5. *And now, O Father, glorify thou me with thine own self* ***with the glory which I had with thee*** *before the world was.*

28. God is the Judge of the whole world.

Psalm 94:1-2. *O LORD God, to whom vengeance belongeth; O God, to whom vengeance belongeth, shew thyself. Lift up thyself,* ***thou judge of the earth:*** *render a reward to the proud.*

29. Jesus is the Judge of the whole world.

John 5:22. *For the* ***Father judgeth no man, but hath committed all judgment unto the Son:*** *That all men should honour the Son, even as they honour the Father. He that honoureth not the Son honoureth not the Father which hath sent him.*

30. God is the Holy One.

Psalm 71:22. *I will also praise thee with the psaltery, even thy truth,* ***O my God:*** *unto thee will I sing with the harp,* ***O thou Holy One*** *of Israel.*

31. Jesus is the Holy One.

Luke 4:33-34. *And in the synagogue there was a man, which had a spirit of an unclean devil, and cried out with a loud voice, Saying, Let us alone; what have we to do with thee, thou Jesus of Nazareth? art thou come to destroy us? I know thee who thou art; the Holy One of God.*

32. God is the only Savior.

Isaiah 43:11. *I, even I, am the LORD; and* ***beside me there is no savior.***

Luke 1:47. *And Mary said, My soul doth magnify the Lord, and my spirit hath rejoiced in* ***God my Savior.***

Jude 1:25. *To the* ***only*** *wise* ***God our Saviour,*** *be glory and majesty, dominion and power, both now and ever. Amen.*

Titus 2:10. *Not purloining, but shewing all good fidelity; that they may adorn the doctrine of* ***God our Saviour*** *in all things.*

1 Timothy 4:10. *For therefore we both labour and suffer reproach, because we trust in* ***the living God, who is the Saviour*** *of all men, specially of those that believe.*

33. Jesus is the only Savior.

John 4:41-42. *And many more believed because of his own word; And said unto the woman, Now we believe, not because of thy saying: for we have heard him ourselves, and know that* ***this is indeed the Christ, the Savior*** *of the world.*

How about some other ***very supportive*** passages that help us know the identity of Jesus Christ, our Lord?

> 1 Timothy 3:16. *And without controversy great is the mystery of godliness:* ***God was manifested in the flesh****, Justified in the Spirit, Seen by angels, Preached among the Gentiles, Believed on in the world, Received up in glory.*
>
> Philippians 2:5-8. *Let this mind be in you, which was also in Christ Jesus: Who,* ***being in the form of God****, thought it not robbery to be* ***equal with God****: But made himself of no reputation, and took upon him the form of a servant, and was made in the likeness of men: And being found in fashion as a man, he humbled himself, and became obedient unto death, even the death of the cross.*
>
> 1 John 5:7. *For there are three that bear witness in heaven: the Father, the Word, and the Holy Spirit; and* ***these three are one****.*
>
> Acts 20:28. *Take heed therefore unto yourselves, and to all the flock, over the which the Holy Ghost hath made you overseers, to feed* ***the church of God, which he hath purchased with his own blood****.*
>
> Acts 7:59. *And they stoned Stephen,* ***calling upon God****, and saying,* ***Lord Jesus, receive my spirit****.*
>
> Colossians 1:13-19. [verse 12: the Father] *Who hath delivered us from the power of darkness, and hath translated us into the* ***kingdom of his dear Son****:* [and then he goes on, speaking of the Son] *In whom we have redemption through his blood, even the forgiveness of sins:* ***Who is the image of the invisible God*** [Paul speaks of a God NOT of flesh and bone], *the firstborn of every creature: For by him were* ***all*** *things created, that are in heaven, and that are in earth,* ***visible and invisible****, whether they be thrones, or dominions, or principalities, or powers: all things were created by him, and for him: And he is* ***before all things****, and by* ***him all things consist****. And he is the head of the body, the church: who is the beginning, the firstborn from the dead; that in all things he might have the preeminence. For it pleased the Father that* ***in him should all fulness dwell****;*

> Colossians 2:9. *For in him dwelleth* ***all the fulness of the Godhead bodily.***

Speaking prophetically of John the Baptist, Isaiah describes who the Baptist prepared the way for, saying,

> Isaiah 40:3. *The voice of him that crieth in the wilderness, Prepare ye the way of the LORD, make straight in the desert a highway* ***for our God.***

The Jews said of Jesus,

> John 10:33. *The Jews answered him, saying, For a good work we stone thee not; but for blasphemy; and because that thou, being a man, makest thyself God.*

And finally,

> Matthew 1:23. *Behold, a virgin shall be with child, and shall bring forth a son, and they shall call his name Emmanuel, which being interpreted is,* ***God with us.***

Just one more: ***God is the Messiah!*** In Handel's Messiah, which the LDS are great at reciting with a tremendous amount of blindness at Christmas time, the composer quotes Isaiah:

> Isaiah 9:6. *For unto us a child is born, unto us a son is given: and the government shall be upon his shoulder: and his name shall be called Wonderful, Counsellor, The* ***mighty God****, The* ***everlasting Father****, The Prince of Peace.*

And yet we also understand that *Jesus is the Messiah!*

> John 4:25-26. *The [Samaritan] woman saith unto him, I know that Messiah cometh, which is called Christ: when he is come, he will tell us all things. Jesus saith unto her,* ***I that speak unto thee am he.***

Unless we believe that He – Jesus – is the ***I AM***, we will die in our sin.

❋ ❋ ❋

"After reading all I could get my hands on about this man, all I can say is it seems to me that in the end he did not fear God in the least."

Joseph Smith and the Bible

We have been going through topics alphabetically this year as they relate not just to Mormonism, but also to the Bible. For example, we've taken the topic of baptism and seen what the LDS have to say about it, and then we look at what the Bible says. In light of this aim, our topic may surprise you: Joseph Smith. "*Joseph Smith*?" you might ask. "*How would the person of Joseph Smith, born in 1806, have anything to do with what is written in the Bible?*"

Well, if you are a Bible believing Christian, you know he doesn't. But if you are a Latter-day Saint, you are likely to believe that the man Joseph Smith, was prophesied of *all through* the Bible, both his individual person and the things he introduced to the world.

Does the Bible speak of Joseph Smith at all? Does it really foretell of the work he introduced? Is it true that Mormons actually believe that the name of Joseph Smith Jr. was included in the Old Testament? I think that I can safely say that the following information will be absolutely shocking to most Bible believing Christians. And, I hope, to some truth-seeking LDS, too.

Now, it is not by coincidence that almost all religious reformers (who started out Christian then drifted) have sought to add their name to what Jesus brought to the world. Reverend Sun Myung Moon did it. David Koresh did it. Jim Jones did it. Marshall Applewhite did it, as have hundreds and hundreds of others. (For an interesting read about these types of people throughout history, check out the book, *God's Lunatics* by Michael Largo.)

Well Mr. Joseph Smith was not one whit different than the rest of these religious charlatans. And as a result of his claims, Mormon men and women have picked up the torch that Smith himself lit and marched through the streets crying that people must receive his person and work in order to be saved.

And as with most intelligent counterfeits, Joseph did not remove Jesus from the picture; he simply placed himself at the same table with the LORD. In one of the standard books of scripture used by Mormons today (the *Doctrine and Covenants*) we read:

> D&C 135:3. Joseph Smith, the prophet and Seer of the Lord, has done more, save Jesus only, for the salvation of men in this world, than any other man that ever lived in it.

According to this LDS "scripture," Joseph Smith has done more for the salvation of men in this world than Abraham, Moses, Isaiah, Ezekiel, Jeremiah, Daniel, Peter, Paul, John the Beloved, Ignatius, Polycarp, Tertullian, Luther, Edwards, Knox, Tyndale, Wesley, Wycliffe, Zwingli, Billy Sunday or Billy Graham?

Joseph Smith – done more – save Jesus Christ?

The man who stared into hats at peep stones and pretended to locate buried treasure underground ... *done more?*

The man who took teenage servants living in his home, to be his polygamist wives ... *done more?*

The man who said, and I quote, "God is my right hand man (*History of the Church* 6:78)" has done more than any other man, save Jesus? Really?

Amazingly enough, over the years, well respected LDS leaders have taken this position and elevated Joseph Smith to an even higher spiritual status by making some extremely bold comparatives between his life and mission and the life and mission of Jesus Christ. I am not making up what I am about to report. These are genuine, authentic quotes about the man Joseph Smith by respected Mormon leaders.

Listen closely how they liken him and his life to that of the Lord Jesus Christ.

Apostle Hugh B. Brown, *An Abundant Life*, page 138:

> Joseph Smith was less than 15 when he had his first vision, 24 when he translated the Book of Mormon, 25 when the Church was organized, and he died a young man – yet he left an imprint upon the world second only to that of Christ the Lord.

President and "Prophet" Brigham Young, as he was prone to do, said all sorts of stuff. Young was very big on making Smith's approval necessary for entering heaven and escaping damnation. Listen to what he said in a sermon on March 29, 1857 (*Journal of Discourses* 4:298):

> I know that Joseph Smith is a prophet of God, that this is the Gospel of salvation, and if you do not believe it you will be damned, every one of you.

Adding more fuel to this position, Young also said on March 8, 1857 (*Journal of Discourses* 4:271):

> If we can pass the sentinel Joseph the Prophet, we shall go into the celestial kingdom, and not a man can injure us. If he says, 'God bless you, come along here,' if we will live so that Joseph will justify us, and say, 'Here am I, brethren,' we shall pass every sentinel; there will be no danger but that we will pass into the celestial kingdom.

Again, Brigham Young said (October 9, 1859, *Journal of Discourses* 7:289):

> … no man or woman in this dispensation will ever enter into the celestial kingdom of God without the consent of Joseph Smith. From the day that the Priesthood was taken from the earth to the winding-up scene of all things, every man and woman must have the certificate of Joseph Smith, junior, as a passport to their entrance into the mansion where God and Christ are – I with you and you with me. I cannot go there without his consent. He holds the keys for that kingdom for the last dispensation – the keys to rule in the spirit-world; and he rules there triumphantly, for he gained full power and a glorious victory over the power of Satan while he was yet in the flesh, and was a martyr to his religion and to the name of Christ, which gives him a most perfect victory in the spirit-world. He reigns there as supreme a being in his sphere, capacity, and calling, as God does in heaven. Many will exclaim – "Oh, that is very disagreeable! It is preposterous! We cannot bear the thought!" But it is true.

Just as Jesus after His death went to Spirit prison to release the Old Testament faithful to God, listen to what LDS President President Wilford Woodruff said of Joseph Smith (*The Discourses of Wilford Woodruff*, page 36):

> When Joseph Smith's body was laid in the grave, his spirit, like unto the Son of God, went into the spirit world with the keys of this dispensation to unlock the prison doors. There were fifty thousand millions' of spirits that never saw the face of a prophet, or heard a gospel sermon in their lives, until Joseph Smith preached to them the message of salvation.

LDS President Joseph F. Smith taught (*Gospel Doctrine* 1939, page 134; reprinted in "Joseph Smith: Restorer of Truth," *Ensign*, December 2003):

> The day will come – and it is not far distant, either – when the name of the Prophet Joseph Smith will be coupled with the

> name of Jesus Christ of Nazareth, the Son of God, as his representative, as his agent whom he chose, ordained and set apart to lay anew the foundations of the Church of God in the world, which is indeed the Church of Jesus Christ, possessing all the powers of the Gospel, all the rites and privileges, the authority of the Holy Priesthood, and every principle necessary to fit and qualify both the living and the dead to inherit eternal life, and to attain to exaltation in the kingdom of God.

A more recent LDS Prophet, Spencer W. Kimball, likened Smith to the Lord Jesus Christ in yet another way (LDS *Conference Report*, April 1946, page 45):

> And his hour had come to seal with his blood his testimony, so often borne to multitudes of friends and foes. His Judas came from his own circle – Governor Ford was his Pontius Pilate, Nauvoo was his Gethsemane, and Carthage his Calvary. There were also modern Pharisees to goad the mobs – and another martyr testified.

Mormon Prophet David O. McKay ("Joseph Smith: Restorer of Truth," *Ensign*, December 2003) said:

> The principles of the restored gospel as revealed to the Prophet Joseph Smith are the surest, safest guide to mortal man.

And good old "Apostle" Bruce R. McConkie wrote, when I was a kid (*Mormon Doctrine*, 1966, p. 670):

> If it had not been for Joseph Smith and the restoration, there would be no salvation.

Many LDS claim this book has been "repudiated," but it has stood firm for twenty-plus years, causing millions to accept statements like this. It is still available from LDS book outlets and the First Presidency has never officially repudiated McConkie's apostleship. So to me, it's still valid to quote.

The Prophet and Apostle Heber J. Grant taught (July 26, 1857, *Journal of Discourses* 5:88):

> You call us fools: but the day will be, gentlemen and ladies, whether you belong to this Church or not, when you will prize brother Joseph Smith as the Prophet of the Living God, and look upon him as a God, and also upon Brigham Young, our Governor in the Territory of Deseret.

Finally, one of the latest LDS prophets, Gordon B. Hinckley said, on Christmas Day, no less ("Joseph Smith: Restorer of Truth," *Ensign*, December 2003) about Joseph Smith:

> We stand in reverence before him. He is the great prophet of this dispensation. He stands as the head of this great and mighty work which is spreading across the earth. He is our prophet, our revelator, our seer, our friend. Let us not forget him. Let not his memory be forgotten in the celebration of Christmas. God be thanked for the Prophet Joseph.

All of this should really be of no surprise when we read the extolment Joseph Smith assigned to himself, and what others have assigned to him since his death. In the following list are all of the appellations that have been assigned to Joseph Smith by LDS sources.

They say he was …

1. **Prophet**
2. **Priest**
3. **Medium of God's anointed** – Doctrine and Covenants 132:7.
4. **Chosen** – *Doctrines of Salvation* 1:184.
5. **Foreordained from foundation of the world** – Doctrines of Salvation 1:184.
6. **Martyr** – *History of the Church* 6:617-619, 627; *Journal of Discourses* 7:289

7. **Choice seer** – 2 Nephi 3:6-7, 15
8. **Military general**
9. **Mayor**
10. **God to all** – *TPJS*, page 363: God made Aaron to be the mouthpiece for the children of Israel, and **He will make me be god to you** in His stead, and the Elders to be mouth for me; and if you don't like it, you must lump it. I have been giving Elder Adams instruction in some principles to speak to you, and if he makes a mistake, I will get up and correct him. (April 8, 1844.) *DHC* 6:318-320.
11. **Meek and lowly** – *Discourses of Joseph Smith*, pages 30-31; *History of the Church* 5:218.
12. **Related to Jesus** – "Great Are the Words of Isaiah," LDS *Conference Report*, April 1929, pages 124-125.
13. **Voice of one crying in the wilderness** – *Discourses of Joseph Smith*, page 200.
14. **Controls minds of mankind** – *TPJS*, page 341: President Joseph Smith again arose and said—In relation to **the power over the minds of mankind which I hold,** I would say, It is in consequence of the power of truth in the doctrines which I have been an instrument in the hands of God of presenting unto them, and not because of any compulsion on my part.
15. **Continues to lead from heaven** – *Teachings of Ezra Taft Benson*, page 101: The Prophet Joseph Smith was not only "one of the noble and great ones," but he gave and **continues to give attention to important matters here on the earth even today from the realms above.** For in the eyes of the Lord, the God of this world under the Father, it is all one great eternal program in which the Prophet Joseph plays an important role, all through the eternal priesthood and authority of God. (*God, Family, Country,* pp. 30-31.)

16. **Knows more than the entire world put together** – *TPJS*, page 350: Now, I ask all who hear me, why the learned men who are preaching salvation, say that God created the heavens and the earth out of nothing? The reason is, that they are unlearned in the things of God, and have not the gift of the Holy Ghost; they account it blasphemy in any one to contradict their idea. If you tell them that God made the world out of something, they will call you a fool. But **I am learned, and know more than all the world put together.** The Holy Ghost does, anyhow, and He is within me, and comprehends more than all the world: and I will associate myself with Him.

17. **Offered a complete sacrifice** – *Joseph Smith, the Prophet, the Man*, pages xxxiv-xxxv: When a man gives his life for the cause he has advocated, he meets the highest test of his honesty and sincerity that his own or any future generation can in fairness ask. When he dies for the testimony he has borne, all malicious tongues should ever after be silent, and all voices hushed in reverence before **a sacrifice so complete** (Dalby).

18. **Shed his blood for truth** – *Joseph Smith, the Prophet, the Man*, page xxxiv: **For the truths that will be taught here,** he gave his life. For the testimonies that will be spoken here, **he shed his blood.** I like these words spoken by one who admired and loved him.

19. **Holds endless priesthood** – "Praise to the Man," *LDS Hymns #27*; *Joseph Smith, the Prophet, the Man*, page 3: Great is his glory and **endless his priesthood**. Ever and ever the keys he will hold. Faithful and true, he will enter his kingdom, Crowned in the midst of the prophets of old.

20. **A Teacher**

21. **His name will never perish** – *Gospel Doctrine*, page 479: God lives, and Jesus is the Christ, the Savior of the

world. Joseph Smith is a prophet of God—living, not dead; for **his name will never perish**.

22. **Intelligence is superior** – *Discourses of Joseph Smith*, pages 4-5.

23. **Has done more than anyone** – *Discourses of Joseph Smith*, pages 22-23; *Journal of Discourses* 24:14-15.

24. **Was as great as Adam and Abraham** – *Mormon Doctrine*, pages 395-396: In the providences of Almighty God, and according to the plan before ordained in the councils of eternity, Joseph Smith, Jr., was born into mortality, December 23, 1805. As a pre-existent spirit he had ranked with Adam and Abraham; he was one of the noble and great ones of whom Abraham wrote (Abra. 3:22-23), a truth which President Joseph F. Smith also saw in vision. (*Gospel Doctrine*, 4th ed., p. 601.) In that prior existence, by diligence and obedience, he gained the spiritual stature and capacity which entitled him to be foreordained to stand as the head of the greatest of all gospel dispensations (*Teachings*, p. 365.).

25. **His work is eternal** – *Gospel Doctrine*, page 481: The work in which Joseph Smith was engaged was not confined to this life alone, but it **pertains as well to the life to come**, and to the life that has been. In other words, it relates to those who have lived upon the earth, to those who are living and to those who shall come after us. It is not something which relates to man only while he tabernacles in the flesh, but to the whole human family from eternity to eternity.

26. **Rough rolling stone** – *History of the Church* 5:401: I am like a huge, rough stone rolling down from a high mountain; and the only polishing I get is when some corner gets rubbed off by coming in contact with something else, striking with accelerated force against religious bigotry, priestcraft, lawyer-craft, doctor-craft, lying editors, suborned judges and jurors, and the authority of perjured

executives, backed by mobs, blasphemers, licentious and corrupt men and women—all hell knocking off a corner here and a corner there. Thus I will become a smooth and polished shaft in the quiver of the Almighty, who will give me dominion over all and every one of them, when their refuge of lies shall fail, and their hiding place shall be destroyed, while these smooth-polished stones with which I come in contact become marred.

27. **Noble and great spirit like Jeremiah** – *A Marvelous Work and a Wonder*, page 278: The spirit of Joseph Smith, **like Jeremiah, was also one of the "noble and great" ones.** The Lord appointed unto him his work and reserved him to come forth in this dispensation to be a prophet and seer unto the nations. That is why the Lord called Joseph Smith while yet a boy, because he knew Joseph and knew of his integrity and greatness.

28. **Joseph and God are partners** – *Handbook of the Restoration*, page 50: There is only one explanation which is tenable. God chose this man. He spoke through him. The virgin, unsophisticated mind of the youth was a fertile field for the planting of spiritual seeds. They grew and matured into a perfect faith that **brought Joseph into partnership with God.** When that came to be, there was nothing unattainable, for as we are told of old, one man and God are a majority.

29. **He bears infirmities of others** – *Discourses of Joseph Smith*, page 28: Notwithstanding my weaknesses, I am under the necessity of **bearing the infirmities of others**, who when they get into difficulty, hang on to me tenaciously to get them out, and wish me to cover their faults (*HC* 5:516.).

30. **He brings purpose to life** – *Handbook of the Restoration*, pg. 50-51: It would seem scarcely necessary to point out the obvious conclusion and purpose of this recital. If any man has received in his heart the witness of the divine

truth embraced in the contributions of the Prophet Joseph, I charge him to be true ... **Glorious purpose will come into life**. Family ties will be sweeter. Friendships will be dearer. Service will be nobler, and the peace of Christ will be his portion.

31. **He kept Church together** – *Discourses of Joseph Smith*, page 31: I have more to boast of than ever any man had. I am the only man that has ever been able to keep a whole church together since the days of Adam. A large majority of the whole have stood by me. Neither Paul, John, Peter, nor Jesus ever did it. I boast that no man ever did such a work as I. The followers of Jesus ran away from Him; but the Latter-day Saints never ran away from me yet (*HC* 6:408-409).

32. **Humble as a child** – *Joseph Smith the Prophet*, page 28.

33. **Heavens rested while Joseph left to mature** – *Life of Joseph the Prophet*, page 6: The great work of opening the dispensation thus accomplished by the august administration of the Father and Son, the heavens rested for a season. There was divine wisdom in this. Joseph was too young at that time to be sent forth with the wondrous proclamation to all nations, kindreds and tongues, that God had called him to be the prophet of a new civilization; too young, at fourteen, to seek out from the multitude strong apostolic men, saying unto them, "Leave your nets and follow me."

34. **Athletic** – *The Lord Needed a Prophet*, page 4: At six feet tall and weighing about two hundred pounds, the Prophet Joseph had an athletic build. He enjoyed hard work and energetic play. Joseph frequently joined the young boys in Nauvoo in outdoor games. He could hit a ball with a bat so great a distance that the other players would call to the boy who was going for the ball to take his dinner while he was at it. Joseph would laugh and go on with the game.

35. **Genius with no education** – *Divine Authority or the Question, Was Joseph Smith Sent of God?*, page 4: How came Mr. Smith, if a deceiver, to think of all this? Did Martin Luther, Wesley, Whitfield, Swedenborg, or Irving think of this? Whence his superior intellect, his depth of understanding, his extensive foresight, that he should so far surpass all former impostors for 1700 years? John testifies that when the everlasting gospel is restored to the earth it shall be by an angel. Mr. Smith testifies that it was restored by an angel, and in no other way. This is another presumptive evidence that he was sent of God.

36. **Mason** – *Encyclopedia of Mormonism*, **page 1018.**

37. **Joseph's consent needed to enter heaven** – *Journal of Discourses* 7:289: No man or woman in this dispensation will ever enter into the celestial kingdom of God without the consent of Joseph Smith. From the day that the Priesthood was taken from the earth to the winding-up scene of all things, every man and woman must have the certificate of Joseph Smith, junior, as a passport to their entrance into the mansion where God and Christ are – I with you and you with me. I cannot go there without his consent.

38. **People studied at the feet of Joseph** – *Joseph Smith, The Choice Seer*, Preface #3: In assessing the marvelous impact of the Choice Seer's work on this dispensation, we will turn first and foremost to the doctrinal teachings of Joseph Smith as set forth in his sermons, letters, revelations, translations, and narrations. In addition, we will rely occasionally on the clarifications and expansions of those who knew Brother Joseph firsthand and studied at his feet, as well as those apostolic and prophetic successors to whom is given the divine mandate to build on the doctrinal foundation he laid.

39. **Joseph holds keys until Christ's return** – Doctrine and Covenants 112:15: Exalt not yourselves; rebel not

against my servant Joseph; for verily I say unto you, I am with him, and my hand shall be over him; and **the keys** which I have given unto him, and also to youward, **shall not be taken from him till I come.**

40. **Was a suffering martyr** - *Joseph Smith the Prophet*, page 63.

41. **A lamb to slaughter** – *TPJS*, page 379.

42. **Joseph had more followers than Jesus** – *Journal of Discourses* 14:202: ... this personage whom we call the Savior of the world, there were not, strange to say, as many per*sons believed on him as have believed on Joseph Smith in the latter days.*

43. **Man of sorrows** – *Joseph Smith, The Choice Seer*, Prologue: Joseph Smith Among the Prophets: The farm boy who grew to become a prophet's prophet was also, to some degree at least, "a man of sorrows, and acquainted with grief."

44. **Had to go away, but will return** – *Journal of Discourses* 13:164: Said he, "You have to round up your shoulders to bear up the kingdom. No matter what becomes of me ..." This language was plain enough, but we did not understand it any more than the disciples of Jesus when he told them he was going away, and that if he went not the Comforter would not come. It was just so with Joseph. ... but none of us seemed to understand that he was going to seal his testimony with his blood, but so it was.

45. **Smith carries your sin** – *TPJS*, page 193: I charged the Saints not to follow the example of the adversary in accusing the brethren, and said, "If you do not accuse each other, God will not accuse you. If you have no accuser you will enter heaven, and **if you will follow the revelations and instructions which God gives you through me, I will take you into heaven as my back load.** If you will

not accuse me, I will not accuse you. If you will throw a cloak of charity over my sins, I will over yours—for charity covereth a multitude of sins. What many people call sin is not sin.

46. **Holds power of Jesus** – *Journal of Discourses* 7:289-290: It was decreed in the councils of eternity, long before the foundations of the earth were laid, that [Joseph Smith] should be the man in the last dispensation of this world to bring forth the word of God to the people and receive the fulness of the keys of **power of the Priesthood of the Son of God**. The Lord had his eye upon him, and upon his father, and upon his father's father, and upon their progenitors clear back to Abraham, and from Abraham to the flood, from the flood to Enoch, and from Enoch to Adam. He has watched that family and that blood as it has circulated from its fountain to the birth of that man. He was fore-ordained in eternity to preside over this last dispensation.

47. **Salvation available because of Smith** – *Mormon Doctrine*, page 396: Since the keys of salvation were restored to the Prophet, it is in and through and because of his latter-day mission that the full redemptive power of the Lord has again become available to men. **It is because the Lord called Joseph Smith that salvation is again available to mortal men.**

48. **Reverence for Smith's name advised** – *Neal A. Maxwell Quote Book*, page 181: Whenever we speak of the Prophet Joseph Smith … it should be in reverent appreciation of the Lord who called him and whom Joseph served so well ("A Choice Seer," p. 113.).

49. **Smith brings assurance of salvation** – *Joseph Smith, The Choice Seer*, Prologue: Praise to the Man #4: Because of Joseph Smith, we know that we are members of the house of Israel and heirs to all the blessings promised to Abraham, Isaac, and Jacob. Joseph Smith did more than

restore a New Testament church. Indeed, the genius of the Restoration is found in the Old Testament. It centers in the covenant God made with father Abraham.

50. **Confessing spirit of Smith is of God** – *Discourses of Brigham Young*, page 435: **Whosoever confesseth that Joseph Smith was sent of God** to reveal the holy Gospel to the children of men, and lay the foundation for gathering Israel, and building up the Kingdom of God on the earth, that spirit is of God, and every spirit that does not confess that God has sent Joseph Smith, and revealed the everlasting Gospel to and through him, is of Antichrist, no matter whether it is found in a pulpit or on a throne.

51. **Greater than the prophet Isaiah** – *Discourses of Joseph Smith*, page 7; In thirty nations are men and women who look upon him as a greater leader than Moses and **a greater prophet than Isaiah**; his disciples now number close to a million [the present figure is over 3.5 million]; and already a granite shaft pierces the sky over the place where he was born, and another is in course of erection over the place where he is credited with having received the inspiration for his Book. (John Henry Evans, op. cit., introduction.)

52. **He is the root of Jesse** – *Doctrine and Covenants* 113:1-6

53. **Visited by Jesus, Moses & others** – *The Lord Needed a Prophet*, page 14: There in the Kirtland Temple **Joseph again saw the Savior as well as the ancient prophets Moses, Elias, and Elijah.** Those heavenly messengers strengthened Joseph's faith, gave him important priesthood authority, and filled him with courage to face the trials that were soon to come.

54. **Jesus' & Joseph's visage "marred" through sacrifices** – *Answers: Straight forward Answers to Tough Gospel Questions*, pages 125-126.

55. **Joseph defies world to refute him** – *TPJS*, page 372: The head God organized the heavens and the earth. I defy all the world to refute me.

56. **Joseph enlarged conception of covenants** – *The Life of the Prophet Joseph Smith*, page 167: Thus has Joseph enlarged our conceptions of the priesthood, of the covenant, of religion.

57. **Joseph holds authority to speak for God** – *TPJS*, pg. 345: I will prove that the world is wrong, by showing what God is. I am going to enquire after God; for I want you all to know him and to be familiar with him; for if I am bringing you to a knowledge of him, all persecutions against me ought to cease. You will then know that I am his servant; for **I speak as one having authority.**

58. **He helped save the world** – *Doctrines & Covenants Speaks* **2:456:** One of Joseph Smith's contributions to the **salvation of men in this world** was the bringing forth of…the Book of Mormon, which he translated by the gift and power of God…(D&C 135:3).

59. **Joseph is heaven's gatekeeper** – *Journal of Discourses* 7:289: He holds the keys of that [the celestial] kingdom for the last dispensation—the keys to rule in the spirit-world; and he rules there triumphantly.

60. **Joseph is greatest fulfillment of the Church** – *Journal of Discourses* 24:15: Through Joseph Smith, God has revealed many things which were kept hid from the foundation of the world in fulfillment of the Prophets—and at no time since Enoch walked the earth has the Church of God been organized as perfectly as it is to-day—not excepting the dispensation of Jesus and His disciples—or if it was we have no record of it.

61. **Joseph never lied?** – *History of the Church* 6:366: When did I ever teach anything wrong from this stand? When was I ever confounded? I want to triumph in Israel be-

fore I depart hence and am no more seen. I never told you I was perfect; but there is no error in the revelations which I have taught. Must I, then, be thrown away as a thing of naught?

62. **Joseph is all he claimed to be** – *Doctrines of Salvation* 1:18: There is no possibility of his being deceived, and on this issue we are ready to make our stand. I maintain that Joseph Smith was all that he claimed to be. His statements are too positive and his claims too great to admit of deception on his part. No impostor could have accomplished so great and wonderful a work. Had he been such, he would have been detected and exposed, and the plan would have failed and come to naught.

63. **Joseph is Jehovah's epic** – *Life of the Prophet Joseph Smith*, page 165: Jehovah's epic! There is no other defining that will adequately express the subject and themes grasped by the genius of the Mormon Prophet.

64. **Three questions to ask about Joseph Smith** – *Neal A. Maxwell Quote Book*, page 181: Yet another way of testing and appreciating the significance of the ministry of the Prophet Joseph Smith is to ask oneself: (1) "What would we know about the holy temples and about the sealing power without the Prophet Joseph Smith?"; (2) "What would we know about the plan of salvation with its different estates without the Prophet Joseph Smith?"; (3) "What would we know about the precious and plain doctrine of premortality of mankind without the Prophet Joseph Smith?" The answer to each question is the same: "Very, very little; certainly not enough ("A Choice Seer.")."

65. **Thousands thank God for Joseph** – *Joseph Smith, Prophet of the Restoration*, page 112: Consequently, as I have said, Joseph Smith is held in reverence, his name is honored; **tens of thousands of people thank God in their heart and from the depths of their souls** for the knowl-

edge the Lord has restored to the earth through him, and therefore they speak well of him and bear testimony of his worth …They speak to his praise, to his honor, and they hold his name in honorable remembrance. They revere him and they love him as they love no other man, because they know he was the chosen instrument in the hands of the Almighty of restoring the Gospel of life and salvation unto them.

66. **Loyalty to Joseph brings rewards** – *Joseph Smith: The Choice Seer*, Epilogue #12: We know that loyalty to Joseph Smith and the Restoration will reap rich rewards for individual members of the Church and will result in miraculous conversions throughout the earth.

67. **Joseph's name known for good and evil** – *Joseph Smith History* 1:33.

68. **Joseph close to omniscience** – *Gospel Through the Ages*, pg. 125: The holy men of the Lord, such as the beloved Prophet Joseph Smith, who understood the unseen world beyond the veil of mortality, not only had a firm conviction that life is eternal, but had a comprehensive philosophy of the stages of progression that men pass through.

Then we have to look at what Joseph actually did with his own name when he was alive. Did you know that he included his own name in the Book of Mormon he supposedly translated from golden plates? Mormon Prophet John Taylor admits it, saying (*Teachings of Presidents of the Church: Joseph Smith*, page 547):

> Who was Joseph Smith? The Book of Mormon tells us he was of the seed of Joseph that was sold into Egypt, and hence he was selected as Abraham was to fulfil a work upon the earth.

But that wasn't enough! Listen: Joseph Smith claimed to have retranslated the book of Genesis in the Bible and included a prophecy about himself in it! I am not kidding you! Listen to Joseph Smith's "translation" of Genesis 50:30-33:

> And again, a seer will I raise up out of the fruit of thy loins, and unto him will I give power to bring forth my word unto the seed of thy loins; and not to the bringing forth of my word only, saith the Lord, but to the convincing them of my word, which shall have already gone forth among them in the last days; Wherefore the fruit of thy loins shall write, and the fruit of the loins of Judah shall write; and that which shall be written by the fruit of thy loins, and also that which shall be written by the fruit of the loins of Judah, shall grow together unto the confounding of false doctrines, and laying down of contentions, and establishing peace among the fruit of thy loins, and bringing them to a knowledge of their fathers in the latter days; and also to the knowledge of my covenants, saith the Lord. And out of weakness shall he be made strong, in that day when my work shall go forth among all my people, which shall restore them, who are of the house of Israel, in the last days. And that seer will I bless, and they that seek to destroy him shall be confounded; for this promise I give unto you; for I will remember you from generation to generation; **and his name shall be called Joseph, and it shall be after the name of his father**; and he shall be like unto you; for the thing which the Lord shall bring forth by his hand shall bring my people unto salvation.

Finally, how about some quotes about what Joseph Smith said about himself?

> I calculate to be one of the instruments of setting up the kingdom of Daniel by the word of the Lord, and I intend to lay a foundation that will revolutionize the whole world. (*History of the Church,* 6:364)

> I could explain a hundred fold more than I ever have of the glories of the kingdoms manifested to me in the vision, were I permitted, and were the people prepared to receive them. (*History of the Church*, 5:402)

> I see no faults in the Church, and therefore let me be resurrected with the Saints, whether I ascend to heaven or descend to hell, or go to any other place. And if we go to hell, we will turn the devils out of doors and make a heaven of it. (*History of the Church* 5:157)

> In your hands or that of any other person, so much power would, no doubt, be dangerous. I am the only man in the world whom it would be safe to trust with it. Remember, I am a prophet (Cited by Ivan J. Barrett, "Joseph Smith—the Chosen of God and the Friend of Man," speech given at BYU, August 12, 1975).

Friends, you have just listened to thirty full minutes on how the "Smith Myth" has been perpetuated. Run for the hills at the very sound of this clap-trap and turn to the living God for your solace, your eternal security, and your salvation.

"From a very young age, Mormon children are taught to stand up in meetings and say: "I know this church is true." Grammatically speaking, their words would be correct if they were speaking of Jesus – 'I know Jesus is true,' because we can only know what is absolutely true, what is unfailing, what will not ever change – only such things or beings can truly be known."

Knowing (or Epistemology)

We know from the Bible that in the end times, but with God's approbation, Satan is going to establish his own unholy trinity of FATHER, SON, and HOLY SPIRIT:

FATHER	→	SATAN
SON	→	ANTI-CHRIST
HOLY SPIRIT	→	BEAST (False Prophet)

Where Jesus was the Hebrew *Messiah*, or, in the Greek, the *Christos*, or the Christ, the unholy trinity will provide the world with an "anti-Christ": a man who is antithetical to everything Jesus was in the flesh. This is a very interesting comparison:

JESUS was	**ANTI-CHRIST will be**
Humble, meek	Proud and powerful
The Truth	Wholly deceptive
Not handsome	Attractive
No place to live	Affluent
Not political at all	VERY political
Glorified Father	Glorify Satan

Using the "things of the world" and by the powers of the "god of this world," this anti-Christ is going to deceive many, many, many people to their absolute destruction. He will succeed in doing this by using the elements of this fallen world with more power and persuasion than we could ever imagine, all given to him by Satan.

Now prior to Jesus leaving earth, He said something VERY important relative to our topic tonight, and to this spirit of anti-Christ.

> John 14:27. *Peace I leave with you, my peace I give unto you: not as the world giveth, give I unto you. Let not your heart be troubled, neither let it be afraid.*

Jesus lets us know at least a couple of things here:

1. This world has its form of peace; and
2. God has His.

Onc peace is from above, and the other is from this world.

Of all the questions we receive in this ministry, one of the most asked, by Mormons AND Christians alike (amazingly enough) is, "How can a person ***know*** God's truth?" When you think about it, there is possibly no greater question for a seeker to ask and to understand, because getting it wrong can open anyone up to all kinds of misdirected influences and counterfeits.

Our topic this time, in our long list of alphabetical topics, is *KNOWING.*

Let's take a historical and Biblical look at how God has operated and communicated with His creations in the past.

God always operates according to His rules and ways, not ours. People are often under the impression that, because God did something one way at one time, He will do the same thing, in the same way, at another. He spoke to Moses in a burning bush; He'll do the same with me. This is where understanding Biblical context plays a very important role.

In the Garden of Eden, God spoke directly with Adam and Eve – no prophets, no scriptures to reference, no intermediaries. God to man. Because God resided in man who were known as Adam and Eve. But man and the world we inhabited fell into sin, and the direct relationship of God "*in us*" ceased. Long story short, and skipping the family patriarchal times, God began to speak His specific communications to specific people called prophets. And He commanded that the words of these prophets be written. They were then compiled into what the Jews call the *Torah* and what Gentiles call the Old Testament and both considered "Scripture," God's Word.

It was trusted, referenced, and was the guide for God's covenantal people. If it was written, it was obeyed by those who loved God. Simple as that, folks. Look how the Jews still reverence it today.

Then God stopped talking. So the writing stopped too. This period is known as the *intertestamental period* and it spans about four hundred years from the end of the prophets of the Old Testament (Malachi) to the beginning of the New Testament, when Jesus Christ was born. Then God began speaking again, *through His Son.*

Still, no writing was done. But eyewitnesses, called apostles, who were gathered by the Lord Himself, learn from Him so as to testify and teach all He said and did. Now Jesus told these special witnesses, as recorded in the gospel of John:

> John 14:26. *the Comforter, which is the Holy Ghost, whom the Father will send in my name, he shall teach you all things, and bring* ***all things*** *to your remembrance, whatsoever I have said unto you.*

Once Jesus died, resurrected, and ascended into heaven, the Holy Spirit did, in fact, bring all things to their remembrance and these eyewitnesses wrote, just as the prophets of old wrote, what had been said and done. And just as the prophets of old wrote the Words of God, as given to them by the Holy Spirit, and considered them Scripture, so did the specially-appointed apostles write about actually seeing the *WORD* of God in the flesh. They reported all He did and said, and their words are considered Scripture to us today right along with those in the Old Testament.

Hebrews makes this clear:

> Hebrews 1:1-2. *God, who at sundry times and in divers manners spake* ***in time past unto the fathers by the prophets****, hath in these last days spoken unto us by his Son, whom he hath appointed heir of all things, by whom also he made the worlds.*

Well, you may wonder: how did God speak to people between the time that Jesus died, resurrected, and ascended into heaven until the writings of the apostles were available to believers? Because this was a time of transition – a time when the Old Testament was converging with a New Commandment – the change of administrations was not an easy or quick one. God the Holy Spirit manifested Himself powerfully in these early days of Christ's church. As a result, marvelous outpourings of His Spirit – outpourings which are still available to us today in the very same way – guided the Church, with the living apostles directing what was allowed and what was not.

On the day of Pentecost, the Holy Spirit, as Jesus had promised, descended upon the apostles and the other disciples who were with them. His magnificent works were made manifest in Jesus' name through them and others. Many were healed, many spoke in tongues, the dead were raised, and the Holy Spirit ignited the world with spiritual fervor. Visions were had, and the fire from God rested strongly in the hearts of these first members of Christ's body.

Remember, the church – and the good news – was not only new, but those who accepted it were being killed right and left for abandoning the faith of the fathers. Nothing short of the Holy Spirit pouring down upon them and imbuing them with His power could have forged the church amidst such conditions and persecution.

At the same time, letters written by first-hand witnesses of Christ, were being penned and sent out to the local churches as they were established and growing. These letters were deemed very instructive and were meticulously copied by people who had a scribal tradition of concern for accuracy. The letters were sent to other churches, which then took great care to repeat the process. As the apostles were killed off by persecution, the letters remained, and became an additional guide to the churches, along with the Old Testament and the Holy Spirit. In time, the letters that were traditional, authenticated and accepted as doctrinal by faithful leaders in the body became standard, while those writings deemed suspicious or of dubious authorship were discounted and done away with.

Were manifestations of the Holy Spirit still possible? Most certainly. Did believers sense and feel direction from on high? Without question – just as we do today. The writings of the apostles were collected as a body of writings, the feelings, promptings, inspirations, and revelations of the Holy Spirit were checked against the recorded words of the prophets and apostles because they had been written by the Holy Spirit in the first place. If the claims of an individual were contrary to what had been written already by the Holy Spirit, such claims were rejected and the established Word of God took precedence. Listen to this. Listen, *the apostles' written words were checked against the Old Testament writings that had come before them.* Did you know that? Did you know that the letters and gospels of the apostles included in the New Testament had to pass the scrutiny of what had been written in the Old Testament? Well, they did; and this is why Christians take the Old and New Testaments in one hand.

Currently, we have the earliest manuscript of John's gospel dating to A.D. 130, which is within 50-60 years of the original. This is remarkable when we consider that, the next earliest manuscript of a work of antiquity, Homer's *Iliad*, dates from about *400 years* after the original! (The *Iliad* also has a mere 643 manuscripts in existence; the New Testament 24,970! See Josh McDowell, *New Evidence that Demands a Verdict*, pages 33-68.) We also have full New Testament manuscripts dating all the way back to before A.D. 200, which perfectly correlate to the King James Bible today. The Catholic faith, as we know it, was not truly formed until A.D. 400, so if we want to say the Catholics took out many "plain and precious" truths from the Bible, we can prove this statement false.

As the apostles died off and organized religion took hold on the world, the Word of God and the Spirit of God was certainly quenched – but not extinguished entirely. Believers were never wiped off the face of the earth nor left to their own devices.

Isaiah 40:8. *The grass withereth, the flower fadeth: but* ***the word of our God shall stand for ever.***

1 Peter 1:23-25. … ***the word of God, which liveth and abideth for ever.*** *For all flesh is as grass, and all the glory of man as the flower of grass. The grass withereth, and the flower thereof falleth away: But the word of the Lord endureth for ever.*

The gates of hell did not prevail nor did God allow the work of Jesus to evaporate. Nevertheless, the Word of God was not in wide circulation, and it wasn't until the advent of the printing press when the Bible was put into print that it could once again influence seeking people as to the ways and will of God.

As the Word of God was made available, so the Holy Spirit began to manifest Himself again strongly. We call this age the *Reformation*, and it was the study of the Word of God along with the Holy Spirit working afresh that illuminated the hearts and minds of many.

Today, along with the promptings, feelings, and directives of the Holy Spirit, believers take the Word of God in hand, read, and let this combination of His Spirit and His Word work their work, which *always* testifies that Jesus lives, that He is King, and that we are saved by Him. The Holy Spirit would never teach against the words He brought to the original writers' minds, which is why feelings, promptings, or revelations that are contrary to God's written word cannot – must not – be considered divinely inspired or reliable. In this manner, God provides those who love Him with a safeguard against beguiling men and women who claim to receive "special revelations" which can be known outside of Biblical direction.

How does the Manual – God's Word – work?

First, scripture interprets scripture. We use *all* of scripture to understand the rest.

> 2 Peter 1:20. *Knowing this first, that no prophecy of the scripture is of any private interpretation.*

What does this mean? It means nobody can or should take any scripture and discern or interpret its meaning based on their own fleshly mind. What is REALLY interesting about this passage is the Greek word translated into the English word, "*interpretation*." You know what it is? It's "*epilusis*." From this word we get "impulse" and/or "impulsive," meaning nobody is allowed to take scripture and "impulsively" translate it out of the personal or self-directed thoughts of his own mind.

But this is exactly – exactly – what Joseph Smith did, as have many other mesmerizers, con men, and mystics staring into crystal balls. Using tried and true techniques to deceive people, these religious charlatans employ several tactics on the unsuspecting and unlearned. These tactics include:

- Convincing people they have a special connection to the heavens, to angels, to spirits, or to even God Himself;
- Claiming the Bible cannot be trusted when it counters their special revelations.
- Stating that, by following them and their special version of truth, they will reach higher states of enlightenment.
- Telling people that they can know that what they are being told comes about mystically, through feelings, through signs, and inner promptings.
- Finally, and typically, these charlatans will often minimize the deity of Jesus in one way or another, even to the point of claiming to author salvation themselves.

And so we come to Mormonism.

Founded by a man KNOWN for first getting people to trust him, then getting them to question the authenticity of the Bible, and then to rely upon their feelings to know truth, Joseph Smith's Mormonism built an entire religion on "feelings," not as God gives, but as the world does. This is a warning from one who has been there: Mormonism's epistemological foundation – how they KNOW – is emotionalism, which is the very element the world employs to convince.

Watch any influential Hollywood film, listen to any moving music, read any touching story and in it you will find "the peace that the world gives."

Rudolf Hess, Adolph Hitler's first deputy, stood before a large audience of Nazis and said (Adolph Hitler, "The Twisted Cross," as cited in Arza Evans, *The Keystone of Mormonism*, page 120):

> Do not seek Adolph Hitler with your brains, you will find him with your hearts.

This is trusting in feelings, emotionalism, and the peace that the world gives, at best. Tears do not convey truth, my friends. Facts do. Facts. The human heart will always hear what it wants to hear, see what it wants to see, and embrace what is most satisfying to its needs and wants, even in exchange for God's will. This is especially true when the heart has not been changed by the Holy Spirit through rebirth.

Objectivity is nearly impossible when emotional issues like personal security, occupation, family, marriage, children, or wealth are weighed in the balance. Our flesh clings too strongly to such trappings and Satan knows it. Add in the proud LDS notions of becoming a god and/or procreating for eternity, and feelings will almost always run roughshod over the truth – what God says.

This show that I do is extremely painful for dyed-in-the-wool LDS people to watch because it calls into question all they have felt, believed, and built their hopes and trust upon. If their resistance could be honestly articulated, it would sound like this:

> "I don't want to hear the facts you present because I really like my ward."
>
> "I don't like your show because I love my job and need it to feed my family."
>
> "You're a liar, Shawn McCraney, because I can't lose the eternal marriage Joseph promised I could have."

And Mormon "*feelings*" reign over the *facts* God makes plain. You see, God gave us facts in His Manual to put a check on our natural inclinations to trust our self-centered feelings. Men like Joseph Smith just completely ignored God's facts and claiming "new revelation," rewrote them and told people to check with their "feelings" to see if they are true. Can you see what a treacherous game it is to rely on feelings alone to know God's truth and will?

A number of years ago, near the end of one of the shows, we had a sweet-voiced woman, who claimed to be LDS, say she has had *"numerous spiritual experiences testifying to the truthfulness of the LDS Church."* She added, as a way to justify her position, that she *"knows a lot of other people in the LDS church who have had the same experiences."* She then claimed, *"I can't deny it. I feel like Joseph Smith who said, I dare not deny it."*

She then went on to "bear testimony" saying "she knows Joseph Smith **truly** had his first vision, that the Church is **true**, that the twelve apostles are **true**...yada, yada, yada. She asked me, *"How do you account for all these people in the church who have had these 'spiritual experiences' just like me?"* I explained that there are many religions where people "share in experiences similar to hers" – how would she account for them (e.g., Wiccans, Jehovah's Witnesses, Muslims, Coptics, Rosicrucians, Greek Orthodox, Catholics, and Seventh-Day Adventists, to name a few)? Our caller was so myopic, so ego-centric, she could not believe or hear anything but her own view. In a not uncommon response, she resorted to the infamous LDS retort,

"But I just know."

I said, *"I think you are sincere and you believe the things you are saying are ... ,"* but she interrupted me matter-of-factly, and said, *"I know it,"* and added, *"I know these things of an assurity."* Herein lies a main difference between Mormonism and biblical Christianity: Mormons lay claim to *subjectively knowing truth by their own feelings and inclinations* and Christians take their feelings and ch*eck them by what has been provided by God in His word.*

When confronted with God's Word, the LDS flee to several defensive positions. One, the inability to trust God's Word; two, that they have additional scripture which takes precedence over His word; or three, they bear this thing they call their "*testimony*" which is a culmination of all they supposedly know. But their claims, often delivered through tears, that they "*know the Church is true*" (or "*that Joseph was a prophet*," or "*that the Book of Mormon is true*," etc.) is not one bit more valid than my claiming, without tears, that I know Mormonism is as false as my grandmothers teeth.

See the problem with unsubstantiated methods of knowing? Facts and truth are irrelevant in the Mormon mind because subjective feelings, which support their false knowing, is all that matters. What will make my arguments or my knowing superior or inferior to theirs? Facts.

What facts do we have by which to test, judge, and examine our feelings? Believe it or not, God does not expect us to believe in Him and His will blindly. He appeals to the faculties He embodied within us to establish Himself. He gives us:

Nature.

The cosmos.

Science.

History.

The Biblical record.

Our minds.

Reason and rationality.

His Spirit.

And above all: His Word, written to convince any who are seeking, by the Holy Spirit, through inspired writers.

Not fables. Not myths. Not feelings. Not tablets falling from the sky or tears or soft music.

In the old World War II movie, *The Twisted Cross*, Hitler is quoted as having said (as cited in Arza Evans, *The Keystone of Mormonism*, page 120):

> Reason can treacherously deceive a man, but emotion is always sure and never leaves him.

But *God* says,

> Isaiah 1:18. *Come now, and let us reason together ...*

You want to KNOW truth? God's Will? Read the Word and the Holy Spirit will testify of Jesus through those writings and with reason.

Then you *shall know the truth, and the truth shall make you free.*

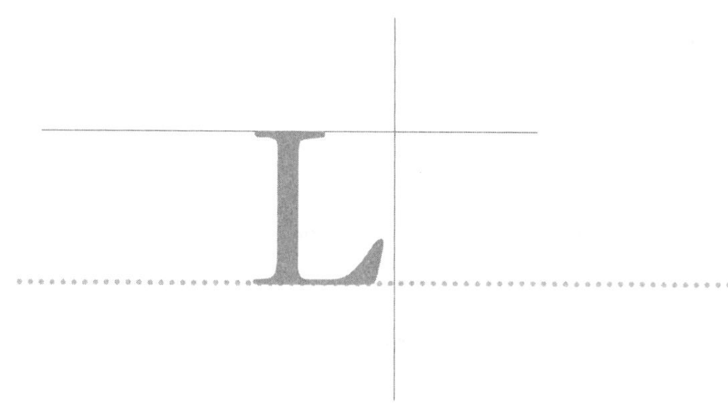

"I am perhaps one of the most lawless individuals that ever walked the face of this earth. Yet God saved me…in spite of myself."

The Law

One of the MAJOR differences, which I have personally experienced, between being a faithful Latter-day Saint and being a faithful Christian is the weight, the burden, and the yoke that comes with being what is hailed as a "faithful Mormon" and the loving liberty that comes with being a faithful Christian. Now there are some long, drawn out, ridiculous arguments Latter-day Saints are making, especially online, claiming that they believe in salvation by grace and grace alone. I mean, from the bloggers to the missionaries, they convincingly claim that Mormons are saved by grace and grace alone.

They want acceptance into the evangelical flock. They want the world to embrace them. They want the office of the President of the United States. And they want to be embraced in order to influence from within.

As is the case with their recent national ads, the perception Mormonism presents to the world is not congruent with reality nor with their official doctrine.

Let's take the idea of salvation by grace. Mormonism has 13 Articles of Faith penned by their founding prophet, Joseph Smith. Any and every active Mormon would agree that these statements capture the essence of the faith. Article of Faith number 3 reads:

> We believe that … all mankind may be saved, by obedience to the LAWS and ORDINANCES of the Gospel.

We [**members of the Mormon church**] believe that [**who?**] all mankind may be [**what?**] SAVED by [**grace? Noooo!**] **BY OBEDIENCE to the LAWS and ORDINANCES of the** [**LDS**] **Gospel.**

Hear this clearly, please: Christianity is emphatic that all mankind may be saved by faith in the shed blood of Jesus Christ alone, period, end of story. But Mormonism, which claims to be Christian, officially states that, *All mankind may be saved by obedience to the LAWS and ORDINANCES of the LDS gospel.*

Aside from the fact that this third Article of Faith is absolutely in conflict with biblical Christianity, what are some of the other problems with it? There are many and they are horrible.

First, what does it actually mean to be "*obedient*"? If a parent sits a child down at the beginning of the year and says, "The only expectation I have for you this year, Junior, is that I want you to make your bed every day before you leave the house, no matter what," and the child does it every day except one, was the child obedient to the parents' demand? No. There was a *failure* to obey. He was disobedient because he disobeyed. Obedience is sort of like virginity, pregnancy, and cancer: you either *are pregnant* or you *are not*. You either *are a virgin* or you *are not*. You either *have cancer* or you *don't* and *you either are obedient or you are not.*

Now, listen carefully! If people are saved by obedience to something, and NOT by faith in someone who was obedient in our place, then their salvation is predicated on their ability to obey the requirements completely. But the problem is that none of us – nobody – has ever, ever, ever been obedient. To really bring the matter home, no human being can actually get through a single day without disobeying God's perfect law in one way or another. So don't fool yourself. No matter who you are, you are disobedient to God.

In fact, let's take this to an extreme which comes out of the Bible. Let's suppose you are one of these types who has very few issues with outright sin. You have decided that you are going to be saved, as Joseph wrote, through *your* obedience to the laws and ordinances of the Mormon gospel. You never envy. You're never hateful, you never gossip, lust, lie; you hold your tongue, and you love God and your neighbors perfectly– except for one mess up in your life. One! Okay, you got it?

Guess what?

That one sin, that one act of disobedience makes it as *IF* you have broken every rule God has ever given. What? Yes.

> James 2:10. *For whoever shall keep the whole law and yet offend in one point, he is guilty of all.*

I didn't say this, God did.

In other words, if you go throughout your whole life and keep all of God's law (which would be impossible) and you break *one point of it*, God says – God says – God says you would be guilty of breaking all of His laws!

Why would God say this? Because He wants you to understand that you CANNOT save yourself by obedience to any set of laws or ordinances. Human obedience is impossible, so therefore all of us are found disobedient by God. Even the very devoted and dedicated Jews failed to be obedient. You see, God gave the children of Israel, His covenant people, a collection of laws at one time. These laws were good, holy, and reflective of God's character, but they were *not* obeyed. Paul tells us that

> Galatians 3:24. *Wherefore the law was our schoolmaster to bring us unto Christ, that we might be justified by faith.*

This verse tells us that the very presence of God's law shows us that we are in dire need of a Savior! Amazing huh? The law was there to show us how disobedient we are (if we're honest) and, in the face of our disobedience, we ought to readily embrace the Savior who was obedient in our place.

This is the first crime in placing people back under law *after the cross*. In so doing, it removes – in their arrogant minds – the need for a Savior. The premise is that they can achieve their own righteousness, and the conclusion is that a Savior becomes either unnecessary or simply another rung on the ladder of exaltation to be climbed by themselves.

Another crime brought about by placing law into the lives of believers is that it burdens them. In the book of Acts, the apostles found themselves being pressured by certain Jewish believers in Christ to reintroduce elements of the Old Testament law upon Gentile believers in Christ, Who had fulfilled the law on behalf of all.

But Peter rose up and said something important. He said:

> Acts 15:10. *Now therefore why tempt ye God, to* ***put a yoke upon***

> *the neck of the disciples, which neither our fathers nor we were able to bear?*

Notice that Peter says that to place the rules, rituals and other elements of the law on the backs of believers in Christ would be like placing a yoke upon them. A yoke he states, that neither their fathers nor the apostles themselves were able to bear! Have you ever had a religion place a yoke or a burden on your back? I don't care if it is one thing or many, have you ever experienced this? Well this is an awful thing to do to anyone because Jesus took it all away once and for all.

What imagery does this lawful yoke invoke in your mind? Bondage, right? Heavy labor: earning and yearning and pulling and striving. And for what? To make God love us, accept us, be our God? Is this the kind of god you know: one to whom you are constantly forced to prove yourself so that he will accept you – *if* you toe the line?

This sounds more like a mean step-father not a loving God.

A third reason it is a crime to require fulfillment of the law in the lives of believers is that it takes what Jesus has *already* done for us, and puts it back squarely into the hands of the people seeking Him! This is another gospel! He bore the yoke for us, my friends! He not only bore the burden of our sin and made the payment for our failures to obey the law, *He actually transfers His righteousness to our account*! And He did it through *His* complete obedience.

Listen!

> 2 Corinthians 5:21. *For he* [God] *hath made him* [Jesus] *to be sin for us, who knew no sin; that we* ***might be made the righteousness of God in him.***

And listen to what Paul teaches the Romans – come on, now –

really listen to this, because in this one verse we are told about the effects of the fall of Adam and what the obedience of Christ does for those who believe on Him. Ready?

> Romans 5:9. *For as by one man's disobedience many were made sinners,* [this is speaking of Adam, his fall, and original sin] *so by the obedience of one* [this speaks of Jesus alone] *shall many be made righteous.*

Because Jesus fulfilled the law perfectly on our behalf, then shed His blood for the same, we are made righteous in the eyes of God through our FAITH on HIM and *NOT* because we earn or obey certain laws ourselves! And what should be the result? Jesus says, and is able to say because of His act of mercy and love on the cross,

> Matthew 11:29. *Take my yoke upon you, and learn of me; for I am meek and lowly in heart: and ye shall find* ***rest*** *unto your souls. For* ***my yoke is easy****, and* ***my burden is light****.*

Fourth, the Bible makes it clear that it is through our faith on Jesus and what He did – not what we do through obeying any laws or doing any ordinances – that we may be saved from the condemnation of our own disobedience to the laws of God. This line of thinking is in direct opposition to Mormon teachings.

Listen:

> Romans 3:28. *Therefore we conclude that a man is justified by faith* ***without the deeds of the law.***

> Romans 10:4. *For* ***Christ is the*** **end** ***of the law*** *for righteousness to every one that believeth.*

> Romans 8:3-4. *For what* ***the law could not do****, in that it was weak through the flesh, God sending his own Son in the likeness of sinful flesh, and for sin, condemned sin in the flesh: that the righteousness*

of the law might be fulfilled in us, who walk not after the flesh, but after the Spirit.

Galatians 2:16. *Knowing that a man is* ***not justified by the works of the law****, but by the faith of Jesus Christ, even we have believed in Jesus Christ, that we might be justified by the faith of Christ, and* ***not by the works of the law: for by the works of the law shall no flesh be justified.***

Galatians 2:21. *I do not frustrate the grace of God: for* ***if righteousness come by the law, then Christ is dead in vain.***

Galatians 3:11. ***But that no man is justified by the law*** *in the sight of God, it is evident: for, The just shall live by faith.*

Galatians 3:13. *Christ hath redeemed us from the* ***curse of the law****, being made a curse for us: for it is written, Cursed is every one that hangeth on a tree:*

And what do the LDS leaders say?

LDS First Presidency member and Apostle Marion G. Romney taught ("How Men are Saved," *Ensign*, November 1974):

> The Church also accepts the scriptural doctrine that following the resurrection each person – then an immortal soul – will be arraigned before the bar of God's justice and receive a final judgment based on his performance during mortal probation, that the verdict will turn on obedience or disobedience to the laws and ordinances of the gospel. If these laws and ordinances have been complied with during mortal life, the candidate will be cleansed [will be cleansed?] from the stain of sin by the atoning blood of Jesus Christ and be saved in the celestial kingdom of God, there to enjoy with God eternal life. Those who have not complied with the laws and ordinances of the gospel will receive a lesser reward.

A final (and this is heavy folks) but extremely dangerous effect of adding to the good news required obedience to "laws and ordinances" is that, by attempting to actually live by the law, we are effectively staying ***in*** a state of sin, not away from sin. How does it do this? By keeping us guilty.

You see, if you are dead to the law, then it has no power over you, and you are free. We are dead to the law *if* we are alive in Christ! Listen to these verses:

> Romans 3:20. *Therefore by the deeds of the law there shall no flesh be justified in his sight: for* ***by the law is the knowledge of sin.***

If the parent never gave the kid the law to make his bed every day, the kid would not be guilty of disobedience. But because there is a law given, sin is the only result possible. And the only solution is to be free from the law! This is why the Bible says,

> 1 Corinthians 15:56. *The sting of death is sin; and* ***the strength of sin is the law.***

Listen to how Paul describes the effect of sin on believers in Jesus and His grace:

> Romans 6:14. *For* ***sin shall not have dominion over you: for ye are not under the law,*** *but under* ***grace.***

And then,

> Romans 7:6. *But now we* [who are believers in Christ Jesus] *are delivered from the law, that being dead wherein we were held; that we should serve in newness of spirit, and not in the oldness of the letter.*

What does that LDS Article of Faith do to people? *It keeps them in sin and it keeps them dead – dead in their sin!*

They think they are without sin by obeying the laws and ordinances of the Mormon gospel, when they are actually *more* sinful – because they can't be obedient to all the law. *Listen!*

> Romans 8:2. *For the law of the Spirit of life in Christ Jesus hath* ***made me free from*** *the law of sin and death.*

Paul gives a stern warning to people who attempt to live their lives by law after receiving Jesus as the Savior of their lives, saying

> Galatians 5:4. *Christ is become of no effect unto you, whosoever of you are justified by the law;* ***ye are fallen from grace.***

Never let a religion tell you that you must follow this rule and that rule. Christ Jesus did it all for us. Look to Him, be free, be liberated, and cease your disobedience, which is the only thing that comes by embracing laws.

❋ ❋ ❋

> "There is no more important characteristic to an individual who claims Jesus as His Lord and King than to love all as defined by 1 Corinthians 13."

Love

We've covered a lot of alphabetized topics this year – thirty-one to date – and all of them significant in the Mormon / Christian debate. Tonight, we are going to speak about a topic that is perhaps more greatly misunderstood the world over than any other. What makes it difficult to properly address are its many facets, universal applications, and what it really amounts to in the life of a true Christian.

The topic? Love.

Almost everyone on earth has some sort of interaction with love. We call it love when we feel a strong affinity to someone or something. We feel loved by people around us. Hollywood portrays its version of love as a highly-charged, intensely romantic, even magically seductive aura of feeling and emotion. Anyone who has investigated the term from a Biblical perspective knows that there are many terms used for love in scripture. We read of *storge:* familial love; *eros:* intimate love; and *philia:* brotherly love.

The New Testament uses another Greek term for love that was not around in classic Greek times (i.e., during the days of Plato). That word is *agape* love. Contained in what Christians refer to as the "love chapter" of the Bible, 1 Corinthians 13, we find an elucidation on this word *agape*. And you're all familiar with it because in the King James version of the Bible it uses another word for the *agape* love: "*charity*." This is not a very good word for English speaking people today because the word *charity* has taken on all sorts of philanthropic ideals and is more associated simply with giving. While those who really *love* do *give*, not all who *give* really do so out of a sense of *agape* love.

Why was the word *charity* used in this chapter when every time we see it, it is a translation of *agape*? *Charity* is a transliteration of the Latin word *caritas*. Because there was no classic Greek origin of the word *agape*, the King James translators went to the Latin for an equivalent, and they found it in the Latin word *caritas*. So every time *agape* was used in the Greek manuscript they wrote *charity*, which is the English transliteration of *caritas*. Then as things go, the word *charity* subsequently was taken and used by the world to represent loving help or giving. And while a truly charitable heart is certainly giving and helping, it is much, much, more than this.

Determining or detecting real *agape* love in people can be almost as difficult as determining a person's true faith in Jesus Christ. Certainly the actions people take can be somewhat of an indication of the presence of genuine *agape* love, but even magnificent works of apparent charity can be misleading. Jesus Himself said:

> Matthew 7:22-23. *Many will say to me in that day, Lord, Lord,*

> *have we not prophesied in thy name? and in thy name have cast out devils? and in thy name done many wonderful works? And then will I profess unto them, I never knew you: depart from me, ye that work iniquity.*

In the Mormon/Christian debate it is vital to examine genuine *agape* love through a Biblical lens, and avoid the more humanist applications of love (like romance, charitable giving, and wonderful outward works) in our attempt to see if there is a difference between the ways Biblical Christians and devout Mormons love. While I have specifically found many LDS to be the living embodiment of *agape* love, I would say when comparing the love Mormonism generates to the love devout Christianity generates, we speak of two very different loves. Let me explain why.

First, genuine *agape* love thrives in the Biblical doctrine of grace but shrinks and dies when doctrines of works and law are present. Our last alphabetical topic was law. It was made manifestly clear that we are dead to the law. Why? Because the law ought to serve to reveal our sin and therefore, serve to bring us to Christ as the solution for our sin.

When placed before peoples' faces, they generally respond in one of two ways to the presence of law. First, they look at its demands and say, *"I am obedient. Therefore I am good or better than others."*

The other response is one of rebellion, causing people to say, *"I'm NOT gonna do that. I'm not going to obey."*

Both responses are antithetical to *agape* love. Because of the legalism that Mormonism employs in terms of dress, tithes, Sabbath day observance, being "temple worthy," etc., etc., etc., and referring to these things as *LAWS*, the *opposite* of *agape* love is being produced in the hearts of their members. I have personally witnessed the results of law and a lack of agape love written largely across the face of the state of Utah in the polarized lives of the people there.

Would you like to witness an amazing societal contradistinction first hand? Get up early on any given Sunday morning and drive through downtown Salt Lake City. At 6 a.m., the homeless shelters boot their occupants out into the street. In many ways, these are the *rebellious to the law*, the mavericks, those who refuse to conform to law. On the other side of the street, as it were, one may also observe the most faithful Mormon law keepers migrating on foot or by car toward their religious destinations.

I've seen the interaction. A few months ago I saw a street person ask for money from an LDS man heading into the temple. The Latter-day Saint stiffly rejected the man and when the LDS man passed, the bum flipped him off. There is little *agape* love being exchanged or shared by either side on these mornings because the presence of law has made most of the people either rebellious … or proud.

But what did Jesus say?

> Matthew 5:43-46. *Ye have heard that it hath been said, Thou shalt love thy neighbour, and hate thine enemy. But I say unto you, Love your enemies, bless them that curse you, do good to them that hate you, and pray for them which despitefully use you, and persecute you; for if ye love them which love you, what reward have ye? do not even the publicans the same?*

What was to happen to all the laws and commandments that had previously been written in stone? Jesus said:

> John 13:34-35. *A new commandment I give unto you, That ye love one another; as I have loved you, that ye also love one another. By this shall all men know that ye are my disciples, if ye have love one to another.*

In many ways, any law – such as the laws the LDS impose on their membership – other than the New Commandment Jesus gave *crushes* our ability to fulfill His new directive. A person cannot live both by grace *and* works, or by love *and* law. There cannot be liberty in Christ and bondage to rules simultaneously; they are contradictory paradigms.

One reason is that laws written in stone produce fear in all who observe them. The human response to fear is, typically, either a spirit of bondage or of rebellion and certainly not the LIBERTY afforded by Christ. We either cower to the law, let it dominate and intimidate us, OR we let it make us feel superior to our neighbor, OR we rebel against it and fight it every step of the way. These are the very results we see physically manifested in the general Utah society.

What does scripture say?

> 1 John 4:18. *There is no fear in love; but perfect love casteth out fear: because fear hath torment. He that feareth is not made perfect in love.*

Imagine you are married to a rule-making despot. "You must do this to be worthy of my love," he says. "You must do that to be worthy to live in the mansion I just built in the mountains." How would you respond to this? You would either live in fear of failing to meet his demands (bondage), or you would rebel against him and his rules and tell him to go hang himself (rebellion). This is NOT what Jesus offers, friends.

> 2 Timothy 1:7. *For God hath not given us the spirit of fear; but of power, and of love, and of a sound mind.*

This only comes by our first being unconditionally loved and accepted as we are.

This brings us to another point. The LDS view of Who Jesus is, what He did for us, and our inability to ever be "worthy" of His free, unencumbered gift makes possessing true *agape* love much more difficult, if not entirely impossible, as compared to Biblical believers. You see, Paul suggests

> Ephesians 3:17-19. *That Christ may dwell in our hearts by faith; that we, being rooted and grounded in love, may be able to comprehend with all saints what is the breadth, and length, and depth, and height; and to know the love of Christ, which passeth knowledge, that ye might be filled with all the fulness of God.*

Listen! This is a bold statement, but absolutely Biblical and true: nobody on earth – not the Dalai Lama, not Thomas Monson, not anyone – can truly fulfill the new commandment to love others *if* they are lacking in knowing and experiencing the real love of Jesus *first*. John makes this plain:

1 John 4:19 *We love him, because he first loved us.*

This passage and all that I am trying to share is illustrated perfectly in a story found in the gospel of Luke, chapter 7. It seems a very legalistic religious leader named Simon invited Jesus to have a meal with him at his home and Jesus accepted the invitation. Starting at verse 37 it says:

> Luke 7:37-38. *And, behold, a woman in the city, which was a sinner, when she knew that Jesus sat at meat in the Pharisee's house, brought an alabaster box of ointment, And stood at his feet behind him weeping, and began to wash his feet with tears, and did wipe them with the hairs of her head, and kissed his feet, and anointed them with the ointment.*

This woman had not been living a good life. She was filthy with sin.

> Luke 7:39-40. *Now when the Pharisee which had bidden him saw it, he spake within himself, saying, This man,* [Jesus] *if he were a prophet, would have known who and what manner of woman this*

> *is that toucheth him: for she is a sinner. And Jesus answering said unto him, Simon, I have somewhat to say unto thee. And he saith, Master, say on.*

And Jesus tells a very simple and a very short story, saying,

> Luke 7:41-43. *There was a certain creditor which had two debtors: the one owed five hundred pence, and the other fifty. And when they had nothing to pay, he frankly forgave them both. Tell me therefore, which of them will love him most? Simon answered and said, I suppose that he, to whom he forgave most. And he said unto him, Thou hast rightly judged.*

We are given a new commandment by Jesus and that is to LOVE – *TO LOVE* – and here Jesus tells us exactly who will fulfill the commandment best: those who have been forgiven of the most sin!

It's hard to hear but true. Jesus came to save sinners. Within Mormonism, Jesus rarely saves because, generally speaking, the faithful members do not see their sin. They're too busy masking it by obedience to the laws of Mormonism, which can only bring pride. And get this: because they don't see their deep and total need and reliance on Jesus as a result of their sin, they love little, and therefore do not truly fulfill His new commandment.

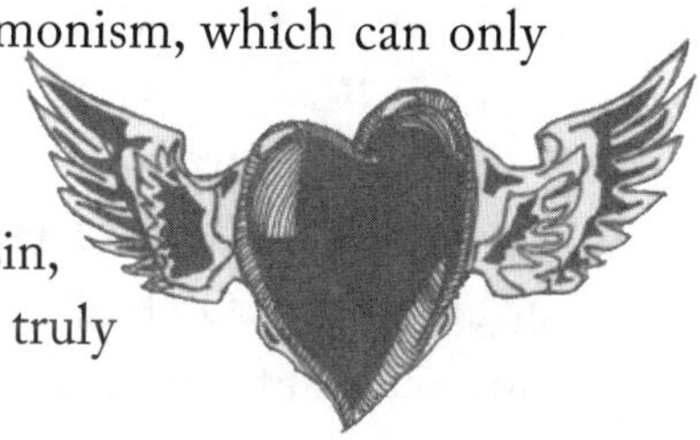

> Luke 7:44-47. *And he turned to the woman, and said unto Simon, Seest thou this woman? I entered into thine house, thou gavest me no water for my feet: but she hath washed my feet with tears, and wiped them with the hairs of her head. Thou gavest me no kiss: but this woman since the time I came in hath not ceased to kiss my feet. My head with oil thou didst not anoint: but this woman hath anointed my feet with ointment. Wherefore I say unto thee, Her sins, which are many, are forgiven;* ***for she loved much:*** *but to whom little is forgiven, the same loveth little.*

Who does this describe, folks? In our day and age of religion, who is Jesus Himself speaking of?

> Luke 7:48-50. *And he said unto her, Thy sins are forgiven. And they that sat at meat with him began to say within themselves, Who is this that forgiveth sins also? And he said to the woman,* ***Thy faith hath saved thee****; go in peace.*

You see, this simple story from the Word of God perfectly lays out the whole entire beautiful gospel of Jesus Christ and how it literally plays out in the life of people. Like the woman in the story, a sinful person recognizes their awful state and their total inability to do anything about it. Then, like the woman, they see Jesus for Who He is: the *only* source of their salvation. Because they see that He first loved them, they are then able to love back with that *agape* love. And that love is manifested in loving, devoted acts of service.

But remember, the acts themselves, the many wonderful works, are meaningless alone if they are not motivated, driven, and prompted by the knowledge of who He is and what He did for us. Get it? You see, when we really see Jesus as the *ONLY* solution to our salvation, that it is by Him and Him alone and not by anything of ourselves, then are we made completely free and at liberty to LOVE all – I mean everybody – without any exception or qualification. This is *agape* love.

However, the law causes us to place limitations on our love, to calculate the merit and worthiness of individuals; this is not agape love. It is grace that allows us to be good and to do good. Being recipients of His grace then moves us to love and serve as God loved and served – unconditionally, saving us when we were unworthy.

It is not without purpose that Jesus in telling the story of the good Samaritan, says that it was a priest and a Levite who walked past the beaten man and a Samaritan who stopped to help. Again, evidence of agape love.

Now, a common comeback that we hear from some LDS, which really isn't a comeback at all, is, "Well, if a person really loves, if a person is really a Christian, he or she will keep His commandments." And then they provide a laundry list of commandments that Jesus has supposedly given, both from their own leaders and by quoting out-of-context statements from Jesus in the Bible.

Let me use some biblical phrases which do, in fact, contextually summarize what it means to keep His commandments. The first thing we know is that the commandments we are expected to keep are easy, not heavy, and liberating.

> 1 John 5:2-3. *By this we know that we love the children of God, when we love God, and keep his commandments. For this is the love of God, that we keep his commandments: and his commandments are not grievous.*

Latter-day Saints frequently say that "His commandments" must be kept, and then delineate them in a way which is absolutely absurd. In one of their temple rites they bind themselves with oaths, under heavy covenants to donate *all* of their time, *all* of their talents – *everything* they physically have and even everything they will be given in the future – to the building up of Mormonism!

But Jesus said, obey His commandments. Well, what are His commandments?

> 1 John 3:22-23. *And whatsoever we ask, we receive of him, because we keep his commandments, and do those things that are pleasing in his sight.* ***And this is his commandment, That we should believe on the name of his Son Jesus Christ, and love one another****, as he gave us commandment.*

As John reports, Jesus Himself told us,

> John 15:10-12. *If ye keep my commandments, ye shall abide in my love; even as I have kept my Father's commandments, and abide in his love. This is my commandment, That ye love one another, as I have loved you.*

"This is my commandment: That ye love one another, as I have loved you."

How did He love us, friends? He loved each one of us even in our sins – as failures, as weaklings, as reprobates. He went to the cross in our place. He followed the will of the Father. He died for us out of love.

Let me conclude with the words of the Lord through John the Beloved Apostle. What He says here is impossible to accomplish in our own flesh, by or through the law, or without knowing who Jesus really is and what He really did:

> 1 John 4:7-16. *Beloved, let us love one another: for love is of God; and every one that loveth is born of God, and knoweth God. He that loveth not knoweth not God; for God is love. In this was manifested the love of God toward us, because that God sent his only begotten Son into the world, that we might live through him. Herein is love, not that we loved God, but that he loved us, and sent his Son to be the propitiation for our sins. Beloved, if God so loved us, we ought also to love one another. No man hath seen God at any time. If we love one another, God dwelleth in us, and his love is perfected in us. Hereby know we that we dwell in him, and he in us, because he hath given us of his Spirit. And we have seen and do testify that the Father sent the Son to be the Savior of the world. Whosoever shall confess that Jesus is the Son of God, God dwelleth in him, and he in God. And we have known and believed the love that God hath to us. God is love; and he that dwelleth in love dwelleth in God, and God in him.*

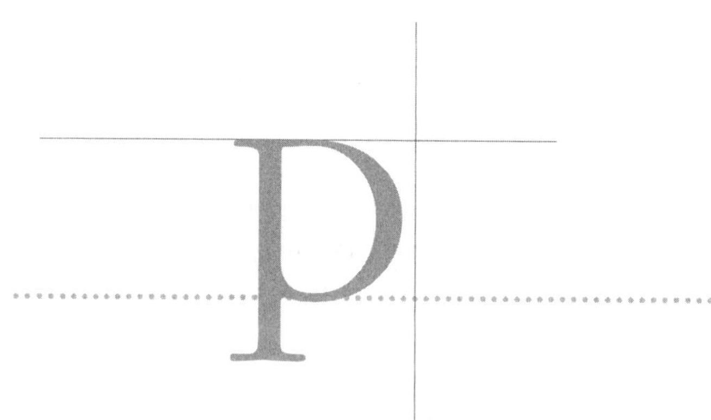

"The LDS love to attack the Christian world for paying its pastors, somehow believing that this method is against God but not knowing that it is actually recommended by Him. In my opinion, if you want to really see a self-serving religious leader, make his or her service 'voluntary,' while simultaneously and wholly predicated on whether he will be offered advancement in leadership in the future. This is the best picture of man-made religion."

Paid Clergy

Across the nation, I'm sure even as we speak, there are LDS missionaries sitting with seeking people and delivering a white-washed version of what they call the restored gospel. Built-in to their sales pitch is a little gem they pull out and use to shine up their whole presentation: the fact, they will claim, that Mormonism does not "pay" those who serve in the Church. In the unofficial but fairly ubiquitous pamphlet, "*The Seventeen Points of the True Church,*" one point plainly states:

The true church must have no paid clergy.

With almost unbearable PRIDE, many Mormons hold up this

claim as if it truly validates them as a religion and a people representing God. But is this true? In this section, we will explore the topic of a paid clergy. We will ask and answer the question, is it a better system, even God's system, for those who are in full time clergy to go uncompensated? Did this idea really come from God or did it originate in the minds of men? And what *does* the Bible say about paid clergy? We'll also ask and answer, what are the effects on a congregation of the LDS system of supposedly non-paid clergy as opposed to a church where the clergy is paid for its labors? We'll conclude by examining how much the LDS Church follows its own claims and the ways they get around it.

So first let's ask: "Are the LDS correct?" Did this idea of no paid clergy come from God or just from the minds of man? What does the Bible say about it? How did the sons of Aaron earn their keep in the Old Testament as they were assigned to the full time employ of doing God's work in His temple? They were supported by those things given to the temple for God's use by the rest of the community!

This fact caused Paul to write, when speaking of whether a person should be paid to teach:

> 1 Corinthians 9:13-14. *Do ye not know that they which minister about holy things live of the things of the temple? and they which wait at the altar are partakers with the altar? Even so hath the Lord ordained that they which preach the gospel should live of the gospel.*

Let's also consider the popular Biblical illustration for those who teach the Word of God, because that is the primary Biblical call for all clergy: to teach the word of God. In the illustration, the Bible refers to teaching the Word of God as *feeding the sheep*.

And as a result we have a title ascribed to those whose job it is to teach and lead in the things of God: shepherd, which in Latin is *pastor*. Tell me, is being "a true shepherd" over a flock a part-time, voluntary position which takes only a handful of hours per week or is it a full-time occupation? Can a truly devoted shepherd really prepare to know and teach the Word while tending to the flock by only working five to eight hours a week? Or does he dedicate himself and his life to serving, feeding, and protecting them from wolves? If an *effective shepherd* does pastor the sheep full time, how is he to earn his living?

Proverbs tells us

> Proverbs 27:18. *Whoso keepeth the fig tree shall eat the fruit thereof: so he that waiteth on his master shall be honored.*

What picture do you have of Jesus and His apostles as they went out into the world? What did Jesus say to the twelve? Jesus said the same thing to His apostles in

> Matthew 10:10. [Take no] *scrip for your journey, neither two coats, neither shoes, nor yet staves: for the workman is worthy of his meat.*

Do you see Jesus and the twelve as corporation leaders: self-sufficient Mormon bishop-types with good jobs, administering and managing their people? Or as humble Christian shepherds who get up every week and teach their flock from the Word of God?

In Deuteronomy we read:

> Deuteronomy 25:4. *Thou shalt not muzzle the ox when he treadeth out the corn.*

What did this mean? It was from God Himself, Who said while an ox is plowing the field do not forbid it from freely eating the grain beneath its feet. How does this apply to our topic of paid clergy? When speaking of this very topic, Paul appealed to this verse. You see, if God commanded that we are not to withhold support and comfort *even from oxen* while they are employed in their work, how much more should human beings who labor in His vineyard be compensated the moneys and goods given to the church?

Paul wrote of this:

> 1 Corinthians 9:9. *For it is written in the law of Moses, Thou shalt not muzzle the ox when he treadeth out the corn. Is it for the oxen that God careth, or saith he it assuredly for our sake? Yea, for our sake it was written: because he that ploweth ought to plow in hope, and he that thresheth, to thresh in hope of partaking. If we sowed unto you spiritual things, is it a great matter if we shall reap your carnal things? If others partake of this right over you, do not we yet more?*

Repeating this premise, he instructed Timothy this way:

> 1 Timothy 5:17-18. *Let the elders that rule well be counted worthy of double honor, especially those who labor in the word and in teaching. For the scripture saith, Thou shalt not muzzle the ox when he treadeth out the corn. And, The laborer is worthy of his hire.*

I mean, really, what else do you need? The word of God is so clear on the matter.

Now, as a means to support the evilness of a paid clergy, the LDS resort to a number of tactics. For starters, in the LDS temple, an instructional, doctrinal film is shown. When I was a member, it had an actor representing a Protestant minister. Satan hires the minister to preach to the children of Adam and Eve (i.e., mankind). The implication is clear: men who are paid to teach the gospel are in the employ of Satan himself.

Secondly, the LDS have a *looooong* history of its leaders, missionaries, and members speaking out against pastors and preachers who are paid for their labor. Joseph Fielding McConkie wrote (*Revelations of the Restoration*, page 964):

> Wherever creeds are found one can also expect to find a paid clergy, the simple truths of the gospel cloaked in the dark robes of mystery, religious intolerance, and a history of bloodshed.

Read that again because that quote literally describes Mormonism much more than it describes Christianity. Think about real Christians and real Mormons when reading the above! Who does it fit best, all things considered?

The late but still respected LDS Apostle James Talmage described paid clergy when he wrote the following (*The Vitality of Mormonism*, page 155):

> Never has been spoken a stronger arraignment of insincere teachers, false pastors, self-seeking hirelings – those who teach for pelf and divine for dollars, robbers who pose as shepherds yet avoid the door to the fold and climb up some other way, prophets in the devil's employ, to achieve their master's purpose, hesitate not to robe themselves in assumed sanctity, and appear in sheep's clothing while inwardly they are ravening wolves (Matthew 7:15).

And the LDS act as if they just love and embrace everyone.

Moving on, LDS apologists and missionaries use several Biblical passages out of context to defend their position. One is found in Isaiah 45:13 which says:

> Isaiah 45:13. *I have raised him up in righteousness, and I will direct all his ways: he shall build my city, and he shall let go my captives, not for price nor reward, saith the LORD of hosts.*

What does this have to do with paid clergy, either directly or indirectly? Nothing. Nothing at all! This passage refers to Cyrus, and what he did for the Jews as a type of Christ, a picture of what God will do for all. It is God showing His faithfulness in His promise to deliver His people, meaning He will do it freely and without ransom or any other grievous condition. The passage is actually an affirmation of *salvation being by God's grace* more than anything else!

Another verse they use, which is at least applicable to the topic in question, is extracted from Peter's first epistle:

> 1 Peter 5:2. *Feed the flock of God which is among you, taking the oversight thereof, not by constraint, but willingly; not for filthy lucre, but of a ready mind;*

But again we must ask, what is the *context* of this verse? Pastors are, without a doubt, called to feed the flock of God, to teach them God's Word. And by what motivation? Well, Peter states, "*not by constraint, but willingly.*" It should be their *vocare* (Latin, "to call"); that is, their *call.* They ought to do it because they want to, not because of any compulsion for money, social or religious pressure, family expectations, or any other "*constraint.*"

And Peter adds, "*Not for filthy lucre, but of a ready mind.*"

Peter says that in order to be an effective and loving shepherd of the Lord's sheep, the pastor's intention for doing it must be based in love and a ready mind.

You'll notice that we receive a number of calls from the LDS wondering how much money I am making doing this. They ask this because they have been taught that anyone who goes into the ministry does so for *filthy lucre.* But true Christians know that anyone who gets into the ministry for money should get out – this is all it is saying. The warning has no bearing on whether pastors or ministers of the gospel are permitted to receive financial support for their labors.

We have proven that scripture clearly supports a paid clergy. This means that God Himself allows people to receive support who teach and shepherd; and if God supports this He must know that, all things considered, this is best for a minister of the gospel. So what, then, does it mean to have shepherds who are ***not paid*** to lead and shepherd a congregation? I have given this a lot of thought over the years and it is as cunning a plan as they come.

You see, when a Christian church pays its pastor, he becomes the servant of the congregation. His main job? It is to feed the sheep from the Word of God, to free them from the bondage of sin and guilt, and to introduce them to the gospel of grace. He is also there to counsel (using God's Word as a basis) and to perform religious services for those in the flock. The body of believers supports him based on his dedication to the Lord and the call on his life. And according to scripture, he is worthy of this remuneration even more than people are worthy of pay from their secular jobs!

Amazing huh?

If he fails to do as the Manual instructs, he will lose his position; if he follows the Manual, he has God on his side and nothing to fear.

But let's look at the LDS system. In it, everyone in the congregation is called based on his personal worthiness, his past performance, and in some cases, his wealth and proven ability to lead the ward. His duty is not to teach the Word of God; in fact, they rarely do. Instead, they serve more as middle managers of a world-wide business conglomeration. They are there for the purposes of:

1. Ensuring obedience and worthiness;
2. Maintaining the status quo;
3. Counseling, aimed at improving the member's performance by use of the prescribed LDS guides; and

4. Advancing their members in the Church's works-based system, which includes the payment of tithes.

Where a paid pastor might encourage its members to support the church financially, people are free to belong without a cost, with full access to any and all programs offered by that congregation. But with a non-paid bishop, he works very hard at getting the rest of his ward to pay tithing, with lack of compliance resulting in denial of the "full benefits" the Church has to offer. In other words, they cannot fully belong without full payment.

See the twist?

A paid pastor of a Christian church is singularly accountable to the Lord and His flock; but members of an LDS ward are beholden to the bishop and the Church, constantly *serving* and *paying* and *doing* in order to be approved by them. When fully approved, the bishop, like any good middle manager, rewards with recognition, better callings, mentions from the pulpit, and of course, the temple recommend. When disapproved, however, the bishop, like any good middle manager, works with them to improve upon their performance, withholding the better callings and the so-called "saving ordinances" until compliance is achieved.

In the end, I cannot help but to consider the LDS lay clergy an oppressive and manipulative system devised by man with only an appearance of goodness.

Which is more "Christian" friends:

A single standing church with a good man serving as pastor, who loves the Lord, studies His Word, and teaches it to His congregation for a fair and reasonable salary, obtained by the free will gifts of the people;

OR

A multi-national institutionalized corporation where everyone is required to pay 10% of their income to not only get into the temple (and thereby heaven) but to also have a shot at "managing" a group of member-peers, too, but rarely ever truly teaching God's Word?

The Lord knew what He was doing when He set up His church.

All of this being said however, the LDS DO HAVE A PAID CLERGY! And some are paid big. All of their Church Educational System teachers are paid – and what is a pastor if not for church education? Church educators are paid. They are employed by the Mormon church full time. All of the Church's apostles are paid. All of the Salt Lake City hierarchy are paid. All of those at Church-owned companies are paid – all of them! Are *they* working for God? Why are they then paid?

A number of years ago I said that I would be willing to bet that Thomas S. Monson, who started full-time as a very, very young leader in the LDS Church, is now a multi-millionaire! How did this happen since almost all of His working adult life he has been in the employ of the Church? Well a great researcher and supporter of our ministry – John M. – did some outstanding digging for us relative to the financial side of Mormonism.

Remember, no "true church," no "restored gospel," could possibly have a paid clergy, right?

The following is according to D. Michael Quinn, formerly of the Church historical department, (*The Mormon Hierarchy: Extensions of Power*, see chapter 6, "Church Finances"):

> Stake Patriarchs used to charge $1.00 per blessing. This increased to $2.00 by the end of the nineteenth century. Strangely

> enough, these patriarchs encouraged the faithful to receive numerous blessings over the course of their lives. "Uncle" John Smith reported that, although he "lived very Poor ever Since we Left Kirtland Ohio," once ordained a patriarch by his nephew Joseph Smith, he "Obtained a Comfortable Living (page 205)." *Hmmmm …*

During Brigham Young's reign, bishops took whatever they desired from all non-cash tithing donations (page 206).

In 1844, John Taylor limited a bishop's take to 8% of the tithing collected while stake presidents got 2% of all the tithing collected by the bishops in their stakes (page 206)!

No PAID CLERGY! Ha! This has been a multi-level clergy upline if there ever was one!

In 1888, Wilford Woodruff established SET SALARIES for stake presidents and set up committees to allocate 10% of the tithes collected in the stakes to go to the bishops (pages 206-209).

At the April 1896 General Conference, the First Presidency announced an end to salaries for local officers and agree to only pay the … *ahem* … apostles (page 206).

By 1904, stake presidents were receiving $300.00 per year for their work, and as late as the 1920s, some bishops reported to still have been receiving 10% of the tithes collected in their wards (page 206).

Now we know this payment of bishops and stake presidents is no longer in force, but what about the apostles and their salaries? These "special witnesses of the Lord Jesus Christ" claim that they are no different in their divine call than the original twelve; how are they … *ahem* … compensated?

First, they do receive money from the coffers of the church. How much I do not know.

Second, they can write books, especially as apostles, and have a built-in market of at least 10 million people willing to buy them.

Finally, and according to Quinn's research in *Extensions of Power* (pages 217-222), the … *ahem* … apostles serve as directors on companies owned by the church or those friendly with the church. Listen to Quinn's quote from his highly-researched book: "By the twentieth century, it was standard policy to give financial compensation to those serving as officers and directors of LDS firms [described earlier by Quinn as those "owned or controlled by the LDS church," page 214]. Such business leadership was primarily the privilege of the First Presidency, Quorum of the Twelve, and the Presiding Bishopric (page 217)." To be a "director" in a company usually means a work load consisting of six, day-long board meetings per year, and a week's worth of committee participation annually.

According to CNN Money.com, the average annual director's compensation in 2006 was as follows:

- A director in the manufacturing sector received $109,000/year.
- A director in financial services received an average of $83,000/year.
- A director in the service sector received an average of $106,250/year.

Quinn researched the First Presidency and the twelve apostles in 1984. They all served on at least one board as a director; some were on as many as twelve (pages 221-223). All, apparently, were being compensated somewhere around one hundred grand per appointment.

The Latter-day Saints must go to the temple in order to live with God in the celestial kingdom. They must mandatorily pay 10% of their annual income to enter this temple. These tithing dollars are used by the church to buy and run businesses. And the prophet and … *ahem* … apostles are then made directors of these businesses and receive directors' compensation as a result.

No paid clergy????? Right.

❋ ❋ ❋

> "To be honest, it was their singular teaching on polygamy that kept me wanting to remain Mormon. I mean, that's quite an opportunity to forfeit if this whole mess turns out to be true in the end." [This was said in jest.]

Polygamy

There is perhaps no issue that has more tenaciously attached itself to Mormonism past and present as that of their doctrine and practice of polygamy. And while we have discussed it before here on our program, our reviews were, for the most part, limited to the founding prophet Joseph Smith Jr. introducing it, secretly practicing it, and what happened after he died to the women he had secretly wed.

Now we are going to embark on a much more extensive look at the LDS practice of polygamy. We're going to pick it up from the death of Joseph Smith through the present. I firmly believe two things can or will occur through our presentation of this information. First, I believe that the information we will cover will blow you away if you open your mind and just listen to the whole matter. Second, I personally think that if you are a female member of the church, you cannot, if you truly listen to the information presented, continue to believe, *in good conscience*, that these LDS leaders were inspired by God in the fabrication of this practice, and, therefore, in the fabrication of many other LDS doctrines that are at odds with God's truth.

Thomas Hobbes, a great mind of ages past, once said something to the effect that, *"organized religion is like a large bitter pill that if swallowed whole, it can cure many pains, but if chewed up and before being swallowed, it will only cause a person to regurgitate."* [The English Works of Thomas Hobbes of Malmesbury, p. 360] We hope this information will cause you to chew on your religion before swallowing it whole, with the hopeful end being a wholesale regurgitation of such man-made beliefs.

There is always present the salacious but understandable idea that the primary purpose for the existence of Mormon polygamy was lust (i.e., men getting "lots o' chicks"). I think this idea needs some clarification. Where Mormon polygamy may have been initiated by lust on the part of Joseph Smith (who once stated, "Whenever I see a pretty woman, I have to pray for grace" [Wilhelm Wyl, *Mormon Portraits, Joseph Smith the Prophet, His Family and His Friends,* page 55]) the practice, by the time it became open and acceptable in Utah, was far more utilitarian: it had become purposeful, pragmatic, and doctrinally based.

In either case, women were treated as chattel.

While Joseph Smith kept the practice hidden throughout his entire life, sharing it only with those who could "bear it," in Brigham Young's and John Taylor's Utah, polygamy was out in the open and even promoted as the means for an LDS man to reach a *"fullness of glory"* (Doctrine and Covenants 132:6). Like many, many things LDS, Joseph publicly denied ever having more than one wife while privately practicing polygamy with at least thirty-three females. I say females because "women" would not be an appropriate title as Joseph secretly made females of all child-bearing ages his, including several teenagers. In order to keep the practice secret, one Ebenezer Robinson, who was approached with the opportunity to embrace polygamy in Nauvoo, Illinois, said a secret location existed twelve miles outside of Nauvoo where impregnated plural wives were sent to be kept from the eyes of inquisitive Gentiles (*One Nation Under Gods* [*ONUG*], page 282).

And while Joseph didn't restrict himself to only single women (he married a number of other men's wives – see Todd Compton, *In Sacred Loneliness: The Plural Wives of Joseph Smith*), not all women approached with the "advanced theological practice" accepted it from him. Orson Pratt, early church leader who was at one time married to Sarah Pratt (who ultimately left Mormonism *and* Orson) was propositioned by Joseph Smith to become his wife while married to Pratt. In an 1886 interview she said (Statement of Sarah Pratt, *Mormon Portraits*, pages 61-62, as cited in Tanner, *Mormonism: Shadow or Reality?*, Fifth Edition, page 220):

> Joseph used to state to his intended victims, **as he did to me**: "God does not care if we have a good time, if only other people do not know it."

She continued:

> He only introduced a marriage ceremony when he had found out he could not get certain women without it...If any woman, like me, opposed his wishes, he used to say: "Be silent, or I shall ruin your character. My character must be sustained in the interest of the church."

If and when Joseph was confronted by those who wanted to investigate "the principle," as it came to be known, Joseph would vehemently deny it. On May 26, 1844, Joseph said in a public response to accusations of his practicing polygamy (*History of the Church* 6:411):

> William Law ... swears that I have committed adultery. I wish the grand jury would tell me who they [meaning his seven wives] are ... I am quite tired of fools asking me. A man asked me if the commandment was given that a man may have seven wives ... I am innocent of these charges ... What a thing it is for a man to be accused of committing adultery, and having seven wives, when I can only find one! I am the same man, and as innocent as I was fourteen years ago; and I can prove them all perjurers.

When Joseph Smith made this public claim, it is true that he didn't have seven wives. He had at least thirty three!

After Smith was killed, and the Saints headed west, Mormon polygamy began to break from the shadows and flourish under the desert sun of Utah. Like Jim Jones after him, who introduced his own farfetched doctrines in the jungles of Guyana, Brigham Young made plural marriage *THE* standard once the Saints were safely secluded from the rest of civilization by 800 miles in any direction: the standard for faithful living, the standard for following the prophet, and the standard for being obedient.

It started becoming publicly accepted when, in 1851, Brigham Young made his first public reference to the principle when he mentioned his *"wives"* from the pulpit (*ONUG*, page 284). Travelers and Gentiles passing through the territory would report seeing unusual living arrangements, which ultimately lead the Mormons to admit the practice more openly.

Finally, in 1852, five years after the Mormons arrived in Salt Lake City, Joseph Smith Jr.'s official revelation on plural marriage – which he purportedly received from God in 1843 – was published and embraced openly (*Mormonism: Shadow or Reality?*, page 204). An 1835 first edition of the Doctrine and Covenants contains a revelation Joseph also claimed to have received from God that actually condemned the practice of plural marriage and promoted monogamy (Section CI, Marriage, page 251). In time, however, this "revelation from God" was removed from the Doctrine and Covenants and replaced with Joseph's more advanced revelation on matrimony, which in my mind can be called the "lots o' chicks" doctrine.

So what really is behind the "lots o' chicks" doctrine found in Mormonism? Why that focus – what would drive a man to take on more than one wife?

From a male perspective, from my personal heart of flesh, polygamy might appear beneficial for the following reasons:

- It could make me feel powerful.
- It could keep me young and moving and virile.
- It could make me the center of attention for many females instead of just one, which would stoke my pride.
- It could help me play god here on earth.
- It would give me variety in the flesh.
- I could pit different wives against each other to get my way.
- I could impregnate more women than one, again feeling more alive, powerful, and virile.
- I could corral them into a giant work force.
- I would not be beholden to any single female.
- I would be served.

However, as the father of three daughters, I have to ask, what is the benefit to the females? Is this the way God would want any of His daughters to live? Would I recommend my daughters to get involved in such a set up?

In order to fully understand Mormon polygamy, we have to go back a ways. Now this going back is really very important because if we understand how polygamy was ultimately justified doctrinally and theologically, we will also understand why Mormonism today – Salt Lake City Mormonism – has not apologized for the practices of the past, has not removed the doctrine in the present, and continues to believe the doctrine has a place in the futures of all faithful LDS men.

Lots o' chicks.

From a Biblical perspective, monogamy is logical, not polygamy. In the beginning, God created heaven and the earth and from the earth, the man, Adam. From Adam he formed one woman: Eve. Not two or three or fifty-three; He formed one woman. Adam had a full rib cage left when God was finished creating his mate.

Theologically, monogamy also makes sense within the confines of Bible believing Christians because New Testament Christianity makes it very clear that marriage is not the end-all of human existence, but rather it is to know and serve the only true and living God. Jesus set marriage in its proper place when He said:

> Matthew 22:30. *For in the resurrection [men] neither marry, nor are given in marriage, but are as the angels of God in heaven.*

In Luke's gospel, He shed further light on the function and scope of marriage when He said:

> Luke 20:34-35. *The children of this world marry, and are given in marriage: but they which shall be accounted worthy to obtain that world, and the resurrection from the dead, neither marry, nor are given in marriage.*

In other words, while marriage is ordained of God, and is a good and permissible thing, according to Jesus it is an institution for life on earth and not part of post resurrection life. Paul, who was himself single, wrote to the Corinthian believers (listen, now):

> 1 Corinthians 7:7-9. *For I would that all men were even as I myself am. But each has his proper gift from God, one according to this manner and another according to that. I say therefore to the unmarried and the widows, "It is good for them if they remain even as I. But if they do not have self-control, let them marry; for it is better to marry than to burn.*

This Biblical, Christian view of the earthly institution of marriage is far afield from the revised LDS view Joseph Smith presented. Where Jesus said the children of **this world only** marry and are given in marriage, Mormonism makes marriage, in some senses, its god. It is presented as the end-all, highest state of human existence because it is only in that state that a person can become a god. This is the view that must be understood – on becoming a god – before we can truly reason with the practice and purpose of polygamy. Because of this, we are going to review the LDS myths relative to the make-up of God, the preexistence, the creation of spirit children – which will enable us to understand the practice of polygamy in Mormon history and the present doctrine about it, which *REMAINS* part of Mormonism today.

There are two ways human beings approach the origins of matter, or things that we can see, touch, smell, and otherwise somehow identify. There are those who believe that all matter was created out of nothing by God. Or, there are those who believe that matter has always existed, that it pre-dates God, and that even God cannot create matter out of nothing. Now listen closely: these are ultimately the only two options. Matter was either created from nothing *OR* matter has always existed.

Got that down?

Christians embrace the former but LDS doctrine teaches the latter. Why the difference?

Because Christians embrace the biblical account that states "*In the beginning, God ...*" When we read *the beginning*, we believe, *the* actual *beginning*. Christians also embrace that "*All things*" – ALL things – "*were made by Him and without Him was not anything made that was made* (John 1:3)." We do not extend any belief beyond this point: we believe God created all matter.

But in Mormonism, Joseph Smith taught the latter concept that **matter has always existed.**

Hang with me now because individually these concepts are radical at best (relative to the Biblical perspective) but taken together we hold in our hands one of the most humanistic and materialistic world views imaginable.

Ready?

The first thing Joseph Smith taught was that everything that could be considered *real* is actually *material.*

> D&C 141:7-8. *There is no such thing as immaterial matter. All spirit is matter, but is more fine or pure, and can only be discerned by purer eyes.*

Mormon doctrine wholly rejects any form of immateriality as being real. There are no invisible, non-material spirits in Mormonism. No non-material anything, anywhere, at anytime. All things, everything, seen and unseen, in Mormonism is material. And when things that are invisible to us – like spirits – are truly examined, Mormonism teaches that they, too, are constructed of material, and the material of all things has always existed and was never created! Mormon doctrine teaches that anything that is not material cannot be considered real; for something to be considered *real* it must be made of *matter*. Early LDS apostle, scientist, and intellectual Parley P. Pratt, said ("Materiality," *The Prophet*, May 24, 1845, as cited in *The New Mormon Challenge*, page 226):

> Nothing exists which is not material. The elementary principles of the material universe are eternal; they never originated from nonentity, and they never can be annihilated. Immateriality is but another name for nonentity – it is the negative of all things, and beings – of all existence.

Remember, hand in hand with this concept is the LDS idea that material has always existed and cannot be created or destroyed. So, in Mormon doctrine, everything that exists is constructed of matter; and this matter – from God, to the Holy Spirit, to angels, rocks and human beings – could not be created and cannot ever be destroyed.

Got all that?

Now, just to let you in on a hint of the argument that calls this position into question, if something must be made of matter to be considered real in Mormonism, what do they say memories, dreams, and thoughts are?

Okay.

So from this philosophical approach to matter, Mormonism steps forward and says through its teachings, the purpose of all this self-existent matter is to advance: to become more purposeful, to grow in strength, glory, and power. Given this position, then, even the Mormon god Elohim, who has always materially existed, has progressed to the point where he became god. And you and I, who have always existed, have progressed to the point where we took on bodies of flesh and bone to house our spirit bodies (which are also material). You see, from the LDS perspective, material progression is to be expected from the material universe. Matter is not meant to be stagnant or inert, but to progress, refine, and to become more and more enlightened. So God, always in the form of matter, progressed to the point where He became God. And you and I, created in his image, also have the opportunity to progress to the point in our material state where we can also become advanced, refined: in other words, a god.

And the trek goes on and on and on, eternally, as we, in turn, gather uncreated matter, form it into spirits, and create more worlds. These notions of matter are foundational when trying to comprehend the LDS belief in plural marriage.

The second influence upon LDS doctrine has to do with **eternal laws and principles.** At the very center of Mormon theology is the belief that any law and/or principle that can be considered good is also self-existent, meaning it has no creator including God, and has always existed in the exact same condition (i.e., is *immutable*). It never changes over eons and eons of time.

Additionally, Mormonism teaches that any law or principle that is temporary or has evolved from an original or mutable source (meaning it has been created by something or someone else) must be considered evil.

In promoting the theology of eternally good and uncreated laws and principles, Joseph Smith said (*TPJS*, page 181):

> Every principle proceeding from God is eternal and any principle which is not eternal is of the devil ...The first step in the salvation of man is the laws of eternal and self-existent principles.

"*Self-existent principles*" are principles that were not created, have no beginning or end, never change, and have eternally existed on their own, by themselves, without a creator or an original source.

Bottom line, Latter-day Saint doctrine teaches that eternal laws and principles existed even *before* God, meaning that laws and principles define, govern, and supersede god, his will, and his ways.

Now, let me tie these two segments – *materialism* and *self-existent principles* – together. To Mormons, everything real is made of matter that has always existed and was never created. The ultimate purpose of all matter is to fulfill its potential.

Human beings fulfill their potential by being obedient to eternally existing laws and principles which even God didn't create but to which He is also subject. By obeying these eternally existing laws, human beings will ultimately progress in glory to the point of becoming a god.

There are blessings from obedience to these laws and cursings associated with disobedience to them. There are a number of scriptural passages in LDS cannon that support this idea.

> D&C 130:20-21. *There is a law, irrevocably decreed in heaven before the foundation of the world, upon which all blessings are predicated. And when we obtain any blessing from God, it is by obedience to that law upon which it was predicated...*

Doctrine and Covenants 82:10 alludes to even God being bound by these eternal laws when it states:

> D&C 82:10 I the Lord am BOUND when you do what I say, but when you do not what I say, ye have no promise.

(I don't think there is any more pernicious doctrine in the LDS Doctrine and Covenants than this.)

According to basic Mormon doctrine, every uncreated, eternally-existing law has a blessing connected to it. If a soul obeys the eternal law, God must respond by blessing that individual – He is bound to. And although the blessings come from God, or through God, it is by *obedience* to that uncreated, eternal law that the person is rewarded and not because God chooses to bless or not bless the soul out of His own will or desire.

So now with a basic understanding of this materialistic LDS worldview, let me tell their story, implementing these beliefs, which are so contrary to biblical Christianity, as a backdrop.

One of the eternal laws and principles of Mormonism is the eternal law of celestial marriage. In order for material human beings to progress toward fulfilling their full potential, they must be sealed for time and all eternity (this occurs in their temples) to their mate. Before the earth was formed, god – a man who progressed to that position by obedience to eternal laws and principles – took eternally existing spirit matter, and with his wife ("*mother in heaven*," one of many of the father's wives in heaven), created spirit children from that matter. Of those children, which included you and me, were many bright creations including Jesus, Lucifer, Abraham, etc. So there we all were – spirit children – gathered around the throne of our heavenly father and his wives.

Now, Heavenly Father and his wives all had physical bodies, (remember, because they had progressed to this point by obedience) and all of us spirit kids desired to get one, too, so he created earth and a plan: all of us pre-mortal life spirits could come down to earth, receive physical bodies, progress through trials and tests, and if found obedient to the self-existent eternal laws and principles just as he once was (which included celestial marriage), we could return to our heavenly parents and someday become gods too.

This plan was presented by the Father and Lucifer said something like this: "No, no, no. I don't like it. I will go down and force everyone to obey, and I will bring them all back to you, father. But if I do this for you, give me all the glory." God replied, "Sorry Lucifer, everyone must choose to obey these laws and principles freely or it is all meaningless." Then Jesus came forth and said, "I will go down and offer my life for all those who sin, and therefore make it possible for those who blow it to repent and then return to you." And god respected this offer.

This angered Lucifer and a war broke out in heaven in which Lucifer, who became *Satan*, was cast out of heaven with one-third of the other pre-mortal spirit children of god the father and heavenly mother. And where did they go? Down here on earth to try and get all of us who accepted god's plan to fail.

Meanwhile, back up in the pre-mortal existence, every single person who has ever been or who will ever be born on earth, had made the decision to go with God's plan. And while awaiting our turn to be born, some of us spent our time progressing, refining, and becoming more enlightened in this non-flesh (yet still material) state. Those who progressed the most came to earth most blessed. Those who squandered their time there, came to earth in less fortuitous conditions.

Latter-day Saints have long emphasized that the most valiant of the pre-existence (you know, those who obeyed the laws and principles most exactly) are born into the LDS faith. It has also long been intimated that those who are born into prominent LDS families were likewise the most faithful in the pre-mortal state.

Listen to the way "Apostle" Mark E. Peterson put it ("Race Problems – as they affect the church," page 11):

> We cannot escape the conclusion that because of performance in our pre-existence some of us are born as Chinese, some as Japanese, some as Indians, some as Negroes, some as Americans,

> some as Latter-day Saints. These are rewards and punishments, fully in harmony with His established policy in dealing with sinners and saints, rewarding all according to their deeds.

Or, how about "Apostle" Dallin H. Oakes ("The Great Plan of Happiness," *Ensign*, November 1993):

> All of the myriads of mortals who have been born on this earth chose the Father's plan and fought for it. Many of us also made covenants with the Father concerning what we would do in mortality. In ways that have not been revealed, our actions in the spirit world influence us in mortality.

It's all about progression through obedience and advancement through personal growth. This lays out the basis for the LDS idea of the pre-mortal existence.

The Bible is clear when it states that God is the First and the Last, the Alpha and the Omega. It is clear, as we read in Genesis, when the Bible states that He is the creator of all things. The Bible is clear that there is only one human being that had a pre-mortal existence: the God-Man, Jesus Christ.

Remember what He said to the people:

> John 8:23. … *Ye are from beneath; I am from above:* ***ye are of this world; I am not of this world.***

He also said *no man had ever seen the Father at any time* (see John 6:46).

Where Joseph Smith replaced the Word of God with a myth, claiming men to be the children of heavenly father and heavenly mother (or mothers), the Bible makes it perfectly clear that we are not His children until we have been born again. We are ONLY His creations, formed from the dust:

> John 1:12-13. *But as many as* ***received him, to them gave he power***

> *to **become the sons of God**, even to them that **believe on his name**: Which were **born**, not of blood, nor of the will of the flesh, nor of the will of man, but **of God**.*

But more to the point, these unique LDS teachings about matter, laws, and pre-existence are the theological groundwork that set the stage for Joseph ultimately introducing the doctrine of plural marriage that Mormons embrace. The stones of this foundation include the LDS belief that *matter has always existed* and was not created by God; that there are *laws and principles that have always existed* that were not created by God; and that *by obeying these eternal rules, men and women can progress as infinite matter*, over time becoming "gods."

When an LDS man takes upon himself a second wife he has multiplied his given domain and sphere of earthly influence and is therefore placed into a higher level of responsibility and glory. This is the ultimate motivation behind the doctrine of plural wives. Add three, five, or a dozen more wives, and you have an LDS man who is literally practicing the heavenly order of god here on earth: the eternal law of polygamy, a principle that has forever existed. Such participation advances material men just as god the father advanced, producing as many children as possible and giving the man more wombs to bear and nourish spirit children in the hereafter. Those children, too, could then continue to advance toward godhood.

Now do not forget, my friends, that the doctrine of plural marriage is STILL embraced by the LDS Church in Salt Lake City today, despite the fact that they spend all sorts of time and money claiming this is NOT true. When a Latter-day Saint tells you that they have "*nothing to do with polygamy today*" or that it was something the LDS "*did in the past, but those who practice it today are excommunicated*," ask them three questions:

1. Is the doctrine and teachings for the practice of plural marriage still in the present day LDS scriptures? (Answer: It is! It's in the *Doctrine and Covenants* section 132.) Then ask
2. Can a man today be sealed to another woman to be his plural wife in the eternities? (Answer: He can!) Is this a form of practicing the principle by the Salt Lake Mormon church? (Answer: It is!) Finally, ask them
3. Is the LDS doctrine of polygamy an *eternal* principle or is it a *created* principle? If they say it was not eternal, then you can say that according to their doctrine, it is evil, because it was a created principle and created principles are evil. And if they say it is an eternal principle, then you can ask them that if it is an eternal principle does that mean they still believe in it?

Bottom-line: they are being deceptive. They want to be popular and they are willing to lie about their doctrine in order to achieve it.

As we've mentioned, once everyone settled in Utah under the power and influence of Brigham Young, polygamy became a way of life. And not just a way a life, a demand on men if they were going to achieve the highest degree of eternal glory. Men were encouraged to build up the kingdom through the practice. If they refused, they were looked down upon, even ostracized.

Now listen, the prophet and the apostles made it known, in no uncertain terms, that the way to exaltation was through the practice of plural marriage. Was the prophet wrong? Did he lead those men and women astray?

This leads to the fourth question to ask the LDS:

4. Were Brigham Young and the apostles wrong in teach-

> ing this about polygamy? Was it true or not, that a man had to practice plural marriage in order to be exalted? If it was true then, why not now? And if it was not the truth, did the prophet and apostles lead these men and women astray?

Where Brigham Young and other leaders like William Clayton and Heber C. Kimball all had room to house their many wives (Young had the Beehive house and the Lion House, Clayton had a big house, and Kimball had one, too), the majority of men who took on other wives did so without any provision. To get a flavor of what life was like for these families who "followed the prophet," I would suggest a reading of a book by one of Brigham Young's ex-wives, Ann Eliza Young: *Wife No. 19*. It was bleak, crude, and placed them in a condition of perpetual, life-long bondage to poverty.

So hot was the demand for wives in the territory that there were few societal regulations for who could marry whom, which led to a type of familial bedlam. Courtship patterns slipped sideways and there was no standard for how many wives could be taken or from where. In Brigham City, one Bishop Smith married two of his own nieces (*Wife No. 19*, page 310). Bishop Johnson in Springville married six of his own nieces, with the OLDEST being only 15 years old (page 310). As the others grew, they were "given to him," the last and youngest being 13 years old when they were sealed (page 311).

Ann Eliza wrote (page 310):

> Uncles and nieces were married; one man would marry several sisters; and it was a very common thing for a mother and daughter to have the same husband (gosh, I'm thankful that wasn't my lot in life!) In one family at least three generations were represented among the wives – grandmother, mother, daughter, and

> a case occurred in Salt Lake City where a man actually married his half sister, and that, too, with the full approval of Brigham Young.

Author Richard Abanes notes (*ONUG*, page 294):

> Brigham Young reasoned that since all people were brothers and sisters born to Heavenly Father, then earthly relationships were of little import when it came to sealing.

A scholar from Brigham Young University, one Jessie L. Embry, acknowledged that as late as 1886, church President Lorenzo Snow held that brothers and sisters could marry (ONUG, page 294).

Fanny Stenhouse, who also defected from Mormonism after being a plural wife, wrote a book called, *Tell It All*, where she stated (as cited in *ONUG*, page 294):

> Marriages have been contracted between the nearest of relatives; and old men tottering on the brink of the grave have been united to little girls scarcely in their teens; while unnatural alliances of every description, which in any other community would be regarded with disgust and abhorrence, are here entered into in the name of God.

In the name of Who? God.

Who? God.

Now, let me say this here and now. I believe completely in the right to let people do as they wish within the law, believe what they wish, and worship how they want. I do NOT agree with teens and children taken, but the idea of polygamy – even inter-relational unions – is not going to receive anything from me in terms of judgment. However, I don't agree with it. I don't like it. I think it is messed up.

But there are thousands of very strange cultural practices out there and I am in no position to police all of them.

HOWEVER, *Mormonism claims to be Christian*. Do these attitudes and actions sound "*Christian*"? If Christian, then why haven't all the Christian scholars and theologians over the ages embraced polygamy as normative? Here is the reason and the rub: this stuff is NOT of Jesus, it never *has been* of Jesus, and yet today, *WHILE RETAINING THIS DOCTRINE AND NOT RENOUNCING IT*, Mormonism wants to claim to be Christian.

LDS "Apostle" Heber C. Kimball said (*Journal of Discourses* 4:209):

> In the spirit world ...we will go to brother Joseph and say, "Here we are, brother Joseph"... He will say to us, "Come along, my boys, we will give you a good suit of clothes. Where are your wives?"

And the men will answer Joseph by saying:

> "They are back yonder, they would not follow us."

And Joseph will say,

> Never mind. Here are thousands, have all you want.

What does that say? What is the attitude toward women that this sort of language presents to men? How would a woman feel about herself in light of sayings like this?

Sound Christian to you?

When Brigham Young was approached by one Phineas Cook, who said that his *"wife was nearly tired out,"* Brigham Young replied that when "*his women got tired, he could take them home and change them for fresh ones* (*ONUG*, page 295)."

Three separate individuals all reported in their private writings that LDS Apostle Heber C. Kimball referred to his women as "*cows*," and was quoted as saying, "I think no more of taking another wife than I do of buying a cow." (*ONUG*, page 295)

Sound Christian?

In fact, let me take a minute and explain something about women and Christianity.

In Genesis we read:

> Genesis 2:23. *And Adam said, This is now bone of my bones, and flesh of my flesh: she shall be called Woman, because she was taken out of Man.*

In Hebrew, the word for man is "*ish*" and for woman, "*isha*." And from the beginning they were ONE – made from the same being. United, fitting together like two puzzle pieces. One woman from one man. With the fall of Adam, the original condition of the man/woman relationship was lost and all sorts of really UGLY stuff came in and made a home:

Competition.
Anger.
Manipulation.
Power-struggles.
Selfishness.

When God brought up his holy nation, Israel, He instituted the law, a code for living in the flesh while under the conditions of the fall. Within this law came a priesthood which served and functioned to bless the children of Israel. ONLY Jewish males could hold this priesthood, not females. In this code there was a demand for all of the men of God to be identified through circumcision. This token set them apart from the rest of the world both as a people, as a nation, and as a priesthood. But God gave nothing in this law for women to receive identification of their own because the woman received her identity through the male figurehead of her life. He was the first, from whom she was taken and he was the head. He was identified; she was not, except through Him.

He, if of the tribe of Levi, held the priesthood. She could not. Under the Jewish dispensation, "church" and state were identical. No one could be a member of the one without also being a member of the other. Circumcision was a sign and seal of membership in both. Every circumcised person thereby bore evidence that he was one of the chosen people, a member of the people of God as they then existed, and consequently also a member of the Jewish commonwealth.

But prior to Christ, and because of the Fall, woman received all her identity through her husband. She essentially had no rights, and could be abandoned for any number of reasons. Needless to say, before Jesus, life was very, very hard on women. Yet this is the *VERY system and attitude* that Joseph Smith and Brigham Young reinstituted to the Latter-day Saints. They went back in time, adopted it, and applied it to their own operation. What they neglected to understand was that about 1,820 years before, a Baby named Jesus was born. And by the end of His short life, He restored things to their Edenic state, spiritually for those who are his.

He not only *fulfilled* the Law, He *abolished* its effects, freeing people from its restrictive ways and introduced living by the Spirit as a result. Since His death and resurrection, no one who knows Him ought to relate to the old law. Priestly duties have been completed in Him. A woman does not need to be married to have an identity in this world for she has an identity in Jesus. Male circumcision has on one hand been abolished as a covenant act in the flesh, while on the other hand it has now been applied to *all* men, not just a select group identified with priesthoods and rituals. Now, we are *all* commanded to have our individual hearts circumcised so as to identify each of us to Him.

Knowing all of this, can you see how much Mormonism rejects the good news and attempts to reimplement what Jesus completed through His death and resurrection? Let me tell you something folks: what the LDS leaders are doing is an abomination in light of what Jesus has done, for where He reversed all the effects of the fall and set in motion freedom and liberty in the Spirit for ALL people, the LDS leadership brought it all back, which makes a mockery of the Lord's work on the cross.

The natural results? Suffering women, the glorification of men, a reinstitution of law, required temple ordinances, and the death of grace. Shame on you, Thomas Monson. Shame on you.

Speaking of the Mormon practice of polygamy in Utah, author Richard Abanes wrote in his book, *One Nation Under Gods* (page 297), that

> After several years in Utah, Mormon men began realizing that their supply of young women was dwindling.

Several pages ago, we discussed how Brigham Young and others viewed women as property, even as cattle, which were to be gathered, owned, and even exchanged. When the women started to run in short supply, something needed to be done. LDS missionaries were therefore instructed to bring back as many females as possible from the mission field to replenish the wanting supply. Concerns began to crop up, however, that the missionaries, who were typically much younger and more appealing than the brethren back home, were taking the "best women for themselves" and leave the graying grandpas with the leftovers.

Heber C. Kimball told departing missionaries the following (*Journal of Discourses* 6:256):

> *You are sent out as shepherds to gather the sheep together; and remember that they are not your sheep: they belong to Him that sends you. Then do not make a choice of any of those sheep*; do not make selections before they are brought home and put into the fold. *You understand* that. *Amen* [italics in original].

He is also quoted as saying (Stanley Hirshon, *The Lion of the Lord*, pages 129-130, as cited in Tanner, *The Changing World of Mormonism*, page 225),

> The brother missionaries have been in the habit of picking out the prettiest women for themselves before they get here, and bringing the ugly ones for us; hereafter you have to bring them all here before taking any of them, and let us all have a fair shake.

Nice eh?

Now, I've got to be honest. If I was the leader of a church that taught that men needed to take on extra wives in order to achieve exaltation, and I desired to surround myself with wives so I could be exalted, I would want the hotties around me too.

Well, word got around overseas that women were going back to Utah (or *Zion* as they called it) and were getting taken in as plural wives. This caused both the LDS leadership and the missionaries to frankly LIE to people about the practice of polygamy in order to convince them to join the church and come to Zion. The same lying is still going on today to investigators by both the missionaries who represent a very limited gospel perspective and the leadership who present a very limited, revised, and spun version of history.

For example, the 1866 version of the LDS Doctrine and Covenants published in Europe denied polygamy; so did the American version up until 1876 when the monogamy revelation was replaced with the polygamy revelation, Doctrine and Covenants 132.

But in 1866 Brigham Young declared (*Journal of Discourses* 11: 269):

> "The only men who become Gods, even the Sons of God, are those who enter into polygamy.

This same year, Brigham Young's successor John Taylor said (*Journal of Discourses* 11:221):

> Where did this commandment come from in relation to polygamy? It also came from God …When I see any of our people, men or women, opposing a principle of this kind, I have years ago set them down as on the highroad to apostasy, and I do today; I consider them apostates …

What is interesting is that while in France in 1850, this very same John Taylor said in a public forum (*Orson Pratt's Works*, page 8, as cited in Tanner, *The Changing World of Mormonism*, page 262):

> We are accused here of polygamy, and actions the most indelicate, obscene and disgusting, such that none but a corrupt and depraved mind could have contrived … These things are too outrageous to admit of belief.

Then he took out the Doctrine and Covenants and read from the edition that disavowed polygamy. At that very moment John Taylor, this future president of the Mormon church, while standing on French soil and denying the doctrine and practice of plural marriage, had twelve wives back in *Zion* who had at that point already borne him eight children (D. Michael Quinn,

The Mormon Hierarchy: Origins of Power, page 597)! He lied in order to get people to convert and come to isolated Zion.

As with the leaders so with the sheep. Mormon missionaries routinely lied – as they do today – in order to deceive their European audiences. These lies were in the form of outright half-truths and misinformation.

Three nights ago I was looking up film reviews for a movie my family was going to see. The site is called MRQE.com and it is a repository for thousands of film reviews by hundreds of critics. Banners at the top of this site advertised the giving away of free Bibles. They prompt people to click on the ads with catchy phrases. I clicked on an ad and was immediately taken to the LDS.org website where I could dialogue with an LDS representative about Mormonism. It was after midnight, but I clicked on the function and was connected to someone named *NORMAN* who presented the most bifurcated, myopic form of "twistianity" I have ever heard. His approach was no different from the early LDS members, missionaries, and leaders who downplayed polygamy in order to deceive European investigators.

Let me share a story about one woman who was deceived into coming to Zion. Her name was Caroline Owens and she had been friends with one John Miles since they were children in England. It seems John Miles migrated to Utah as a Mormon, but on a return trip to England, asked Caroline to be his wife, saying they would be wed once they arrived back in Zion. Caroline asked about polygamy, and Miles reassured her that only a few men were allowed more than one wife; young men like himself had but one. The couple came to Utah and Caroline reported that she was treated cordially and with love, but the entire charade revealed itself just hours after her wedding. She recounted (*ONUG*, page 300):

> I can never tell the horrors of the next few hours ... I went to my room and dressed for the reception, which took place at Cannon's other house where he kept his other three wives. When I went down, there was a crowd there, among the rest a plain looking girl in a calico dress, to whom I was introduced. It was Emily Spencer ... I told her to get up. Miles came forward and said, "Sit still, Emily Spencer, my wife." I felt as though I had been shot

This deception ultimately led to a Supreme Court case, Miles vs. the United States of America.

Before Englishman William Jarman and his wife came to Utah, they too, had been deceived by LDS missionaries. According to Jarman, the elder who converted them never denied polygamy, but when asked about it said what missionaries continue to say today (William Jarman, *U.S.A., Uncle Sam's abscess; or Hell upon earth for U.S., Uncle Sam*, page 44):

> Polygamy is very rarely followed; the prophet Brigham and one or two others practise [sic] it because God revealed to them that they must do so.

The elder continued to the Englishman's wife:

> But Mrs. Jarman, it is not essential to salvation, as you seem to think, that men must become polygamists.

Remember, two years earlier, Brigham Young had actually taught that it was, indeed, essential.

What was the fallout if an LDS man or woman refused or spoke against practicing polygamy? The very same fallout if a man or woman refuses or speaks against something the Mormon leaders say today, with some added pressure.

For instance, there is the documented case of one Bishop Snow, an LDS polygamist living in Manti. It seems old Bishop Snow, a believer in the principle, in the *Book of Mormon*, in modern-day prophets, etc., etc., had his eye on a buxom young LDS woman and approached her with an offer to be another one of his wives. The girl thanked Snow but declined, saying she was in love with and engaged to a younger man, one Thomas Lewis, much nearer her age. Bishop Snow, invoking God's name and claiming it was "*His will*," explained that her beau could be "gotten rid of or sent on a mission;" still the girl refused.

Her refusal was unheard of. Just like today, refusing your bishop when he says something comes from the LORD is not in harmony with LDS protocol. Her behavior caused "the brethren" to call Thomas Lewis in to counsel him to give up his love. Lewis said, "No way." For his insolence, he was held down by a bunch of believers in Joseph's gospel and brutally castrated by Bishop Snow, who used a bowie knife to do the job (*ONUG*, page 299; see also Quinn, *The Mormon Hierarchy: Extensions of Power*, pages 250-251).

Now, before you pass this off as a singular aberration, there are some things to consider relative to this act of castration that Bishop Snow ruthlessly, selfishly, and demonically did to Thomas Lewis:

- It was done by a man in authority, angry at not getting what he wanted;
- It was done by a true believing Mormon leader;
- He was held down by other true believing Mormons;
- It would NEVER be done by Bible believing Christians;
- it was a by-product of Mormon doctrine and policy; and here's the important one…
- THEY ARE STILL CASTRATING MALES TODAY WHO REFUSE TO DO THEIR WILL.

How?

By telling them they will lose their wives in the eternities to other worthy LDS men. By telling them they will lose the ability to procreate in the hereafter if they leave the Church. By refusing to put independent men in positions of authority, thereby rendering them theologically impotent.

From the seed springs a tree, from the tree springs the fruit, from the fruit springs the seed, and on, and on, and on.

Sadly, horribly, disgustingly, the girl ended up marrying Bishop Snow. His counselor recorded in May of 1857 that Thomas Lewis "has now gone crazy." In Historian D. Michael Quinn's book, *The Mormon Hierarchy: Extensions of Power*, he notes that when Brigham Young was informed of the castration he stated that he felt, "inclined to sustain him," and then in July, Young wrote to Bishop Snow and said "Just let the matter drop, and say no more about it, and it will soon die away among the people (pages 250-251)."

Just like Mountain Meadows, right Brigham?

The year is 1885. LDS Church President John Taylor and his two counselors have fled the country because of their polygamous status (*The Mormon Hierarchy: Extensions of Power,* page 44). Two years later, in 1887, politicians passed the power-packed Edmonds-Tucker Act, which required wives involved in polygamy to actually testify *against* their husbands in courts of law ("Polygamy: The 'Relic of Barbarism' that Won't Go Away," *ABA State and Local Bar News*, Volume 31, Number 4, Summer 2008).

The Edmonds-Tucker Act also made adultery a felony and then hit the Mormon Church right where they could not stand to be hit: in their assets. The Church was disincorporated and the seizure and liquidation began of all Church real estate valued at over $50,000 (*The Mormon Hierarchy: Extensions of Power*, page 325). Suddenly, the Mormons started to deny publicly the practice altogether - again. And plural marriage went underground, where it has remained, even to some extent, to this day.

By 1890 nearly 1300 Mormons had been jailed for polygamy. Wilford Woodruff had taken over as the new prophet of the church in 1889 and he literally inherited a nightmare. Personally, Woodruff believed in and practiced polygamy, and had even announced essentially that nothing could stop it from continuing on. Woodruff believed that a favorable ruling from the Supreme Court would challenge the constitutionality of the Edmunds-Tucker Act. But he believed wrong.

Bottom line, Woodruff was faced with either allowing federal marshals to dismantle and then sell off the unfinished Salt Lake temple or to discontinue polygamy. Let me re-phrase that: to make a Mormon *announcement* that polygamy was to be discontinued. Woodruff, after on a number of occasions having defended the existence of plural marriage and claiming it would not ever go away, released an official manifesto on September 25, 1890 which admonished every Mormon to no longer enter into plural marriage. Said Woodruff (Official Declaration – 1):

> Inasmuch as laws have been enacted by Congress forbidding plural marriages, which laws have been pronounced constitutional by the court of last resort, I hereby declare my intention to submit to those laws, and to use my influence with the members of the Church over which I preside to have them do likewise.

Author Richard Abanes points out in his book *One Nation Under Gods* that the "revelation" differed dramatically from other revelations that had ever been given to the Saints, because (page 324):

- Before being issued, this so-called "revelation" was written, re-written, edited, and re-edited many times behind closed doors by various persons ranging from Mormon politicians, to LDS apostles, to non-Mormon legal advisors.

- It was addressed "To whom it may concern," a decidedly secular phrase that failed to hold the authority of a "Thus saith the Lord" declaration.
- It was publicly issued as a press release from Washington by Utah delegate in Congress John T. Caine, rather than being presented to the congregation by church authorities at a church conference, which was how other revelations had been presented.
- It was not signed by the First presidency, but only signed by Wilford Woodruff.
- Woodruff carefully worded the Manifesto to read "I now publicly declare that my advice to the Latter-day Saints is to refrain from contracting any marriage forbidden by the law of the land [emphasis added]," which meant that the entire declaration was Woodruff's personal advice, rather than a command from God. Thus, a sort of theological loophole was given for disobedience.

The point: Mormonism's head man, their prophet, seer and revelator Wilford W. Woodruff, issued a statement that would appease federal officers and the Supreme Court so that the liquidation of LDS assets would cease and their petition for statehood would be granted. In the end, faithful Latter-day Saints continued to practice polygamy with the illegal marriages being secretly performed by leading members of the Church. Lying, either to bring about a perceived "greater good" or to protect the image of the Church has always been an acceptable practice within Mormonism. Even the missionaries today, in most cases, think they have the right to withhold information from seeking investigators. They will, for the good of the cause, not reveal all that the investigator needs to know about the religion he or she is buying into. Most members will do the same thing. Deception is part of the founding church and is alive and well today – justified especially if it is so done in the name of "*sharing the gospel*" or defending the good name of the Church.

While the facts today have proven absolutely contrary, Wilford Woodruff swore in court that polygamous men were to only live with one wife and that polygamy was prohibited. You can go to UTLM.org and read about it all. My friends, there is no easy way to put this other than this: the man the LDS called their prophet, Wilford Woodruff, was a liar. His testimony was simply not true.

In reference to this testimony, Abraham Cannon wrote in his journal that Wilford Woodruff told his apostles the he "was placed in such a position on the witness stand that he could not answer other than he did (*ONUG*, page 326).

Yes, he could.

In 1911 Apostle Matthias Cowley said in his statements before the Council of the Twelve (*ONUG*, page 326):

> I am not dishonest and not a liar and have always been true to the work and to the brethren. I have always been true and faithful myself. We have always been taught that when the brethren were in a tight place that it would not be amiss to lie to help them out. One of the Presidency of the Church made the statement some years ago when I was in the presidency of one of the stakes of Zion in Idaho that he would lie like hell to help his brethren

My friends, LDS President Wilford Woodruff was a liar.

Brigham Young and Joseph Smith Jr. were confirmed liars too. I don't know about John Taylor, the third president of the LDS

Church. But what I do know is three of the four first prophets, seers, and revelators of Mormonism are proven liars.

And why did Woodruff lie? So that Mormonism could retain its assets and Utah could become a state. Trusting that this religious group was telling the truth, the U.S. government in 1896 granted statehood in good faith to the Utah territory.

Guess what happened? The number of Utah polygamous marriages rose immediately, causing *The Salt Lake Tribune* to accuse LDS leaders of deception. The very year statehood was granted, a future president of the Church, Joseph F. Smith, while speaking at a meetinghouse dedication, defied the manifesto, saying (*ONUG*, page 326):

> Take care of your polygamous wives; we don't care for Uncle Sam now.

Wilford Woodruff suddenly died in 1898 and Lorenzo Snow, a practicing polygamist, took the helm. When LDS historian B. H. Roberts was denied a seat in the House of Representatives because he was a polygamist, the Mormon leadership tried to circumvent the illegal nature of polygamy by authoring the Evans Bill, which would make aspects of it legal again (*ONUG*, page 327). Even though the bill was vetoed by Utah's governor, the American people got wind that the Mormons were trying to reintroduce polygamy; with Utah now a state in the union, a nationwide uproar commenced.

This culminated in an exhaustive investigation into the LDS Church by the U.S. senate. One Mormon senator by the name of Reed Smoot found his congressional seat hanging by a thread as a result of this investigation.

In 1901, President Lorenzo Snow died and Joseph F. Smith, a man who had taken more wives even after the manifesto and had encouraged others to do the same, took office. Between 1902 and 1904, he personally allowed at least sixty-three plural marriages to occur in secret (*ONUG*, page 328). But even though Smith was in favor of the Mormon eternal principle, U.S. governmental pressures forced him to take some drastic measures to end it as an acceptable practice among the Utah LDS faithful.

Naturally, Smith was a liar like most of the "prophets" who preceded him. But this time, the investigation that became known as the "Reed Smoot hearings" exposed the theater of lies these supposed spiritual leaders of Mormonism had told and continued to tell.

Mormonism would recover.

The actual practice of polygamy was, ultimately, excised and the Mormons regained some national forgiveness by instituting a public relations campaign that started slowly and has continued to thrive to this very day. Still, just as in years gone by, they never, ever, present the whole truth, but only what they want you to hear and know. And so the practice of saying one thing publicly and doing another privately has in many ways, become a way of life among the Mormons.

It continues even today. It is present in every missionary discussion. It is alive every time a Mormon shares their faith. And it oozes out of every public relations campaign and commercial they air.

You've been warned.

❋ ❋ ❋

> "When a Latter-day Saint admits to me that they believe god had a father, who had a father, who had a father, regressing back into the eternities, I tell them, 'Well, when you get back to the God who started the whole thing, that's the God I worship.'"

Polytheism

The first four words in the Bible plainly lays bare everything we might want to know about the origins of matter, space, time, earth, and man. Those words speak to God's make-up and to monotheism, polytheism, and henotheism.

The four words?

In the beginning, God …

Every single human being has a choice when presented with these words: to believe them, receive them, and embrace them OR to doubt them, add to them, and deny them.

Believe it or not, these four simple words and how they are either received or rejected, define a person's Judaism, a person's Islam, or a person's Christianity because *the beginning* either means "the beginning" or it doesn't. And God was either at this beginning or He was not. Devout Jews, Muslims, and Christians fully receive these four words as they are:

In the beginning, God …

Taking examples from the Old Testament, we read other passages that help establish the eternality and singleness of God.

In Exodus, God is clear about how He wants to be seen by the children of Israel, saying:

Exodus 20:2. *I am the LORD thy God, which have brought thee out of the land of Egypt, out of the house of bondage. Thou shalt have no other gods before me.*

Emphasizing the first four words of Genesis, God reiterates through the prophet Isaiah:

Isaiah 45:21. …*who hath declared this from ancient time? Who hath told it from that time? Have not I the LORD? And there is no God else beside me; a just God and a Savior; there is none beside me.*

If God is demanding anything, He is demanding that He and He *alone* is God, that there is none before Him or after Him, and that there never will be any other God … *ever*! This does not mean there are no other “*gods*” (LOWER CASE *g*). In this world there are many. But when speaking of God omniscient and God omnipotent, there was, is and forever will be only one.

Speaking to those who receive Him, He says:

Isaiah 44:8. *Fear ye not, neither be afraid: have not I told thee from that time, and have declared it? ye are even my witnesses. Is there a God beside me? yea, there is no God; I know not any.*

And the Psalmist adds,

Psalms 90:2. …*even from everlasting to everlasting, thou art God.*

While we differ vastly in many other areas, Christians, Jews, and Muslims fully embrace this fact. Mormons do not. Why not? What do Mormons believe about God, and why do they believe what they believe and how do these beliefs affect everything else they do? I think you will be amazed by the answers.

This section is going to the “*heart of the matter*” on how Mormonism is neither Christian, nor Jew, nor Muslim. In fact, it will do more to show that in this respect, in this respect, mind you, Mormonism is more pagan, even atheistic, than anything else.

I don't think I need to spend more time proving that Christianity holds God as the preeminent, uncreated, eternal, immutable first cause of all things. But no matter what Mormon missionaries are saying to hook people into joining the church today, the LDS have a very different view of God. To understand their view of God, we really have to first understand the Mormon doctrine of matter; you know, the material or "stuff" of which everything on earth is composed.

Let me share an either/or fact with you: *Matter has either always existed OR it was created out of nothing.* That is it; there are no other options. Matter has either always existed OR it was created (by God) out of nothing.

Pretty wild thought, huh?

Bible believing Christians embrace the Biblical idea that God, the eternal One, the First and the Last, created everything, all matter, out of nothing. The fancy phrase for this is "*creatio ex nihilo.*" We get this belief from passages like the first four words in the Bible:

In the beginning, God …

And from passages in the New Testament which, speaking of Jesus, say things like:

> John 1:3. *All things were made by Him and without Him was not anything made that was made.*

So you got that? Christians believe that God Himself originally created everything from nothing.

Now this belief is contrary to non-believers. In their minds, matter or material has ALWAYS existed and as a result there is no need for a God. We know these people by some familiar names – Marxists, materialists, atheists, evolutionists – and I would like, in this specific area, to formally add *Mormon*s to this list. You see, like "materialist atheists" or guys like Karl Marx who offered the world a godless form of thinking called "dialectical materialism," Joseph Smith also believed that matter has always existed, and that it cannot ever be created nor destroyed, NOT EVEN BY GOD.

Just think about this, folks. Joseph Smith taught that God cannot create matter and this teaching is foundational to the thrust of all things Mormon. I'll explain how and why in a while. But this stance alone places Mormonism in opposition to the Bible, to all of Judaism, Islam, and Christianity, and squarely in the corner of people who deny the power (and even the existence) of God. But Smith went even further. Not only did he claim that matter has always existed, he also stated that principles like virtue, thriftiness, hope, faith – any principle of which we are aware – is *also* self-existent, meaning that it exists without God. To Smith, eternal principles precede God! They existed *before* He was God and as God, He is beholden to obey them.

Listen to what Smith taught (*TPJS*, page 181):

> Every principle proceeding from God is eternal and any principle which is not eternal is of the devil ... the first step in the salvation of man is the laws of eternal and **self-existent** principles [emphasis Shawn's].

So Joseph Smith taught two things which have undergirded the LDS view of God. The first is that *matter* has always existed and that God Himself cannot create or destroy it. And the second is that all *principles* that exist are eternal – self-existent in nature – meaning God did not create them, either.

Therefore, where the first four words of the Bible read, *"In the beginning, God ..."* Mormon doctrine says, "*In the beginning, self-existing material ...*" and "*in the beginning, self-existing principles*

..." Automatically we have a system in place that does *NOT* honor the living God, but cheapens, demeans, and reduces Him in terms of omniscience and omnipotence.

These basic theological building-blocks of Mormonism lead us straight into our topic, which is the LDS idea of there being many Gods (with a capital G). You see, if God cannot create matter from nothing and if He is subject to rules that existed before He was God, then the God known and worshipped by Christians is a myth.

Just before Joseph Smith was killed in a shoot-out at Carthage jail, the Mormon founder and prophet spoke at a funeral for a man named King Follett (*History of the Church* 6:302-317):

> We have imagined and supposed that God was God from all eternity; I will refute that idea, and take away the veil, so that you may see.

Psalms 90:2 says God is "*everlasting to everlasting,*" meaning He was God from all eternity, has no beginning and no end; but Joseph Smith said, "*I will refute that idea!*"

LDS defenders will say that the King Follett comments are sketchy because they were all recorded in personal journals. Well, let's hear from other LDS leaders over the ages to see what *they* think of God being God from all eternity.

LDS apostle Orson Hyde said (*Journal of Discourses* 1:123):

> Remember that God our Heavenly Father was perhaps once a child, and mortal like we are, and rose step by step in the scale of progress, in the school of advancement; has moved forward and overcome until He has arrived at the point where He now is.

James Talmage, another respected but long-deceased apostle for the Mormon Church said (*Articles of Faith,* pages 430-431):

> We believe in a God who is Himself progressive, whose majesty is intelligence; whose perfection consists in eternal advancement – a Being who has attained His exalted state by a path which now His children are permitted to follow, whose glory it is their heritage to share. In spite of the opposition of the sects, in the face of direct charges of blasphemy, the Church proclaims the eternal truth: "As man is, God once was; as God is, man may be."

These quotes and many like them essentially reinforce the LDS view of God and its grand plan of eternal progression. Let me explain. Where Christianity begins with, *In the beginning, God…*

Mormonism begins with …

There was once a man who lived a mortal, material life, perhaps on an earth just like this. This man obeyed all the eternal principles, including marriage; he died, was resurrected, and overcoming sin and death, in time became a father in heaven. He and his eternal wives, in resurrected bodies of flesh and bone, formed spirit bodies out of eternally existing matter. These spirits, housed in physical bodies which were also put together from eternally existing matter, ultimately came to earth and made up the human race. That's you and me.

As heavenly Father and heavenly Mother's literal children, we all have an opportunity to advance, by obedience to eternally existing laws and principles, to overcome sin and death, and to become Gods, (upper case G), too. This story of progression toward Godhood is FOUNDATIONAL to the Mormon faith and it places Mormonism unequivocally outside of monotheistic Christianity and into the realms of polytheism.

How is Mormonism polytheistic? First, it states that God the Father, who was once a man, had a heavenly Father. And this heavenly Father had a heavenly Father. And so on, and so on, into an eternal regression of Gods. Then, Mormonism states that all human beings who embrace Mormonism also have the opportunity to become Gods. Both of these positions, however, defy the words of God as found in Isaiah which say:

> Isaiah 44:8. *Is there a God beside me? yea, there is no God; I know not any.*

In the Mormon / Christian debate, the facts are laid bare and every single person gets to willingly decide which set they embrace. Ready?

Mormonism says:	The Bible says:
God was a man	God is eternal
God has a father	God is uncreated
God cannot create matter	God created all things from nothing
God didn't create laws or principles	God was before all things
Man can become a God	There will never be any other God

Everything Mormons do somehow supports this humanist idea of eternal progression. It's the premise behind their clean living, their temple attendance, their perfectionism, and their large families. They want to ascend on high and become Gods and this life is their training ground to get themselves ready.

In 1993, Terry J. Moyer, an LDS Church employee, wrote in an LDS Church publication ("The Family—Now and Forever," *Ensign*, June 1993):

> The stunning truth, lost to mankind before the Restoration, is that each of us is a god in embryo. We may become as our heavenly parents. We, too, in exalted families, may one day preside in our own realms …

Prophet Spencer W. Kimball said ("President Kimball Speaks Out on Morality," *Ensign*, November 1980):

> In each of us is the potentiality to become a God – pure, holy, influential, true, independent of earthly forces. We learn from the scriptures that we each have eternal existence, that we were in the beginning with God (see Abr. 3:22). That understanding this gives to us a unique sense of MAN'S DIGNITY [emphasis Shawn's].

Now, laid bare, this stuff can be pretty frightening to the general public. Because Mormonism wants to be accepted by the general public, especially when we take their political desires into account, we find them spinning this information more and more. But paradoxically, because the idea of becoming a God can be very appealing to the pride and ego of fallen men, they continue to subtly stand behind it. This can make understanding what Mormonism really teaches regarding God, and becoming God, quite confusing to the untrained observer. So in order to see through their cunning, let's examine a few examples of the LDS trying to play "both sides" of the message.

Back in 1997, in an interview with a reporter from the San Francisco *Chronicle*, rather than proclaiming this fundamental belief, LDS Prophet Gordon B. Hinckley was rather vague. The reporter asked (San Francisco *Chronicle*, April 13, 1997, section Z1, page 3):

> Don't Mormons believe that God was once a man?

Hinckley's response?

> I wouldn't say that. There was a little couplet coined, "AS man is, God once was. As God is, man may become." Now that's more of a couplet than anything else. That gets into some pretty deep theology we don't know very much about.

I watched this very interview and my mouth about dropped to the floor in the face of this highly deceptive response.

Then in an August 1997 interview in *Time* magazine, senior correspondent Richard Ostling asked Hinckley a question regarding the doctrine that God was once a man. Hinckley responded (*Time* Magazine, August 1997, page 56):

> I don't know that we teach it. I don't know that we emphasize it. I haven't heard it discussed for a long time in public discourse. I don't know. I don't know all the circumstances under which that statement was made. I understand the philosophical background behind it. But I don't know a lot about it and I don't know that others know a lot about it.

I was flabbergasted. Just one year earlier, writing about God in the Church-published *Ensign* magazine, BYU professor Robert Millet stated ("The Eternal Gospel, *Ensign*, July 1996):

> Knowing what we know concerning God our Father … that He is an exalted and glorified being; that He was once a man and dwelt on an earth …

What was going on? Hinckley was flat out being deceptive – and millions called him a living prophet. Well, President Hinckley got some heat from his own people for his televised response. At the very next General Conference, October 1997, Hinckley made the following statement ("Drawing Nearer to the Lord," *Ensign*, October 1997):

> You need not worry that I do not understand some matters of doctrine. I think I understand them thoroughly.

To cap it all off, just one year later, and in an act of sheer duplicity, he stood up in another LDS General Conference and provided a coded message that would be both consistent with his public interviews and at the same time support the Saints' absolute knowledge that they believe God was once a man. This is how he did it. He rhetorically asked from the conference pulpit ("What Are People Asking About Us?" *Ensign*, October 1998):

> What is the Mormon doctrine of deity, of God?

Then he quoted from Joseph Smith himself, saying:

> The Prophet Joseph declared, "It is the first principle of the Gospel to know for certainty the Character of God, and to know that we may converse with Him as one man converses with another (*Teachings of the Prophet Joseph Smith*, sel. Joseph Fielding Smith [1976], 345)."

Why was his using this quote duplicitous? Because he didn't finish it! And any stalwart member with ears to hear knew it. Had he finished it, he would have quoted *all* of what Smith said, which was (*TPJS*, pages 345-346):

> It is the first principle of the Gospel to know for certainty the Character of God, and to know that we converse with Him as one man converses with another **and that He was once a man like us; yea, that God himself, the Father of us all, dwelt on an earth, the same as Jesus Christ did**, and I will show it from the Bible [emphasis Shawn's].

Right there Hinckley was leading the LDS Church into an era of doctrinal spin doctoring regarding this uniquely LDS belief. Where earlier LDS President Joseph Fielding Smith had written in *Doctrines of Salvation* (2:47):

> Our Father in heaven, according to the Prophet, had a Father, and since there has been a condition of this kind through all eternity, each Father had a Father, until we come to a stop where we cannot go further, because of our limited capacity to understand;

and Brigham Young said (as recorded in *Journal of Discourses* 7:333):

> How many Gods there are, I do not know, But there never was a time when there were not Gods and worlds, and when men were not passing through the same ordeals that we are now passing through. That course has been from all eternity and it is and will be so to all eternity;

the new and more duplicitous LDS Prophet Hinckley said:

> I don't know that we teach it. I don't know that we emphasize it.

In a more academic form of denial, online LDS apologists are attempting to spin away from the term *polytheist* by applying the term *henotheistic* to themselves. Henotheism, a word coined by a nineteenth century expert on Hinduism, Max Muller, merely states that a polytheist worships many gods but that a henotheist worships only one god while recognizing the existence of others. Big freaking "academic" deal. A polytheist, by any other name, is still a polytheist.

Finally, LDS missionaries and other official and unofficial spokes-apologists for the Church are lately claiming that people can become "*like* God," instead of becoming "*a* God," a distinction they hope will add legitimacy to their claims of being Christian. Besides the fact that this modified doctrine is also false – in Isaiah 40:25, God tells us there is NO ONE LIKE HIM – this has never been the LDS teaching and an honest Mormon will admit it. But then, in the way that only such a cunning enterprise can, many LDS have been convinced and are still endorsing the ideology.

My friends, *choose ye this day whom ye will serve* (Joshua 24:15): Almighty God who from everlasting to everlasting created all things; or Mormonism's God, a glorified man who has a father who has a father who has a father, who is finite, who is *not* the original source, and whom you can *be* (or *be like*, depending upon your audience) if you do as they say.

❋ ❋ ❋

"Of all the difficult doctrines Latter-day Saints have to overcome, the myth of a premortal existence (along with that of an anthropomorphic God) are usually the toughest. I attribute the difficulty to the soulish nature of the teaching itself. Sure it makes sense to believe we came from somewhere and that God the Father lives in a body of flesh and bones, penis and all. But this is human logic we're relating to, and the Bible, when read contextually, teaches the exact opposite."

Pre-Existence

It is vitally important in the search for God that we make a concerted effort to separate and distinguish between truth and error, facts and fables, *true* doctrines of Jesus Christ and the imaginations of men. Of fables, Paul warns Timothy (and us):

> 2 Timothy 4:3-4. *For the time will come when they will not endure sound doctrine; but after* ***their own lusts*** *shall they heap to themselves teachers, having itching ears; and they shall* ***turn away their ears from the truth, and shall be turned unto fables.***

The heathen religions have always abounded with fictions and fables. Even the Jewish teachers were renowned for the number of fables which had been introduced into their beliefs. This, too, caused Paul to write:

> Titus 1:14. [Don't give] *heed to* ***Jewish fables****, and* ***commandments of men****, that turn from the truth.*

Speaking to the faithful believers of his day, the apostle Peter wrote:

> 2 Peter 1:16. *For we have not followed cunningly devised fables when we made known unto you the power and coming of our Lord Jesus Christ, but were eyewitnesses of his majesty.*

Cunningly devised fables can sprout, take root, and flourish quickly within a body of believers. They often make sense to our fleshly minds and sometimes they can seem more inviting than the truths of the Word, which truths have always been considered foolishness to the wise of this world. The ONLY effective deterrent to controlling and eliminating fables is an effective and liberal understanding of the Word of God. Correctly and contextually understood, the Word exposes fables and the commandments of men. The farther away a person walks from the Word, the closer they are to embracing fables.

Fables, myths and fairytales are often presented to entertain and tantalize the undisciplined mind. Sometimes fables are created to help people cope with the brutalities of the truth. When I was eight or nine years old I was scheduled to have my tonsils out. Instead of telling me the doctor goes down my throat with a pair of razor sharp scissors or a scalpel to cut the things out of my head, my mom created a fable as a means to help me cope with the event and provide me with peace and reassurance. Maybe – *maybe* – some myth-making is acceptable when speaking to children about an uncomfortable event or situation. Storks, Santa Claus, and the tooth fairy are things we all outgrow; but when it comes to God and His Word there is nothing more pathetic than grown men and women who would rather believe in a lie to comfort them than face the hard truths of God.

Two Biblical facts Joseph Smith found untenable and worthy of revision were the fact that human existence begins in the womb and the fact that we all begin life in this fallen world as creatures. The idea that God formed us from the dust of the earth and breathed the *beginning of life* into human beings was preposterous to Joseph. Borrowing from heretical Greek philosophy, he gave the Mormons a fable called *the pre-existence.*

Boyd K. Packer, one of the twelve LDS apostles has said ("The Mystery of Life," *Ensign*, November 1993):

> There is no way to make sense out of life without a knowledge of the doctrine of premortal life. The idea that mortal birth is the beginning is preposterous. There is no way to explain life if you believe that.

Hence, the fable.

A second Biblical fact Joseph disliked was the idea that all human beings at birth are merely God's creatures – *similar* to animals but with opposable thumbs and an ability to reason – and that it is only through faith on His Son that any and every human creature becomes a child of God. In the face of this Biblical teaching, Joseph taught that we are born children of God, rightful heirs to His kingdom and His throne, *if* we earn it.

Supporting this fable, stories, paintings, and songs have been composed within Mormonism. Plan of salvation charts are drawn to teach little children about their pre-existent state as children of heavenly Father and heavenly Mother. One of the most beloved LDS hymns stands in direct opposition to biblical truth. Where a Biblically accurate song might say:

> *I am a creature of God*
> *Sinful, dumb and wild*
> *And in the state I will remain*
> *'Til I become His child …*

the LDS instead sing (*Hymns*, number 301):

> *I am a child of God.*
> *And He has sent me here.*
> *Has given me an earthly home.*
> *With parents kind and dear.*
> *Lead me, guide me, walk beside me*
> *Help me find the way.*
> *Teach me all that I MUST DO*
> *To live with him one day.*

This fable of a pre-existence is so forcefully and repetitively presented to the LDS that people who leave Mormonism typically have the most difficult time letting this one go. Admittedly, when it is placed before you as part of a grand fairytale-like theme, the idea has some appeal to the carnal mind. Who wouldn't want to believe that they have existed forever as a spirit, with Jesus as their spiritual brother in the life before this one? Who wouldn't want to embrace as truth this appealing but fictional heavenly heritage?

Histories can play a powerful role in establishing a person in life, in giving them a worldview, and in grounding them with purpose and identity. When I was enrolled in the School of Ministry in Southern California, I was friends with a man named Mark.

Mark grew up hearing stories of his family's ties to French aristocracy. Castles, valor, wealth and power were his heritage. Then one day in his early twenties he learned that he was adopted and that his parents were actually some messed up people from Chicago. The fairy tale died for Mark, and he was left without a history, without moorings, and without a name. The beautiful thing was that this was exactly where he needed to be because after a season of rebellion, Mark came to know the Lord, his real Father through *adoption by faith*.

Now, when I was a teenager, an LDS man wrote a play called *Saturday's Warrior*, which was based entirely on the make-believe fable of the LDS plan of salvation.

It was creative, it was musical, and it reassured everyone who saw it that they did, in fact, come from this mythical pre-existent place. The Osmond family also produced an album one year called The Plan (through the "Kolob" record label, by the way), and I remember to this day the first line of one of the first songs on it:

"Before the beginning, We were winning ..." meaning that we all came from a place before this earth life where we lived with our heavenly parents and were making decisions that would affect our lives here on earth.

Speaking of this pre-mortal state, *The Encyclopedia of Mormonism* states (2:549):

> The Father, Elohim, is called the Father because he is the literally father of the spirits of mortals. [It then refers the reader to the book of Hebrews, 12:9, before continuing by stating...] This paternity is not allegorical. All individual human spirits were begotten (not created from nothing or made) by the Father in a premortal state, where they lived and were nurtured by Heavenly Parents.

LDS Apostle Boyd K. Packer said ("The Mystery of Life," *Ensign*, November 1983):

> Dear brethren and sisters, the scriptures and the teachings of the apostles and prophets speak of us in premortal life as sons and daughters, spirit children of God. Gender existed before, and did not begin at mortal birth.

There are four or five main passages – literally interpreted and selectively chosen from the body of the Word – which the LDS and their missionaries use to "prove" that the fable of a pre-existence is true. These are:

Job 38:7
Ecclesiastes 12:7
Romans 8:16
Jeremiah 1:5
John 9:1-16

Let's take these one by one and address them.

Job 38:4-7

As the entire drama and trial of Job nears its conclusion, God steps in and speaks with Job, asking him some probing questions. Let's read:

> Job 38:4-7. *Where wast thou when I laid the foundations of the earth? declare, if thou hast understanding. Who hath laid the measures thereof, if thou knowest? or who hath stretched the line upon it? Whereupon are the foundations thereof fastened? or who laid the corner stone thereof; When the morning stars sang together, and all the sons of God shouted for joy?*

The Lord asks Job rhetorically where he was when all of creation happened, by which question God means to say, *Job, you weren't even around*! Therefore, since humans were not around, the *morning stars* and *all the sons of God* must refer to something other than human beings. Who were they?

When we read Genesis 1:1 – *"In the beginning God created the heavens and the earth"* – we are not told what is included in *the heavens*, but we do know, by checking with the totality of God's Word, that MAN was not there. In the *Chaldee* language – the language that Abraham spoke – the Biblical text reads "a*ll the troops of angels*" in place of the "*all the sons of God* (Adam Clarke, *The Holy Bible Containing the Old and New Testaments … Volume 2*, page 859)." This reference, then, is a reference to intelligent, *created* angelic hosts of heaven, who were first in God's order of creation, created before the visible, physical creation.

Ecclesiastes 12:7

> Ecclesiastes 12:7. *Then shall the dust return to the earth as it was: and the spirit shall return unto God who gave it.*

The LDS missionaries will say to the unsuspecting and untrained, "*The Bible even says the spirit will return to God who gave it.*"

Whoa! the investigator thinks. ***I must** have existed in the spirit world before this life.*

Looking back to Genesis, which is where Christians gain their understanding of the origin of men and women, we learn that after making Adam from the dust God breathed into him the breath of life (Genesis 2:7). By and through this breath of God, Adam and the rest of humanity became living souls. This breath, this *Ha Ruach* in Hebrew, was from God and was God's.

This breath or spirit is another way human beings are differentiated from animals. Animals are bipartite: they have a soul and a body. But human beings are tripartite, or three in one – body, soul, and spirit – and we associate with God through the spirit of life that God breathed into us at the start:

> Zechariah 12:1. *The burden of the word of the LORD for Israel, saith the LORD, which stretcheth forth the heavens, and layeth the foundation of the earth, and **formeth the spirit of man within him.***
>
> Job 27:3. *All the while my breath is in me, and **the spirit of God is in my nostrils.***

The spirit God placed within man, which became corrupted as a result of Adam's fall, will depart from this life either unregenerated – NOT BORN AGAIN – and will go to hell; OR, it will have been changed by the blood of Jesus Christ – BORN AGAIN, BORN FROM ABOVE – and will go cleansed and acceptable to the God Who gave it.

Romans 8:16-17

Romans 8:16-17 is a perfect example of the LDS taking a single passage or set of passages and attempting to use them to prove one of their fables. It reads:

> Romans 8:16-17. *The Spirit itself beareth witness with our spirit,*

> *that we are the children of God: And if children, then heirs; heirs of God, and joint-heirs with Christ; if so be that we suffer with him, that we may be also glorified together.*

There could be no more true passage of scripture in the Bible *when it is applied to believers who have come to know Jesus through their spirits*. But what does the Bible say about the condition of men and women who have NOT experienced Jesus by faith?

> Job 25:4, 6. *How then can man be justified with God? or how can he be clean that is born of a woman? ... How much less man, that is a worm? and the son of man, which is a worm?*

> Isaiah 40:7. *The grass withereth, the flower fadeth: because the spirit of the LORD bloweth upon it: surely the people is grass.*

> Isaiah 64:6. *But we are all as an unclean thing, and all our righteousnesses are as filthy rags; and we all do fade as a leaf; and our iniquities, like the wind, have taken us away.*

And what does the Bible say about us being God's children? How does it happen? By physical birth and right? Or by conversion and faith?

> John 1:12. *But* ***as many as received him, to them gave he power to become the sons of God****, even to them that* ***believe on his name: Which were born, not*** *of blood,* ***nor*** *of the will of the flesh,* ***nor*** *of the will of man,* ***but of God****.*

> Romans 8:15. *For ye have not received the spirit of bondage again to fear; but ye have received* ***the Spirit of adoption****, whereby we cry, Abba, Father.*

> Galatians 3:26. *For ye are all the children of God* ***by faith*** *in Christ Jesus.*

John the Beloved makes it perfectly clear that all of us here on earth are not – *NOT* – children of God:

> 1 John 3:1. *Behold, what manner of love the Father hath bestowed upon us, that we should be called the sons of God: therefore the world knoweth us not, because it knew him not.*

Jeremiah 1:5

How about this LDS favorite?

> Jeremiah 1:5. *Before I formed thee in the belly I knew thee; and before thou camest forth out of the womb I sanctified thee, and I ordained thee a prophet unto the nations.*

Can I re-read this with some different *emPHAsis* on some different *sylLABles*?

*BEFORE **I** formed thee in the belly, **I** knew thee; and before thou camest forth out of the womb **I** sanctified thee, and **I** ordained thee a prophet.*

The "*I*"s refer to His foreknowledge and His omniscience; these are directly tied to the belly and the womb. The very fact that LDS misapply this passage illustrates their misunderstanding of the omniscience of God. God knows all things beginning to end, so of course He knows what Jeremiah would do and be, and of course He sanctified him in this work! This passage speaks to the *eternality* and *power* of GOD, NOT the eternality and existence of Jeremiah!

This leads us to the last of the favorite passages the LDS use to try to support the pre-existence fable: John 9:1-16.

John 9:1-16

We read:

> John 9:1-2. *And as Jesus passed by, he saw a man which was blind*

> *from his birth. And his disciples asked him, saying, Master, who did sin, this man, or his parents, that he was born blind?*

The LDS believe that this passage proves that we lived in a pre-existent state before this life – how else could the man born blind have sinned if he didn't live before?

A little historicity and study explains this clearly. First of all, the fable of a pre-existent state for man had been around *long* before Joseph ever incorporated it into his teachings. The Pythagoreans, for example, believed the souls of men were sent into other bodies for the punishment of some sin which they had committed in a pre-existent state. Ironically enough, the LDS claim Christianity was warped by the infiltration of Hellenistic ideas and yet in this fable, Joseph embraced one of the most widespread beliefs found throughout Greek, and other, mythology.

Most of the Asiatic nations have believed in the doctrine known as transmigration of the soul, the idea that a soul may pass out of one body and reside in another (human or animal) or in an inanimate object. The Hindus believe that most of their misfortunes arise out of the sins of a former birth; and, in moments of grief may break out into exclamations such as, "*Ah! In a former birth how many sins must I have committed, that I am thus afflicted!*"

Even from the very remotest antiquity some Jewish rabbis have had the same belief, and even did in Jesus' day. Origen cites, in an apocryphal book of the Hebrews, the patriarch Jacob saying (Clarke, *Commentary on the Whole Bible*), "I am an angel of God; one of the first order of spirits. Men call me Jacob, but my true name, which God has given me, is Israel ..." Many Jewish doctors have believed that the souls of Adam, Abraham, and Phineas have successively animated the great men of their nation. The Jewish philosopher Philo said (William Barclay, *The Letters to the Galatians and Ephesians*, page 114) "There are spirits flying everywhere through the air ... The air is the house of the disembodied spirits."

Josephus (*Antiquities of the Jews,*. b. xvii. c. 1, s. 3, and *Wars of the Jews*, b. ii. c. 8, s. 14,) said the Pharisees believed that only the souls of those who were pious were permitted to reanimate human bodies, and this was rather by way of reward than punishment; and that the souls of the vicious are put into eternal prisons, where they are continually tormented, and out of which they can never escape. Finally, John Lightfoot (*A Commentary on the New Testament from the Talmud and Hebraic*) taught that some rabbis believed that it was possible for an infant to sin in the womb, and to be punished with some bodily infirmity as a consequence.

So this unscriptural, erroneous notion of human spirits pre-existing is nothing new. This distortion of the truth existed even before Jesus' earthly ministry.

Returning to the passage, the disciples questioned the Lord: *Did this man sin in a pre-existent state, that he is punished in this body with blindness? Or, did his parents commit some sin, for which they are thus plagued in their offspring?* Jesus, in His simple and effective way, clears the whole matter up:

> John 9:3. *Neither hath this man sinned, nor his parents: but that the works of God should be made manifest in him.*

What *does* the WORD say to refute the idea of a pre-mortal existence?

It says plainly and clearly that we are beings created out of the dust of the earth – star dust as my friend Ken would say - and animated by the breath of God. It states clearly that there is only one pre-existent being to ever walk the earth and His name was *Yeshua*, the Messiah. John the Baptist said of Jesus,

> John 3:31. *He that cometh from above is above all: he that is of the earth is earthly, and speaketh of the earth: he that cometh from heaven is above all.*

Only Jesus existed with the Father, and only Jesus came forth to us to bear witness of Who God is. Speaking to the Jews, Jesus said,

> John 8:23. *Ye are from beneath; I am from above: ye are of this world; I am not of this world.*

Realizing from where Jesus had come, and the truth of His words, His disciples looked on Him and claimed:

> John 16:30. *Now are we sure that thou knowest all things, and needest not that any man should ask thee:* ***by this we believe that thou camest forth from God.***

By embracing the fable of a pre-existence, the LDS not only are teaching something untrue, they are teaching that all of us share in a heavenly heritage, just like Jesus. In writing to the Corinthian believers, Paul makes clear the distinction between earthy things like us, and heavenly things like the Lord Jesus. Referring to Adam, Paul wrote:

> 1 Corinthians 15:47-49. *The first man is of the earth, earthy: the second man is the Lord from heaven. As is the earthy, such are they also that are earthy: and as is the heavenly, such are they also that are heavenly. And as we have borne the image of the earthy, we* ***shall*** *also* ***bear*** *the image of the heavenly.*

We are of the earth, but we "*shall bear*" the image of the heavenly Jesus, if and only if we are born again. The doctrine of a pre-existence is misleading and mythological, causing acceptance of a fairy tale gospel in the minds of men, as they ignore the plain saving truths contained in God's written Word.

❋ ❋ ❋

"We used to wonder as kids how important our Aaronic priesthood could really be, especially when you consider the activities boys are typically involved in between the ages of twelve to eighteen."

Priesthood (Aaronic)

As we continue on with our alphabetized topics comparing Mormonism and biblical Christianity, our present topic is priesthood, part I.

The LDS set up this huge, albeit false, premise of priesthood authority, which many unsuspecting people buy, hook, line, and sinker; and the false premise goes something like this: In the Old and New Testaments, God authorized only certain people to act on His behalf. They use the example of the Levites in the Old Testament who were, truly, the ONLY ones who were allowed by God to officiate in priestly temple duties among the children of Israel (see Exodus 40:12-15; this command is reiterated in the book of Deuteronomy, for example 7:35 and chapter 8 in its entirety). What the LDS do with this information is they jump to our day and age and state that this exclusive authorization or authority to act in God's name instituted back in the Old Testament continues to be the case today, that His exclusive, divinely assigned priesthood is only given to worthy male members of the LDS church.

If you ask a worthy LDS male where he got his fictional priesthood, he will say he received it (or was ordained to it) from another worthy male member who holds or held the priesthood first. Then when you ask that person from where he received the priesthood, he will say that he received it from another faithful LDS male before him. This "line of authority" just keeps going back and back and back all the way, according to the LDS, to Jesus Christ Himself.

Is this true?

Depends on how you define "*truth*." Is truth defined as "*corresponding to reality*?" Or is it your view that something is true merely because you have chosen to believe it?

Working back from the present day, worthy LDS males claim that they can literally demonstrate their "priesthood line of authority." But these claims all hinge on the claims of one man: Joseph Smith. You see, in 1830 or so, Joseph Smith claimed he received these fictional priesthoods when resurrected beings came to earth and bestowed them upon his head by the laying on of hands. He then passed it on to other men who believed his story and this is how the LDS claim their line of authority straight from Jesus Christ.

Joseph claimed that two "priesthood restorations" happened to him. The first, he said, occurred when John the Baptist appeared, laid his hands on the heads of Joseph and Oliver Cowdery (his scribe) and bestowed the "Aaronic priesthood" upon them. Later, Joseph Smith claimed that the apostles Peter, James, and John appeared and bestowed upon him what he coined the "Melchizedek" priesthood.

In this section, we are going to examine the LDS claims to the Aaronic priesthood. In the next, we'll look at the Melchizedek.

First, let me speak about priesthood in general. Going back to Adam, man was his own priest and presented his own sacrifices to God. Recall the story of Cain and Abel. Each brought his own offering to God, not relying upon a priest to mediate in his stead. Later, the office of priest went to the male head of each family. We find that:

- Noah (Genesis 8:20),
- Abraham (Genesis 12:7),
- Isaac (Genesis 26:25),
- Jacob (Genesis 31:54), and
- Job (Job 1:5)

all offered sacrifice to God without the intermediation of a priest.

The first time the word "priest" is used in the Bible is when it is applied to a mysterious Old Testament figure named Melchizedek (Genesis 14:18). Like I said, we'll talk about Melchizedek in the next section.

When Moses led the children of Israel out of Egypt, the ancient manner of "head-of-household" priests was still being observed by them. But on Mount Sinai, a change in this ancient practice was made. Exodus 28 teaches us that God had a hereditary priesthood take over. The heritage assigned to the priesthood line was the tribe of Levi.

Why the Levites? Exodus 32:26-28 says it was because they did "*according to the word of Moses.*" It is important to note that they were *not* chosen because they were sin-free. Remember it was Aaron who instigated the production of the golden calf!

There are two important things to remember: first, there were *priests* in this hereditary priesthood; and second, there were *high priests*. A man's Levitical lineage determined the two. You see, Levi had three sons whose names were Gershon, Merari, and Kohath (Genesis 46:11). Kohath had a son named Amram (Exodus 6:18); and Amram had sons named Aaron and Moses (Numbers 26:59).

Got that? ONLY those men who came from the Levi/Kohath/Amram/Aaron line could be *high priests* while the rest of the sons of Levi - the offspring of Gershon and Merari - acted as *priests*, subordinated to Aaron's line in the their temple duties.

How important were these hereditary lines in this priesthood? Well, let me blow your mind a bit here. Not even JESUS himself, being from the tribe of Judah, could officiate in the Levitical priesthood duties as either a high priest or a priest. Don't believe me?

> Hebrews 7:14. *For it is evident that our Lord sprang out of Juda; of which tribe Moses spake nothing concerning priesthood.*

Okay; you got all that so far?

Now Joseph Smith claimed that while he and Oliver Cowdery were translating the *Book of Mormon* in May of 1829, that they retired to the woods and had John the Baptist appear and give them this very elite Aaronic priesthood! Numbers chapter 3 says ONLY the Levites could hold this priesthood or the result would be death (verse 10)! But Joseph claimed John the Baptist showed up and gave it to him!

We have to ask ourselves what do the LDS do with this Levitical priesthood today? They "give it" to all male members of the Mormon church who are between the ages of twelve and eighteen! This is pure misappropriation! Listen to what the Bible says about those who held the Levitical priesthood:

> Numbers 4:3. *Take the sum of the sons of Kohath from among the sons of Levi, according to their families, by their fathers' house,* ***from thirty years old and upward even to fifty years****, all that enter into the service, to do the work in the tabernacle of the congregation.*

I want you to imagine something for a moment. Aaron and his sons are called by God to officiate in the Levitical priesthood. And they do so with extreme dedication and devotion. This was so serious a call that when two of Aaron's sons mingled "*strange fire*" outside the temple, God torched them to death in front of all of the children of Israel (Leviticus 10:1-2)! And they were Aaron's very own sons.

Now further imagine for a minute that Aaron somehow visits the earth today. He visits an LDS ward and discovers a dozen or more *boys*, between the ages of 12 and 18, chewing gum and cutting up and having done God-knows-what the night before, claiming to hold this priesthood to which he and his family dedicated their everything thousands of years ago? Are you beginning to see where the LDS truly err in this Aaronic priesthood application? It is simply another piece of evidence of Joseph Smith applying Biblical truths selectively and inappropriately.

We must ask, "How were these priests prepared to use this priesthood, the priesthood that is supposedly given to twelve year old boys in Mormonism today?" They went through an arduous and cumbersome process of purification which may be read about in Leviticus chapter 8. This process included:

- A ceremonial washing
- Prayer over the head of a bull
- Slaying the bull
- Sprinkling its blood and offering the sacrifice by burning
- Offering bread
- Sacrificing two rams

Then the descendent of Aaron would be separated from the people for seven days. During those seven days more animals would be sacrificed. And then the Aaronic priest would be reintroduced to the congregation.

And how are LDS boys prepared for their duties in the Aaronic priesthood? They turn 12 and are interviewed by their bishop.

What exactly did the Sons of Aaron and the Levitical priests do in the tabernacle once they were purified? First, they dressed themselves in a very specific and ritualistic fashion for each respective function in which they officiated. They attended to a plethora of duties which are meticulously described in Exodus (27:20,21; 29:38-44), Leviticus (6:12; 10:11; 24:8), Numbers (10:1-10), Deuteronomy (17:8-13; 33:10), and Malachi (2:7); and here is perhaps the most important point: *EVERYTHING* these adult priests did pointed to the finished work of Jesus Christ which was to come!

Let me repeat this: Everything these priests did pointed to the *finished work* of Jesus Christ.

This leads us perhaps to the most important point relative to the misapplication of the Aaronic priesthood today by the LDS. The Aaronic priests represented the people before God, and offered the various blood sacrifices which were all *shadows of the coming Messiah*!

Once a year, on the day of atonement, the high priest

- Who came from the Kohath line of Levi,
- Who had to be between 30 and 50 years of age,
- Who had been purified ritualistically like no other,
- Who had to be dressed in severely restricted and detailed ways,
- And who would perform rites and rituals *exactly* as God commanded him…

…would enter the Holy of Holies alone and once a year offer sacrifice to God for the sins of the people *as a type of the Messiah who was to come*! This was the purpose of the Aaronic priesthood. This was the reason it was on the earth! It pointed to the *finished work* of Jesus.

The FINISHED WORK.

Once that ultimate sacrifice had been given by the only true, innocent, and acceptable offering – Jesus Christ – there was no need for an Aaronic priesthood any more. Let me explain why this is the case. The tabernacle/temple for the children of Israel was composed of three parts (in one building – are you stating to notice a pattern here?): ☺

- An outer court,
- An inner court, and
- A Holy of Holies.

The outer court was an area for the Gentiles. The inner court was an area for animal sacrifice, singing, and worship toward God. The Holy of Holies was separated from the rest of the building by a 5-inch thick veil. The veil could ONLY be parted once a year when the Aaronic high priest entered to offer blood sacrifice on the day of atonement. Inside the Holy of Holies sat the ark of the covenant which was overshadowed by gold cherubs on either side. Inside this ark was a golden pot of manna, Aaron's budding rod, the tables of the law, and a golden censer. Before the high priest entered to sprinkle the shed blood of an unblemished animal for the covering of the sins of the people, he had bells attached to his robe and a rope tied about his waist so in the event he died or passed out, he could be dragged out without defiling the sacred place of God.

Now what was the significance of all of this? It all pointed to Jesus Christ and His final and finished work on the cross. How? To get the full answer, read the book of Hebrews in its entirety! But let me summarize:

Just as the high priest was of the proper lineage of Aaron, Jesus was of the perfect lineage: He was God! Where unblemished animals could only temporarily cover sins, it took the blood of the unblemished God/Man Jesus Christ to permanently wash sin away:

> Hebrews 9:12. *Neither by the blood of goats and calves, but by his own blood he entered in once into the holy place, having obtained eternal redemption for us.*

And while the high priest entered every year into the Holy of Holies to offer sacrificial blood for the people, Jesus entered once and for all to atone for the sins of the world.

> Hebrews 9:25. *Nor yet that he should offer himself often, as the high priest entereth into the holy place every year with blood of others;*

And as the high priest entered into an earthly Holy of Holies where God temporarily visited, Jesus now entered and resides permanently in the heavenly Holy of Holies where God permanently dwells.

> Hebrews 10:12. *But this man, after he had offered one sacrifice for sins forever, sat down on the right hand of God;*

As the veil in the temple once barred all men access to the throne of God and required a special priesthood holder to access it, the veil that once separated all of us from God's presence was torn in two when Jesus died, and became the flesh of Jesus Himself.

> Hebrews 10:20. *By a new and living way, which he hath consecrated for us, through the veil, that is to say, his flesh;*

Everything in the temporary temple or tabernacle - from the table, the shewbread, the censer, the manna, and the Levitical priesthood to the mercy seat, the ark of the covenant, the tabernacle, the Holy of Holies, the veil, and the shed blood of every animal – all of it foreshadowed and was made reality in the life, death, and resurrection of JESUS.

There is no need for a continuation of an Aaronic priesthood, not in any way! In any shape! In any form!

Let me give you a final illustration as to why. Suppose a young teenage girl has a dream one night. And she dreams she is going to be a mother some day and that her baby will have curly red hair, freckles, and dimples. The next day she sees a picture of a baby in a fashion magazine with curly red hair. And though it doesn't look anything like the baby of her dreams, she tears out the ad and pastes it in a journal as a memento, a reminder of her dream. Years pass, and the same girl has another dream where her red-headed child becomes a world class basketball player. And the next day she tears a picture out of a magazine showing a tall, lanky red-haired pro-basketball player. In her twenties, when the girl is engaged to be married, she has another dream that the son she will bear will also become a medical doctor someday, saving the lives of many. And she locates yet another picture of a red-haired doctor and pastes it in a journal, as a reminder of what she expects to occur.

Ultimately, the girl marries, and within a few years has her first child. It's a boy with curly red hair, freckles and dimples. Where should the young woman's attentions go now that she actually has a living child in her care? To the reality of the living child. But suppose our young mother, who has now been blessed with the actual fulfillment of her dreams – a living, breathing, red-headed, curly-haired baby – spends the majority of her time as a mother staring at the pictures she cut from the magazines instead of caring for her actual boy? She lights candles in a weekly processional to the images of him and ritualistically places flowers at the foot of the images she pasted in her journal over the years, which merely served to foreshadow the coming of her son. This would not only be a strange and weird practice, it would mock the very life of the living child, right?

It would be a case where the idea, the image, and the foreshadowing of the object have a greater place in her heart than the actual living object itself. I mean, the boy gets drafted into the NBA, is playing on television, and setting records all over the place but the mother keeps looking back at the picture of the basketball player instead of to her actual son! Would this make any sense?

The parallels are exact to a re-establishment of a priesthood when the priesthood had been fulfilled in the living Christ! The Bible is perfectly clear about why an Aaronic priesthood was established: it was all a *foreshadowing* of things to come, things fulfilled by God's own Son! Re-establishing the Aaronic priesthood is akin to a bakery making the world's most delicious pies; but once they are done, taking them out of the tins, stacking the pies in the back of the store and putting the tins on display to be admired by paying customers!

The priesthood *pointed* to Jesus and Jesus has come. Joseph Smith ignored this fact and, once again, reinstituted something God had long fulfilled in His Son.

What a sham and a shame.

❋ ❋ ❋

"Years ago we had a faithful LDS man call in to our television program. In the course of the call he attempted to rebuke me by the 'power' of his (supposed) 'Melchizedek priesthood.' Nothing happened. I asked him about his position in the church and he stated boldly and proudly, 'I'm a high priest!' I reminded him (with as much boldness) that he was not a high priest, and that there was only one High Priest worthy of such a title – the Lord Jesus Christ."

Priesthood (Melchizedek)

Most objects or systems we use in life begin at a sufficient and acceptable level then progress to a better, more advanced state as time moves on. Our once black and white television sets, for example, have now progressed into color, flat screen, high-definition, surround-sound entertainment centers. Rigid business models usually transform into better, dynamic, open-ended applications adept at handling mass response. Even parenting skills frequently evolve from being overly legalistic and punitive (with that poor, first, "experimental" child) to a far better, more patient and loving approach as the later ones come along.

The book of Hebrews, particularly chapter 7, teaches us that Jesus introduced to the world a *better way* than the Levitical system, which we talked about in the last section. Just as the Model T was not an extremely comfortable ride, the Mosaic Law was not a very comfortable system with which to live. But it was "sufficient and acceptable" for the time, pointing, as it did, to a better day and better way.

When Jesus came He not only fulfilled the law and the prophets but shattered the barrier which stood between man and God. Ripping the veil, as it were, by His death, He parked the Model T of the Mosaic Law and introduced a new model to the world, one in which He is in the driver's seat, not men. This was not an easy thing for the early Christian-Jews to embrace. We see in scripture that many of them sought to return to their Model Ts, finding the luxurious grace of a relationship with Jesus in control actually too liberating for their religious hearts and minds.

The book of Hebrews was written to these Christian Jews to help them transition into the better way. It teaches that

- Jesus is the "better way"
- Relationship is a "better way"
- The promised Messiah offers an eternal and unchanging covenant because it is based on Him and His righteousness and not on the works or righteousness of men and women.

Hebrews teaches that Jesus is superior to angels (Hebrews 1:4). What He provides is superior (a better way) to what Moses provided (Hebrews 3:3). His work was better than the work of human priests; His sacrifice was better than their sacrifices (Hebrews 7:20-28). The book of Hebrews teaches that Christianity – a personal relationship with Jesus by faith – surpasses Judaism because it is a "*better covenant*" (Hebrews 8:6) which offers a *better sanctuary* (Hebrews 8:1-2) and a *better sacrifice* (Hebrews 10:1-14) for sin.

Chapter one teaches, among other things, that Jesus is greater than angels. Chapter three teaches that Jesus is greater than Moses. Chapter four teaches that Jesus' priesthood is greater than the Old Testament priesthood (which we discussed in the last section). Then in chapter five the writer of Hebrews mentions a very mysterious person named Melchizedek.

Now in the book of Genesis (chapter 14), after Abraham and Lot parted company, there was a confederation of five kings that conquered the area where Lot lived and took him captive and spoiled several cities. Abraham heard about it, got his servants together and went out against these five kings and won, rescuing Lot and taking from them the spoils they had acquired from conquering these cities. As Abraham was returning with the spoils there came to him a character by the name of Melchizedek. This is all that is written of this Old Testament figure:

> Genesis 14:18. *And Melchizedek king of Salem brought forth bread and wine: and he was the priest of the most high God. And he blessed him, and said, Blessed be Abram of the most high God, possessor of heaven and earth: And blessed be the most high God, which hath delivered thine enemies into thy hand. And he* [Abraham] *gave him* [Melchizedek] *tithes of all.*

There is only one other reference to Melchizedek in the Old Testament, and I'll talk about it in a minute.

Now, as he was accustomed to do, it seems that whenever there was a mysterious event or person in the Bible, Joseph Smith, founder of Mormonism, would take it and offer some far-fetched extra-Biblical interpretation of its meaning. Consider what he said about John the Beloved and the Three Nephites "never dying" but living on the earth even to our day. Or how about Enoch? We know from the Bible (Genesis 5:24) that after walking with God 365 years, "*he was not, for God took him*;" we know little else. But Joseph Smith taught that not only was he translated, but a whole city that carried his namesake went up, too! Cain, in Mormon lore, was not only the father of a cursed black race, but Mormons claim he was never to die, leading some LDS to believe that he wanders around the world today as some sort of "Big Foot" or sasquatch. If there is a mystery or uncertainty in the text of the Bible, Joseph addressed it, expanded on it, and then called it "revealed truth." Well, there is perhaps nothing more misappropriated by Joseph Smith than the role and meaning behind this Biblical image named Melchizedek.

Last week, we covered Joseph Smith's total misapplication of the Aaronic priesthood to the LDS Church. Well, according to a very suspect timeline, somewhere between May of 1829 and June of the same year, Joseph said the apostles Peter, James, and John paid him a visit and restored what Joseph termed the "*Melchizedek priesthood*" to the earth.

> D&C 84:19-22. And this greater priesthood administereth the gospel and holdeth the key of the mysteries of the kingdom, even the key of the knowledge of God. Therefore, in the ordinances thereof, the power of God is manifest. And without the ordinances thereof, and the authority of the priesthood, the power of Godliness is not manifest unto men in the flesh; for without this no man can see the face of God, even the Father, and live.

Deceased LDS Apostle Bruce R. McConkie wrote (*Mormon Doctrine*, page 479):

> ... the presence or the absence of this priesthood establishes the divinity or falsity of a professing church.

He adds (page 480),

> If there is no Melchizedek Priesthood on earth, the true church is not here and the gospel of Christ is not available to men. But where the Melchizedek priesthood is, there is the kingdom, the Church, and the fullness of the Gospel [emphasis in original].

Now, I must admit, that without a scriptural backing, this might all seem to make some sense. I mean, there *was* a Levitical Priesthood and there *was* a Melchizedek priesthood – it seems only natural that they would still be doctrinally valid, right? Why not go along with it?

Now to truly do justice to this subject, we would need to go through the book of Hebrews chapter five, six, and seven verse by verse, and I highly recommend that be done. But there's not enough time in this venue. So I am going to give you a thumbnail sketch, a little portrait of Mormon claims regarding the Melchizedek priesthood compared to what the Bible tells us. Ready?

Latter-day Saints believe Melchizedek was literally a man who held a priesthood which was passed down from Adam. Simply put, they liken it to a higher priesthood, with the priesthood of Aaron being a lesser. Mormonism teaches that the name of this priesthood is God's priesthood but that the name "Melchizedek" was given to this higher priesthood to avoid too frequent repetition of the name of Deity (*Doctrine and Covenants* 107:2-4). Additionally, the *Book of Mormon* teaches that the man Melchizedek was the greatest high priest ever (Alma 13:19).

Mormonism also teaches that it was called an eternal priesthood because God has always operated by it; therefore, it is eternal. Apostle McConkie (*Mormon Doctrine*, page 477) taught that while this higher priesthood was first given to Adam and that it was passed down generationally, the children of Israel "*rebelled, rejected the higher law, and the Lord took...the fullness of the priesthood from them.*" As a result, the Aaronic priesthood, or Levitical priesthood, became the authority on earth until Jesus came, Who brought the restoration of this higher priesthood with Him, even passing it on to the twelve apostles. Then, Mormons teach that this Melchizedek priesthood was lost from the earth with the death of the last apostle and was out of operation until Joseph Smith restored it to the earth in 1830, when Peter, James, and John appeared on some unknown date at some unknown place and gave it to him.

Mormon doctrine also states that now the LDS Church is the only church/religion that has this power of God (or Melchizedek priesthood) here on earth. And today, the Mormons claim to give this priesthood to men (18 years of age and up) who are worthy to receive it. So let's take a contextual look at what the Bible says about Melchizedek, his person and his priesthood.

When we read the Old Testament, it is vital to understand the use of "*types*." A type is a figure or representation of something else, something to come. In the last section we explained how everything that the Levitical priests did in the temple – even the temple itself – was a type of Christ, the Messiah which was to come. Some other examples of types include:

- Egyptian bondage was a type for the bondage of sin.
- Moses was a type for the Messiah.
- The Exodus was a type for leaving the world behind.
- Entering into the Promised Land was a type for entering into a saving relationship with Christ.
- The Passover Lamb was a type for the shed blood of Jesus.
- Manna from heaven was a type for Jesus, Who is the bread of life.
- Water from the rock was a type for Jesus, the Living Water and the Rock.
- Leprosy was a type for sin.

We know from reading the New Testament that Jesus was both 100% man and 100% God, the fullness of God dwelling in mortal flesh. Is there a type for this found in the Old Testament? Absolutely: it is the ark of the covenant.

> Exodus 25:10-11. *And they shall make an ark of shittim wood... And thou shalt overlay it with pure gold, within and without shalt thou overlay it, and shalt make upon it a crown of gold round about.*

Now shittim, or acacia, wood is gnarled and thorny, representing human flesh. And gold is pure and costly, representing God. The ark was wood. The ark was gold. Jesus was all man. Jesus was all God. And the types of this sort go on and on and on!

So who was Melchizedek? We know very little about him, but let's talk about what we do know. WHAT WE DO KNOW paints a perfect picture of who he is. Genesis 14:18-20 tells us that

1. Melchizedek was King of Salem.
2. He brought forth bread and wine to Abraham after the battle.
3. He was the priest of the most high God.
4. Abraham paid tithes of the spoils from the warfare to Him.

Then we hear the name again in Messianic Psalm 110, written one thousand years later …

5. Psalm 110:4. *The LORD hath sworn, and will not repent, Thou art a priest for ever after the order of Melchizedek.*

Then we jump all the way forward to the book of Hebrews, where the Writer there gives us a few more details about Him, saying he was

6. Hebrews 7:3. … *without father, without mother, without descent, having neither beginning of days nor end of life, but made like unto the Son of God, abideth a priest continually.*

So let's take these points one by one and explain the Biblical stance on Melchizedek. Let's start with the name, Melchizedek, and his kingdom.

1. Melchizedek was King of Salem.

Melchizedek's name in Hebrew is "*Malki Tzedek*," which means "my righteous king," or "king of righteousness." From his name we can see that Melchizedek had a pure and righteous administration of his government – get it? He was the "*KING of Righ-*

teousness." He was also known as the King of *Salem*, which means King of *Peace*. Melchizedek: King of Righteousness and King of Peace. Hmmmm...Who *was* this Melchizedek?

Now, where was Salem? Massachusetts? No. Have you ever heard of a place called Jeru*salem*? That was where Melchizedek reigned. Now listen! Speaking of the Messiah, Psalm 76 says:

> Psalm 76:1-2. *In Judah is* **God** *known; his name is great in Israel. In* ***SALEM*** *also is his tabernacle, and his dwelling place in Zion.*

Next point:

2. He brought forth bread and wine to Abraham after the battle.

This *type*, named Melchizedek, brought some interesting elements to Abraham, the father of our faith. These are the very elements Jesus introduced to the twelve as memorial elements of Himself, of His sacrifice for sin! Hmmmm ... Who was this Melchizedek?

Next Genesis tells us that

3. He was the priest of the most high God.

Hebrews chapter seven helps us understand who Melchizedek was as a type. You see, we know that in the Levitical priesthood, a high priest from the line of Aaron would *once a year* enter into the Holy of Holies chamber of the tabernacle or temple and offer up the shed blood of an unblemished animal for the atonement of sin. That word "*atonement*" in the Hebrew meant *a covering* not *a payment* like it does in the Greek. And being a mere man, this Levitical high priest would have to first have his own sins covered through purifying rituals; then he, the mortal man, would then enter annually into the most sacred place as a high priest.

But these mortal high priests died and had to be replaced by other mere mortals. And these mortal men had to enter in year in and year out to do this work. But the book of Hebrews points out that another High Priest, after the order of this mysterious type named Melchizedek and offering a far *better* way, would enter once and for all into a heavenly Holy of Holies and remain there, mediating on our behalf between man and the most high God (see Hebrews chapter 7). Hmmmm … Who was this Melchizedek?

The fourth point is we know

4. **Abraham paid tithes of the spoils from the warfare to Him.**

So even father Abraham paid tithes to this Melchizedek! And well before tithing was demanded in the Scripture. What was the purpose of this? Abraham was certainly at the top of the heap in authority, wasn't he? In a heated dialogue with the Jews in John chapter 8, Jesus said:

> John 8:56-59. *Your father Abraham rejoiced to see my day:* ***and he saw it,*** *and was glad. Then said the Jews unto him, Thou art not yet fifty years old, and hast thou seen Abraham? Jesus said unto them, Verily, verily, I say unto you,* ***Before Abraham was, I am.*** *Then took they up stones to cast at him …*

The book of Hebrews, especially chapter 7, makes it very clear to the self-righteous Jews, who were having trouble of letting go of the law, that Jesus came and provided a better way, a way that superseded their Aaronic priesthood, a way that was honored even by Abraham, who was the father of their faith.

Are you yet beginning to see who this Melchizedek was?

Over a thousand years passed from the time of Genesis where Melchizedek is first mentioned; and then, out of the blue, David includes his name in Psalm 110, which happens to be … a *MESSIANIC* psalm! And what did David say, speaking of Jesus?

5. **Psalm 110:4 The LORD hath sworn, and will not repent, Thou art a priest forever after the order of Melchizedek.**

Now, the Aaronic order was established on the *ritual* righteousness and *ritual* purity and mortality of man, officiated as it was *by* mortal men, on behalf of Israel. But the Messiah, who was from the tribe of Judah, would take His place as the true and only High Priest. The LORD swore through David's psalm, that this High Priest, Jesus, would hold this priesthood forever.

How? Why?

Because in the Old Testament we had a covenant based on the worthiness of men.

But under the New Covenant, we have a covenant based on the worthiness and righteousness of Christ. As a result, this covenant is not subject to failure; it is eternal, and its product is peace.

Describing this mysterious Melchizedek in even greater detail, the Writer of Hebrews, another thousand years later, wrote that he was

6. **Hebrews 7:3. …** ***without father, without mother, without descent, having neither beginning of days nor end of life, but made like unto the Son of God, abideth a priest continually.***

Now, you've got to think here, because the payoff is worth it. *If* Melchizedek was a real person, could he have really *not* have a father or mother? Might he really *not* have descendants? Is it possible for a man to be really *without* a beginning and an end!? It couldn't be.

So we have two options here regarding the person of Melchizedek. Either he was a real human being and the Writer of Hebrews left his personal information out in order to paint him as a picture of the coming Messiah; OR Melchizedek was *Christ Himself, a pre-incarnate visitation in human form*, or what theologians call a *Christophany*.

I stand by the latter. Let's read this passage again:

> Hebrews 7:3. *without father, without mother, without descent, having neither beginning of days nor end of life, but made like unto the Son of God, abideth a priest continually.*

Who else could this describe, my friends, but Jesus Christ, Who, as uncreated God,

- ***Was without father and mother***
- ***Was without descent***
- ***Was without beginning of days nor end of life***
- ***Was made like unto the Son of God***
- ***Remains a high priest continually!***

Let's wrap this up by letting the Holy Word of God reiterate what we have already discovered about Melchizedek, who was nothing more and nothing less than a type for the Lord Jesus Christ. In the context of the Aaronic priesthood, the Writer of Hebrews states:

> Hebrews 7:22-27. *By so much was Jesus made a surety of a better testament. And there truly were many priests, because they were not suffered to continue by reason of death: But this man [Jesus], because he continueth ever, hath an* ***unchangeable priesthood.*** *Wherefore he is able also to save them to the uttermost that come unto God* ***by him****, seeing he* ***ever liveth*** *to make intercession for them.* ***For such***

> ***an high priest came to us, who is holy, harmless, undefiled, separate from sinners, and made higher than the heavens; Who needeth not daily, as those first high priests, to offer up sacrifice, first for his own sins, and then for the people's: for this he did once, when he offered up himself.***

Oh my friends, Jesus is our one and only High Priest. He and He *alone* represents us before the Father. This mediation is everlasting and eternal because the righteousness required is based on Him and not man, not on failing mortals.

But just listen to the LDS description of this high priesthood and upon where they place the focus (*Encyclopedia of Mormonism* 1:415):

> When **worthy men** receive the Melchizedek Priesthood, **they** enter into a covenant relationship with the Lord. **They** covenant that in faithfulness and obedience **they** will magnify their priesthood callings – that is, wholeheartedly honor and fulfill **their stewardships**. By keeping this covenant, the priesthood holder receives the oath of the Father, which leads to receiving the Father's Kingdom, and all that the Father hath. Those who violate or break this covenant and altogether turn from it, **shall not have forgiveness of sins** in this world nor in the world to come [emphasis Shawn's].

Repent, you holders of a black, false priesthood which was forever abolished by the shed blood of the true King of Salem, Jesus Christ.

Repent and come to Him and Him alone.

⁂ ⁂ ⁂

> "The idea that the LDS prophets are considered 'prophets like unto Moses,' always brings a smile to my face. I mean, when we look back over the course of Biblical history, the prophets and apostles spent all their time and energy either proclaiming God's word without hesitation or testifying of the resurrected Christ: that they saw Him, that they are His special witnesses, and that He lives. The cost for their witnessing? Their very lives. Mormonism's 'living prophets and apostles' are nothing but errand boys for the multi-national, multi-billion dollar religious conglomerate which they dutifully serve and promote. I'd like to hear just one of them claim to have seen, let alone die for, the resurrected Lord."

Prophets

They say a lot of things about him:

- That "He speaks for the Lord."
- That "He is the only person on earth who holds all the authority to act in God's name."
- That "If you follow him, you will not go astray."
- That "He speaks with God today as Moses spoke with God yesterday."
- That "He is a prophet, a seer, and a revelator."

Who is he? The LDS or the Mormons call him "the prophet."

He is categorized by the Latter-day Saints as a "modern-day prophet." The first modern-day prophet of the LDS Church was Joseph Smith, Jr. Brigham Young was second. Since 1830, there has been a succession of men leading the LDS Church who have willingly accepted the lofty title of "*Prophet, Seer, and Revelator*" for the Church. The prophet, seer, and revelator of the LDS Church today is a man named Thomas S. Monson.

At LDS General Conferences, held in April and October of every year, avid Mormons stand when he enters the room and often they will sing (*Hymns* #19):

> We thank thee, O God for a prophet, to guide us in these latter-days …

When Mormon missionaries speak to people, they will often ask, *"Mr. and Mrs. Investigator, in ancient times heavenly Father loved people so much that He sent them living prophets. You remember Moses, and Abraham, and Isaiah?"*

The investigators will nod *"yes!"*

Then the missionaries will ask, all gentle and sweet-like, *"Mr. and Mrs. Investigator, do you think heavenly Father loves us as much today as he loved people anciently?"*

After a moment of perplexity, they might say, *"Well…yeeessss?"*

And the missionaries will say, *"Well of course He does! And guess what?"* [They'll add this bit while flipping open to a photograph of Thomas S. Monson] *"the Lord has given us a living prophets to lead and guide us too! – because He loves us so much."*

Are living prophets *"like unto Moses"* needed to guide people in "*these latter-days*"? If God did not send us living prophets would it mean He doesn't love us as much as He loved ancient Israel? Does the Bible support the idea that prophets like Moses and Elijah would continue to lead the body of Christ after the death and resurrection of the Lord? Do we need living prophets who claim to speak with God on our behalf to bring forth new revelation to the world?

From a very young age, LDS children are inculcated through pictures, talks, lessons, and songs, on the importance of following the living, modern-day prophet. They sing (*CS*, pages 110-111):

Follow the prophet!
Follow the prophet!
Follow the prophet!
Don't go astray - ay.

Follow the prophet!
Follow the prophet!
Follow the prophet!
He knows the way.

It's a powerful song. And when Mormon children graduate to adulthood, they shift into an adult version of the praise by singing, "We Thank Thee, O God, For a Prophet" and "Praise to the Man (*Hymns* #27)," a hymn written about Joseph Smith, Jr.

Pictures of, lessons from the life of, life histories about, and personal lessons from these men are shown and taught more frequently in the LDS Church than pictures and studies from the New Testament. Argue that point all you want. Like it or not. It's true.

And it is sickening.

Now why do you suppose it is that out of all of the scholars and students of God's Word and century upon century of born again believers, who read regularly the Word of God, none have laid claim to having a "living prophet" leading and guiding the body of Christ today? Wouldn't you think that if there was even the slightest question of the necessity of a "living prophet," that more churches than not would lay claim to the office? Sure they would. And that's exactly the point – it is not a question at all. Let me use the Bible to show you why.

Proof #1: The use of the phrase, "*All the prophets*" in the New Testament.

Just listen to the way prophets are spoken of in the New Testament:

> Luke 11:50. [Jesus said] *That the blood of* ***all the prophets, which was shed*** *from the foundation of the world, may be required of this generation.*
>
> Luke 13:28. *There shall be weeping and gnashing of teeth, when ye shall see Abraham, and Isaac, and Jacob, and* ***all the prophets*** *in the kingdom of God, and you yourselves thrust out.*
>
> Luke 24:27. *And beginning at Moses and* ***all the prophets,*** *he expounded unto them in all the scriptures the things concerning himself.*
>
> Acts 3:18. *But those things,* ***which God before had shewed by the mouth of all his prophets,*** *that Christ should suffer,* ***he hath so fulfilled.***
>
> Acts 3:21. *Whom the heaven must receive until the times of restitution of all things, which God hath spoken by the mouth* ***of all his holy prophets since the world began.***
>
> Acts 3:24. *Yea,* ***and all the prophets from Samuel and those that follow after, as many as have spoken, have likewise foretold of these days.***
>
> Acts 3:25. *Ye are the* ***children of the prophets****...*
>
> Acts 10:43. ***To him give all the prophets*** *witness, that through his name whosoever believeth in him shall receive remission of sins.*

The prophets "like unto Moses" were before Christ Jesus, they pointed to Jesus Christ, told of Jesus Christ, spoke of Jesus Christ and they revealed God's will *until* Jesus Christ came. When Jesus came, their job was done, because Jesus was the ultimate ***revelation of God*** and *His perfect will* in the flesh!

Proof #2: The parable of the wicked husbandman.

Jesus tells a profound parable which is found in every one of the synoptic gospels:

- Matthew 21:33-37
- Mark 12:1-11
- Luke 20:9-16

Ready? In the parable, Jesus says

> Matthew 21:33-34. *Hear another parable: There was a certain householder, which planted a vineyard, and hedged it round about, and digged a winepress in it, and built a tower, and let it out to husbandmen, and went into a far country: And when the time of the fruit drew near, he sent his servants to the husbandmen, that they might receive the fruits of it.*

This is a picture of the children of Israel. God planted a vineyard (a people) and then placed it into the hands of religious leaders to be the husbandman of the vineyard. And when He wanted to collect the fruit of the vineyard, he sent his servants (the prophets) to receive them:

(verse 35 states)

> Matthew 21:35-37. *And the husbandmen took his servants [the prophets] and beat one, and killed another, and stoned another. Again, he sent other servants more than the first: and they did unto them likewise. But* ***last of all*** *he sent unto them his son, saying, They will reverence my son.*

And of course, they killed Him, too. But the point is, even in the parable of the Lord Himself, the prophets served a purpose and were persecuted for it. But ***last of all*** God sent His Son! Mark recounts what Jesus said that the "*Lord of the vineyard,*" the "*certain Householder,*" would do in response to the killing of His son. Was it to send even *more* servants? No. There were to be no more "*servants*" sent. Instead,

> Mark 12:9. *What shall therefore the lord of the vineyard do? **he will come and destroy the husbandmen, and will give the vineyard unto others.***

Supporting this premise, we turn to the book of Hebrews, which is our third point. And what does it say?

Proof #3: Hebrews chapter 1.

> Hebrews 1:1-2. *God, who at sundry times and in divers manners **spake in time past** unto the fathers **by the prophets, Hath in these last days spoken unto us by his Son,** whom he hath appointed heir of all things, by whom also he made the worlds.*

How? How does God speak to us by His Son? In so many wonderful ways, my friends. And this is why Christians place Jesus preeminently – not merely prominently, but preeminently – in their lives. He is number one among nothing else

- There is no need for priesthood – He is our High Priest.
- There is no need for prophets – God spoke to us once and for all by and through Him!
- There is no need for the Law – He is our Law.

And by and through His sacrifice we are able, out of gratitude and love, to live lives pleasing and acceptable to God. Do you see why Christians do not have their churches headed up by some human being called a prophet? Jesus is their prophet.

Now, this passage from Hebrews says that God *in times past spoke unto the fathers by the prophets* BUT *has in these last days* [there's that word "last" again] *spoken unto us by His Son*. You see, prophets once spoke with words, but the Word was made flesh, and dwelt among us – Jesus. And prophets revealed the will of God to man. But Jesus came, not merely to reveal the will of God;

He fulfilled the will of God perfectly. And prophets of old revealed the law of God, but Jesus came and fulfilled both the law and the prophets! And prophets had revelations regarding the nature of God; but Jesus came as God in the flesh, once and for all revealing the invisible God to mankind. Finally, as the Author and Finisher of our faith (Hebrews 12:2), Jesus' shed blood makes it possible for God to speak to us, to lead us, to guide us, to walk beside us directly! How? Through the Holy Spirit, Who dwells within all who believe! This takes us to the fourth proof!

Proof #4: The Holy Spirit at Pentecost.

Why would we need a Joseph Smith, a Brigham Young, or a Gordon B. Hinckley to "*guide us in these latter-days*" when we have the Holy Spirit *AND* the living Word?

> John 14:26. *But the Comforter, which is the Holy Ghost, whom the Father will send in my name, he shall teach you* ***all*** *things, and bring* ***all*** *things to your remembrance,* ***whatsoever I have said unto you.***

God wants a relationship with each of us directly. ***He*** wants to teach us. ***He*** wants to tell us, ***He*** wants to lead us and guide us. This was why He created Adam in the first place – for direct fellowship! When we are born again, the Holy Spirit moves in and direct fellowship with God is reestablished just as it was in the garden before the fall! There were no prophets in the garden before the fall. There is no need for a prophet once the effects of the fall are rendered dead and gone, as they were at the cross!

Men seek the advice of and trust in other men because they are afraid to walk by faith! They are afraid to wholly trust in God. They want to turn their thinking over to a person or institution to escape the challenge of leaning upon Jesus. False religious institutions know this, and so they interject all sorts of answers for people – programs, manuals, prophets, popes – and none of them are part of the New Covenant, which is in and through

Jesus. This is why there is more emphasis on modern prophets than on Jesus in Mormonism today, because they have arrogantly placed themselves in between God and man as His earthly mediators! What a sickening lie.

When I was interviewed by LDS interviewer John Dehlin, I made the statement that I had absolutely no respect at all for the LDS brethren. This is why. They place themselves in between God and man.

Proof #5: The Mount of Transfiguration.

As recorded in Mark, chapter 9:

> Mark 9:2. *And after six days Jesus took Peter and James and John and led them up into a high mountain, apart by themselves. And He was transfigured before them.*

What does this mean? It means that Jesus, Who at the time was between the suffering in the wilderness and the suffering on the cross, was transformed! There was a visual manifestation of His glory shining out from beneath His flesh.

> Mark 9:3. *And His clothing became shining, exceedingly white as snow such as no fuller on earth could whiten them.*

Now besides Peter, James and John, who else was there?

> Mark 9:4. *And Elijah with Moses was seen by them, and they were talking with Jesus.*

Now of all the prophets, why Moses and Elijah? Why were they there when the glory of Jesus was revealed? Why not Isaiah? Why not Samuel? Or Abraham? Because these two represented respectively the law (Moses) and the prophets (Elijah), which two elements of the Old Covenant were about to be fulfilled in Jesus' imminent work on the cross.

Moses represented the law: through Moses was the law delivered to the children of Israel.

And Elijah represented the prophets. Why Elijah? Of all the prophets, Elijah was the prophet of prophets, who had the most radical of radical ministries of the Old Covenant. Both Moses' and Elijah's deaths were uncommon, possibly because they would be using their bodies at the transfiguration of Jesus. Moses supposedly died, but was buried by the Lord Himself, without his burial place being known to men (Deuteronomy 34:5-6) and Elijah was taken up into heaven in a fiery chariot (2 Kings 2:11). And interestingly enough, both of them returned here in their bodies that had so strangely disappeared at the times of their apparent passing. Why?

The Jerusalem Targum [see section on "Jesus"] connects the coming of Moses with that of the Messiah. Another Jewish tradition predicts the Messiah's appearance with that of Elijah ("The Transfiguration," *Smith's Bible Dictionary*).

What did Moses and Elijah talk about with Jesus as He was transfigured? Luke tells us:

> Luke 9:31. *And they spake of his death which he should accomplish at Jerusalem.*

The cloud which overshadowed the witnesses Peter, James, and John was bright or light-like and luminous (Mark 9:5); of the same brightness was the cloud at Sinai when Moses spoke with God; the same as when Elijah disappeared in the heavens via chariot; and this bright cloud was the same that was seen at the ascension of the Lord.

Moses and Elijah being there was a witness that the spirits of *the lawgiver and of the prophets* accepted the sufferings and the death of the Messiah in fulfillment of the Old Covenant; AND it furnishes to us striking proof of the unity of the Old and New Testaments and the mysterious intercommunion of the visible and invisible worlds. In other words, both the law and the prophets *meet* in Jesus Christ; He is the connecting link between the Old and New Testaments, between heaven and earth, between the kingdom of grace and the kingdom of glory, between God and man.

It is very significant that at the end of the scene the disciples saw no man save Jesus Himself, alone:

> Mark 9:8. *And suddenly, when they had looked round about, they saw no man any more, save Jesus only with themselves.*

Moses and Elijah, the law and the prophets – types and shadows – passed on and turned it all over to a better way. And Jesus remains, the only one who can lead us to God.

Now when Christians who understand their Bible criticize the LDS for claiming the need for a living prophet "like unto Moses" the LDS respond with a few standard arguments from the Bible to try and prove their point. Let's review them so you're prepared.

The first is an inane and juvenile use of an Old Testament passage which is taken from the book of Amos. It says:

> Amos 3:5. *Surely the Lord GOD will do nothing, but he revealeth his secret unto his servants the prophets.*

There are several responses a Christian ought to have for the LDS use of this verse from the Old Testament. First and foremost, context. If God says in the Bible, "don't kill," (which He does), but then in another place He says, "kill," (which He does), we would need to examine the context of the verses in question in order to understand the true meaning of each utterance.

It is so easy to select a passage, build an entire doctrine on it, and interpret it improperly. For example, do the Lord's words to a would-be disciple prohibit believers from holding funerals?

> Matthew 8:2. *Follow me; and let the dead bury their dead.*

Or, must followers of Jesus hate their families? After all, Jesus said,

> Luke 14:26. *If any man come to me, and hate not his father, and mother, and wife, and children, and brethren, and sisters, yea, and his own life also, he cannot be my disciple.*

Or how about this verse:

> Deuteronomy 23:1. *He that is wounded in the stones, or hath his privy member cut off, shall not enter into the congregation of the LORD.*

Does this apply today? Can a man enter the congregation of the Lord who got hit in the stones the day before with a Frisbee or had a really messy accident with a weed eater when he was a kid?

This "*prophets*" passage in Amos needs the same common sense analysis, friends. To understand it properly, we consider the context of the Bible in its entirety; we examine the broad context of the book containing the passage; we look at the immediate context of the chapter; we look at the passage itself.

In the context of the book of Amos, God was about to bring judgment upon the children of Israel because of their disobedience. The first verse of the chapter says:

> Amos 3:1. *Hear this word that the Lord hath spoken against you, O* ***children of Israel*** *…*

The Lord clearly addresses the *Israelites*; the words that follow in Amos 3 contain the words of judgment that God had Amos speak to them. When we get to the verse in question, it is simply a reminder to the children of Israel that God is not going about punishing them without having given them fair warning first! That is the context.

The subject of the book of Amos is NOT an edict stating that God will never do anything ever on this earth without revealing His secrets to a living prophet. If that were so, then Thomas S. Monson should have warned the people of Sri Lanka about the tsunami headed their way and the people of New Orleans about hurricane Katrina and the subsequent flooding, right? This passage is used by the LDS because it is conveniently worded; it is taken selectively and applied broadly, denying its context and its true meaning. Their use of this verse to justify the existence of their "living prophets" does not hold even a drop of water.

And as we have seen, having a "prophet like unto Moses" – all the "law" and the "prophets" – was fulfilled in Christ! That is the message of the Bible in its entirety.

The second set of "proof texts" the LDS love to use is two singular verses from the book of Ephesians (again, chosen selectively and applied broadly). They love to say that these verses support the LDS Church having a living prophet today.

The first is in Ephesians 2:20, which is usually the only verse of the passage they will read. It says:

> Ephesians 2:20. *And are built upon the foundation of the apostles and prophets, Jesus Christ himself being the chief corner stone;*

In the previous verses, verses 11-18, Paul has made the point that Jesus came and, because of Him, the religious barriers ("*middle wall of partition,*" verse 14) dividing Jew and Gentile with regard to ordinances have been broken down. And that all people – Jew and Gentile alike – are now welcome into the household of God. *THEN* he writes (preach it!):

> Ephesians 2:19-22. ***Now therefore*** [i.e., as a result of Jesus breaking down the barriers Paul had been speaking of] *ye are no more strangers and foreigners, but fellowcitizens with the saints, and of the household of God; And are built upon* ***the foundation of the apostles and prophets,*** *Jesus Christ himself being the chief corner stone; In whom all the building fitly framed together groweth unto an holy temple in the Lord: In whom ye also are builded together for an habitation of God through the Spirit.*

Verse 19 starts out, "*Now, therefore …*" The word "*therefore*" ("as a result of" something) refers the reader back in the passage to what came before. In context then, these passages not only tell us that, NOW, EVEN FOR GENTILES, the Jewish prophets and apostles make up the floor of the invisible temple known as the "*household of God,*" but also that the temple today is made of believers who are "*builded together for a habitation of God through the Spirit,*" Who lives in them!

Then the LDS use another favorite from Ephesians:

> Ephesians 4:11-12. *And he* [meaning God] *gave some, apostles; and some, prophets; and some, evangelists; and some, pastors and teachers; For the perfecting of the saints, for the work of the ministry, for the edifying of the body of Christ.*

The first passage, Ephesians 2, refers to the prophets of old – like unto Moses – who now serve as the foundation to the church. But this passage refers to the gift of prophecy, which is truly found in the church today. But the gift of prophecy is more like the gift of teaching revealed truths and not so much foretelling the future, as the office of prophet did in the Old Testament. Listen to how Paul describes "prophets" in the New Testament sense:

> 1 Corinthians 14:3. *But he that prophesieth speaketh unto men to edification, and exhortation, and comfort.*

One who "prophesies" is one who speaks to edify, exhort, and comfort. Paul says nothing about foretelling the future, although there may be those to whom God gives that gift who are able to do so. Nevertheless, the gift of prophecy found in the body of Christ today is just one of many gifts with which the Lord blesses His church.

Notice the order here: first, apostles, *then* prophets:

> 1 Corinthian 12:28. *And God hath set some in the church, first apostles,* ***secondarily*** *prophets, thirdly teachers, after that miracles, then gifts of healings, helps, governments, diversities of tongues.*

These things – apostles, prophets, teachers, miracles, healings, helps, etc. – are the gifts God gives to the believers in the body of Christ and have nothing to do with modern day living prophets like unto Moses.

Again, all of this boils down to Jesus, folks. They claim to have him, but …

Why do you need a prophet when you have Jesus?

Why do you need a priesthood when you have Jesus?

Why do you need temple rites when you have Jesus?

You don't.

When the LDS missionaries ask, "*Do you think God loves us as much today as He loved His children back in Moses day?*" the response ought to be, "Maybe even more: '*For God so loved the world, that he gave his only begotten Son, that whosoever believeth in him should not perish, but have everlasting life.*'"

"As with most things in the faith, Mormonism states that the fault for many problems in the world lies in the pre-mortal actions of the individual experiencing them. The LDS logic about race, particularly the black race, is no different. Mormons have historically had no problem telling people of color that everything about the condition of their lives is essentially because of their failures in this fabled pre-existence."

Race

Part1

By endeavoring to examine the role of racism in Mormonism, there is more at stake than just looking at the doctrines and attitudes of the past within the religion. We must also ask, "*If racism actually played a part in the establishment of Mormonism, have those seeds been eradicated from its spiritual foundations? Or do they continue to live on today?*"

Another equally vital question is, "*How trustworthy is the spiritual leadership of the LDS prophets, who, at one time, not only condoned but promoted racism within the ranks of the LDS, but now refute it?*"

Or, *"How can a Latter-day Saint know that the spiritual advice he is getting today – which is supposed to be eternal – will not also be refuted in the future?"*

And finally, *"What is at the core of racism? Does the Bible support racism, bigotry, or exclusion, particularly since Jesus came and broke down the veil with the good news?"*

We'll try and answer these and other questions with regard to race and the LDS Church.

In order to really get a handle on racism within the LDS Church, we must go to their scriptures – particularly, the Book of Mormon and the *Pearl of Great Price.* From these modern "revelations" which are presented and accepted as being "of God" by most believing LDS, we find the earliest seeds of racism present. Early in the Book of Mormon, a vision is recited by one of the main characters in the book, and in his description he says:

> 1 Nephi 13:15. And I beheld the Spirit of the Lord, that it was upon the Gentiles, and they did prosper and obtain the land for their inheritance; [READY?] and I beheld that they were white, and exceedingly fair and beautiful, like unto my people, before they were slain.

The line stating that the Gentiles seen in this vision were *"white, and exceedingly fair and beautiful"* is key to understanding the mindset of early Mormonism relative to race. White was akin to beautiful and worthy. Dark was akin to ugly and rebellious.

Later in the Book of Mormon, it describes what God did when He divided the bad sons of a family from the good ones:

> 2 Nephi 5:21. And he had caused the cursing to come upon them, yea, even a sore cursing, because of their iniquity, for behold, ***they had hardened their hearts*** against him, that they had become like unto flint, wherefore, as they were white, and exceedingly fair and

> delightsome, that they might not be enticing unto my people, ***the Lord did cause a skin of blackness*** to come upon them.

Notice the correlation between the *hardness of their hearts* and their *skin color*: in order to keep the "*delightsome*" from being *enticed* by the *hard-hearted*, God caused "*a skin of blackness to come upon them.*"

In the next section of the book, Jacob, the author describes the Lamanite people (who were the dark-skinned descendants of a character named Laman) by saying:

> Jacob 3:5. *Behold the Lamanites, your brethren, whom **ye hate because of their filthiness and the cursing which had come upon their skin** ...*

Got that? Then two verses later, the writer shares a concern he has for his white skinned brothers, saying:

> Jacob 3:8. *O my brethren, I fear that unless ye shall repent of your sins that their skins* [referring to the skins of the evil Lamanites] *will be whiter than yours, when ye shall be brought with them before the throne of God.*

So here, in the Book of Mormon, the supposedly ancient writer feared that, unless his white brethren repented, the skin of their evil brethren would become whiter than theirs. Dark skin = evil and unrepentant! White skin = good and humble!

Also in the Book of Mormon, Alma chapter 3, the writer explains what evil existed in the Lamanites that originally caused their skin to go from white to black. It says:

> Alma 3:6. *And the skins of the Lamanites were dark, according to the MARK which was set upon their fathers, which was a curse upon them because of their transgression and their rebellion against their brethren, who consisted of Nephi, Jacob, and Joseph, and Sam, who were just and holy men.*

And then later, toward the end of the book in 3 Nephi, the writer describes an amazing dermatological event that was occurring in the land:

> 3 Nephi 2:14-16. And it came to pass that those Lamanites [the dark-skinned people] who had united with the Nephites [the white and delightsome people] were numbered among the Nephites; and their curse was taken from them, and their skin became white like unto the Nephites; And their young men and their daughters became exceedingly fair, and were numbered among the Nephites ...

So, right here in the Mormons' most important spiritual book, there is a doctrine that dark people are loathsome and are dark because of the hardness of their hearts; but they can and will become white and delightsome, if they join the side of the spiritually enlightened.

This teaching is contained in the Book of Mormon. That is one of the main justifications for the racism that existed, and continues to exist, in Mormonism yesterday and today.

Got that?

Those Book of Mormon passages set the racist stage for the Indians and most other people of color.

Then there is another scriptural reference which has given life to Mormon racism past and present. It is found in a short reference in the book of Moses, which is Joseph Smith's re-translation of the Biblical book of Genesis and which is included in the LDS volume of scripture called the *Pearl of Great Price*. It reads:

> Moses 7:22. And Enoch also beheld the residue of the people which were the sons of Adam; and they were a mixture of all the seed of Adam save it was the seed of Cain, for ***the seed of Cain were black, and had not place among them.***

This "scripture," provided by Joseph Smith as was the Book of

Mormon, once again uses skin color as a barometer for righteousness; but this time, black skin – sometimes called *the mark* – came from the sinful loins of Cain. These are the primary scriptural sources within Mormonism that have to do with skin color: the Book of Mormon passages referring to the Indians and the book of Moses referring to black folks. Take these two skin-pigment positions and add a third influential factor that came from another popular teaching that originated from one of Joseph Smith's fanciful revelations.

The third factor influencing Mormon racial doctrines is found in the book of Abraham, which is also located in the *Pearl of Great Price*. The book of Abraham (3:22) discusses the "*noble and great ones*" who lived a premortal existence before coming to earth and gaining bodies. According to Joseph Smith, he learned while looking at some old papyrus that father Abraham had a vision of this pre-existence, and saw a premortal grand council where all these *noble and great ones* were gathered together. Referring to a sermon preached by Joseph Smith in which he referenced this premortal council and the noble and great spirits that were invited to participate, recently deceased LDS apostle Neal A. Maxwell quoted from the journal of George Laub, a Latter-day Saint who was present when Smith taught the following doctrine (Neal A. Maxwell, *But For a Small Moment,* page 93):

> Brother Joseph Smith was chosen for the last dispensation or seventh dispensation. [At] the time, the grand council [sat] in heaven to organize this world, Joseph was chosen [as] the last and greatest prophet to lay the foundation of God's work of the seventh dispensation.

How did this "revelation" of Joseph Smith's contribute to its racist position? Well, if there had been many *noble and great ones* in the premortal existence, then there must have also been "not-so-noble and lowly" ones, too. And guess who those would be, once they came to earth? Why, anyone who didn't have white and delightful skin, of course!

So, to summarize for clarity, what we have in place that has fostered a tremendous and long-lived racist mentality among the LDS is:

- The belief that skin color and righteousness are linked, as taught in the Book of Mormon and the book of Moses.
- The narrative that American Indian folk have dark skin as the result of a cursing of their forefathers for their evil; and that black people have a curse on their skin also due to the evil nature of their murderous forefather, Cain.
- Finally, the idea that if there were great and noble souls (like Joseph Smith) who existed before the world was, then there must also have been *LESSER* than noble souls who deserved a lesser life here on earth, souls given dark skin based on their lives and actions in the preexistence.

So there's the scriptural foundation from which LDS racism grew. And boy, did it ever grow!

Now, let me briefly speak to several modern defenses the LDS use to justify their racism of the past and, I believe, of the present as well. I once used these defenses as an LDS missionary for the Church and as an active member thereafter. Why did I do so? Because they were handy, ready-made statements of convenience, programmed into me over a lifetime that I never really took the time to think through. But I have now.

The first line of defense that is often used says something to the effect that, "*God Himself could be called a racist because of His dealings with ancient Israel! I mean, He only allowed the literal descendents of Aaron to hold the priesthood, right?*"

Now listen carefully. There is a big difference between God saying ONLY a specific line of men could perform the priesthood duties in the temple, and God saying "Everyone can perform these duties *except* black people!" The arguments are not one and the same. It is *not* racist to exclude all but one people group from performing particular functions; it *is* racist to allow all people groups but one to perform particular functions. Get the difference? Besides that, the Levites were the same race as all the other Israelites and were not chosen based upon anything even remotely related to their skin color.

Another defense, used frequently today, is that the ban was lifted in 1978. *"So why worry about it now? I mean, today we love the blacks and Indians, Shawn. Look around – we even adopt them into our homes!"*

First of all, just like polygamy, the doctrine and teachings on skin color and pre-existence are STILL present in what the LDS accept as scripture! Second, the seeds are still present today in the hearts of the majority of Latter-day Saints who have been members since before 1978 – or people over 35 years of age who have been raised in the Church. And these people are the ones who, for the most part, fill the leadership positions of the current Church. Who cares what you *allow*: the questions are, what is your doctrine and what do you believe in your heart of hearts? I therefore suggest that these racist ideas are still alive and well and that they cannot help but be passed from the old guard to the new.

Finally, there has never been an apology. There have only been justifications and fallacious reasoning about why racism was allowed to run amok in Mormonism. How a black person – or a brown or yellow or red or even a deeply suntanned individual – could ever participate in this religion KNOWING full well that those teachings are still in place, still doctrinal, and that no apology has ever been given is beyond me, unless those people of color accept the demeaning doctrines about themselves as true!

Once the teachings of Joseph Smith were in place – that skin color was a result of personal righteousness both here and in the make-believe premortal existence – the stage was set to begin the exclusion of certain races and people from total acceptance into the religion. I presume unaware of God's view regarding black men and the priesthood, Joseph Smith, early on, actually gave a black man named Elijah Abel the priesthood and ordained him into what the LDS called a the office of a "seventy" in the Church. Some members today use this as evidence of the prophet's magnanimous heart; others say he hadn't received the fullness of the gospel yet. But 11th President of the Church, Harold B. Lee, addressed the situation in a speech given at BYU on April 19, 1961. Lee was an ardent proponent of the "curse of Cain" myth and the idea that our actions in a pre-existence determined our position and skin color in this life. This is what he said relative to Joseph Smith ordaining Elijah Abel back in the day ("Do the Right Things for the Right Reasons," April 19, 1961):

> Some are heralding the fact that there was one of colored blood, Elijah Abel, who was ordained a Seventy in the early days. They go to the Church chronology and find the date of this ordination, and hold that up as saying that we departed from what was started way back, but they forget that also in Church history is another interesting observation. President Joseph F. Smith is quoted in a statement under date of August 26, 1908, when he referred to Elijah Abel who was ordained a Seventy in the days of the Prophet and to whom was issued a Seventy's certificate. This ordination, when found out, was declared null and void by the Prophet himself and so likewise by the next three presidents who succeeded the Prophet Joseph. Somehow because of a little lapse, or a little failure to do research properly, some people

> reach a conclusion that they had wanted to reach and to make it appear as though something had been done way back from which we had departed and which now ought to be set in order. The Prophet Joseph Smith said, "That person who rises up to condemn the Church, saying that the Church is out of the way while he himself is righteous, then know surely that the man is on the road to apostasy, and unless he will repent he will apostatize as surely as God lives."

Let's take a minute and ask ourselves some reasonable questions. First, what kind of God makes changes to the skin pigmentation of people, from white and pure to dark and loathsome, based on their attitudes, actions, and ideals? The Willy-Wonka God? Come on. And why hasn't God used this "pigmentology" practice on any other people groups throughout the history of world? How come Nazi Germans remained white and delightsome? Why did the Bolsheviks stay pale? The Charles Manson family? Old Charlie Manson is to this day as white as a toilet seat.

You see, the explanations regarding race that Joseph included in the *Book of Mormon* were couched in the backwoods ideals of his day, and he included them in order to provide answers, no matter how ridiculous they sounded. America was getting settled and suddenly the white folk discovered all these red-skinned savages roaming around their back yards in loin cloths. "*Damn! Where on earth did these red folks a-come from*!" Enter Joseph Smith who, having borrowed from popular theories already being bantered about in his day and age was willing to promote additional theories and then claim they came from God!

Now, I'm uncertain as to what the percentages of the world are relative to skin color, but I would guess that at least 80% of the world is neither white nor delightsome. So, while not only giving people a fairly fanciful answer, Joseph gave whitey an ethnocentrically pleasing response, one which not only made all "white" people delightsome, and all "dark" people loathsome, but told them they were this way based on their own pre-mortal righteousness. Gosh, that was appealing. "We really *are* better, aren't we?" Those Aryan guys up in northern Idaho are doing the same thing today.

As this stuff accumulated in his head, it helped Joseph to flesh out, over time, an entire religious system that I call "*progressive theology*": the doctrines on how men become gods. And where did all this conjecture go once it left Joseph's pen and paper? Where all man-made ideas go that are ascribed to God and stamped with His authority: to heartlessness, exclusion, piety, and pride.

Now because of all this stuff we've been talking about on the show, we've had some interesting responses from our viewing audience. Let me tell you, I couldn't have scripted it or written this stuff myself. First, we had a guy named Josh (I think) from the Provo/Orem area. He introduced himself as a "filmmaker" and tried to spin the LDS racist scriptures as not *necessarily* being racist – that what we as men call "racist" does not mean that God *means* it to be racist. So then what is racism? I mean, can't we state that if one group of people are EXCLUDED from certain things based on the color of their skin that that is racist? According to the filmmaker Josh, the answer is no. Josh's approach to racism within Mormonism is ... *SPIN!* Don't call it what it is; rather, play games with semantics.

Then we had an LDS caller named Virginia who called with a message that said she didn't think the passages regarding pre-existent "great and noble ones" were racist passages. To this I agreed. But what Virginia failed to notice was that the idea of pre-existent worthiness *IS* foundational to the LDS racist views. This will become more than apparent shortly, when we listen to some statements from LDS leaders about race. Virginia then presented another errant defense of Mormon racism, one that ignored the facts before her (that Mormonism has always been racist).

The next caller stepped up to the plate and took yet another approach to defending the faith. He introduced confusion. The caller's name was Boyd and he referred to himself as an LDS "researcher." Boyd repeated an incomprehensible mantra over and over again: *"We just have to get to the beginning!"* I tried to understand what the heck he meant, but what he meant existed only in his head. So he just kept repeating, *"We have to get to the beginning!"*

Boyd's call – full of spin and vagaries – presented us with yet another method the LDS use to defend their faith: wholesale confusion. They say so much meaningless stuff in so many convoluted ways that people just give up and say, *"Oh, I'm just gonna stick to what I've been taught all my life because it's all too confusing to try and explore."*

Finally, we had a call from a guy named Bob. Now, our screener wrote that Bob was a first time caller, but when I heard Bob's voice, I knew that he was not only NOT a first time caller, but I recognized that he was an LDS man who really considers himself an apologist who writes an online blog and promotes himself by way of internet videos, much of which is aimed against me. He has called the program numerous times but is so boring and so focused on nitpicking certain miniscule variables that the simple truths never get a chance to shine. This Bob, in my opinion and experience, is mean and highly deceptive. So mean that he calls people who listen to the show "Santa's broken toys" and so deceptive, that last week he told our operator he was a first time caller when he wasn't. So here we were presented with yet another LDS method to defend their faith: deception.

You see, these types need fodder to stay alive in their quest for recognition. Bob "needs" to have conversations with me so as to then build an entire blog about what is said through literally pages and pages of spin and straining at gnats. This gives people like Bob an identity. A name. Recognition. A life. Validation. Importance. All this is achieved through spin, selective scripture selection, and making mountains out of single words.

So what did the Bob want when he called in and lied to get on the air? He asked me a question about Elijah Abel, the black man who was ordained with the priesthood by Joseph Smith. Bob asked me when that priesthood given to Elijah Abel had been rescinded. He was trying to imply that this priesthood was *never* rescinded, which was an attempt to make Mormonism appear friendlier to the blacks. I happened to have a quote on hand from Harold B. Lee, taken from the speech we quoted above (Brigham Young University, 1961) in which Lee said that, when discovered, Elijah Abel's priesthood ordination had been rescinded. Lee said, in fact, that Abel's ordination …

> … was declared null and void **by the Prophet himself** and so likewise **by the next three presidents** who succeeded the Prophet Joseph.

What did the Bob say in response? That the LDS apostle Harold B. Lee "was mistaken." The LDS apostle, considered a *prophet, seer, and revelator*, was mistaken! And now Bob, from Fruit Heights, Utah, is the authority. The LDS apostle who was trusted as a literal mouthpiece for God, while speaking to thousands at BYU – well, *he* was mistaken; but Bob…now he has the real teachings. Let me assure you that the folks listening at BYU back in 1961 trusted apostle Lee as an apostle. They believed him, just like the people believe their …*ahem*… "apostles and prophets" today.

My question is why? If the apostle made a mistake like this then what mistakes are they making today? This is really the whole point of our program tonight. Racism is just one vehicle of many that prove it. How come these yahoos get to call themselves prophets and apostles, say whatever they want, cause whatever hatred they choose, and then once they're dead, Latter-day Saints have the very convenient ability to say they were wrong all the while?

Listen, the Word of God – the Bible – is trustworthy, yesterday, today, and forever more. These men, from Harold B. Lee, to Brigham Young, to Joseph Smith, to the Bob, the Boyd, the Virginia, and the Josh, are not. Their whole purpose is to somehow try to defend and to justify a lie. Trust God's Word. Trust Him. Trust nothing else.

Part 2

So, the scriptural foundation had been laid for racism within Mormonism by Joseph Smith himself. To review, these foundations said that:

1. Dark skin color was *a curse,* placed upon the American Indians by God because of the sins of their fathers (and actually for their own sins); *and* that the skin color placed upon black people was also a curse placed by God upon them because of the sins of their forefather, Cain.

2. There is the LDS idea that the skin color and the socioeconomic status of every individual born on earth are indicators of their pre-existent "worthiness." If a person is born white, wealthy, and LDS, he was the best of the best in the mythical pre-existence. If a person is born poor or

> black (whether in Harlem or the Congo), it was because his actions lacked "valiance" before the world was!

Even though most of these views are denied by LDS *defenders* today, the ideas and the opinions live on within the hearts of most LDS members. I want to know why no Latter-day Saint has ever called the show and agreed with the teaching honestly. This is the irritant in my heart.

Let's now examine how the scriptural pronouncements we mentioned last week affected the hearts of LDS leaders and members for over 175 years, even up until this day. Our first heart is that of Joseph Fielding Smith (*Doctrines of Salvation* 1:61),

> There is a reason why one man is born black and with other disadvantages, while another is born white with great advantages. The reason is that we once had an estate before we came here, and were obedient, more or less, to the laws that were given us there. Those who were faithful in all things there received greater blessings here, and those who were not faithful received less.

How about another from Joseph Fielding Smith (*Doctrines of Salvation* 1:65-66):

> There were no neutrals in the war in heaven. All took sides either with Christ or with Satan. Every man had his agency there, and men receive rewards here based upon their actions there, just as they will receive rewards hereafter for deeds done in the body. The Negro, evidently, is receiving the reward he merits.

Joseph Fielding Smith, 10th President of the LDS Church, also wrote (*The Way to Perfection*, page 107),

> It was well understood by the early elders of the Church that the mark which was placed on Cain and which his posterity inherited was the black skin. The Book of Moses informs us that Cain and his descendants were black.

In the same volume, Joseph Fielding Smith is also on record saying (*The Way to Perfection*, page 101),

> Not only was Cain called upon to suffer, but because of his wickedness he became the father of an inferior race.

The above statement is interesting because Joseph Fielding Smith said elsewhere that (*Answers to Gospel Questions* 4:170),

> The Latter-day Saints have no animosity towards the Negro. Neither have they described him as belonging to an "inferior race."

LDS President John Taylor said (*Journal of Discourses* 23:336),

> Why is it, in fact, that we should have a devil? Why did the Lord not kill him long ago? Because he could not do without him. He needed the devil and a great many of those who do his bidding to keep men straight, that we may learn to place our dependence on God, and trust in Him, and to observe his laws and keep his commandments. When he destroyed the inhabitants of the antediluvian world, he suffered a descendant of Cain to come through the flood in order that he might be properly represented upon the earth.

Defending segregation LDS Apostle Mark E. Peterson stated in a speech at BYU ("Race Problems – as they affect the church," August 27, 1954),

> When [God] placed the mark upon Cain, He engaged in segregation. When he told Enoch not to preach the gospel to the descendants of Cain who were black, the Lord engaged in segregation. When He cursed the descendants of Cain as to the Priesthood, He engaged in segregation.

And there are several dozen additional quotes from that speech that are just as biting; I am not going to take the time and space to include them here but go to www.utlm.org to read them.

Now, let me make a comment here so as to put this whole thing in a fair light. I understand racism. I don't like it, but I have made racist comments and told racist jokes in my life. I think most fallen men and women are racist by nature. I think Satan loves racism and bigotry and hatred and so I am not so dumb as to think it does not exist in the hearts of people in every walk of life, even today.

So here is the problem with Mormon racism: they laid it all upon God! They created a doctrinal position for racism and placed it in God's hands. This is a very different matter than a single individual who is LDS being racist. And this is why we cover the matter today. LDS scriptures, prophets, and apostles – the most trusted men in the religion – were not only racist themselves, they taught racist doctrine and belief and even practiced it *AS A RELIGION* – AS GOD'S ONLY TRUE RELIGION. Now cross reference this with what James teaches us:

> James 1:13. *Let no man say when he is tempted, I am tempted of God: for God cannot be tempted with evil, neither tempteth he any man.*

So we have a few options here. Either …

> Option A: Racism is not evil;
> Option B: God *can* do evil, contrary to James 1:13; or
> Option C: Mormonism did the evil and its prophets and apostles actually have the audacity to put the blame on God for it.

The answer is Option C. In fact, listen as one of the most popular LDS writers of the 1960s, a guy named John Stewart, chose to actually throw down on God rather than allow Mormonism to appear unfair. In his book, *The Glory of Mormonism*, written in 1963, Brother Stewart wrote (page 154):

> When God allows a spirit to take a negroid body, do you sup-

> pose He is unaware of the fact that he will suffer a social stigma? Therefore, if you say that this church is unjust in not allowing the Negro to bear the priesthood, you must, to be consistent, likewise say that God is even more unjust in giving him a black skin.

Oh, wait … that's right, John Stewart wasn't an official spokesman for the Church. Well, how about Joseph Fielding Smith, LDS prophet who said (as cited in John J. Stewart, *The Glory of Mormonism*, page 154):

> It is NOT the authorities of the church who have placed a restriction on him regarding the holding of the priesthood [meaning the black man] … IT WAS THE LORD [emphasis Shawn's]!

Nice one there, JSF.

In any case, the bottom line was this: if you were of a color of skin other than white you were considered inferior in one way or another for the first 138 years of Mormonism. Now remember, with all these racist ideas, it wasn't just about being banned from holding the priesthood. It also included being banned from the temple (where a Mormon is required to go in order to live with God after this life) as well as a ban from interracial marriage. No mixing the vanilla with the chocolate at the ward ice cream social because GOD was a racist, *not the church!* Never the church!

Well, things started a changin' at the hands of some of the less racist-minded leaders. At first, these changes were, frankly, quite humorous and pathetic, but they did show some early signs of hope. In an article published by "*APOSTLE*" Spencer W. Kimball in the LDS church magazine the *Improvement Era* (December 1960, pages 922-923), the leader suggested that he had witnessed some rather remarkable happenings among the Lamanites. In the article, Apostle Kimball described how he was witnessing first-hand the progress and growth of the native

American Indians living on a reservation that he had frequented for several decades. Wrote Kimball:

> I saw a striking contrast in the progress of the Indian people today as against that of only fifteen years ago. Truly the scales of darkness are falling from their eyes, and they are fast becoming a white and delightsome people.

After hailing all the growth and accomplishments of these reservation Indians, Apostle Kimball again referenced the Book of Mormon verbiage and claims by saying:

> The day of the Lamanites is nigh. For years they have been growing delightsome, and they are now becoming white and delightsome, as they were promised.

Then he spoke of a photograph of Indian missionaries he had seen:

> In this picture of the twenty Lamanite missionaries, fifteen of the twenty were as light as Anglos; five were darker but equally delightsome.

In the 1960s and 1970s, there was a program conducted by the LDS to take Indian kids from off the reservations and place them in the homes of Caucasian Latter-day Saints. They called it the "*Home Placement Program.*" In this article, Apostle Kimball referred to those who were in the program:

> The children in the home placement program in Utah are often lighter than their brothers and sisters in the hogans on the reservations!

Can you believe this schnit?! And this racist man, proclaimed to be an apostle, goes on and on and on with it!

Now, this was 1960. I was born in 1961 and I cut my religious teeth on this crap. I trusted my leaders. I believed they were really apostles of the Lord Jesus Christ, who said junk like this! And for the first 17 years of my existence, prior to 1978, I believed this mythology; I believed that this racist garbage actually came from GOD!

As a Christian, I read the Bible – passages like these from the Apostle Paul:

> Romans 2:11. *For there is no respect of persons with God.*
>
> 1 Corinthians 12:13. *For by one Spirit are we all baptized into one body, whether we be Jews or Gentiles, whether we be bond or free; and have been all made to drink into one Spirit.*
>
> Galatians 3:28. *There is neither Jew nor Greek, there is neither bond nor free, there is neither male nor female: for ye are all one in Christ Jesus.*

Now listen to this verse:

> Colossians 3:11. *Where there is neither Greek nor Jew, circumcision nor uncircumcision, Barbarian, Scythian, bond nor free: but Christ is all, and in all.*

Now when Paul writes "*Barbarians*," the word as used in Scripture speaks of ANYONE who was not a Greek. The Greek word *barbarov* properly denotes anyone who speaks a foreign (or "babbling") language. And anyone who was not a Greek, no matter who he was, was included and able to receive the gospel in its FULLNESS!

The word "*Scythians*" referred to the most savage and untamed humans on earth. Again, the meaning here is that even such a ferocious and uncivilized people were not excluded from the gospel, but were as welcome as any other and were entitled to the same privileges as all others. ALL OTHERS. When Jesus died, and the veil of the temple was ripped in two, the FULLNESS OF THE GOSPEL WAS OPEN TO ALL OTHERS.

The questions looming over Mormonism are why and how so many people allowed these men to infect them with racist ideas, claiming they were from God and how does Mormonism continue to grow today in spite of these doctrines? Someone, anyone, throw me a lifeline, please. Explain to me how and why. I mean, were these LDS leaders right or were they wrong? *Tell me!* Was skin color an indicator of righteousness? Could skin color really change if a person's righteousness changed? Are all non-white races and cultures inferior because of some pre-existent failures on the part of those people? Please, call and tell me why.

In 1966, Pulitzer-prize winning journalist Wallace Turner wrote a book entitled *The Mormon Establishment*. In it, he wrote (page 218):

> The most serious problem facing the LDS church today is the negro question.

He went on to say that as long as Mormonism practiced racism it would be a political and social cancer (page 228).

It goes without saying that the 1960s brought with it a culture seeking more tolerance. The American Civil Rights movement was afoot; but Mormonism, fronted by a leadership that spewed racist ideologies, was apathetic to the national press. Turner accused the Mormons of "indifference [and] inattention" toward the Civil Rights movement and pointed out the "smug-satisfaction" that existed among the Saints because so very few Negroes lived in areas of the country where the Mormons lived (page 229).

Right about this time, Mormonism got a new leader, David O McKay. According to LDS sociologist Armand Mauss, McKay was different from past General Authorities in that he was "remarkably free of traditional notions about marks, curses, and the like (Gottlieb and Wiley, *American Saints: The Rise of Mor-*

mon Power, page 179)." As quoted in Gottlieb and Wiley's book, *American Saints: The Rise of Mormon Power*, McKay even went so far as to state, in private, that (page 241):

> Sometime in God's eternal plan the Negro will be given the right to hold the Priesthood.

And while many thought that McKay would be the one to allow all worthy men access to the LDS priesthood, it wasn't going to happen as long as there remained several frothing racists in the ranks of LDS leadership, namely Ezra Taft Benson, Joseph Fielding Smith, and Harold B. Lee, all of whom would become prophets of the LDS Church after McKay passed away in 1970.

I don't think it would be fair to discuss the role of racism in Mormonism without mentioning the courage and valor of one unsung LDS boy. His name was Steven Holbrook. While serving his LDS mission in 1963, Holbrook was taken aside by Church leaders and told "not to work with the poor and to tell the blacks that they should attend the church of their choice, but not the Mormon Church (*American Saints*, pages 179-180)." This made Holbrook sick inside. He listened to his conscience over his desire to follow orders, left his mission, and returned to Utah. He began working with the NAACP, which was staging demonstrations in Utah against the LDS doctrines of "non-white inferiority." The NAACP had argued that the Church's policies fostered prejudice because of their contention that "negroes deserve to be the subject of disadvantaged living conditions while living their lives here on earth (*American Saints*, page 180)."

Hats off to Steven Holbrook for his fearless courage to stand up to the giant. If people like Steven Holbrook hadn't challenged the LDS doctrine and leadership, I would suggest that things would have remained the way they were to this very day! I wonder: where are the Steve Holbrooks within Mormonism today?

Where are those who will stand up against these racist doctrines that are STILL present in their beloved Book of Mormon? Where are the Steve Holbrooks who will stand up against Doctrine and Covenants 132 and say, "Take the fetcher out! Now! Or no more tithing!" Where are the Steve Holbrooks who will courageously say, "As someone who loves Jesus I am not going to accept that damned forgery called The Book of Abraham in the *Pearl of Great Price*!" Where are you? How can you, week in and week out, listen to this stuff and do NOTHING about it? Come on! There are thousands – even millions – of people now and in future generations who could be freed from this evil – if you would just stand up and be heard.

Once LDS racists Joseph Fielding Smith and Harold B Lee died, Apostle Spencer W. Kimball, who wrote that garbage about Indians turning white, became the new LDS "prophet, seer, and revelator." And while Kimball was responsible for actually writing one of the most horrific books ever written in Mormon history, *The Miracle of Forgiveness,* which, in my opinion made gaining forgiveness as a Mormon a miracle in and of itself, he did have the foresight to recognize the need for a change in doctrine regarding blacks.

You see, when the survival of Mormonism is threatened, revelations come.

It was this way with the "*revelation*" on polygamy and it was this way when Kimball received his 1978 "*revelation*" that blacks could receive the LDS priesthood. What prefaced it? Subtle things at first. A BYU basketball game was interrupted by protesters regarding the LDS policy against blacks. Then a riot erupted at the University of Wyoming when black athletes wore armbands protesting BYU's presence there. Then Stanford University and the University of Washington boycotted all sporting events that involved BYU. Then the NAACP asked third-world countries to deny visas to LDS missionaries until the black doctrine was repealed. Finally, discrimination charges were brought against the LDS Church for allowing whites to be patrol leaders in their scout troops, while refusing to allow blacks the same position (*ONUG,* page 369).

All this mounted in the mind of Kimball. But the biggie was when LDS Apostle LeGrand Richards came to Kimball in 1978 with a problem. It seems that three years earlier, in 1974, the LDS church had announced plans to build a temple in Brazil. Now that it was almost complete, they had realized that much of the money and time invested to build it came from men and women who, God forbid, had at least one drop of black blood in their veins. Apostle Richards told Prophet Kimball, *"If we don't change, then they can't even use it after they've got it!* (*ONUG*, page 369)."

The result? REVELATION!!!!!!!!!!!!

And as of (I think) June of 1978, black men could receive the LDS priesthood, which meant they could enter the temple, which meant they could have eternal life.

Wouldn't all of this have been much less painful had Mormonism just trusted the Bible?

❋ ❋ ❋

> "I've got no illustration for repentance. Too much wrong has already been done in the cause to enforce it; I didn't see any sense in adding to the mess. If you want to know what I mean by this, read the book written by past LDS president and prophet, Spencer W. Kimball, *The Miracle of Forgiveness*. He paints his picture of what repentance is and isn't. After I read it as a teen, I came to believe it would be a miracle if anyone could ever be forgiven."

Repentance

This topic is one of the most misunderstood topics not only in the Mormon / Christian debate, but in Christianity as a whole, which makes teaching it doubly difficult. The topic?

Repentance.

I'm not so sure I have the ability to stress both the importance of a proper understanding of repentance for those seeking to comprehend the good news of Jesus Christ as well as a proper description of what repentance really means. So pray for me, and pray for your own spiritual enlightenment as I make an attempt.

If we looked up the word "*repent*" or "*repentance*" in a modern dictionary we would find a number of misleading definitions. They say things like, "to turn from sin; to amend one's life; to feel regret" and/or "to change behaviors and attitudes about previous actions and beliefs." As a result of these modern definitions of the word "repent," millions of people – if not billions – use the word in a way that is not only wrong but it is *the opposite meaning* needed for a true grasp on the good news of Jesus Christ.

So let's begin this analysis with a very brief explanation of the "good news" of Jesus Christ. There were several churches that

Paul founded in the territory of Galatia. Men came in to some of those congregations and began to pervert the gospel of grace or the good news of Jesus Christ. This prompted Paul to write, refuting these perversions. According to the first chapter of his letter to the Galatians, these men had begun to preach something Paul called "*another gospel*" (verse 6), which label he then qualified by saying that it really "is not another" gospel (verse 7). In reality, "*gospel*" means "good news" and if you tell me God will forgive me all of my sins, past, present, and future, and count me righteous if all I do is simply believe on Jesus Christ and trust in His goodness and His shed blood … well, THAT really is good news. And it is the *only* gospel or good news.

But if you tell me that I must THEN follow the rules and regulations of the law, and keep fully the law of God in order to earn righteousness or be accepted by God, that is *NOT* good news. Nobody has *ever* been successful at that; and the result in their lives of making the attempt is bondage (see Acts 15:10). Bondage is a yoke, a burden, on a man and is NOT what Jesus gave His life for.

Now, when most people use the word repent today they mean it in the sense of our modern dictionaries; and when confronted by something a sinner or a saint does that is unbecoming they will say, "*you need to repent*," meaning "stop your sinning … amend your life … feel regret" and/or "change your behaviors and attitudes about previous actions and beliefs." Listen: this is NOT the real meaning of repent, my friends. Yes, you will hear even Christian authorities indicating that "to repent" includes these Webster definitions; but in this dispensation of grace this is *NOT true* – not in the least.

Repent, in the New Testament sense of the term means, and means only, "*to change your mind.*" When reading in the gospel of Mark, for example, the words say:

> Mark 6:12. *And they went out, and preached that men should repent.*

But the meaning is this: *"And they went out, and preached that men should change their minds."*

Where John the Baptist says,

> Matthew 3:2. *Repent ye: for the kingdom of heaven is at hand ...*

... the passage could and should be read, *"Change your mind, for the kingdom of heaven is at hand."*

So that is the first problem with the use of the word repent: too many people think it means change your actions; to stop; to act, or to be, humble; to cry; or to conform outwardly. This is not so; it means to change your mind. Unfortunately, many people today – especially Mormons but many Christians as well – when they use the word *repent* in the Webster's-dictionary-like way, they mean to suggest that if a person does not CONFORM or STOP, they stand in jeopardy of going to hell.

This brings us to the second problem with the use of the word repent: people use it as the requisite qualification for staying out of hell. NOTHING, folks, *NOTHING* could be further from the truth. We do not go to heaven because we have repented (in the "changed our actions" sense of the word) any more than we go to hell because we have not repented. We go to heaven by the grace of God through faith; we miss hell by the grace of God through faith. Period. When we use the word *repent* in the sense of "stop or turn from your actions or behaviors" and then tie this erroneous definition of repentance to placement in heaven or hell, we have slipped into another gospel, and the good news is, once again, lost.

And let me tell you, the misuse of the word repent and repentance makes it one of the most horrible words in religious language. Let's use Mormonism as a model for this diabolical use of the word repent/repentance. Mormonism teaches that in order to truly repent, a person must perform certain steps. On my LDS mission, we taught the steps to repentance using the "*RSCARF*" method. Ready?

A truly repentant person must first:

- **R**ecognize that they have sinned.
- Feel **S**orrow for the sin.
- **C**onfess the sin to God and Bishop.
- **A**sk forgiveness of God and others.
- Make **R**estitution for the sin.
- **F**orsake the sin forever and ever.

Now, this method was suitable in the Old Testament. Under the law, there had to be some sort of systematized or formalized method in place. Why? Because Israel had not been redeemed. They were under a blessings/cursing economy. And even though God wanted their hearts, repentance for them, under the law, was more of a turning from their actions and less of a changing of their minds. What was required is that they do what they were commanded. But they couldn't succeed because no one can consistently do right when their hearts and minds have not changed. Paul tells us that the law was given as a "schoolmaster" (Galatians chapter 3) to teach the Israelites of their sinfulness; it was not meant to produce personal righteousness sufficient for salvation.

Well, Mormonism, having utterly ignored the good news, has re-adopted elements of legalistic living from the Jews and has placed its people under a yoke of repentance performance. And you have never been in bondage until you've lived under this regime. Listen to some quotes from LDS leaders regarding repentance. President Joseph F. Smith wrote this horrible passage as reported in *Gospel Doctrine*, pages 100-101:

> True repentance is not only sorrow for sins, and humble penitence and contrition before God, but it involves the necessity of turning away from them, a discontinuance of all evil practices and deeds, a thorough reformation of life, a vital change from evil to good, from vice to virtue, from darkness to light. Not only so, but to make restitution, so far as it is possible, for all the wrongs we have done, to pay our debts, and restore to God and man their rights – that which is due to them from us. This is true repentance, and the exercise of the will and all the powers of body and mind is demanded, to complete this glorious work of repentance; then God will accept it.

LDS Prophet and Seer Harold B. Lee said (*Ye Are the Light of the World: Selected Sermons and Writings of Harold B. Lee*, page 321):

> In one sentence, repentance means turning from that which we have done wrong in the sight of the Lord and never repeating that mistake again. Then we can have the miracle of forgiveness.

Mormon Prophet Spencer W. Kimball wrote all of the following in his utterly evil book, *The Miracle of Forgiveness*:

> Our loving Heavenly Father has given us the blessed principle of repentance as the gateway to forgiveness. All sins but those excepted by the Lord – basically, the sin against the Holy Ghost, and murder – will be forgiven to those who totally, consistently, and continuously repent in a genuine and comprehensive transformation of life. (page 14)

> There is one crucial test of repentance. This is abandonment of the sin. (page 163)

> Trying is not sufficient. Nor is repentance complete when one merely tried to abandon sin. (page 164)

> Repentance must involve an all-out, total surrender to the program of the Lord. That transgressor is not fully repentant who

> neglects his tithing, misses his meetings, breaks the Sabbath, fails in his family prayers, does not sustain the authorities of the Church, breaks the word of Wisdom, does not love the Lord nor his fellowman. A reforming adulterer who drinks or curses is not repentance. The repenting burglar who has sex play is not ready for forgiveness. God cannot forgive unless the transgressor shows a true repentance which spreads to all areas of his life. (page 203)

And finally for Kimball's *Miracle of Forgiveness*:

> Your Heavenly Father has promised forgiveness upon total repentance and meeting all requirements, but that forgiveness is not granted merely for the asking. There must be works – many works – and an all-out, total surrender, with a great humility and a "broken heart and a contrite spirit." It depends upon you whether or not you are forgiven, and when. It could be weeks, it could be years, it could be centuries before that happy day when you have the positive assurance that the Lord has forgiven you. That depends on your humility, your sincerity, your works, your attitudes. (pages 324-325)

Some LDS today say that Kimball's *Miracle of Forgiveness* has been shelved by present-day leaders, but as late as November of 2004, LDS Apostle Richard G. Scott referred to it as "*Spencer W. Kimball's masterly work,*" encouraging those seeking repentance to consult it ("Peace of Conscience and Peace of Mind," *Liahona*, November 2004). *Ugggggggh.*

In an LDS General Conference this so-called prophet said ("To Bear the Priesthood Worthily, *Ensign*, May 1975):

> There can be no forgiveness without real and total repentance, and there can be no repentance without punishment. This is as eternal as the soul.

Mormon Apostle Bruce R. McConkie wrote (*The Promised Messiah: The First Coming of Christ*, page 242):

> All must repent to be free. All must obey to gain gospel blessings. All must keep the commandments to merit mercy.

LDS Apostle Boyd. K. Packer, as reported in the LDS *Ensign* Magazine, said ("The Brilliant Morning of Forgiveness," November 1995):

> Even that grace of God promised in scriptures comes only after "all you can do."

Finally, the LDS 1997 Gospel Principles manual states (page 125):

> To make our repentance complete we must keep the commandments of the Lord.

And now, back to the truth.

True repentance is *changing our minds* about a matter. When Peter preached to the Jews and told them to repent and be baptized in the name of Jesus Christ, he was telling them to "change their mind" about who the Messiah is, and then be baptized. But repentance to the Jews – what they needed to change their minds about – was very different than what we Gentiles need to change our minds about.

John the Baptist came to prepare the way for the house of Israel. Jesus came to the house of Israel. The twelve apostles came to the house of Israel.

But Paul was called and especially sent to the Gentiles, and his approach was VERY different (Romans 11:13; Galatians 2:7-8; 2 Timothy 1:11). If you look at the word *repent* in the gospels and in Acts, you find it mentioned 14 times. But in the Pauline epistles you find it only twice, and neither time is it in the sense of a command. Are Gentiles supposed to repent? Absolutely. But in a *good news* way and not in a legalistic one.

How does this work? First, remember: what does repentance mean? **"To change our minds."** Don't forget this because it is key to understanding this concept. Next, let me present you with two "ifs" and ask two "whats":

- If we are saved by grace through faith and not of works; *and* …
- If Jesus paid for all sins, past, present, and future; *then* …
- Of what are gentiles repenting; and …
- What does repentance "do" if our sins were paid for 2000 years ago?

First, there is repentance (or changing our minds) unto salvation. *Faith* and *changing our minds* are two sides of the same coin: the coin of salvation. When a Gentile comes to the realization of the kind of life he (or she) has been living (usually by the hearing of the Word and **always** by the working of the Holy Spirit), *especially* as it relates to the Holiness of God …

… And then he recognizes that the *only* solution to his predicament – his sinful life – is the shed blood of Jesus Christ, he *repents* or *changes his mind* about the kind of person he has been and the kind of life he has lived! He *repents* or *changes his mind* about the way he has viewed God in the past. Finally, he *changes his mind* about the way he has always perceived the purpose of his life, about the value of his former life's interests and efforts, about the priorities he has had in the past, and about the goals he has for the future. He changes his mind.

That is repentance unto salvation.

That is how faith and repentance (or changing of the mind)

saves us. To put it a better way, *IF* a person really has faith, *THEN* he will really change his mind!

Get it?

Changing our minds alone won't save us, and changing our actions alone certainly won't save us; but faith alone can and does!

And yet on the other side of that salvation coin repentance: the natural changing of our minds, about God and about our sinful selves. Now this is important – what causes us to have that natural change of mind? Fear may, although I find it to be very tenuous. But in most genuine rebirths, it's the love of God! We are brought to this state of faith and a changed mind by the GOODNESS of GOD not the threats of God! Paul asks Gentiles why they …

> Romans 2:4. … *despised the riches of God's goodness (and His forbearance and His longsuffering); not knowing that* ***the goodness of God leads people to repentance?***

So this is the first repenting (changing of the mind) a person does: seeing his life for what it is; seeing God for what He is; and knowing that he deserves death and destruction but instead sees the "goodness of God" – *this* recognition leads him to *change his mind* about everything. Again, this is faith *unto* repentance.

But let me ask another question. Will the person continue to sin even though he has changed his mind about whom he is and about Whom God is? The answer is yes. Do these sins remove him from God's presence, love, or salvation? Never!

In discussing this very phenomenon, remember what Paul (a saved, believing, born again follower of Christ; indeed, an apostle!) said about himself:

> Romans 7:22-25. *For I delight in the law of God after the inward*

> *man* [my heart, my mind, my spirit]*: But I see another law in my members* [that is, my flesh], *warring against the law of my mind, and bringing me into captivity to the law of sin which is in my members. O wretched man that I am! who shall deliver me from the body of this death? I thank God through Jesus Christ our Lord. So then with the mind I myself serve the law of God; but with the flesh the law of sin.*

Here is where the LDS step in and really do a number on people. How? First, they continue to claim that repentance means a person has to change his behavior or stop his actions. Second, they say that it is *only* through "doing" these repenting practices (remember *RSCARF*?) that God will be with us here by His Spirit. Third, they say that if we don't repent by changing our behavior or stopping all sinful action, we will completely miss heaven.

All three of these premises are lies. Let's evaluate them one by one.

"First, [the LDS] continue to claim that repentance means a person has to change his behavior or stop his actions."

Once a person comes to a saving relationship with the Lord, he needs to continue to change his mind about one thing: his failing to trust and rely on God. It is only by faith that we can please God (Hebrews 11:6); as saved Christians, sin is a result of our lack of faith and trust in the Lord. Our repenting (mind changing) as believers, then, is aimed at changing our minds about *how* we trust and believe in Him and His strength; it's never about our own strength or abilities. It's a matter of growing in trust – that belief, that faith that He is big enough to handle our lives – which results in the elimination of sin from us. Any other approach puts us right back on the religious hamster wheel of self-perfection of the flesh.

"Second, [the LDS] say that it is *only* through 'doing' these re-

penting practices (remember *RSCARF*?) that God will be with us here by His Spirit."

If this is true, then the good news is false – that's the long and the short of it. And, if true, we are destined *forever* to striving and churning and struggling to appease the living God. *This is why Jesus came, my friends:* He came and appeased God *on our behalf.* It is by our goodness or purity that we are saved or accepted by Him and it is not our evil or failures that cause Him to leave! Everything, to a believer, is based on our faith in and on Him and Him alone.

"Third, [the LDS] say that if we don't repent by changing our behavior or stopping all sinful action, we will completely miss heaven."

Did you know that it was the book of Galatians that ignited the protestant reformation? You see, Martin Luther was a devoted Catholic monk. And Catholicism taught Luther to focus on specific sins, the repenting or changing of which would make him right with God. And so he tried. Boy, he "repented" (in the false sense) like no other. Every night he would look at the closing day in retrospect and try to repent of every misdeed, foul thought, or lazy indifference to the things he could have done better. Luther went to Rome and, climbing a set of stairs in the holy sanctuary, he was told that if he knelt on each step and recited the *pater noster* (the Lord's Prayer in Latin) before ascending to the next step, he could receive the forgiveness of sins he had committed up until that day (http://www.spindleworks.com/library/faber/faith.htm)! But when the climb was over, he said aloud, "Who can tell?" (meaning, who can tell if my sins were forgiven through such action).

It was the book of Galatians in which Luther first learned that we are all justified by faith! This was the good news of that book: that incessant repenting was the tool of religion, wielded to keep people in chains, but that Jesus had broken those chains and set all men free who but *change their minds* about who He is and then change their mind about how they are saved.

In closing, consider these words from the Apostle Paul:

> Romans 3:21-28. *But now [i.e., since the cross] the righteousness of God* ***without the law*** *is manifested, being witnessed by the law and the prophets; Even* ***the righteousness of God which is by faith of Jesus Christ*** *unto all and upon all them that* ***believe****...For all have sinned, and come short of the glory of God;* ***Being justified freely by his grace*** *through the redemption that is in Christ Jesus: Whom God hath set forth to be a propitiation* ***through faith*** *in his blood, to declare* ***his righteousness for the remission of sins*** *that are past, through the forbearance of God; To declare, I say, at this time* ***his righteousness****: that he might be just, and the justifier of him which believeth in Jesus. Where is boasting then? It is excluded. By what law? of works?* ***Nay: but by the law of faith. Therefore we conclude that a man is justified by faith without the deeds of the law.***

His righteousness saves us, not our own (we have none). All that is required of us is that we *change our minds*, and believe Him.

"I never really understood as a Latter-day Saint why the Sabbath day was so important...especially when we were on vacation or needed something from the store."

Sabbath-Day

For those of you who aren't aware, Latter-day Saints call Sunday the "Sabbath-day," and have a number of written and unwritten rules and expectations for its observation. When I was a child, I remember singing a song in primary called *Saturday*, that went something like this (*CS*, page 196):

> *Saturday is a special day, it's the day we get ready for Sunday;*
>
> *We clean the house and we shop at the store, so we won't have to work until Monday;*
>
> *We brush our clothes and we shine our shoes, and we call it our "get-the- work-done" day;*
>
> *Then we trim our nails and we shampoo our hair, so we can be ready for Sunday!*

Mormon leaders have said all sorts of stuff about Sunday or what they call the Sabbath day. LDS Prophet Spencer W. Kimball counseled (*Miracle of Forgiveness*, pages 96-97):

> The Sabbath is a holy day in which to do worthy and holy things. Abstinence from work and recreation is important but insufficient. The Sabbath calls for constructive thoughts and acts, and if one merely lounges about doing nothing on the Sabbath, he is breaking it. To observe it, one will be on his knees in prayer, preparing lessons, studying the gospel, meditating, visiting the ill and distressed, sleeping, reading wholesome material, and attending all the meetings of that day to which he is expected. To fail to do these proper things is a transgression on the omission side.

Elder L. Tom Perry of the Quorum of the Twelve implied that the way we dress on Sunday is of great import, saying ("'And Why Call Ye Me Lord, Lord, and Do Not the Things That I Say,'" *Ensign*, November 1984):

> When [the Lord] instructed us to be unspotted from the world [D&C 59:9], I believe He not only expected us to stay away from worldly places on the Sabbath, but also to dress appropriately on His day. I often wonder what happened to the good old saying, 'Sunday best.' If our dress deteriorates to everyday attire, our actions seem to follow the type of clothing we wear. Of course, we would not expect our children to remain dressed in their church clothes all day, but neither would we expect them to dress in clothes that would not be appropriate for the Sabbath.

Despite these admonitions from "living prophets," UTLM.ORG makes an interesting observation ("No Passover?" Salt Lake City *Messenger* #74, February 1990) :

> The Book of Mormon ... seems to be deficient with regard to the "Sabbath day." A search for the words ***Sabbath*** and ***Sabbaths*** revealed that they were used 171 times in the Bible, but appeared

> just 5 times in the Book of Mormon. It's also interesting to note that 3 of the 5 cases (Mosiah 13:16, 18, 19) are derived directly from the Bible, Exodus 20:8, 10, 11. It seems almost incredible that the Book of Mormon, which was supposed to have been written by Jewish people, would almost completely disregard the day which was held so sacred by the ancient Israelites.

Now, Orthodox Jews have all sorts of restrictions regarding the Sabbath day. With them, I do not begrudge this practice one bit. They have an eternal covenant with God regarding that day.

So what's my problem with the LDS view of what they refer to as "*the Sabbath*?" We need to go to the Manual folks! That is where we learn about things like Sabbath days! And what exactly is the Sabbath day according to the Bible? Is it something to be trifled with? When did it begin, to whom was it given, and is it applicable to Christians today? Are there dangers in embracing Sabbath day observances and then not keeping it? Is it errant to have a day set aside for worship?

I am going to offer seven concepts regarding the Sabbath in anticipation of today's most common assumptions, questions, and misinterpretations of it. It is a hot topic as there is so much misunderstanding of it even within the body of Christ.

Okay, first a clarification: I do not believe it is my place (nor any person's place) to judge what people do relative to gathering, worshipping, or honoring God on a specific day of the week. There is liberty in Christ – freedom to do as we are so lead. If someone wants to observe the Sabbath day, the Lord's day, the year of Jubilee, or whatever, go for it. I think God honors it when it comes from the heart and is motivated out of love for and a desire to worship Him. But it is very important to understand the Biblical presentation of what is being observed in order to help eradicate the bondage that many religious institutions place on unsuspecting people regarding the observance of certain days and especially when it comes to making it a requirement of people's "worthiness." So, if you follow a day because in your heart you desire to do so, then God bless you. And if you don't because you believe in your heart it is not necessary, well, God bless you, too. ***But if you impose a day on others in the name of God, like the LDS do, and make it a requirement for worthiness, well then we've got a problem.***

Okay, here goes:

Concept #1: There is one Sabbath day and one only; it is on Saturday.

Sunday cannot be a Sabbath day any more than your dog can be a cat. Your dog might act like a cat, purr like a cat, walk like a cat, and even eat cat food, but your dog is still a dog. The Sabbath is on Saturday. It has always been on Saturday and there are good, Biblical reasons for this, which we'll discuss below.

When a member of the LDS church says, "*Do you obey the Sabbath?*" and applies it to observances and actions on a Sunday, it is a misnomer at best, and a complete bastardization of God's Word at worst. Why?

Let's take a minute and examine the day. First, the word Sabbath means "*rest*" in Hebrew. What does it mean? Rest. It is associated with God's rest after He finished creating the world. Now God was not tired and had to rest; the rest means He stopped creating. The act of creation was at an end. The creation was finished and so He stopped. It was a break in the creation. The true Sabbath hearkens back to what God did at the end of creation:

> Genesis 2:2-3. *And on the seventh day [which is Saturday] God ended his work which he had made; and he rested on the seventh day*

> *from all his work which he had made. And God blessed the seventh day, and sanctified it: because that in it he had rested from all his work which God created and made.*

Concept #2: The practice of Sabbath observance did not begin at creation.

But there is a very important point to understand here. The Sabbath *rest* was NOT, I repeat, was NOT, *instituted* at creation. Adam and Eve did not observe a Sabbath day. Why would they? What did they have to rest from in the garden of Eden? Nothing! GOD WAS WITH THEM! And there was no labor to complete because *they* were complete! Then why is the Sabbath day mentioned in Genesis?

For the same reason Eve was called the "*mother of all living*" (Genesis 3:20) prior to her having children; the same reason Judas was referred to in the gospel of John as the *betrayer of Jesus* before he committed the betrayal: as an explanation. The Genesis record was written as an explanation of why there was a Sabbath, not as evidence of there *being* a Sabbath *at the time.* Remember, Moses wrote Genesis in retrospect. He wasn't there with Adam and Eve. And when he wrote, he tied in many things to provide to the children of Israel a Biblical explanation as to "*why*" many of their practices existed.

How do we know this? Let's read in Nehemiah. Speaking of God, Nehemiah writes:

> Nehemiah 9:13-14. *Thou camest down also upon mount Sinai, and spakest with them from heaven, and gavest them right judgments, and true laws, good statutes and commandments:* ***And madest known unto them thy holy sabbath****, and commandedst them precepts, statutes, and laws,* ***by the hand of Moses*** *thy servant.*

The Israelites observed the Sabbath *after* the events revealed in Genesis; it was not practiced *before* Sinai. So let's drop the idea that the Sabbath day was a practice from the beginning. It wasn't.

Concept #3: The Sabbath day is a commandment – one of the ten! Isn't it?

Absolutely. But what was the context of that command? In order to fully get the gist of the Sabbath day first mentioned in Exodus 20, it must be seen in the context of the people to whom it was given: he children of Israel. This is why the practice of it is so important to correctly understanding it.

> Deuteronomy 5:1. *And Moses called* ***all Israel****, and said unto them, Hear,* ***O Israel****, the statutes and judgments which I speak in your ears this day, that ye may learn them, and keep, and do them. The LORD our God made a covenant* ***with us*** *in Horeb.*

The ten commandments then begin at verse 6. When we read the ten commandments in their context (Exodus 19-24) they are inseparably connected with the *OLD COVENANT* of the law given to the Israelites. Gentiles, on the other hand, are under the *NEW COVENANT* of grace, *as all the law was fulfilled in Christ* in Whom we now live *by faith*:

> Hebrews 8:13. *In that he saith, A new covenant, he hath made the first old. Now that which decayeth and waxeth old is ready to vanish away.*

Now there are always, *always* people who want to burden others with aspects of the Old Covenant or the law. They want to apply what God had with the Jews to His new relationship with the Gentiles. Lacking faith, they want to require outward demands which tend to make compliant people feel holy. Religion wants to impose law over grace.

Herbert W. Armstrong, self-proclaimed "God's apostle" of the

Worldwide Church of God, emphasized Sabbath observance, dietary demands, and even grooming standards for women. But Hebrews explains the Lord's view of those who attempt to minimize the grace of His Son by reintroducing aspects of the law as mandatory for salvation and worthiness:

> Hebrews 10:29. *Of how much sorer punishment, suppose ye, shall he be thought worthy, who hath trodden under foot* ***the Son of God****, and hath counted the blood of the covenant, wherewith he was sanctified, an unholy thing, and hath done* ***despite unto the Spirit of grace?***

Now the ten commandments are good. But how do they operate under the New Covenant of grace by faith found in the Lord Jesus? ***They are simultaneously amplified in Jesus and made possible through Jesus.*** Let's take a few examples:

> Commandment number six (Deuteronomy 5:17): *Thou shalt not kill*! What did Jesus say about *Thou shalt not kill*? He said (Matthew 5:22), don't even get angry (amplified). And how do we not even get angry? Through faith in Him as He has paid the price for all anger (made possible by Jesus).
>
> Commandment number seven: (Deuteronomy 5:18): *Thou shalt not commit adultery*! He said (Matthew 5:28), don't even look upon a woman with lust (amplified). How? Through faith in Him who carried our sin and provides the strength to overcome that inclination (made possible by Jesus).
>
> All things are amplified and made possible through Him! *HIM*! He becomes everything to the believer. He is not one among many things; He is *first* and *only* among all things. He is not merely prominent; He is pre-eminent!

I'll explain the Sabbath day according to this amplification/fulfillment of the law with Him as our key to success in obeying it in a moment.

Concept #4: The Sabbath is said to last forever and be perpetual!

In Exodus, God said:

> Exodus 31:16-17. *Therefore the* ***sons of Israel*** *shall keep the Sabbath, to observe the Sabbath* ***throughout their generations****, for an everlasting covenant. It is a sign* ***between Me and the sons of Israel*** *forever. For in six days the LORD made the heavens and the earth, and on the seventh day He rested, and was refreshed.*

First of all, God is clear that this is an agreement between Israel and God. Period.

Second, if phrases like these are going to be literally applied today to both the church and the Jewish nation, then everything in the Old Testament that is said to be *perpetual* should be continuing today, right? How about the following, all said to be perpetual:

- Burnt offerings (Exodus 29:42)
- Incense burnings (Exodus 20:8)
- Ceremonial Washings (30:21)
- Passover Feast (12:14)

And then, so should all the covenants and all the obligations of the Old Testament, too; things like tithing, dietary laws, circumcision … etc. But the Writer of Hebrews is explicit in explaining that the entire Old Covenant has been replaced by something better!

> Hebrews 8:6. *But now hath he obtained a more excellent ministry, by how much also he is the mediator of a better covenant, which was established upon better promises.*

If the New Covenant is *better*, then New Covenant must be different. Old Covenant = writing on parchment with ink and quill. New Covenant = writing with a word processor or even a voice activated processor.

Is there anything good for us with regard to the old? Certainly. Are the writings on the old still viable? Sure. Are the words on the parchment less applicable? No. Paul writes,

> Romans 15:4. *For whatsoever things were written aforetime were written for* ***our learning****, that we through patience and comfort of the scriptures might have hope.*

The scriptures written "*aforetime*," i.e., the Old Covenant, were written for our *learning* and our *hope* – but *NOT* for our doctrine.

Is there a "better" way? Yes. Is it more advanced? Certainly. Has it replaced parchment writing? Yes. Is it a completely new approach? Not completely. It is *based* on the method of parchment writings, but is expanded into a host of other processes and applications. The Old Covenant morality remains in place, but it is actuated through the New Covenant worldview.

Don't kill says the sixth commandment of the Old; d*on't even be angry,* says the new. *Pay tithes*, says Malachi; g*ive all*, says the gospel of Jesus Christ. All is *amplified* through Christ and all is *made possible* through Christ.

Concept #5: According to the gospels, Jesus kept the Sabbath. Shouldn't we follow His perfect example?

You know, I have to admit that I hate it when people use Jesus as their personal puppet to manipulate others into guilt or shame over their little pet doctrines. If you do something they feel is wrong by *their* standards, Jesus becomes their little tool: "*Jesus would never have done that.*" But by the same token, they ignore His example on issues that are unimportant to them. "Jesus would have forgiven that," you tell them. *"We'll I'm not Jesus,"* comes the response. You can't have it both ways!

Yes. Jesus observed the Sabbath. But why?

> Galatians 4:4-5. *But when the fulness of the time was come, God sent forth his Son, made of a woman,* ***made under the law,*** *To redeem them that were under the law, that we might receive the adoption of sons.*

Simply put, the Old Covenant could NOT end until the death of Jesus and did not end until the outpouring of the Holy Spirit at Pentecost. The New Covenant in His blood is what we operate by today (Hebrews 13:20), not by prophets and Old Covenant observances.

During Jesus' life, the law was still in effect and He observed all of its requirements perfectly, so as to save all from the demands of the law. If Jesus had not kept the whole of the Law, missing it even in the smallest point, he would have been disqualified as the Messiah. But the veil of the temple being torn in two at His death signified that it was finished …***just as God was finished on the 7th day and rested, or completed, His work!*** Isn't that beautiful? Where the last day of the week was a day of rest – the Sabbath – for those under the law, Jesus said, "*Come unto me …***and I** *will give you rest*" (Matthew 11:28); not just on one day of the week but every day of your regenerated life! Here, we see another example of Jesus *amplifying* the law: Jesus becomes our Sabbath; He becomes our rest, not just for one day but for every day, and through Him it is made possible!

In that the Jews do not yet recognize Jesus as the Messiah, and that they are continuing under the Old Covenant demands, it only makes sense that they continue to observe the genuine Saturday Sabbath. But for Christians to try and observe a completely different day of the week as a commandment and calling it "Sabbath" is not only unnecessary but impossible and out of character with the amplification/completion of the law which Jesus introduced to all who believe.

Do you see the inanity of tying Sabbath day observances to personal worthiness? Yet in light of all this, people still push to observe a special day of the week and call it a Sabbath.

Concept #6: Paul regularly went to the synagogue on the Sabbath after the New Covenant began, didn't he?

Of course he did. But, come on, now! What is the context of his doing so? The early members of the body – believers – were, for the most part, Jewish. Steeped in thousands of years of Judaism, they continued temple practices even after placing faith in Jesus Christ as their Messiah. Old things take time to die and new things take time to grow. This is the entire thrust of the book of Acts: the transition out of the Old Covenant and into the New. Paul simply went to the temple to evangelize Jews.

The ebb and flow of the Old to the New Covenant as evidenced in the book of Acts was an arduous and at times bitter event. It took time. God allows for things to pass away and to grow at the same time! There is a natural overlap and exchange that occurs when God deals with humanity. Paul also wrote,

> 1 Corinthians 9:20, 22. *And unto the Jews I became as a Jew, that I might gain the Jews; to them that are under the law, as under the law, that I might gain them that are under the law … I am made all things to all men, that I might by all means save some*

And even though Paul visited the temple on the Sabbath day to reach unconverted Jews, he continued to preach the New Covenant to Gentiles as well, as a means to nourish tender roots toward maturity. Regarding the Sabbath day, Paul, the "*apostle to the Gentiles*," wrote to the Gentiles and Christian Jews:

> Colossians 2:10, 16-17. *And ye are complete in* [Christ] ... *Let no man therefore judge you in meat, or in drink, or in respect of an holyday, or of the new moon, or of the Sabbath days: Which are a shadow of things to come; but the body is of Christ.*

Have you ever been judged by others based on the food you eat, the drinks you drink, or the inattention you give to a day of the week? Ever eat out on a Sunday and find yourself receiving stares ... from other people eating out on Sunday too?

The hypocrisy and judgments kill me.

In the same passage, Paul writes in verse 14 that Jesus:

> Colossians 2:10. [Blotted] *out the handwriting of ordinances that was against us, which was contrary to us, and took it out of the way, nailing it to his cross;*

As an interesting and important side note, the Sabbath of the Old Covenant was not just the last day of the week, Saturday; it also included monthly and annual rest days. It even included a fiftieth anniversary YEAR of rest! Why don't the LDS practice the monthly "*new moon*" Sabbath days, or the yearly Sabbatical festivals based on the law found in Leviticus 25:1-22? Why don't the LDS take one full year out of fifty and celebrate the Sabbath Jubilee (verses 8-24)? The answer is because they practice smorgasbord religion, choosing a little law here, a little grace there, mix in a bit of dogmatism, and add a dash of liberality to suit. But as a whole, the theology is a blatant misapplication and misappropriation of the law, errantly resurrected from the past, applied to the present, and used to control the spiritual lives of good people who *could, WHO COULD* have daily, worshipful rest in JESUS.

Concept #7: But the Bible doesn't specify an alternate day of worship for Christians.

Specifically, this is true. It is also true that the apostles did not lay out a day to be observed by believing Gentiles. However, we do know a few things about meeting on the Lord's day or what scripture calls the first day of the week.

We know from Acts that:

> Acts 20:7. . . . *upon the first day of the week* [Sunday], *when the disciples came together to break bread, Paul preached unto them, ready to depart on the morrow; and continued his speech until midnight.*

We know that on the *first day of the week*, the risen Lord Jesus first appeared to His disciples with a commission to evangelize (John 20:19-23).

We know that on the *first day of the week*, the first recorded sermon was preached about the death and resurrection of Jesus (Acts 2:1, 22-36; the day of Pentecost was on a Sunday). We also know that, on that same day, the *first day of the week*, the first recorded converts after Christ's death, burial, resurrection, and ascension were gathered into the body and baptized (Acts 2:41).

We know that on the *first day of the week*, believers laid aside their gifts for the Lord's work (1 Corinthians 16:2)

And to Christians, the first day of the week is both traditional and filled with beautiful significance. But it is not a Sabbath day and it comes with no legislation of activities.

Summary: *The whole LDS idea of a Sabbath is just altogether wrong.*

The children of Israel were under the burden of the law and were commanded to take a day of rest on Saturday, a month-end rest, an annual rest, and a whole year rest (every 49 years) as part of their required Law of the Sabbath. The LDS do not practice a Sabbath according to *any* of these legitimate Biblical applications; none of them!

The punishment for breaking the Jewish Sabbath was death. The LDS have in their past history believed in putting people to death for other perceived spiritual failures – like interracial unions – but never for Sabbath breaking. Authentic Sabbath observance, if it was truly an "everlasting covenant," would have to include the same punishments today.

To conclude, where the true Sabbath (Saturday) was a day that mirrored God's "finished work" in the creation, Christians look to Jesus' "finished work" on the cross; we find rest in Him every day of the week. Every day in the life of a saved believer is a Sabbath, as we find our devotions, our rest, and our focus on Him.

May the covenant of grace wash over the LDS Church, releasing its members to rest in Him every day of their lives, no longer seeking a false sense of rest and worthiness based on a fictitious day of the week.

"I think perhaps the earliest doubts or questions I had about Mormonism occurred when I was a kid and our deacons quorum advisor told us that if we were ever approached by a spirit, we should to ask to shake its hand; that way we would be able to tell where it came from: heaven or hell. Right then and there, my bumpy little head started thinking, '*Something's not right with all of this*.'"

Satan / Lucifer

After presidential candidate Mitt Romney announced that he was quitting the 2008 race for the White House, the host on a

Salt Lake City radio program made the comment – the ridiculous comment – that Romney "lost the Republican nod because Huckabee publicly said '*Don't Mormons believe that Jesus and the devil are brothers*?'" In light of LDS teachings and doctrine, what was wrong with the question? As we have mentioned, Latter-day Saints believe that every single being that has lived, is living, or will live on this earth "pre-existed" in a spirit world prior to coming to this earth. All of these spirits were formed by God (and his wife or wives) out of intelligent spirit-matter which, according to Joseph Smith, Jr., has always existed as some kind of spiritual intelligence.

According to the *Pearl of Great Price*, a book of scripture the LDS hold to be as viable as the Bible, and the revelations of Joseph Smith, God the Father gathered these intelligences in some unknown way and formed spirit children out of them. Among these spirit children were those who were at the top of the glory pyramid (because they were exceedingly bright and exceptional) and then all the rest of these spirit beings sort of trail down in gradations of glory. The brightest of these spirit formations was Jesus, who was followed closely by a being the LDS call "Lucifer," which means "Son or Star of the Morning" or "Morning Star" or "Day Star."

Then the grandest of the patriarchs and prophets, like Abraham, were put together, followed by leaders in the Mormon Church, then members of the Mormon Church here on earth, and then the rest of the inhabitants of earth. As a point of pure conjecture among many LDS leaders, teachers, and members, it was long assumed (at least when I was a member and before) that black people (or any persons of color) were a compilation of the lowest spirit intelligences in the cosmos. When people ask, "*Don't Mormons believe that Jesus and the devil are brothers*?" this is to what they are referring.

And yes, in Mormon doctrine they are spirit brothers, just like the rest of us are spirit brothers and sisters of Jesus and of the being who was once called Lucifer. Now to the LDS, this teaching is perfectly reasonable. Since Jesus Himself was a spirit child of God the Father – a created being – then all the rest of the mythological characters make sense. Jesus was a created spirit child, Lucifer was a created spirit child, and we were all created spirit children.

To the Christian ear, however, the idea is categorically reprehensible. You see, Bible believing Christians have read the Manual and understand Jesus according to His Biblical identity, not the opinions of man. And the Bible is manifestly clear that Jesus is an uncreated Being; that He was in the beginning; that He is the Alpha and the Omega; and that He, in fact, created all things. All things. To put Him in the same class as the devil or man or angels is just unconscionable to regenerated Christians.

Now take a moment and ask yourself, does the doctrine of Jesus being your spirit brother make you want to worship Him more or less than the doctrine that He is Holy God, Creator of all things, Who came down and offered Himself for you and your sins? Which teaching causes more adoration for the Lord in your heart, and which teaching legitimizes Him more in your heart?

Now after the supposed creation of Jesus, and of this spirit being they called Lucifer, and of the rest of us, the LDS continue the pre-existence fable by stating that, in order for all of us spirit children to have the opportunity to progress, God the Father presented a plan where we would all get to come to earth and get bodies, and thereby learn to walk by faith, eventually returning to live with Him again *if* we are found faithful at the end of our mortal probation. Lucifer, not liking God's plan, came up with a plan of his own: *he* would come down to earth and force all of God's children to comply with the rules so that no one would be lost. As a result of Lucifer's great work in forcing all of God's children back to heaven, he, Lucifer, would get all the glory. Jesus, however, offered to come to earth and give His life as a ransom for sin and give humans the freedom to choose to return or not. God rejected Lucifer's proposal, and the spirit children of God divided: two thirds going with God and one third of them rebelling with Lucifer. A war in heaven broke out and in the end, Lucifer and his angels lost. Lucifer, cast down to earth with his angels (spirits), became "*Satan*" or the devil, who spends all his time and energy trying to get human beings who did not follow him and his plan to sin and fight against God the Father and Jesus.

Now, allow me to talk about this name *Lucifer* for a moment. In the Old Testament, there is a passage which reads:

> Isaiah 14:12. *How art thou fallen from heaven, O Lucifer, son of the morning! how art thou cut down to the ground, which didst weaken the nations!*

Joseph Smith took this Bible passage, applied the name Lucifer to Satan, and incorporated the character into the story of his fall in the pre-existence. As a result, the LDS commonly refer to Satan, prior to his fall from grace, as Lucifer. This is not such a big deal as many Christians have made the same error in thinking that Lucifer was a pre-earth name for Satan based on the same passage. The problem lies in the fact that Joseph did not teach referentially or as a process of discovery; rather, he taught that his insights came directly from God, and are therefore not subject to revision. The context of this verse, unfortunately for Joseph's interpretation, is explicitly speaking about Nebuchadnezzar. The text says nothing at all concerning Satan, or his fall, or his name ever being Lucifer. In fact, *Lucifer* means "*day star*" and this is a title that truly belongs to Christ, "*the bright and morning star*" of Revelation 22:16.

So where do *Christians* think Satan came from? What does the Bible have to say on the topic and how do the LDS use Biblical passages to support their extra-biblical beliefs? When it comes to the topic of Satan, Christians know very little about his origins, and what we do know in reference to Him is quite inconclusive. (By the way, as a rule of thumb: when a person or institution claims to have most of the answers to the unknown, it's time to be very cautious of that person or institution.)

Now, there are nine verses in the book of Ezekiel that many Christians believe speak of Satan, his beginnings, and what placed him as the darkness of this world. Literally, these passages are NOT about Satan, but are about the King of Tyre; the context of the chapter prior to these verses is predicting the fall of Tyre. But it is possible, like other passages of scripture in the Old Testament, that there is a secondary application of these passages (sometimes there is even a tertiary application) and that they speak to Satan's identity. Let's read them.

> Ezekiel 28:11-19. *Moreover the word of the LORD came unto me, saying, Son of man, take up a lamentation upon the king of Tyrus, and say unto him, Thus saith the Lord GOD; Thou sealest up the sum, full of wisdom, and perfect in beauty. Thou hast been in Eden the garden of God; every precious stone was thy covering, the sardius, topaz, and the diamond, the beryl, the onyx, and the jasper, the sapphire, the emerald, and the carbuncle, and gold: the workmanship of thy tabrets and of thy pipes was prepared in thee in the day that thou wast created. Thou art the anointed cherub that covereth; and I have set thee so: thou wast upon the holy mountain of God; thou hast walked up and down in the midst of the stones of fire. Thou wast perfect in thy ways from the day that thou wast created, till iniquity was found in thee. By the multitude of thy merchandise they have filled the midst of thee with violence, and thou hast sinned: therefore I will cast thee as profane out of the mountain of God: and I will destroy thee, O covering cherub, from the midst of the stones of fire. Thine heart was lifted up because of thy beauty,*

thou hast corrupted thy wisdom by reason of thy brightness: I will cast thee to the ground, I will lay thee before kings, that they may behold thee. Thou hast defiled thy sanctuaries by the multitude of thine iniquities, by the iniquity of thy traffick; therefore will I bring forth a fire from the midst of thee, it shall devour thee, and I will bring thee to ashes upon the earth in the sight of all them that behold thee. All they that know thee among the people shall be astonished at thee: thou shalt be a terror, and never shalt thou be any more.

Much of this could be applied to Satan. But in the end, Christians do not have a definitive answer as to his exact origins. Most believe he was a cherub – an angel - who, because of pride, fell from grace and from the service of God in heaven. I personally believe these passages in Ezekiel speak to both the King of Tyre and to Satan's existence and fall.

Now this is what the Word definitively says about Satan:

- The name means *adversary* (1 Peter 9:8) and *accuser* (Revelation 12:9-10).
- In the New Testament "Satan" is used interchangeably with "*diabolos*," or the devil, more than thirty times (e.g. Matthew 4:8,10; Matthew 12:24-28; Luke 4:6-8; Revelation 20:2; etc.).
- He is called "the dragon" and "the old serpent" (Revelation 12:9 and 20:2); "the prince of this world" (John 12:31 and 14:30); "the prince of the power of the air" and "the spirit that now worketh in the children of disobedience" (Ephesians 2:2); "the god of this world" (2 Corinthians 4:4)
- He is called "Beelzebub, the prince of the devils" (Matthew 12:24).
- His power is very great in the world; he is described as a "roaring lion, seeking whom he may devour" (1 Peter 5:8). People are said to be "taken captive by him" (2 Timothy 2:26).

- Christians are warned against his "devices" (2 Corinthians 2:11) and are called upon to "resist" him (James 4:7).
- Hebrews interestingly says that he "had the power of death," (Hebrews 2:14).
- We know from 2 Corinthians 11:14 that Satan can transform himself into an angel of light.
- We also know he can work all sorts of powers and wonders (2 Thessalonians 2:9).
- Christians also know from the book of Job that, as rebellious and independent as he is, Satan answers to God and that he must be obedient to God's rule and will; and that God allows Satan to test and tempt and try human kind.

There are several Bible verses the LDS use to support their teachings that Satan was a created spirit just like Jesus (and just like us) who fell from God's presence after a war in heaven. In addition to Isaiah 14:12, these other verses include:

Job 38:7
Revelation 12:7
2 Peter 2:4

Let's take a quick look at them before we go on.

Job 38:7

God asks Job rhetorically where he was in the beginning, i.e., at creation. God says, *Where were you…*

> Job 38:7. *…when the morning stars sang together, and all the sons of God shouted for joy?*

To the LDS mind, this is evidence that there was a pre-existence, that a plan was presented, which caused the "*sons of God*" to "*shout for joy.*" Strangely, some LDS believe that God's question of Job, *Where were you when the morning stars sang together for joy* was actually God reminding Job that he was, in fact, there?! But to Christians, the phrase, *the morning stars sang together* refers to angels, a completely different order of creation than man (see Hebrews chapter 1, where the Author differentiates between God, men, and angels); this was God's way of telling Job, "*Wake up, dude. You weren't even around yet when I was creating everything.*"

If Job had have been there when the *morning stars sang together* and *the sons of God shouted for joy,* he would have told God, "I was there!" Instead, what was Job's response to God?

> Job 40:4-5. *Behold, I am vile [compared to a Holy God]; what shall I answer thee? I will lay mine hand upon my mouth. Once have I spoken; but I will not answer: yea, twice; but I will proceed no further.*

I mean, doesn't this make sense?

Interestingly enough and as previously mentioned, the Chaldaic Bible says, "*all the troops of angels,*" instead of the phrase "*all the sons of God.*"

The Word is replete with references to angels being a different order, and having been created at a different time, than man (remember Hebrews chapter 1, for example). We know there are angels who exist exclusively to praise God and to cry endlessly "*Holy, Holy, Holy.*" We know that they are organized into troops as a hierarchy (Psalm 68:17; Matthew 26:53); their existence as part of heaven is supported in God's Word (Isaiah 6:1-3; Revelation 4:6-8).

Revelation 12:7-9

Next we have a great set of verses that the LDS use to confirm the fable of their involvement in this war in heaven.

Now, it is *nice* to be able to take passages and apply them to whatever doctrine *you* personally favor; false teachers do it all the time. In just this way, the LDS take these passages from Revelation out of context and use them to support Joseph's tall tales! Listen:

> Revelation 12:7-9. *And there was war in heaven: Michael and his angels fought against the dragon; and the dragon fought and his angels, And prevailed not; neither was their place found any more in heaven. And the great dragon was cast out, that old serpent, called the Devil, and Satan, which deceiveth the whole world: he was cast out into the earth, and his angels were cast out with him.*

First and foremost, there are all sorts of interpretations of the meaning of this passage, especially in light of the context of the entire book of Revelation. And the various Biblical interpretations are profoundly scriptural. **NONE** of them reflect the LDS idea of a pre-existence-era war. But even if – and that is a big *even if* –there was a war in heaven before the world was, these passages *do not* mean that humans were present!

This was the great skill of Joseph's: taking a verse or set of verses, removing them from their context, and using them as a proof text for his imaginative teachings.

2 Peter 2:4

A final verse the LDS and their missionaries use is in 2 Peter:

> 2 Peter 2:4 God. *spared not the angels that sinned, but cast them down to hell, and delivered them into chains of darkness, to be reserved unto judgment.*

Naturally the LDS view this passage as additional support for their false teaching of a pre-existent war involving all humanity. It is no mystery that "*God spared not the angels that sinned*" against Him nor that He will deliver them into chains of darkness; but like the other verses, these passages do not support the extra-biblical ideas taught by Joseph Smith. Let's look at the context of this verse to see what Peter is actually writing about:

> 2 Peter 2:1-9. *But there were false prophets also among the people* [of ancient Israel], *even as there shall be* ***false teachers among you****, who privily shall bring in* ***damnable heresies****, even denying the Lord that bought them, and bring upon themselves swift destruction. And* ***many shall follow their pernicious ways****; by reason of whom* ***the way of truth shall be evil spoken of****. And through covetousness shall they with feigned words* ***make merchandise of you****: whose judgment now of a long time lingereth not, and their damnation slumbereth not. For if God* ***spared not the angels that sinned****, but cast them down to hell, and delivered them into chains of darkness, to be reserved unto judgment; And* ***spared not the old world****, but saved* ***Noah*** *the eighth person,* ***a preacher of righteousness****, bringing in the flood upon the world of the ungodly; And* ***turning the cities of Sodom and Gomorrha into ashes condemned them*** *with an overthrow, making them an ensample unto those that after should live ungodly; And* ***delivered just Lot****, vexed with the filthy conversation of the wicked: (For that righteous man dwelling among them, in seeing and hearing, vexed his righteous soul from day to day with their unlawful deeds;) The Lord knoweth how to* ***deliver the godly out of temptations****, and to* ***reserve the unjust unto the day of judgment*** *to be punished.*

Peter warns that "false teachers" are a reality within Christianity. Many will fall prey to their "damnable heresies" and be made "merchandise" of. Because of them and their followers, the way of truth will "be evil spoken of." They will not be spared God's judgment, which is sure, just as surely as He cast "the angels that sinned" out of heaven; just as surely as He destroyed the evil "old world" with a flood; just as surely as He turned "Sodom and Gomorrah into ashes." And just as He delivered "Noah … a preacher of righteousness" and "just Lot" from those destruction, He knows how to deliver the godly from temptation and "reserve the unjust unto the day of judgment" yet to come.

The unjust will be destroyed; the just will be spared from destruction. Peter is using *types* in this passage to describe future events (see the section on "Melchizedek Priesthood" for a discussion on the Biblical use of types). No mention is made of a pre-existent war involving pre-existent humanity.

"I doubt there has ever been a Latter-Day Saint who has walked out of the temple for the first time and said, 'Boy that was a normal, comforting experience centered on Jesus.'"

Temples

Part 1

In this section, we will be examining *temples.*

For clarity's sake, let's go back – way back – to the tabernacle of ancient Israel. Why? Because their tabernacle was actually referred to as *"the temple of the LORD"* (1 Samuel 1:9). The tabernacle was portable and very small, a tent, actually, and consisted of three compartments: an outer court, an inner court and a Holy of Holies, the place where God's presence would be manifested.

The rites and rituals in the tabernacle are laid out explicitly in Leviticus. You can read them in that book today. These rites included ceremonial washing of priests and offering animal and vegetable sacrifices to God in a place made of very specific materials and surrounded by very specific and symbolic furnishings and décor.

There was one tabernacle and one only, no matter how many people were in the house of Israel. Hundreds of years later, King David wanted to build God a permanent temple, but being a man of blood (or violence) God forbade him to do it himself. Before his death David had "*prepared abundantly*," with all his "*might*," taking great "*trouble*" in gathering materials for the building of the temple on the summit of Mount Moriah (1 Chronicles 22:5,14; 29:2; 2 Chronicles 3:1), on the east of the city of Jerusalem. Genesis tells us that this is the mount where Abraham had offered up Isaac (Genesis 22:1-14).

When it came to this permanent temple, there was only ONE for all of Israel; it was this one temple that David's son Solomon erected in glorious splendor. Even today, there is one and only one temple site recognized by the Jews, no matter how many Jews are on earth or where they may live. For this reason even orthodox Jews have gone without making the required sacrifices as detailed in Leviticus – the Jews do not today control the temple mount location in Jerusalem. So important was this location that Solomon, needing more land surface, would not relocate to a more spacious site. Instead, he had a huge wall of solid masonry (in some places rising more than 200 feet high) raised across the south of the hill. He added a similar wall on the eastern side as well [Josephus, *War of the Jews* - BOOK 5, CH. 5).

1 Kings tells us that Solomon's temple was put together under the direction of skilled Phoenician builders and workmen, in the fourth year of Solomon's reign, about 480 years after the Exodus (1 Kings 6:1-38; 2 Chronicles 3:1-17). The sacredness of the building was vitally important and solemnity was maintained as it was built. According to 1 Kings 6:7, no sound of hammer or axe or any tool of iron was heard as the structure rose, thus showing respect and honor to God and His sanctuary. More than seven years after it had been begun, the temple

was completed in all its architectural magnificence and beauty (1 Kings 6:38).

So holy was the edifice that it stood for 11 months on the summit of Moriah, silent and unused (1 Kings 6:38 and 2 Chronicles 5:2-3; The temple was completed in the eighth month of Solomon's eleventh year and the dedication took place in the seventh month of the following year.). At that time, the dedication of the temple was held on a scale of the greatest magnificence (2 Chronicles 5:2-7:10), when the ark of the covenant (which, by the way, the LDS Church does not own, have, or possess, even though the myths suggesting it does are abundant) was solemnly brought amidst great ceremony, from the tent and deposited in the place prepared for it in the temple (2 Chronicles 5:2-14). It was then that the glory cloud, the symbol of the Divine presence, "*filled the house of God*" (verse 14), which was a picture of the incarnation of Jesus.

This new permanent temple consisted of:

1. The ***porch*** or ***vestibule*** (2 Chronicles 3:4). This entryway stood on the east side of the temple. A great court surrounded the temple (2 Chronicles 4:9-10) and contained an altar for burnt offerings, a brazen sea, and ten lavers for ceremonial washings (2 Chronicles 4:1-6).
2. The ***holy place***, ***sanctuary***, or ***nave*** (2 Chronicles 3:5), containing the golden altar of incense, the golden table for the bread of the Presence; and ten golden lampstands, five on the north and five on the south (1 Kings 7:48-50).
3. The ***oracle*** or ***most holy place*** or ***Holy of Holies*** (1 Kings 6:19). This room was to contain the ark of the covenant. This was the dwelling place of God.

There was no "endowment" done in this temple on Mount Moriah.

There were no baptisms for the dead.

There were no sealings or marriages for time and all eternity of couples or families.

There was an outer court for the masses.

There was a sanctuary for the priests.

There was a Holy of Holies housing the ark of the covenant under the outstretched wings of two golden cherubim where once a year the high priest would enter and offer sacrificial blood for the atonement of the people.

This temple erected by Solomon lasted a little over 360 years, finally being pillaged and destroyed in 587 B.C. by Nebuchadnezzar, who burned the temple, and carried all its treasures with him to Babylon (2 Kings 25:8-15). The book of Ezra tells of Israel's return to Jerusalem, the reestablishment of Judah's national calendar of feasts and sacrifices, and the completion of a second, more modest temple around 516 B.C. It did not house the ark of the covenant or the tablets of the law. While in the exact location as Solomon's temple, spiritually this second temple is a shadow of its former self.

In an effort to gain the favor of the Jews, Herod the Great, who loved opulent and grand building projects, proposed to rebuild it for them. This project began in 20 B.C. and took several decades and was not complete at the time of his death.

That temple was nearly completed in A.D. 70. Within forty years after our Lord's crucifixion, his prediction of its overthrow was accomplished (Matthew 24:2; Mark 13:1-2; Luke 21:5-6). The Roman legions took the city of Jerusalem by storm, and even though Titus preferred to preserve the temple, contrary to his orders his soldiers set fire to it in several places, and it was utterly destroyed. It has never been rebuilt.

The temple mount today, called in Arabic the *Haram esh-Sharif* ("the sacred enclosure" or "the noble sanctuary") is occupied by an Islamic sanctuary known as the Dome of the Rock. This is in the same place as the Jewish temple site on Mount Moriah. It is an important locale to the Jews and will continue to be even after Christ returns.

However, for Christians, the New Testament uses the word "*temple*" figuratively in referring to Christ's human body (John 2:19-21). That's interesting, isn't it? But it makes sense because everything in the Old Testament is a type or picture of Jesus in the new, as we have seen. So where the ancient Jews came to a physical place to worship God and offer sacrifices during the "pre-Messiah years," once He came and offered the final sacrifice, it is only logical that we now come to worship and meet Him in spiritual places. Paul calls believers the "*temple of God*":

> 1 Corinthians 3:16-17. *Know ye not that ye are the temple of God, and that the Spirit of God dwelleth in you? If any man defile the temple of God, him shall God destroy; for the temple of God is holy, which temple ye are.*

How is this? Because God no longer dwells in buildings made with hands; He now dwells within people who have been spiritually reborn.

> Acts 7:48. *Howbeit the most High* ***dwelleth not in temples made with hands.***

> Acts 17:24. *God that made the world and all things therein, seeing that he is Lord of heaven and earth,* ***dwelleth not in temples made with hands.***

You see, the reason 1 Kings 6:7 says that "*no sound of hammer or axe or any tool of iron was heard as the structure arose*" was because this pre-Jesus temple was symbolic of the final temple of God, the spiritual place within each of us believers, which no one can see or hear being built. When we are recreated as new creatures in Christ, is there hammering or chopping heard? No; that would be the work of men and religion and materials. The true temple today is without the constructs or constructions of men. Ancient Israel's temple was a singular picture with God's ultimate end in mind!

> 2 Corinthians 6:16 for ***ye are the temple*** of the living God; as God hath said, I will dwell in them, and walk in them; and I will be their God, and they shall be my people.

> 2 Corinthians 5:1 For we know that if our earthly house of this tabernacle were dissolved, we have a building of God, an house not made with hands, eternal in the heavens.

No longer does God just visit men temporarily as He did in Israel's Holy of Holies. By virtue of His Son's shed blood He is with us ALL the time, dwelling within us. Ephesians tells us that the church (meaning the body of believers, not a physical building) is also designated "*an holy temple in the Lord*":.

> Ephesians 2:19-22. *Now therefore ye are no more strangers and foreigners, but fellow citizens with the saints, and of the household of God; And are built upon the foundation of the apostles and prophets, Jesus Christ himself being the chief corner stone; In whom all the building fitly framed together groweth unto an holy temple in the Lord: In whom ye also are* ***builded together for an habitation of God through the Spirit.***

God's temple today is also the corporate body of believers "*fitly framed together*" and "*growing into an holy temple in the Lord*" builded together for what? "*an habitation of God through the spirit!*" So we have a double whammy as believers today. We individually are His temple, and He resides within us; and collectively we form a temple when we stand united with other believers!

Finally, the book of Revelation says that *heaven* is also called a *temple* (3:12; 11:19; 14:17; 15:5; and 16:17).

So this is the biblical perspective on the location of temples, or the dwelling places of God:

- in ancient Israel's tabernacle;
- in King Solomon's glorious edifice;
- in the Lord's physical body;
- in the body of individual believers;
- in the corporate body of the Church today; and
- in heaven, ultimately.

With this accurate understanding of temples and their Biblical place and purpose, how do LDS temples fit in as a "thread which runs from the beginning to the end of the holy gospel of salvation (*Discourses of Brigham Young*, page 195)?" What motivated Joseph Smith to come up with the idea of modern day temples and from where did he get all the things they do in their temples since they obviously don't come from the book of Leviticus? With these questions we stand at somewhat of a cross-roads in religious history, my friends. You see, the good news carried forth and expressed not only in the Bible but firmly understood by all Christians is that Jesus saved sinful man from certain eternal death. I am sure this is what every Christian church was teaching in and around Joseph Smith's time. But by turning from the good news and focusing on the betterment of man, the improvement of society, of bringing heaven down to earth and ultimately turning men into gods, Joseph looked to another source for inspiration other than the Bible: Free Masonry. You see, this was the aim of Free Masonry: to make men and society better.

Now, there is absolutely NO evidence of any ancient origins of Free Masonry no matter what people try to suggest. What we do know is the Free Masons employ allegorical myths to try and create an ancient history because having an ancient history lends to authenticity. Sound familiar?

Some say Masonry is tied to Solomon's building of the temple in ancient Israel; ALLEGORICAL MYTH. Some say Euclid, Pythagoras, the Rosicrucians, Moses, the Essenes, the Druids, or the Gypsies started it. MYTH. MYTH. MYTH. Many maintain that they are tied to the remnant of the Knights Templar. Maybe but this theory is UNFOUNDED. There are dozens and dozens of theories, but what do we KNOW?

The earliest records we have of Free Masonry and their guilds dates back to around 1390. There were men who were stone masons and they roamed about and worked where they were needed and where they desired. They were FREE; that is, they were not serfs, required to render service to a lord. And what did these free men do? They cut and placed and formed and centered stones and rock for cathedrals and churches. And they were allowed to work and travel *at* will. They were free masons.

Now, generally speaking, the only other people at this time who were free to move about Europe were the clergy. Because these masons were some of the only free people in Europe, they held a social status that was very desirable and envied. And the only way you could become one of these independently operative masons was to become apprenticed to a master mason, who took you into his confidence and taught you the secrets of the trade. Such an apprenticeship almost ensured a secure, creative, and liberating lifestyle for those fortunate enough to learn the secrets of the craft. All of these factors led to the stone masons to form themselves into cliques or groups or guilds. And they protected their trades upon a foundation of secrecy: secret oaths, secret handshakes, secret covenants, secret promises, and secret passwords. In order to protect their group's or guild's secrets, the masons also implemented promises of retribution, or penalties, which a "brother" might experience if he shared his oaths with an outsider.

Now, as these things always happen, a highly organized guild formed in Scotland, around A.D. 1600, becoming an official lodge. In fact, it was the Scots who first allowed a "non-operative" mason into their lodge, meaning a guy who wasn't a real stone mason, just a guy who wanted to be in the group. Acceptance of a non-mason or non-stone cutter into the guild indicates that the guild was becoming something more than just a trade union out to protect its secrets. It was becoming a social order, a fraternal organization growing in communal power and control. From that time forward, references to Free Masonry began popping up in personal journals and diaries. And the guilds began to spread.

In England, the groups usually met in bars or taverns, and on June 24, 1717 (St. John the Baptist Day) two large taverns joined forces and called themselves "The Grand Lodge of England." Five years later a manual or Constitution to be used in the lodges was printed in London. It was here that the writer, a guy named Anderson, totally fictionalized Masonic history, tying it to the Bible, the Romans, and the Greeks. These rumors and myths continue even today.

In 1734, a guy named Benjamin Franklin reprinted this manual in the city of brotherly love – Philadelphia, PA – and was elected Grand Master of the Masons of Pennsylvania. Many of the towns in early America were founded on Masonic themes introduced by active Freemasons. America's national capital, Washington, D.C., is one example.

These themes were all around when Joseph Smith Jr. came into the world. By the time Joseph could feed himself, the Masonic lodges in America were essentially fraternal organizations aimed at making men strong, pure, successful, and free of tyranny. The lodge would introduce a new member (or an initiate) to a series of rites (processes) that they call "degrees." These degrees represented the initiate's acceleration toward knowledge and an understanding of Masonry. In the beginning, these levels of light and understanding represented real trade secrets of stone masons. But as non-stone masons were allowed to join, the advancements began to evolve into a representation of ideals which purported to help men progress and become better people, better businessmen, better fathers and better members of the community. Toward, one might say, the exaltation of man.

The United States was a wonderful incubator for Masonic lodges as men sought to establish themselves among other men through a refuge of brotherly trust, a place where they shared a bond, and a unity stronger than death. They called each other "brother." Without a national religion, Masonic lodges became a perfect place for men to learn morals, to practice valor, and to belong to something bigger than themselves. Unlike functional Freemasonry in the fourteenth century, American Freemasonry was a closed and secret fraternal organization which promoted brotherhood, unity, protection, economic support and unity among adherents.

In Kenneth Winn's Exiles in a Land of Liberty, the author suggests how Freemasonry grew in early America, saying that it was by unifying themselves under oaths, grips, signs, tokens, words, and the threat of penalty of death, the Masons became a powerful group that infiltrated early American life as they grew in number, allegiance and strength.

In a sense, the Freemasons morphed into a sort of white Mafia: powerful, united, and capable of doing great good, along with some evil. In fact, when powerful Masons decided to murder one of their own who was about to expose their secrets in a book, it signaled the beginning of the end of powerful Masonic lodges in America. The man the masons murdered was named Morgan. As has been noted, Joseph Smith took Morgan's widow as one of his polygamous wives. With Freemasonry under a dark cloud from the murder of Morgan, Joseph Smith not only took the man's wife as his own, he then borrowed HEAVILY from its secret rites, rituals, and passwords, and merged them into his imaginative, non-Christian religion.

Now it is really important to know that Joseph Smith admitted to being a Freemason in his *History of the Church*, volume 4, page 551. This was prior to his revealing the LDS temple endowment or its rituals to the Church. Under the date of March 15, 1842, Joseph notes:

> In the evening I received the first degree in Free Masonry in the Nauvoo Lodge, assembled in my general business office.

The entry for the next day reads (page 552),

> I was with the Masonic Lodge and rose to the sublime degree.

Clothed in the Masonic garb of white underclothes, a robe, a sash, an apron of fig leaves and a cap, Joseph Smith was led through the Masonic rituals over a two-day period. Less than two months after having gone through these masonic rites and rituals, on May 4, 1842, Joseph introduced his own rites he called the endowment ceremony in Nauvoo. (*History of the Church* 5:1-2).

I'd like to ask my LDS brothers and sisters, whom I love and care about, three things:

1. Is that temple on which you place so much emphasis

from God or from the minds of men seeking to "exalt man?"

2. Has going inside that temple made you feel more humble, mournful, poor in spirit, as a sinful person whose souls rests entirely on Jesus? Or do you enter and exit feeling more superior, exalted, and accomplished than other human beings?

Finally, have you EVER wondered why 95% of the stuff you do in those temples doesn't even remotely resemble the plain descriptions in the book of Leviticus?

Part 2

Let's look at how LDS temples sort of took form, what they are about, and how they've changed over time.

Understand two things about Joseph Smith: first, he was a fantastic synthesizer of information (meaning he took things from everywhere, adjusted them, and made them his own); and second, he thought big – really big – in this morphing, moving, rolling fashion. Like Adolph Hitler, Joseph Smith's dreams and visions may have started small, with a mere book, but they were conceived on a universal scale. And in everything he did, he looked to out-do others who came before him, or tried to overtake him. God's ten commandments were written on stone; Joseph's Book of Mormon was written on gold. Noah built an ark; Joseph's Jaredites built ancient submarines. He could introduce snowball ideas, start them down the hill of nineteenth century gullibility, and get away with it … for a time.

His temple ideas were no different. While we know he eventually borrowed from Masonic rites and ancient Israel temple concepts, Mormon temple ideas started way, way back in LDS Church history. Around 1832, Joseph formed a snowball he called the "School of the Prophets." I suggest that this school was a precursor to the temple as the School of the Prophets was intended to be a place of instruction, a place for the men to purify themselves, and a place where holiness was stressed. In it the students were challenged by God Himself (according to Joseph) to:

> D&C 88:74. *Sanctify yourselves, yea, purify your hearts, and cleanse your hands and your feet before me, that I may make you clean.*

They were warned, like members today are warned in the temple, to mind their carnal thoughts, their light-mindedness, and their lustful desires. And, like the temple today, the perfecting or exaltation of man was the focus in the school. These elements and more (practices such as lifting their hands and repeating certain words) would eventually work their way into Joseph's endowment ceremonies.

As these internal temple ideas rolled in and out of Joseph's mind, he began to incorporate ideas of planning into his Mormon communities. In his societal visions, Joseph naturally incorporated Masonic elements. LDS author and defender Richard Bushman notes that, in Joseph Smith's day (*Joseph Smith: Rough Stone Rolling*, page 219),

> City planning ... was common for utopian and religious visionaries. In many respects, the Zion format, with its square blocks and central squares, resembled plans devised by other town founders in these years.

Many early American towns were laid out by Masons, who, with their own temples on the brain, laid cities out based on the Masonic square. Joseph took their approach and made it his own.

(I remember being taught how evident it was that Brigham Young was a prophet of God due to his miraculous layout of

Salt Lake City, with its temple at the helm and all the streets laid out in N/E/S/W squares. No one ever told me this was standard fare for both religious visionaries and for the Masons who came before them. Additionally, nobody ever told me it was Joseph who actually had laid out Salt Lake City before his death, not Brigham.)

So the Mormons went first to Kirtland, Ohio. At the same time, another group of them went to Jackson County Missouri, which Joseph, by revelation, claimed was to become Zion or the New Jerusalem. When plans were drawn up for a temple in Kirtland, a second temple was planned for Missouri. In each town, the temple was to be the centerpiece. Conflict led to the Mormons being kicked out of Missouri which ended its temple plan along with Joseph's revelatory claim that it was to become Zion.

But the Kirtland temple moved on full steam. The Kirtland temple was built at great expense. The first ritual –Joseph called it "*washing and anointing*" – was done there in 1836. This washing and anointing was nothing like the ritual of the same name done in LDS temples today, but was more like a total bath, and was literally used to clean people up. The tubs used for the washings grew to the point where they would hold several naked men or women in one tub (genders separately). The Salt Lake City temple once had these large tubs for communal washings.

Temples at the time also provided a foot washing ceremony and a time for the people to eat a sacrament of bread and wine. What Mormons today call the "*endowment*" did not exist; there was merely a sort of seeking of a spiritual confirmation.

Morph, morph, morph.

The Kirtland temple still stands today. It was unique in that it related architecturally to levels of priesthood and the order of the Kingdom of God as Joseph saw it. As a city, Kirtland fell apart because of the Church's involvement in the Kirtland Safety Society, a failed bank. The leadership moved its headquarters to Far West, Missouri. There, plans were made for a temple but construction never took place because the Mormons had left Missouri altogether by 1838.

But in 1839, having found a new home in Nauvoo, Illinois, the Saints were commanded once again to build a house of the Lord (*Doctrine and Covenants* 124). Now some time had passed with a respite from major trials. Time and experience always gave Joseph more from which to draw in creating his doctrines and practices, so the Nauvoo temple was conceived and planned on a much grander scale of "snowball rolling." You've got to try and picture this: Joseph was free to build his own dream community because the city charters had allowed him tremendous freedoms. Hand in hand with his secret practice of polygamy he began to reconstruct his temples and expand their purposes. It was in Nauvoo that temples began to serve as ordinance houses for the living and the dead.

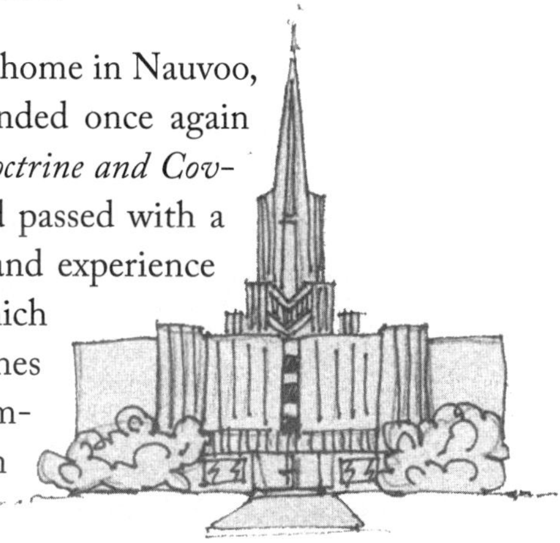

There on the second floor of his red brick store, Joseph was able to create his own "Jonestown," fresh with new rites and rituals. What did they do? They decorated the room with murals and white veils and carpets.

(Is any of this sounding Christian?)

Basking in the warmth of his unrestrained imagination, Joseph concocted his very own heavenly utopia, fueled by the power and prestige of politics (he ran for President of the United States while in Nauvoo), the luxury of having a bit of money, and the verve of intimately "knowing" many women – some with husbands and some not. Upon this foundation, upon this history, upon these purposes, the Mormon temples of today stand. The Nauvoo temple only operated for a very short time – months, if memory serves – before the Saints left it for the move west. It was later decimated by mobs.

Out west, Brigham Young, like the Freemasons before him, and as instructed by Joseph, located the temple based on the City of Zion plan and placed four of them in the centers of specific cities around the state. All were larger than Nauvoo. The first to be completed was St. George, followed by Logan, Manti, and finally, Salt Lake City.

Then temple building stopped until around 1910 when Joseph F. Smith announced two more: one in Hawaii and one in Canada. And as if poised for some future use, Mormon temples continue to be strategically built around the world. Contrary to the very words of Jesus, Who promised that wherever two or three are gathered together in His name, there He would be also. Late LDS Apostle Bruce McConkie said (*Mormon Doctrine*, page 781):

> Where [Latter-day temples] are not, the Church and kingdom and the truth of heaven are not.

Spencer Kimball said:

> Only through celestial marriage can one find the straight way, the narrow path. Eternal life cannot be had in any other way. (*Deseret News*, Church Section, November 12, 1977)

Celestial marriage, of course, is only available through an LDS temple.

Perhaps Brigham Young best stated the purpose of the temples of the LDS Church (*Journal of Discourses* 2:31):

> Your endowment is, to receive all those ordinances in the House of the Lord, which are necessary for you, after you have departed this life, to enable you to walk back to the presence of the Father, passing the angels who stand as sentinels, being enabled to give them the key words, the signs and tokens, pertaining to the Holy Priesthood, and gain your eternal exaltation in spite of earth and hell.

The first time a person does a particular ordinance, it is for himself. When I first went through a Mormon temple, which was in Los Angeles, I went in representing myself. I received all the ordinances or rites for my own salvation and exaltation. After I had personally received all the special rites or rituals and ordinances, then whenever I returned to the temple, I was doing so on behalf of someone who was dead. This is why the LDS do so much genealogy: to find the names and birthdates of ancestors who need to have their "temple work" done for them.

Do you get that?

The first time a member goes through the temple rituals, they receive all the rites for themselves. Every time they return, they are doing "the work" in the name of someone who is dead. In this way, the dead have all the required rites done for them and supposedly then can choose to either receive those works or reject them in the spirit world. By setting up this system, Joseph Smith not only added the burden upon his followers to save themselves, he also burdened them with the responsibility to save the dead. Fourth Prophet Wilford Woodruff stated (*Journal of Discourses* 18:114):

> The Lord holds us responsible for going to and building Tem-

> ples, that we may attend therein to the ordinances necessary for the salvation of the dead.

People often want to know what actually happens when a Latter-day Saint goes into the temple; I will try to explain. There are several works or ordinances that are done in Mormon temples. The rites and rituals done for the dead in the Mormon temple, initially, are these:

- Proxy baptism
- Proxy confirmation of the Holy Spirit
- Proxy priesthood ordinations

When all these ordinances – baptism, confirmation, and if male, receiving the Aaronic and Melchizedek priesthoods – are completed by a living person on behalf of a dead one, then the other temple rites are available to them. (Baptism, confirmation and ordinations for a living person are performed outside of the temple.) The first of these other rites is what is called "washing and anointing." Water and oil are spread over a person in a ritualistic fashion; upon completion, they are told, they are clean of sin.

I'm not kidding.

It is during the washing and anointing that a person is given his white under garments to wear. Then a temple worker "seals" the washing and anointing upon the individual by laying hands upon him, and the ritual is done.

The next rite is called the "endowment." This takes about an hour and forty-five minutes and includes a progression of instructions that are supposed to lead a person to higher and higher stages of enlightenment and understanding. Much of the endowment comes from Freemasonry. During the endowment, each person is taught four essential steps or stages; with each of these stages comes a special handshake, and a secret password, and a change of dress. The endowment concludes when everyone who has "received" these handshakes and passwords comes to a tall cloth doorway called the veil. On one side of the veil stands a temple worker who is supposed to represent the LORD. The person who has received the endowment approaches the tall white veil; the temple worker on the opposite side sticks his hand out through the cloth, whereupon the person rehearses all the passwords and handshakes he or she learned in earlier. One of the passwords is a secret name that everyone receives and is commanded never to reveal the secret name except at the veil. This is believed to be yet another safeguard for keeping unworthy people out of heaven.

After the person shares all the information and handshakes and secret names with the hand of God sticking out through the veil, they are allowed to enter "through the veil" (the curtain is pulled to the side) into a room called the celestial room, which is supposed to represent the LDS celestial kingdom. That is called the endowment.

The Masons called it being "endued." On the east side of the Salt Lake Mormon temple, above a door, there is a figure carved into the stone depicting two hands clasped in a secret way, illustrating the secret Masonic system used inside.

Once a person has been endowed, he or she can then be sealed to an endowed mate "for time and all eternity" by going to a special sealing room and having a ritual by the same name performed.

To Christians, marriage is for time.

For Mormons who are "sealed" in their temples and who then obey everything they covenant to obey, their sealing is for an eternity. And it is the ONLY way for them to become gods and goddesses. In the sealing ceremony, the couple (dressed in the whole regalia of temple garb) will hold hands over an altar using one of the special grips and will unite themselves to each other forever, and ever, ever – as illustrated by a set of eternal mirrors flanking the altar, which are used as an example by most officiators.

Those are the Mormon temple rituals.

Once a man or woman has done all of these rituals for themselves, they are supposed to return to the temple (at least monthly) and perform the same rituals "in the name of" someone who has died so that they, too, can be worthy and ready to enter heaven, having completed all Joseph Smith commanded them to do.

"*Well, so what?*" people often say to me. "*So what if Mormons build temples and go inside them and call it part of their religion. Why should you care? Leave them alone.*" Listen carefully to something Jesus said. He said it for a reason.

> Matthew 24:4. *Take heed that no man deceive you.*

Every now and again, someone pops up with a system that is not only utopian in nature, but it is presented as the only solution to eternal this or eternal that. When LDS President Thomas S. Monson (*To the Rescue*!) visited Rome to break ground for another temple there, someone asked him what the temple means to the Latter-day Saints. He said ("Rome Italy Temple groundbreaking: 'This is one of the greatest blessings that has ever come to Italy,'" *Church News*, October 23, 2010):

> It means EVERYTHING to Latter-day Saints [emphasis Shawn's].

I pray for the day when a future Mormon prophet will stand up and say that about Jesus Christ and Jesus Christ alone.

❋ ❋ ❋

"The Bible says give cheerfully. Mormonism says pay ten percent or you cannot receive all that is necessary to become a God. Hmmm?"

Tithing

Tithing. A controversial topic in the Christian church, tithing is demanded in Mormonism *if* you are going to qualify for a number of different things. Let me start off by telling what they are.

The first reason tithing is demanded in Mormonism is that tithing is an eternal principle, just as they say ALL principles are eternal – like polygamy. LDS Prophet Brigham Young stated, point blank (*Discourses of Brigham Young*, page 177):

> The law of tithing is an eternal law.

The first premise of tithing is that God's requirement for people to give ten percent of their income is an eternal principle. What this means in laymen's terms is that the idea that man should pay 10% to God has always existed; it was not authored by heavenly Father and it will never go away. (See the section on "Polytheism" for a discussion of so-called eternal laws or principles.)

The second reason tithing is demanded is that Mormon doctrine teaches that if you pay 10% of your annual income to the Mormon Church you will not be "burned up" when Jesus returns to earth. I'm not kidding! In the LDS scripture Doctrine and Covenants, Joseph Smith supposedly received a revelation wherein Smith has God Himself say:

> D&C 64:23-24. Behold, now it is called today until the coming of the Son of Man, and verily it is a day of sacrifice, and a day of

> the tithing of my people; for ***he that is tithed shall not be burned at His coming.*** For after today, cometh the burning – this is speaking after the manner of the Lord – for verily I say, tomorrow all the proud and they that do wickedly shall be as stubble, and I will burn them up, for I am the Lord of Hosts; and I will not spare any that remain in Babylon.

As a result of this revelation, Mormons believe that if you pay a full tithe – 10% of your income – God will not torch you upon Jesus' return to the earth.

A third reason tithing is required: Would you like an assurance that you will never leave the LDS church? Guess what you need to do? Pay your tithing! That's right. According to Joseph F. Smith, as recorded in *Teachings of Presidents of the Church: Joseph F. Smith*, (page 277):

> I have said, and I will repeat it here, that a man or a woman who will always pay his or her tithing will never apostatize… it is a law of the Lord; it is a source of revenue for the Church; it is God's requirement, and He said that those who do not observe it are not worthy of an inheritance in Zion. No man will ever apostatize so long as he will pay his tithing … Why? [**listen to this**] Because as long as he has faith to pay his tithing he has faith in the Church and in principles of the Gospel, and there is some good in him, and there is some light in him. As long as he will do this the tempter will not overcome him and will not lead him astray.

Fourth reason tithing is demanded is that Heaven will pour down blessings upon you if you pay it. LDS sacrament meetings are riddled with stories that go something like this: an old woman has an electric bill pending in the amount of $200.00 and a tithing amount of the same figure and chooses to pay the tithing, only to the get the full amount – plus a hundred more – back in some miraculous and timely way. Eighth LDS President

Heber J. Grant confirmed this promise. Quoting an Old Testament passage of scripture found in Malachi, he said (*Teachings of Presidents of the Church: Heber J. Grant*, page 124):

> I am a firm believer that faith without works is dead, and I am a firm believer that the Lord meant what He said when He promised to open the windows of heaven and pour down a blessing on us if we would pay our tithing [see Malachi 3:10].

Finally, and fifth in the line of reasons why tithing is mandated in Mormonism is that a Latter-day Saint must be a full tithe payer if he or she is ever going to be asked to serve in the more responsible roles in the Mormon wards, stakes, and hierarchy. It's not that they make *tithe paying* the qualifier, but instead they make having a *temple recommend* the qualifier – but the only way to get a temple recommend is ... Thaaaassss right! Only by paying a full tithe can one receive a temple recommend.

Tenth LDS President Joseph Fielding Smith said in the 1940 April General Conference (quoting Lorenzo Snow, *Conference Reports*, page 97):

> How do you feel when you give a [temple]) recommend to a person to come into our Temples who pays no tithing, who only pays half a tithing? How will you feel after this? You will feel that you are taking a sacred responsibility in doing that which God does not approve. He [God] has said that a man who fails to pay his tithing shall have no place among the people of God.

Is this true? Are believers – Christians – expected by God to pay ten percent of their annual income in order to be worthy enough to be called among "*the people of God?*" Are Bible-believing Christians required to pay a minimum of ten percent to the church they belong to?

When it comes to the absolute hypocrisy of LDS tithe-paying, I am sitting on literally sixty-four full pages of research. I am going to use this research in the future analyses of the kingdom called Mormonism. But for now, it doesn't make much sense for me to attack the LDS position on tithe paying when there are many, many Bible believing Christians (pastors included) who believe things like "ten percent is a minimum for a Christian to give," or who even use the word "tithing" to describe the giving they do.

Because we know where the LDS stand relative to tithing: that essentially members must pay it if they are to be considered anything in the eyes of God or the Mormon church, I think we should explore what tithing really is – from a Biblical perspective – and see whether it plays a role in the life of a believer today or not.

We'll deal more with Mormon money in future shows.

Now, as a warning, our ministry has literally lost supporters over my position on this topic because some believers insist on calling their financial contributions "tithes" as well as stating that it is the "minimum amount" a true Christian ought to give. I beg to differ.

The tithe was a requirement of the law in which all Israelites were to give 10% of everything they earned (or grew) to the tabernacle/temple. References are found in Leviticus 27:30; Numbers 18:26; Deuteronomy 14:24; and 2 Chronicles 31:5. But as a matter of fact, the Old Testament law required multiple tithes from the children of Israel:

- one tithe for the Levites;
- one tithe for the use of the temple and the great feasts; and
- one for the poor of the land.

These demands would have actually pushed the total to more

than 23%, higher than the 10% generally considered the tithe or tenth part today. I mention this just to point out that the LDS are not even close to paying the tithes ancient Israel was commanded to pay by law.

Let me offer five main reasons why the word *tithe* and/or mandatorily paying tithing could not be part of Christianity today.

Reason #1: Making a percentage of a Christian's income part of "mandatory minimal giving" flies completely in the face of the liberty all believers have in Christ.

Our Lord accomplished all things on the cross. All of the law was fulfilled and completed in Him. Beneficiaries of His free gift are freed, or released, or given complete liberty from all aspects of religious legal demands.

A day of the week for worship? Gone.

Certain rites or rituals for cleansing? Gone.

Specific prayers, holy day observances, clothing styles, forbidden foods?

Gone, baby, gone.

To re-incorporate a mandatory minimum for giving flies in the face of what it means to be saved by grace. I would go so far as to call it, counter good news.

Reason #2: Tithing, in terms of it being a demand upon believers to obey, is nowhere mentioned in the New Testament.

The word itself – whether it be *tithe*, *tithes*, or *tithing* is found seven times in what we consider the New Testament – once in Matthew, twice in Luke, and four times in the book of Hebrews. Two of the references, Matthew and Luke, are of Jesus telling the scribes and Pharisees that they were hypocrites for the way they paid tithes; a second reference in Luke was made by a Pharisee, in a parable, in the midst of professing how good he was:

> Luke 18:12. *I fast twice in the week and I give tithes of all that I possess.*

The four Hebrew references, found in consecutive verses in chapter seven, reference the fact that tithes were paid to the Levitical priests, not to teach that tithes ought to be paid now, but to illustrate a completely different point. Nothing in the New Testament instructs a believer to embrace tithing.

If it was so important in the New Testament economy, the apostles from Peter to Paul would have surely written something about it. Nowhere in the New Testament is tithing commanded or even recommended to Christians as a part of a legalistic religious system. Now certainly, the New Testament talks about the importance and benefits of freewill giving. Paul states that believers should set aside a portion of their income in order to support the church (1 Corinthians 16:1-2). But the 10% figure – which is the tithe – is not associated with these passages, not at all. Believers are to give as they are led and as they are able. Sometimes that means giving more than 10%; sometimes that may mean giving less. It all depends on the ability of the Christian, the needs of the church, and, most importantly, how they are led of God. Every Christian should diligently pray and seek God's wisdom in the matter of giving and/or how much to give. This is where passages like James 1:5 come into play.

But most importantly, and above all, tithes and offerings should be given with pure motives and an attitude of worship to God and service to the body of Christ. Giving is a form of worship; it ought not ever to be formulaic but open, free, and from the heart. One of the few New Testament passages regarding giving is found in 2 Corinthians:

> 2 Corinthians 9:7. *Each man should give what he has decided in his heart to give, not reluctantly or under compulsion, for God loves a cheerful giver.*

There is nothing here about fire insurance, nothing about paying making a person worthy, and nothing about ensuring against apostasy. Just giving cheerfully – just as we ought to worship cheerfully.

Now, as the LDS say, God did make a promise to the Israelites in the book of Malachi about giving tithes, but New Covenant Christians (New Testament Christians) were not the intended audience for this passage. How can I say that? Because we are told in Hebrews 7:22 and other places that the covenant God has for believers in His Son is a ***better*** covenant. A better covenant of grace, not of rules and percentages.

Reason #3: The fact that Abraham paid tithes to Melchizedek cannot somehow mean that Christians ought to do the same.

The very first time we read of the payment of a tithe in the Bible is in the book of Genesis, well before God incorporated it in the law. It is found in the telling of the narrative of Abraham. For this reason, many Christians believe that tithing remains part of the Christian church: it came before Moses and the Law. The fact that Abraham paid a "tithe" to Melchizedek, however, is NOT about making mandatory the giving of a tenth. It is about Abraham's freewill offering in which he gave one tenth.

Let me say that again. The description of Abraham paying tithes to Melchizedek is NOT about paying a tenth; it is about a freewill offering in which Abraham gave a tenth *to God.*

If you are a Christian who thinks we should still tithe because tithing came before the law, then for you let's take a look at the examples of tithes being paid prior to the law. The first prelaw incident, found in Genesis chapter 14, as we have observed, deals with Abraham (Abram, as he was called then):

> Genesis 14:17-20. *And the king of Sodom went out to meet him* [Abraham] *after his return from the slaughter of Chedorlaomer, and of the kings that were with him, at the valley of Shaveh, which is the king's dale. And Melchizedek king of Salem brought forth bread and wine: and he was the priest of the most high God. And he blessed him, and said, Blessed be Abram of the most high God, possessor of heaven and earth: And blessed be the most high God, which hath delivered thine enemies into thy hand. And he gave him tithes of all.*

What happened was that Lot, Abraham's nephew, was taken captive by a man named *Chedorlaomer* and some other kings who were his allies. Hearing of this, father Abraham went out and rescued Lot, then took all the booty from kings he had conquered. (Now, if you haven't already, you need to stop and read the entire passage about Abraham's tithe in Genesis 14. Reading the story for yourself will open you up to some things you may not have noticed before.) Verse 12 gives us the reason that Abram went after the four kings. Lot had been carried off with all the lawless people of Sodom and Gomorrah. Lot was not guilty of the sins that the people of those two towns were committing. According to 2 Peter 2:7-8, Lot was considered a righteous man. So Abraham made up his mind to go rescue him.

Upon his return from victory over the four kings, he was first met by the king of Sodom. It seems like it may have been a three-way meeting which included the mysterious high priest Melchizedek. Whether the three of them were standing in one place at the same time is not important. What is important is what was said by each person.

Melchizedek blessed Abraham (verse 19) because he was "*of the most high God*"; for that reason, God had delivered Abraham's enemies into his hand. Abraham then, verse 20 says, gave Melchizedek a tenth (or a tithe) of *everything* he had taken as a spoil of war with the four kings (see also Hebrews 7:4) – one tenth of everything he plundered *back from* the four kings who had plundered Sodom and Gomorrah and taken all the people captive along with Lot. The tenth or tithe was a portion of what Abram had obtained from his invasion, *not* a portion of everything that he owned.

There is no scriptural evidence that this tenth-giving was a normal part of Abraham's giving. It was a one-time event. More importantly, Abram was free to do basically whatever the local traditions allowed him. According to the King of Sodom (verse 21), it was within Abraham's every right to keep all the goods and valuables for himself. At that point, Abram shared with the king of Sodom the oath he (Abram) had previously given to the Lord (verses 22-24). You see, Abram had already decided and promised to God that he personally was not going to accept anything at all from the king of Sodom. This means Abraham didn't consider the plunder to be his own. Therefore, it had been from spoils he did not even consider his own that Abram gave Melchizedek a tenth.

The Bible doesn't tell us where the balance of the plunder went. It seems it went either to the king of Sodom and/or back to the people who were originally plundered. So here's a few things you need to consider:

1. Abraham's gift to Melchizedek was a **free will gift**. There was no law in effect and there is no evidence that God whispered "*you must pay a tenth*" in his ear.
2. Abraham's gift was clearly a **one-time event**. Abraham and Lot both were prosperous already and had not gained their prosperity from paying tithes. Abraham was prosperous because God had promised He would bless

him back in chapter 12 (Genesis 12:1-3). Abraham did not have to pay a tenth (or any amount) to God to receive the blessings promised. God also told Abraham that he would "*be a blessing*;" according to Galatians 3:13-14 that same blessing is available to all believers now, and it is the blessing of the "*Spirit through faith*." Unfortunately the church has believed for too long that we have to somehow pay our way into getting God's blessings by tithing or by sowing. **We get God's blessing in our lives by having faith in Jesus Christ and NOT by having faith in our tithing or faith in our sowing.**

3. Abraham's gift to Melchizedek did not come from money or resources that Abraham had claimed for himself. His personal valuables were safely at home. Remember that the king of Sodom said that Abraham could have all the valuables he wanted but Abraham refused to accept anything from the king for himself.

4. The only thing Melchizedek said to Abraham was that God had given gave him the victory.

Now I would say that, yes, Abraham's gift to Melchizedek is an *example* for believers to follow; but it is NOT an example of how we must *give a tithe*. Instead, it is an example how to *give free will gifts*! Abraham was free to give anything he wanted and he decided to give a tenth. We, too, are free to decide, as God moves us.

Reason #4: The fact that Jacob vowed to pay a tenth to the Lord in no way means Christians must do the same.

The second incident involving tithing prior to the giving of the law is recorded in Genesis 28, where Jacob made a vow promising to give God "*the tenth*" of all he had *if* God will be with him, provide for him, watch over him on this journey, and bring him back safely to his father. Kind of typical of old Jacob (whose name means "*supplanter*"), eh?

> Genesis 28:20-22. *And Jacob vowed a vow, saying, If God will be with me, and will keep me in this way that I go, and will give me bread to eat, and raiment to put on, So that I come again to my father's house in peace;* ***then*** *shall the* LORD *be my God: And…I will surely give the tenth unto thee.*

This is not an example of how to pay freewill offerings from the Christian heart! We give without condition and consider it gone, sometimes even expecting things to get more difficult for us because Christ taught that His followers are often persecuted.

Reason #5: The fact that a widow paid her mite (as found in the Gospels) cannot somehow mean that Christians must pay tithing.

This might blow your minds: contrary to popular belief, the widow's story is NOT an example for believers to follow. No widow ought to pay in her last mite – unless so directed by God.

Let's read the story:

> Mark 12:41-44. *And Jesus sat over against the treasury, and beheld how the people cast money into the treasury: and many that were rich cast in much. And there came a certain poor widow, and she threw in two mites, which make a farthing. And he called unto him his disciples, and saith unto them, Verily I say unto you, That this poor widow hath cast more in, than all they which have cast into the treasury: For all they did cast in of their abundance; but she of her want did cast in all that she had, even all her living.*

Now the place to start to really understand what Jesus was saying is to first read what the scriptures taught about widows; in Exodus, for example:

> Exodus 22:22. *Ye shall not afflict any widow, or fatherless child.*

And Deuteronomy:

> Deuteronomy 14:28. *At the end of three years thou shalt bring forth all the tithe of thine increase the same year, and shalt lay it up within thy gates: And the Levite, (because he hath no part nor inheritance with thee,) and the stranger, and the fatherless, and the widow, which are within thy gates, shall come, and shall eat and be satisfied.*

Throughout scripture, God is always caring for the widows and the fatherless, not exacting from them. In God's heart the disadvantaged deserve special treatment. Knowing this, let's read the story of the widow's mite *in context.* We'll do that by starting a few verses earlier, at verse 38 instead of 41:

> Mark 12:38-40. *And he said unto them in his doctrine, Beware of the scribes, which love to go in long clothing, and love salutations in the marketplaces, And the chief seats in the synagogues, and the uppermost rooms at feasts: Which devour widows' houses, and for a pretence make long prayers: these shall receive greater damnation.*

Jesus is an excellent teacher. He first told the disciples what the teachers of the law were doing: they "*devour widows' houses.*" Then to demonstrate how these teachers were doing it, Jesus goes and observes offerings being made. As if on cue, along comes a poor widow and puts everything she had to live on in the coffer. Why on earth would a poor widow do that? Jesus shows his disciples exactly how the teachers of the law were plundering the poor widows; God didn't tell that woman to give that offering. That was *what she has been taught to do by the leaders*; believing them, she gave up all she had left. ***Rather than being an example of the type of giving that pleases God, this is really an example of the kind of exploitation the religious leaders were doing to the poor widows at that time!***

Yes, Jesus did say that the poor widow *put more into the treasury than all the others*; but she is NOT the model for poor people to imitate. Jesus was not teaching that. As believers, we are NOT supposed to furtively try and out-do the rich folks. As believers we are to give freely so that widows, the fatherless, and the poor can have their needs met.

When we understand what God wants us to do, we will notice several things:

1. No feelings of guilt about the amount given.
2. No feelings of guilt about the amount we are not able to give.
3. No feeling more special to God because of the amount given.
4. No feeling less special to God because of the amount given.
5. No feeling the need to make up for not paying a full tithe by tithing your time: making knitted socks, singing in the choir, driving the church bus, shoveling snow or anything else.

People are incorrectly taught that it is a good thing to give up all they have to their local church institution, just like the widow in scripture did. Often this story of the widow and her mite is used to encourage believers to somehow prove that they too, "really love the Lord." It does not show that at all. What it does show is that millions of Mormons (and Christians, too) are victims of the same plunderers that the poor widow experienced in Jesus' time: those who falsely teach that the amount you give is a determinant of your love for God, or your salvation.

Jesus brings total freedom. Freedom to worship Him as you please, freedom to live, and the absolute total freedom to give whether it be nothing, a little, or a lot.

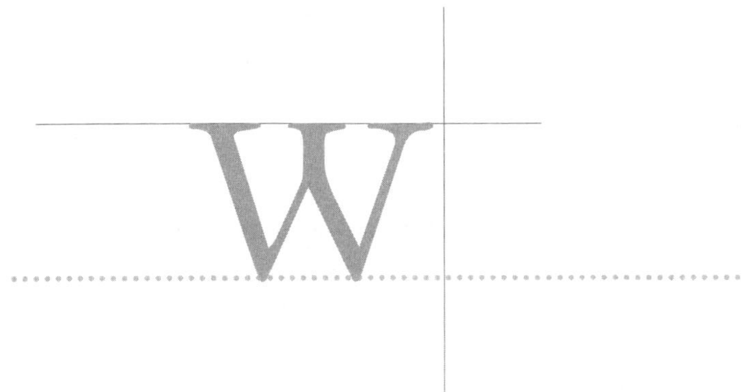

"When the philosophy of, *'if you do you are unworthy'* is introduced to a group of religious people who believe they are saved by their works and personal holiness, then an environment of *'some people are going to be treated badly and without love'* is soon to follow."

Word of Wisdom

Part 1

There are a few things that truly distinguish members of the LDS Church from people of other faiths. The practice and doctrine of polygamy or plural marriage seems to reign supreme in the minds of outsiders. Wearing temple undergarments is another. Having those extra books of scripture is right up there, too. But perhaps most widely observed is the outward practice of avoiding all tobacco products, drinking no alcohol whatsoever, consuming no coffee or tea and/or using "harmful drugs" unless prescribed by a licensed physician.

Within Mormonism, the command for abstaining from these things comes from a revelation Joseph Smith claimed to have received known as the *Word of Wisdom* (WOW), which can be located in section 89 of the LDS scriptures called the Doctrine and Covenants. I have observed that most Latter-day Saints use obedience to the WOW as the PRIMARY indicator of an individual's righteousness; this observation is valid whether the person is LDS or not, but especially if he is.

What is determined to be "obedience" to the WOW, however, is a relative matter. To some, obedience means abstaining from everything mentioned before but also including cola drinks, Mountain Dews, Dr. Peppers, meats, and eating lots of hand ground grains. To others in the Church, there are more or less egregious infractions of the law. Drinking alcohol is always verboten, as is using tobacco, but everything else is sort of open game.

Like most things LDS, there are countless applications and countless interpretations. But one thing can be said with certainty: obedience to the WOW is a badge of honor, worn proudly on the sleeve of every compliant believer. At the risk of sounding sardonic, obedience to the WOW – especially to LDS youth, teens, and horrifically naïve parents, usually mothers – is perhaps more important to members of the Mormon Church than a living and abiding faith in the Lord Jesus Christ. I will be criticized for saying this, but I think the evidence is there to support the claim. More often than not, Latter-day Saints will identify themselves by what they *won't* and *don't* smoke or drink more than in whom or what they place their faith and trust.

I wish we could somehow poll active and faithful Latter-day Saints and ask questions like:

> Can a person who drinks coffee go to heaven? How about tea? Beer? Wine? Whiskey?

OR ...

What would please God more, a man who drinks wine and truly loves and serves his neighbors and God or a man who would never be caught dead touching alcohol or cigarettes, coffee or tea, but is controlling?

I would like to ask LDS parents, *Would you rather have a teenager who smoked like a chimney but read the Word and loved the Lord and others or a teen who obeyed the word of wisdom, served a mission, and always tried to do the right, but was sort of mean, gossipy, and pious?*

Based on my experience teaching early morning seminary I think the honest LDS answers to such questions, if given, would be shocking to Christian believers.

Now don't get your neckties all twisted up in a knot. I think that making healthy choices can be a blessing to people and I think Christians are under some obligation to try to care for the bodies God has given them. Avoiding tobacco is a good thing. Abusing alcohol and drugs is a bad thing.

Coffee? Tea? Whatever.

With the exception of red wine and green tea, I happen to think the advice in the WOW is, in and of itself, wise, and that anyone who chooses to follow it would *probably* live a healthier life. So what's the deal, here? Can't I just leave this LDS issue alone, maybe even compliment Joseph for creating it (or claiming to have received it from God)? No way.

In fact, the more I have endeavored to examine it, the bigger I realize the thing is. We're going to spend the next section talking about why. I think you'll be surprised by what you learn and hear. I want to thank my dear friend and Christian sister Sandra Tanner for supplying me with some good information on the topic as well as numerous other researchers who have taken the time to find out the truth over the myth.

Ready?

There are seven general areas we are going to cover regarding the WOW:

1. We're going to look at LDS claims that the WOW is evidence of Joseph's inspiration as a prophet, well ahead of his time and the scientific evidence.
2. We will look at the setting from which this "*revelation*" came to Joseph Smith.
3. We'll examine Joseph Smith's own level of commitment to the WOW.
4. We will discuss the evolution of its enforcement in the LDS Church, from its inception to the present day.
5. We are going to look at whether or not the WOW is doctrine.
6. We will see how the LDS Church has altered its own history so as to remove unpleasant events related to the WOW.
7. Finally, we will look at how the Bible stands on such doctrines as the WOW.

To start out, let's look at the historical setting surrounding the various health movements prior to the coming forth of the WOW and during that era of time. Latter-day Saints love to use the existence of the WOW as "evidence" that Joseph Smith was divinely inspired; according to them, he revealed it (in 1833) well before modern science knew the dangers of alcohol and tobacco, coffee and tea, and meat. Before providing evidence to the contrary, let me read most of the revelation called the *Word of Wisdom* given February 27, 1833 at Kirtland, Ohio:

SECTION 89

D&C 89:1-21. *A WORD OF WISDOM*, for the benefit of the council of high priests, assembled in Kirtland, and the church, and also the saints in Zion—To be sent greeting; not by commandment or constraint, but by revelation and the word of wisdom, showing forth the order and will of God in the temporal salvation of all saints in the last days—Given for a principle with promise, adapted to the capacity of the weak and the weakest of all saints, who are or can be called saints. Behold, verily, thus saith the Lord unto you: In consequence of evils and designs which do and will exist in the hearts of conspiring men in the last days, I have warned you, and forewarn you, by giving unto you this word of wisdom by revelation— That inasmuch as any man drinketh wine or strong drink among you, behold it is not good, neither meet in the sight of your Father, only in assembling yourselves together to offer up your sacraments before him. And, behold, this should be wine, yea, pure wine of the grape of the vine, of your own make. And, again, strong drinks are not for the belly, but for the washing of your bodies. And again, tobacco is not for the body, neither for the belly, and is not good for man, but is an herb for bruises and all sick cattle, to be used with judgment and skill. And again, hot drinks are not for the body or belly. And again, verily I say unto you, all wholesome herbs God hath ordained for the constitution, nature, and use of man—Every herb in the season thereof, and every fruit in the season thereof; all these to be used with prudence and thanksgiving. Yea, flesh also of beasts and of the fowls of the air, I, the Lord, have ordained for the use of man with thanksgiving; nevertheless they are to be used sparingly; And it is pleasing unto me that they should not be used, only in times of winter, or of cold, or famine. All grain is ordained for the use of man and of beasts, to be the staff of life, not only for man but for the beasts of the field, and the fowls of heaven, and all wild animals that run or creep on the earth; And these hath God made for the use of man only in times of famine and excess of hunger. All grain is good for the food of man; as also the fruit of the vine;

> that which yieldeth fruit, whether in the ground or above the ground—Nevertheless, wheat for man, and corn for the ox, and oats for the horse, and rye for the fowls and for swine, and for all beasts of the field, and barley for all useful animals, and for mild drinks, as also other grain. And all saints who remember to keep and do these sayings, walking in obedience to the commandments, shall receive health in their navel and marrow to their bones; And shall find wisdom and great treasures of knowledge, even hidden treasures; And shall run and not be weary, and shall walk and not faint. And I, the Lord, give unto them a promise, that the destroying angel shall pass by them, as the children of Israel, and not slay them. Amen.

When I was a kid, I remember countless discussions about how Joseph was told by God about the evils in the world before anyone else in his time could understand.

It's important to realize that issues related to health were a hot and growing topic in the early nineteenth century.

Mormon historian Lester E. Bush noted that ("The Word of Wisdom in Early Nineteenth-Century Perspective," *Dialogue*, Volume 14, Number 3, page 51):

> … from a few thousand advocates late in the 1820s, the **American Temperance Society** had grown to **well over a million** members by 1834.

He also wrote (page 51):

> The leaders of the movement were most often clergymen …

What people ate and drank, and how they cared for their bodies, was a topic within the body of Christ and in the secular world long before Joseph Smith was even born! In the century prior to Joseph's "*revelation*," John Wesley's *Primitive Physic* (1747) was published and remained a prominent "*self-help system*" in Joseph's day that "*vigorously condemned*" the sorts of things found in the WOW, including strong drinks (Bush, page 51). According to Bush, Sylvester Graham (the guy who invented the graham cracker) and a Dr. William Alcott also crusaded strongly against other stimulants like "*coffee and tea,* [and] *all meats* (Bush, page 52)." Often these crusaders of health tied the relative benefit of any food to the season of its consumption. This information, in my opinion, makes Joseph's "*revelation*" on the subject of health just another in a long list of plagiarisms.

Where Joseph Smith said God told him in 1833 to eat, "*flesh … only in times of winter, or of cold, or famine*" (verses 12, 13) and "*every herb in the season thereof …*" (verse 11), one Edward Hitchcock wrote in 1831, "But in spring … the food generally, but animal food in particular, should be diminished in quantity …" (*Dyspepsia Forestalled*, as cited in Bush, page 54). Additionally, a contemporary of Joseph's, Dr. Caleb Ticknor, wrote in his 1836 book, *The Philosophy of Living; or, The Way to Enjoy Life and Its Comforts* (as cited in Bush, page 54):

> And not only is animal food proper in winter, but the flesh of old, of fullgrown animals, which is much more stimulating than that of the young of the same kind, is then the more suitable for us. As the warm season approaches, nature has provided in her bounty a diet more bland and less exciting, in the tender flesh of young animals; and during the heat of summer she has given us a variety of succulent vegetables and fruits …

But popular topics of the day that became "revelations" in Joseph's mind didn't end with meat and vegetables. Eliminating tea and coffee from the American diet was another health reformist cause at the time, too, especially when these drinks were served hot. Speaking of hot coffee and tea, Andrew Combe wrote in his 1836 book *The Physiology of Digestion Considered with Relation to the Principles of Dietetics*, (as cited in Bush, page 55):

> When made very strong or taken in large quantity, especially late in the evening, they not only ruin the stomach, but very seriously derange the health of the brain and nervous system.

I recite these quotes to you so that you can see for yourself that opinions regarding substances like alcohol, tobacco, coffee, tea, and meat were frequently discussed in Joseph Smith's day and age and to show how his revelations were right on target with what the most vocal health advocates were claiming. Even John Wesley, a Christian theologian writing *in the previous century,* had warned that coffee and tea were "extremely harmful" to those with weak nerves (Bush, page 55).

And what about tobacco? The WOW notion that tobacco could be used as an herb for bruises dates back as far as 1633, research has uncovered (Bush, page 57). For centuries, tobacco, which was referred to as "the weed" had been used for all sorts of concoctions and poultices (Bush, page 56). This is just another example of good old Joseph taking current events and philosophies and transforming them into revelations from God.

Now, admittedly, it had been thought for some time that tobacco smoke would help prevent the spread of certain diseases, such as the black plague (Bush, page 56). But by 1830, a strong anti-tobacco lobby had begun to take root on American soil which was all part of the Popular Health Reform Movement that began in New England and had spread all the way to Ohio where Joseph had resided for a spell (Tanner, *The Changing World of Mormonism*, page 469).

This Health Reform movement was spearheaded by people like Sylvester Graham, Ellen G. White (of Seventh-Day Adventist fame), the Kellogg family (yes, the Tony the Tiger Kellogg people), and C. W. Post (yes, the Grape-nut breakfast cereal family). These health reformers condemned alcohol, tobacco, tea, coffee, opium, and other "stimulants" including meat well before God supposedly told Joseph His opinion on the matter. In his book, *The Burned over District,* Whitney R. Cross (which is a great read, by the way) devotes the first six to eight pages of an entire chapter to the subject (Chapter 13, "A Moral Reformation," pages 211-217).

So while the advice found in the WOW may have some basis (some) of being good advice, why don't the LDS ever recite the story within an honest contextual setting instead of presenting Joseph as this divinely inspired guru of healthy living? We know why.

So how did the so-called revelation come about anyhow? For the most part, Church history admits the setting. In the preface to Doctrine and Covenants, Section 89 it states:

> As a consequence of the early brethren using tobacco in their meetings, the Prophet was led to ponder upon the matter; consequently he inquired of the Lord concerning it. This revelation, known as the Word of Wisdom, was the result. The first three verses were originally written as an inspired introduction and description by the Prophet.

Brigham Young, however, adds a little more information to the queue, stating (*Journal of Discourses* 12:158):

> I think I am as well acquainted with the circumstances which led to the giving of the Word of Wisdom as any man in the Church [always so humble, that Brigham] although I was not present at the time to witness them. The first school of the prophets was held in a small room situated over the Prophet Joseph's kitchen ...When they assembled together in this room after breakfast, the first thing they did was light their pipes, and while smoking, talk about the great things of the kingdom, and spit all over the room, and as soon as the pipe was out of their mouths a large chew of tobacco would then be taken. Often when the prophet

> entered the room to give the school instructions he would find himself in a cloud of tobacco smoke. This, and the complaints of his wife at having to clean so filthy a floor, made the prophet think upon the matter, and he inquired of the Lord relating to the conduct of the Elders in using tobacco, and the revelation known as the Word of Wisdom was the result of his inquiry.

Interestingly, David Whitmer, who was one of the witnesses to the *Book of Mormon*, gave other insights into events preceding the revelation, which were printed in the Des Moines *Daily News*, Saturday, October 16, 1886 (as cited in Tanner, *Mormonism: Shadow or Reality?*, page 406):

> ... quite a little party of the brethren and sisters being assembled in Smith's house. Some of the men were excessive chewers of the filthy weed, and their disgusting slobbering and spitting caused Mrs. Smith (who, Mr. Whitmer insists, was a lady of predisposed refinement) to make the ironical remark that "It would be a good thing if a revelation could be had declaring the use of tobacco a sin, and commanding its suppression." The matter was taken up and joked about, one of the brethren suggesting that the revelation should also provide for a total abstinence from tea and coffee drinking, intending this as a counter "dig" at the sisters. Sure enough the subject was afterward taken up in dead earnest, and the "Word of Wisdom" was the result.

Convenient revelations which were often tied to and even plagiarized from current events are located throughout most of Joseph Smith's work, from the Book of Mormon to much of the Doctrine and Covenants.

In the next section, we'll examine the depth of Joseph's own commitment to this convenient revelation.

Part 2

We will next be taking a look at how committed was Joseph

Smith himself to his own revelation, the Word of Wisdom, and how Doctrine and Covenants 89 was once understood relative to how it is understood today.

So how committed was Joseph Smith personally to the WOW and how has the enforcement of the WOW evolved since 1833 when it was introduced? LDS author John L. Stewart wrote a book called *Joseph Smith the Prophet*. Page 90 of this book presents a very typical representation of Joseph Smith to the reader:

> The Prophet himself carefully observed the Word of Wisdom, and insisted upon its observance by other men in high positions.

These types of characterizations are the bread and butter of LDS Sunday school teachings because they serve to keep the myth of Joseph alive while at the same time creating a false role model for LDS believers to follow. LDS scholar Hugh Nibley asked in his book, *Sounding Brass* (page 72):

> Where is the evidence that Joseph Smith drank alcohol?

Statements like this are especially evil because they come from a respected LDS scholar and so automatically anyone reading it would assume, he wouldn't ask such a question if evidence existed. This assumption is incorrect.

Prior to the WOW revelation, Joseph certainly consumed alcohol. Where is the evidence? You can read about it in *History of the Church*, Volume 2, page 26. But this was permissible and not hypocritical in the least. I would suppose that most people in that day would sneak a nip here and there. The real question is, did Joseph drink or approve of drinking alcohol *AFTER* the 1833 "*revelation*" known as the Word of Wisdom came forth?

Absolutely:

> *History of the Church* 5:380 – May 3, 1843: Called at the office and drank a glass of wine with Sister Jenetta Richards, made by her mother in England, and reviewed a portion of the conference minutes [Ten years later!].
>
> *History of the Church* 2:369 – January 14, 1836: We then partook of some refreshments, and our hearts were made glad with the fruit of the vine.
>
> *History of the Church* 2:378 – January 20, 1836: Elders Orson Hyde, Luke S. Johnson, and Warren Parrish, then presented the Presidency with three servers of glasses filled with WINE, to bless. And it fell to my lot to attend to this duty, which I cheerfully discharged. It was then passed round in order, then the cake in the same order; and suffice it to say, OUR HEARTS WERE MADE GLAD while partaking of the bounty of earth which was presented, until we had taken our fill; and joy filled every bosom ... [emphases Shawn's]

Even on the day he died, *History of the Church* records that the prophet consumed alcohol, WELL AFTER the WOW had been delivered (6:616):

> Before the jailor came in, his boy brought in some water, and said the guard wanted some WINE. JOSEPH gave Dr. Richards two dollars to give the guard; but the guard said one was enough, and would take no more. The guard immediately sent FOR A BOTTLE OF WINE, pipes, and two small papers of tobacco; and one of the guards brought them into the jail soon after the jailor went out. Dr. Richards uncorked the bottle, AND PRESENTED A GLASS TO JOSEPH, WHO TASTED, AS BROTHER TAYLOR AND THE DOCTOR, and the bottle was then given to the guard, who turned to go out [all emphases Shawn's].

We also know that as mayor of Nauvoo, Joseph Smith passed an ordinance authorizing the sale of alcohol within the city and then he established a bar right in his own house:

> *History of the Church* 6:111 – December 12, 1843: The Council also passed "An ordinance for the health and convenience of travelers and other persons." Ordinance on the Personal Sale of Liquors. Section 1. Be it ordained by the City Council of Nauvoo, that the Mayor of the city be and is hereby authorized to sell or give spirits of any quantity as he in his wisdom shall judge to be for the health and comfort, or convenience of such travelers or other persons as shall visit his house from time to time. Passed December 12, 1843. JOSEPH SMITH, Mayor. WILLARD RICHARDS, Recorder.

When *Emma* protested (good ol' Emma) Joseph shut it down (Tanner, *Mormonism: Shadow or Reality?*, page 408).

Juanita Brooks reported that wine was used amply during the construction of, and inside of, the Nauvoo temple (*John D. Lee*, pages 86-87, as cited in Tanner, *Mormonism: Shadow or Reality?*, page 408).

What about Joseph's tobacco use? In his Brigham Young University Master's thesis, Gary Dean Guthrie cited early Mormon leader Amasa Lyman, who related ("Joseph Smith as Administrator," May 1969, page 161),

> Joseph Smith tried the faith of the Saints many times by his peculiarities. At one time, he had preached a powerful sermon the Word of Wisdom and immediately thereafter, he rode through the streets of Nauvoo SMOKING A CIGAR [emphasis in original].

Recently Truman Madsen did a program about Mormonism's very own "day of Pentecost," which purportedly occurred in the Kirtland, Ohio temple. LDS reporters and propagandists paint this event as though it was a second day of Pentecost such as the one that occurred after Jesus' ascension (Acts chapter 2) when the Holy Spirit fell upon Peter and the other apostles and three thousand Jews were saved. Joseph Smith and the Mormons at Kirtland had been waiting for their own spiritual Pentecost and as the LDS tell it, they received it there in the Kirtland temple one evening. Listen to how Mormon Prophet Joseph Smith described the event (*History of the Church* 2:428):

> Brother George A. Smith arose and began to prophesy, when a noise was heard like the sound of a rushing mighty wind, which filled the Temple, and all the congregation simultaneously arose, being moved upon by an invisible power; many began to speak in tongues and prophesy; others saw glorious visions; and I beheld the Temple was filled with angels, which fact I declared to the congregation. The people of the neighborhood came running together (hearing an unusual sound within, and seeing a bright light like a pillar of fire resting upon the Temple), and were astonished at what was taking place.

What the LDS leaders don't include in the retelling of this supposedly blessed event is how much alcohol was consumed just prior to its occurrence.

William Harris, author of *Mormonism Portrayed* (1841) reports the following (Tanner, *Mormonism: Shadow or Reality?*, page 412):

> In the evening, they met for the endowment. The fast was then broken by eating light wheat bread, and drinking as much wine as they saw proper. Smith knew well how to infuse the spirit which they expected to receive; so he encouraged the brethren to drink freely, telling them that the wine was consecrated, and would not make them drunk ... they began to prophecy, pronounce blessings upon their friends, and curses on their enemies. If I should be so unhappy as to go to the regions of the damned, I would never expect to hear language more awful, or more becoming the infernal pit, than was uttered that night.

Charles Walker, a faithful Latter-day Saint, recorded the following in his journal ("Diary of Charles L. Walker," page 35, as cited in Tanner, *Mormonism: Shadow or Reality?*, page 412):

> Sun., Nov. 21, 1880 … Bro. Milo Andress … Spoke of blessings and power of God manifested in the Kirtland Temple. Said he once asked the Prophet [why] he (Milo) did not feel the power that was spoken of as the power that was felt on the day of the Pentecost? ... when we had fasted for 24 hours and partaken of the Lord's supper, namely a piece of bread as big as your double fist and a half pint of wine in the Temple. I was there and saw the Holy Ghost descend upon the heads of those present like cloven tongues of fire.

In a February 27, 1885 statement, one Mrs. Alfred Morley said (*Naked Truths About Mormonism*, page 2, as cited in Tanner, *Mormonism: Shadow or Reality?*, page 412):

> I have heard many Mormons who attended the dedication, or endowment of the Temple say that very many became drunk... The Mormon leaders would stand up to prophesy and were so drunk they said they could not get it out and would call for another drink. Over a barrel of liquor was used at the service.

Isaac Aldrich also stated (*Naked Truths About Mormonism*, page 3, as cited in Tanner, *Mormonism: Shadow or Reality?*, page 412):

> My brother, Hazen Aldrich, who as president of the Seventies, told me when the Temple was dedicated a barrel of wine was used and they had a drunken "pow-wow."

Another witness having information regarding this incident, Stephen H. Hart, commented (*Naked Truths About Mormonism*, page 3, as cited in Tanner, *Mormonism: Shadow or Reality?*, page 412):

> Mr. McWhithey, who was a Mormon...said he attended a service which lasted from 10 A.M. until 4 P.M., and there was another service in the evening. The Lord's Supper was celebrated

> and they passed the wine in pails several times to the audience, and each person drank as much as he chose from a cup. He said it was mixed liquor and he believed the Mormon leaders intended to get the audience under the influence of the mixed liquor, so they would believe it was the Lord's doings ... . When the liquor was repassed, Mr. McWhithey told them he had endowment enough, and said he wanted to get out of the Temple, which was densely crowded.

The Des Moines *Daily News* reported the following on October 16, 1886, including a statement from David Whitmer, one of the three witnesses to the Book of Mormon (Tanner, *Changing World of Mormonism*, pages 109-110):

> The great heavenly "visitation," which was alleged to have taken place in the temple at Kirtland, was a grand fizzle. The elders were assembled on the appointed day, which was promised would be a veritable day of Pentecost, but there was no visitation. No Peter, James and John; no Moses and Elias, put in an appearance. "I was in my seat on that occasion," says Mr. Whitmer, "and I know that the story sensationally circulated, and which is now on the records of the Utah Mormons as an actual happening, was nothing but a trumped up yarn ..."

Finally, and certainly the most convincing source for a seeking Latter-day Saint, are the comments from LDS Apostle George A. Smith which indicates that wine was used liberally at the event. In a sermon preached at the Salt Lake tabernacle, he said (*Journal of Discourses* 2:216)

> ... after the people had fasted all day, they sent out and got wine and bread ... they ate and drank...and continued to do so until some of the High Counsel of Missouri stepped into the stand, and, as righteous Noah did when he awoke from his wine, commenced to curse their enemies.

This is just one more example of the myth-making used in Mormonism to keep *YOU* believing in its fairy tale of a story.

Let me give you something to think about regarding the junk the "brethren" have pulled to keep people in the dark about the reality of their history. What does it say to you when you read of a supposed revelation from God to Joseph and Joseph doesn't follow it himself? Do you think Joseph really received such a revelation? What does it say to you when in one of the most important "historical moments" of Mormon spiritual history – the Kirtland Pentecost – that great amounts of alcohol had been provided, consumed and, yes, even prescribed? What does it say to you when the Church you accept as true *alters* the historical record? Why do you want to stand up and defend something that has lied to you?

Again, I think the WOW is great advice. But that is all it is. Walk into any chain bookstore on earth and you can find advice on what to eat, drink and avoid. But Joseph presented his advice as a direct revelation from Almighty God, and then had the audacity to not even comply with it. What does that say about him and his supposed revelatory claims?

Part3

In the journals and Histories of the Church, as well as other reliable historical places, the evidence is ample that the early Latter-day Saints understood the WOW in vastly different ways. After all, it was given by way of sound advice, and not as a commandment. Remember, that in general the Christian community was far more legalistic in these matters of drink and smoke than the Mormons were in their first 70 years of existence, with men in leadership – like Joseph Smith, Brigham Young, and B. H. Roberts – greatly enjoying in partaking of the fruits of the earth.

In 1898, nearly 45 years after the death of Joseph Smith, the First Presidency and Quorum of the Twelve Apostles sat down and deliberated over the WOW. Lorenzo Snow, who was the president of the twelve apostles, believed that the WOW should be lived to the letter, including abstinence from meat except in extreme circumstances. His reason was because Joseph Smith taught that animals have spirits. The prophet at the time, Wilford Woodruff agreed, but said they should hold off on enforcing it, especially the not eating meat part.

The minutes of that meeting read (Thomas G. Alexander, "The Word of Wisdom: From Principle to Requirement," *Dialogue: A Journal of Mormon Thought*, Volume 14, Number 3, page 78):

> President Woodruff said he regarded the Word of Wisdom in its entirety as given of the Lord for the LDS to observe, but he did not think Bishops should withhold [temple] recommends from persons who did not adhere strictly to it.

That was 1898.

Now, either the WOW was from God's mouth or it was not. Either it was to be obeyed as a display of worthiness, or it was not. Either a man was defiled by having a drink, or a smoke, or he was not. But it seems that even after the turn of the century, LDS leaders couldn't agree upon what was true and right and what was not.

After Lorenzo Snow became president of the Church he again stood fast for strict obedience to the WOW – including NOT eating meat – but some of the twelve apostles did not believe this included drinking beer, especially good Danish beer and currant wine (Thomas G. Alexander, "The Word of Wisdom: From Principle to Requirement," *Dialogue: A Journal of Mormon Thought,* Volume 14, Number 3, page 78).

Apostles Anthon H. Lund and Matthias Cowley enjoyed Danish beer and currant wine, as did Charles W. Penrose. Emmaline B. Wells, a member of Relief Society presidency and later its president, enjoyed an occasional cup of coffee, and George Albert Smith took brandy "for medicinal reasons" (Alexander, pages 78-79).

Hey, that's why I drink tequila! (That's a joke, by the way!)

Apostles George Teasdale and President Woodruff thought eating pork was a far more serious crime than drinking coffee or tea. Heber J. Grant appears to have been the most vocal in favor for total WOW adherence; he was a leader in the state prohibition movement. Grant was outraged – outraged – when some of the apostles actually opposed the prohibition of beer sales at the Saltair Saloon (Alexander, page 79).

When Lorenzo Snow died, and Joseph F. Smith took his place, he echoed Heber J. Grant's strong opinions for the WOW – but restrictions on the use of meat were dropped altogether at this time (Alexander, page 79).

I love it when the word of God is sort of just open to what suits you.

By 1902, the First Presidency and twelve agreed "not to fellowship with anyone who operated or frequented saloons" (I wonder if this would have included the Marriott Hotel guys at the time?) and they urged the stake presidents to refuse to give flagrant violators of the WOW temple recommends. They did suggest leniency for those old men who liked tobacco and old ladies who enjoyed their tea (Alexander, page 79).

By mid-1905 the campaign to either obey the WOW or be denied Church leadership positions began to take hold under the leadership of the First Presidency. In staying consistent with this focus, they made an administrative change, beginning July of 1906, to replace the sacramental wine in their temple meetings with water (Alexander, page 79).

Now, really pause and think about this. Jesus *HIMSELF* drank wine and commanded us to drink wine in remembrance of His shed blood. And the LDS drink water! In fact, it is often rotten, filthy tap water that has sat in the pipes for a week and tastes absolutely horrific. I mean, there is just no respect for the LORD. Couldn't they at least use purified water? More to the point, couldn't they at least use wine of the grape as Jesus did?

Now if you are LDS, this may seem insignificant to you. But it's not. It is symbolic of His shed blood by which Christians are cleansed!

Between the years of 1907 and 1917, there were a number of factors that led to a greater allegiance and enforcement of the WOW, including the prohibition movement and some other pressing political issues faced by the Church.

In 1915, President Joseph F. Smith took the enforcement a little farther, saying (Alexander, page 82):

> Young or middle aged men who have had experience in the Church should NOT be ordained to the priesthood nor recommended to the privileges of the House of the Lord [**meaning no temple attendance allowed**] unless they will abstain from the use of tobacco and intoxicating drinks [emphasis Shawn's].

And the noose just kept getting tighter and tighter, to the point where only those who outwardly conformed were allowed the opportunity for true salvation: the celestial kingdom. In 1921, under Heber J. Grant, church leadership made adherence to the WOW a requirement for admission to the temple. With prohibition under way, the 1920s also introduced some legislation to ban the sale of tobacco in Utah (Alexander, page 82). A 1923 *Improvement Era* article "argued that tobacco users naturally linked themselves with evil persons such as profaners, criminals, vagrants, and prostitutes (Alexander, page 83)."

You know what, this might actually be true. I mean on scale, I think we would find that those lower on the social and socio-economic scale are smokers. But this isn't the issue. The issue is who the hell do they think they are? Really? Now I've got a daughter who likes to smoke the weed. And she enjoys alcohol at times. And while I think she would be far better off without them in her life, she has got a heart, and a soul, and a gift of love unlike many I have ever seen!

Who do they think they are? And do they really believe that God is impressed with them for these perspectives? GOSH!

With the proscriptions in the original revelation regarding the use of meat being ignored, some members of the church started getting the idea that there were some other substances that needed to be banned: caffeinated drinks! In March of 1917, Frederick J. Pack of the University of Utah published an article in the LDS magazine, Improvement Era, which asked the question, *"Should the LDS drink Coca-Cola?"* His answer was NO. Why? Because even though it was not prohibited in the WOW, such drinks contained the same ingredients as coffee and tea (Alexander, page 84).

One rule establishing "worthiness" will always lead to more. So rabid was the anti-caffeine sentiment that the Coca-Cola company paid a visit to President Heber Grant, complaining that, as a result of this fanaticism, lies were being circulated about their product, like for example, that it contained five times as much caffeine as coffee (when it was able to be shown that there are

1.7 grams of caffeine in a cup of Joe and only .43 grams in the same amount of Coke) (Alexander, page 84). The LDS leadership has not taken an official stand on the use of caffeinated soft drinks but merely say that members should not use any substance that is harmful to the body or addictive.

Since obedience to the WOW became requisite for exaltation in Mormondom, various opinions and trends have surfaced among its members as to what is "allowed" and what is not. Nevertheless, a temple recommend is almost never given to a person who consumes coffee, tea, alcoholic beverages of any sort, tobacco products of any kind, and/or drugs without a prescription from a licensed medical practitioner.

Perhaps the most important thing about the WOW is its canonicity. Is it doctrine?

Now, I have LDS people adamantly contend that the Adam/God teaching was not doctrine, because it was never canonized. So, on the one hand, was *Doctrine and Covenants* section 89 canonized? There was a sustaining vote taken in 1880 that the *Doctrine and Covenants* be binding on the Church membership – which passed (Alexander, page 85). So, based on this evidence, I could agree that the WOW is LDS doctrine.

BUT ... *BUT* ... what *IS* the doctrine? What *DOES* the revelation say? It says that it was "given as a principle with promise ...not by commandment or constraint ..." So, if the WOW as it was received was canonized, and truly LDS doctrine, what is the doctrine? The canonized doctrine is THAT THE WOW was given *NOT* as a commandment but a principle. There is *NO* contemporary edict, announcement, or alteration from the LDS church to alter this.

The true value in this issue really has nothing to do with the

WOW or the contents or obedience to it itself. It has to do with inconsistency in Mormon apologetics. It has to do with authority and power and manipulation taking precedence over God's gentle love in people's lives. It has to do with salvation and with God's acceptance being twisted to meet institutional demands so as to control the masses.

Part 4

In this next section, we're going to read what the Bible was to say about such things as the Mormon Word of Wisdom. I think you will be surprised.

To review: We've had a brief but good look at what the LDS call their Word of Wisdom, or code of health: you know, no tea, coffee, alcohol, tobacco, or harmful drugs. We've looked at the origin of the revelation, and Joseph's subsequent failure to obey it, and how it was optional for seventy five years but today has become a mandate for salvation – salvation defined as an afterlife with God – and a primary indicator of whether or not one is a "good" person.

Well, just what does the Bible say about what human beings eat and drink, smoke or ingest? Let's step back a moment and look first at what God had in mind relative to what His people consumed. (Now, as we move along through this discussion, gently ask yourself, why did our great God Almighty – Creator of all things – create coffee beans, and tea leaves, and grapes that ferment, and animal meat that taste so good?) Now originally, God granted the use of vegetables and fruits for the food of man, with the exception of the fruit of the tree of knowledge of good and evil. We read in Genesis,

> Genesis 1:29. *And God said, Behold, I have given you* ***every herb*** *bearing seed, which is upon the face of all the earth, and* ***every tree,***

> *in the which is the fruit of a tree yielding seed; to you it shall be for meat [i.e., food].*

I am of the personal opinion that the use of animals as food was probably not known to the antediluvians (the people prior to Noah). I may be wrong about this, though. Nevertheless, it seems that after the flood, Noah is then given a direct word from God on the subject of eating animals:

> Genesis 9:2-4. *And the fear of you and the dread of you shall be upon every beast of the earth, and upon every fowl of the air, upon all that moveth upon the earth, and upon all the fishes of the sea;* ***into your hand are they delivered. Every moving thing that liveth shall be meat for you; even as the green herb*** *have I given you all things. But flesh with the life thereof, which is the blood thereof, shall ye not eat.*

Pretty straightforward stuff, eh?

When the children of Israel fled from Egypt, God wanted to raise up and protect His peculiar people and prevent them from mixing with the surrounding pagan nations. He had a covenant bloodline to continue from which Messiah was promised. Because of this, He instituted a number of things that would keep them separate – and their dietary laws were very effective at accomplishing this. We can read about them in Leviticus chapter 11. These restrictions automatically and immediately segregated the children of Israel from the rest of the pagan world.

This was, in my opinion, the primary motivation for the law. There were health issues, too, but primarily it was to set them apart.

But where Joseph Smith's WOW has God saying that meat was not so good, and that strong drink and wine are not so good, there was actually a lot of liberty in God's plan for the children of Israel in what they could eat and drink. In fact, listen to the tenor of the Lord's commands when it came to this liberty:

In Deuteronomy 14:25 there is a discussion about money, then in verse 26 it says

> Deuteronomy 14:26. *And thou shalt bestow that money* ***for whatsoever thy soul lusteth after****, for oxen, or for sheep, or for wine,* ***or for strong drink****, or for whatsoever thy soul desireth: and thou shalt eat there before the LORD thy God, and thou shalt rejoice, thou, and thine household.*

So where God's covenant people were permitted to eat as much meat of those types as they so lusted after, and to buy and drink strong drink and wine, Joseph's God out-did himself with the Mormons by saying, "*no, no, no*" to such things, even though Joseph continued to say, "*yes, yes, yes.*" It's pure *MAN*-ipulation.

Being introduced to the One true and living God and to the law with its dietary commands served to keep the Israelites peculiar and separated from the cultures surrounding them; but it did *little* to separate them from sin and rebellion. This fact underscores the difference between the Israelites living by the law and Christians living by faith in this dispensation of grace. Grace can and does do just that: separate the believer from sin and rebellion.

In Acts chapter 15, well after Jesus ascended into heaven, a group of Pharisees attempted to reinstitute part of the law – the rite of circumcision – back upon the backs (or other parts) of Gentile converts. In response to this Pharisaical appeal to religion, Luke observes that,

> Acts 15:6-11. … *the apostles and elders came together for to consider of this matter. And when there had been much disputing, Peter rose up, and said unto them, Men and brethren, ye know how*

that a good while ago God made choice among us, that the Gentiles by my mouth should hear the word of the gospel, and believe. And God, which knoweth the hearts, bare them witness, ***giving them the Holy Ghost, even as he did unto us;*** *And put no difference between us and them,* ***purifying their hearts by faith.*** *Now therefore, why tempt ye God,* ***to put a yoke upon the neck of the disciples, which neither our fathers nor we were able to bear?*** *But we believe that* ***through the grace*** *of the Lord Jesus Christ we shall be saved, even as they.*

The apostles knew what it would take to keep them and Gentile converts from their sinful and rebellious ways; it was not circumcision, special days of worship, or restrictions from eating or drinking certain foods, but by grace through faith! Herein lies a main difference between the law and grace, religion and relationship, outward adherence verses inward change. In preparation for what He was about to accomplish, Jesus began to introduce to His followers some transitional thinking that moved them away from outward observances and toward inward allegiance, saying in Matthew:

Matthew 15:11. *Not that which goeth into the mouth defileth a man; but that which cometh out of the mouth, this defileth a man.*

Did you hear that, bishop? Stake president? Thomas Monson?

After Jesus said this, the disciples came to Him and told Him that such teachings were "offending the Pharisees" (Matthew 15:12).

Jesus replied:

Matthew 15:17-18. *Do not ye yet understand, that whatsoever entereth in at the mouth goeth into the belly, and is cast out into the draught? But those things which proceed out of the mouth come forth* ***from the heart; and they defile the man.***

Listen: *I would place ALL my money on the drinker, the smoker, the addict who knows the Lord's Gospel of grace a trillion times over a teetotaling ascetic who thinks never smoking or drinking makes him worthy or righteous for the kingdom of heaven.* And yet Mormonism today has resurrected these legalisms and declares that all must obey who want to receive what they say is necessary for salvation: their temple rites, and rituals, and legalisms.

Paul made the point perfectly clear in Romans where He wrote:

> Romans 14:17. *For the kingdom of God is not meat and drink; but righteousness, and peace, and joy in the Holy Ghost.*

You see, once Jesus erased sin, death, disease, and outer and inner filth permanently from the lives of all who believe, past, present, and future, what people choose to eat or drink became a big, fat, non-event. Excuse me? Excuse me, but did you just hear what I said? I said:

> Once Jesus erased sin, death, disease, and outer and inner filth from the lives of all who believe …

There is no need for special dietary rules and regulations any longer to keep people separate and peculiar. God's covenant has been fulfilled in Christ. *All* are invited into the kingdom as the way had been cleared for all to enter in. Did you hear that part, too? The way was open to all: black people, white people, Gentile people, Jewish people, women people, men people, slave people, midget people, gay and straight people, sinful people, smoker people, drinker people, people who dress badly people, people who dress goodly people, rich people, poor people, armless and legless people – all freaking people, *REGARDLESS* of who they are, what they have done, OR even what they continue to do to enter into the unconditional love, peace, forgiveness, and joy that comes through faith in Jesus. You get it? Huh?

How about some more?

Paul wrote:

> 1 Corinthians 8:8. *But **meat commendeth us not to God:** for neither, if we eat, are we the better; neither, if we eat not, are we the worse.*

Speaking of legalisms, just the sort Mormons try to enforce, Paul wrote to the Colossian believers:

> Colossians 2:16. *Let no man therefore judge you in meat, or in drink, or in respect of an holyday, or of the new moon, or of the sabbath days …*

Does this sound like Mormonism?

Paul wrote to Timothy that,

> 1 Timothy 4:1-3. *Now the Spirit speaketh expressly that in the latter times some shall depart from the faith, giving heed to seducing spirits, and doctrines of devils; speaking lies in hypocrisy [hypocrisy means saying one thing and doing another, Joseph]; having their conscience seared with a hot iron [that means acting and speaking outside of God's will without a care]; Forbidding to marry, and **commanding to abstain from meats**, which God hath created to be received with thanksgiving of them which believe and know the truth.*

All this being said, there is perhaps no better summation of the biblical Christian approach to eating and drinking of any and all things than what is found in Romans chapter 14.

So profound, so important, *so contradictory* is this chapter from the LDS demands for Word of Wisdom worthiness that I think it worth the time to read all of it. It won't take too long. So let's look at Romans 14 and read yet another biblical teaching that is at odds with contemporary Mormon doctrine and practice:

Romans 14:1-23. *Him that is weak in the faith receive ye, but not to doubtful disputations. For one believeth that he may eat all things: another, who is weak, eateth herbs.* ***Let not him that eateth despise him that eateth not; and let not him which eateth not judge him that eateth:*** *for God hath received him. Who art thou that judgest another man's servant? to his own master he standeth or falleth. Yea, he shall be holden up: for God is able to make him stand. One man esteemeth one day above another: another esteemeth every day alike. Let every man be fully persuaded in his own mind. He that regardeth the day, regardeth it unto the Lord; and he that regardeth not the day, to the Lord he doth not regard it. He that eateth, eateth to the Lord, for he giveth God thanks; and he that eateth not, to the Lord he eateth not, and giveth God thanks. For none of us liveth to himself, and no man dieth to himself. For whether we live, we live unto the Lord; and whether we die, we die unto the Lord: whether we live therefore, or die, we are the Lord's. For to this end Christ both died, and rose, and revived, that he might be Lord both of the dead and living. But why dost thou judge thy brother? or why dost thou set at nought thy brother? for we shall all stand before the judgment seat of Christ. For it is written, As I live, saith the Lord, every knee shall bow to me, and every tongue shall confess to God. So then every one of us shall give account of himself to God. Let us not therefore judge one another any more: but judge this rather, that no man put a stumblingblock or an occasion to fall in his brother's way.* ***I know, and am persuaded by the Lord Jesus, that there is nothing unclean of itself: but to him that esteemeth any thing to be unclean, to him it is unclean. But if thy brother be grieved with thy meat, now walkest thou not charitably. Destroy not him with thy meat, for whom Christ died.*** *Let not then your good be evil spoken of:* ***For the kingdom of God is not meat and drink; but righteousness, and peace, and joy in the Holy Ghost. For he that in these things serveth Christ is acceptable to God, and approved of men.*** *Let us therefore follow after the things which make for peace, and things wherewith one may edify another.* ***For meat destroy not the work of God.*** *All things indeed are pure; but it is evil for that man who eateth with offence. It is good neither to eat flesh, nor to drink wine, nor any thing whereby thy brother stumbleth, or is offended, or is made weak. Hast thou faith? have it to thyself before God.*

> *Happy is he that condemneth not himself in that thing which he alloweth. And he that doubteth is damned if he eat, because he eateth not of faith: for whatsoever is not of faith is sin.*

My friends, ANY FOOL can make a rule and ANY leader can talk like Peter (that second line is an original) but the liberty of the gospel of Jesus Christ cannot be counterfeited or feigned. There is no “worthiness” that God sees in you because of what you eat or drink. Righteousness and worthiness were singularly offered in the form of God’s Son, once and for all.

Eat well? Sure. Avoid addictions? Absolutely! It’s good. But don’t ever think you are worthy or better than another because you have been wise where others have stumbled, tripped or fallen. Because where you might have clear lungs and a healthy body, they may possess the better part: a heart for the Lord.

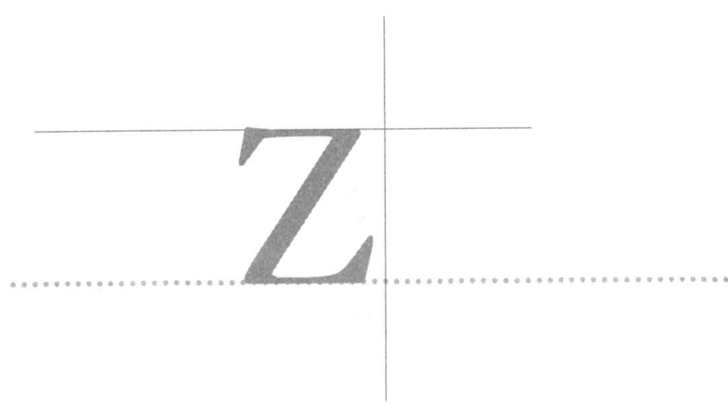

"In attempting to make Mormonism the new Israel (so to speak) you have never read a more confusing and babbling body of writings than their writings of Zion. And yet they continue to press to make this world *their* world, and to call it Zion."

Zion

Step back with me for a minute – back almost 190 years, back to the eastern states of a new America. Mormonism started not with a teenage boy, but with a family by the name of Smith. Before Joseph Smith, the founder of Mormonism, was even born, his family – grandparents, parents, and uncles – believed that there should only be one "true church" on earth, that it needed to be restored because it was completely lost, that every single person on earth would experience some sort of salvation, and that the author of such a restoration would come out of the Smith home.

This family had a father who had lost everything in a failed business venture, turned to alcohol and treasure seeking, and passed along his "skills" for using rods and stones to his middle son, whom he had become convinced would restore the lost primitive church of Jesus Christ back to earth. This same father had also had vivid visions and dreams, the second of which included the following. In this dream or vision (Lucy Mack Smith, *Biographical Sketches of Joseph Smith the Prophet and His Progenitors for Many Generations*, pages 48-50, as cited in Grant Palmer, *An Insider's View of Mormon Origins*, page 71):

> I was traveling in an **open, desolate field** ... **My guide** ... said, "This is the **desolate world**"... and I came to a narrow path ... I beheld a **beautiful stream of water** ... I could see a rope, running along the bank of it ... [I saw] **a tree** such as I had never seen before. It was exceedingly handsome ... Its beautiful branches ... **bore a kind of fruit** ... as **white as snow** ... I drew near and began to eat of it, and I found it **delicious beyond description** ... [and I thought that] I must bring my wife and children, that they may partake with me. Accordingly, **I brought my family** ... [and] we all commenced eating ... We were **exceedingly happy**, insomuch that our joy could not easily be expressed. While thus engaged, I beheld **a spacious building** ... [that] **appeared to reach to the very heavens.** It was **full of ... people**, who were very **finely dressed** ... [T]hey **pointed the finger of scorn** at us ... But their contumely [arrogance] we utterly disregarded ... [in preference to] the fruit that was so delicious. He **[the guide] told me it was the pure love of God**, shed abroad in the hearts of all those who love him ..." [L]ook yonder [he said], you have **two more [children], and you must bring them also**"... I asked my guide what was the meaning of the spacious building which I saw. He replied, "[I]t is Babylon, it is Babylon, and it must fall."

This dream, reported by Joseph Smith Jr.'s mother, Lucy Mack Smith, was dated 1811, when Mormonism's founder was only six or seven years old. ***Remember this dream of Joseph's father for later.***

Now, official LDS church history today tells us that in 1820, when Joseph Smith was a fourteen-year-old boy, he retired to a grove of trees to ask God which church of all the churches on earth was true.

But the real story is far afield from what the LDS Church teaches people today. First of all, road survey records indicate that Joseph Smith could not have even lived in the area he claimed to until he was either sixteen- or seventeen-years-old. That would have been around 1823, the same year when Joseph Smith claimed an angel named Moroni visited him about some buried golden plates. What does this imply?

There was no first vision.

No journal from the time contains anything about a young teen claiming to have seen God. No biography or autobiography, no clergyman's personal journal, no newspaper, mention a first vision, even though the newspapers and journals of the day were full of claims that a teen claimed to discover golden plates.

Why nothing about a first vision? It was created later, folks.

Not even a record from Joseph Smith himself referenced a first vision until almost twenty years *after the supposed fact*! Look at the first published Mormon history, collaborated on by Joseph Smith and Oliver Cowdery in 1834; it ignored the event altogether! And then, once attempts to create "a first vision" came about, they completely contradict each other. Don't believe me? Watch our archived shows in February and March of 2007 on the First vision – it will blow your mind (www.hotm.tv).

Friends, God warns us in the Old Testament:

> Jeremiah 14:14. *The prophets prophesy lies in my name: I sent them not, neither have I commanded them, neither spake unto them: they*

> *prophesy unto you a false vision and divination, and a thing of nought, and the deceit of their heart.*

So we move on.

Before, during, and after the fictional "first vision," Joseph Smith spent many years with his father *scrying* (seeing or peeping) for buried treasure using a peep stone in a hat. Then, after a long night of scanning the dark land for buried booty, the night of the autumnal equinox in 1823 (which, according to folklore magic was the best day of the year to find buried gold), Joseph claims to have retired to his room for the night when an angel by the name of Moroni appears to him and tells him there are some golden plates buried in a hill by his home. Long story short, and some six or seven years later, Joseph tells people he is finally to be allowed by the angel to obtain these golden plates and translate them.

How does he do it? He does it with the very same rock-in-the-hat trick he used with his father to locate buried treasure. (If you don't believe me, go to www.utlm.org and read about it from LDS archives.) Now, unknown to the majority of Mormons today but according to Joseph Smith himself, many "spirits from the past" had constant interaction with Joseph teaching him about and assisting him with the supposed translation. (If you don't believe me, read Dan Vogel's book, *Joseph Smith: The making of a Prophet,* or go to www.utlm.org.) Once the book was done, Joseph Smith Jr. called it the *Book of Mormon*. What did it supposedly contain? A history of the American Indians and another witness of Jesus Christ coming to America.

But what did it really contain? A compilation of thoughts, themes, topics, and direct quotations from sources readily available and popular in Joseph Smith's locale. Much of it can be construed as biographical, including themes of the Smith family's wanderings, the failures of his father, the strength of one early character named Nephi and even the use of seer stones. The book contains impossible to explain blunders, including quotes from the Bible (errors and all); the anachronistic use of Greek names which would not have been available to the fictional *Book of Mormon* people; and great narrative incongruities. A comparison of the towns in the *Book of Mormon* to the towns around the Smith home at the time is almost comical.

But perhaps most revealing are the popular nineteenth century topics which were rampantly discussed by people in and around where Joseph Smith lived. Somehow the following found their way into the *Book of Mormon* narrative, including:

- Anti-Catholic themes
- Anti-Masonry themes
- Mound building myths
- Market economy topics
- Anti-Jacksonian messages
- An agrarian work ethic
- Anti-deism themes
- What the name of God's church needs to be
- A number of popular Indian themes
- Fears of tyranny and anarchy
- Joseph Smith's own name
- Revivalistic language
- Puritan idiom
- Origins of the American Indians
- A whole host of other thoughts promoted by Campbellite restorationists
- And the promotion of a national theocracy

The Book of Mormon also included a litany of plagiarized ideas, words, sentences and paragraphs from other authors. As stated, Joseph borrowed mostly liberally from the Bible (using King James English, by the way) but he also borrowed manuscript ideas from everything from Ethan Smith's *A View of the Hebrews* and the local newspapers to direct quotes taken verbatim from popular preachers of the day! To top the whole thing off, Joseph added in a number of prophecies after the fact, just to make the thing sound historical. These include references to Columbus discovering America, the gathering of Israel, early American colonizing, Jesus' birth, death, and resurrection, and an impossible to prove (at the time) description of whole civilizations of people called Nephites and Lamanites who battled it out in a mega turf war using steel swords and armor, of which not one piece of evidence remains anywhere in the world today!

The book was published. When the reader gets to around the fourteenth page, he can read a very interesting story supposedly taken from the golden plates. It is located in 1 Nephi chapter 8. Nephi's father recounts *a dream* he's had (remember Joseph's father's dream I described earlier?) and it starts this way:

> 1 Nephi 8:2. And it came to pass that as *my father* tarried in the wilderness he spake unto us, saying: Behold, I have dreamed a dream; or in other words, I have seen a vision.
>
> 1 Nephi 8:5-7. And it came to pass that I saw ***a man***, and he was dressed in a white robe; and he came and stood before me. And it came to pass that he spake unto me, and ***bade me follow him***. And it came to pass that as I followed him I beheld myself that I was in a ***dark and dreary waste*** …
>
> 1 Nephi 8:9-17. And it came to pass after I had prayed unto the Lord I behold a ***large and spacious field***. And it came to pass that I beheld ***a tree, whose fruit was desirable*** to make one happy. And it came to pass that did go forth and partake of the fruit thereof; and I beheld that it was ***most sweet, above all that I ever before tasted***. Yea, and I beheld that the fruit thereof was ***white, to exceed***

> ***all the whiteness that I had ever seen.*** And as I partook of the fruit thereof it filled my soul with exceedingly ***great joy***; wherefore, I began to be ***desirous that my family should partake of it*** also; for I knew that it was desirable above all other fruit. And I cast my eyes round about, that perhaps I might discover my family also, I beheld ***a river of water***, and it ran along and it was near the tree of which I was partaking the fruit. And I looked to behold from whence it came; and I saw the head thereof a little way off; and at the head thereof I beheld your mother Sariah, and Sam, and Nephi; and they stood as if they knew not whither they should go. And it came to pass that I beckoned unto them; and I also did say unto them with a loud voice that they should come unto me, and partake of the fruit, which was desirable above all other fruit. And it came to pass that they did come unto me and partake of the fruit also. And it came to pass that ***I was desirous that Laman and Lemuel*** should come and partake of the fruit also; wherefore, I cast mine eyes towards the head of the river, that perhaps I might see them …
>
> 1 Nephi 8:19-20. And I beheld a ***rod of iron***, and it ***extended along the bank*** of the river, and led to the tree by which I stood. And I also beheld a strait and narrow path, which came along by the rod of iron, even to the tree by which I stood; and it also led by the head of the fountain unto a ***large and spacious field, as if it had been a world …***
>
> 1 Nephi 8:26-27. And I also cast my eyes round about, and beheld, on the other side of the river of water, ***a great and spacious building***; and it ***stood as it were in the air, high above the earth.*** And it was ***filled with people***, both old and young , both male and female; and their ***manner of dress was exceedingly fine***; and they were in the attitude of mocking and pointing their fingers towards those who had come at and were partaking of the fruit …

Later, after seeing the tree in a vision of his own, the angel in the vision asks Nephi,

> 1 Nephi 11:21, 22. Knowest thou the meaning of the tree which thy father saw? And I answered him, saying: yea, ***it is the love of God*** ... wherefore, it is the most desirable above all things

Friends, ask yourselves: where have you heard of this dream before? How many times did Joseph's father recount it to him before he incorporated it into his Book of Mormon?

Jesus said:

> Matthew 24:24. *For there shall arise false Christs, and false prophets, and shall shew great signs and wonders; insomuch that, if it were possible, they shall deceive the very elect.*

Deceive Joseph did, because his stories and tales, such as his father's own dream that he turned into scripture, moved many good honest God-seeking people to embrace this counterfeit and follow him.

Now while purporting to translate the Book of Mormon, Joseph claims to have received a visit from John the Baptist, who bestowed upon him the authority to baptize; he then claimed to hold a fictitious priesthood that he called by the name Melchizedek. But again – again, my friends – the story of these visitations were created after the fact, to fill in the blanks of Joseph Smith's ever morphing religious fraud.

How can I say this? Listen to the following facts.

Soon after the Book of Mormon was published, in April of 1830, the Mormon Church, then called the Church of Christ, was organized. Prior to this official event, both Joseph Smith and Oliver Cowdery had baptized each other in the Susquehanna River. Shortly thereafter, when Joseph and Oliver were at David Whitmer's home, they received additional authority, but were told that a meeting would be held where they could ordain each other using this new found power. So they received the calling to ordain each other and then they performed the ordaining at the first Church meeting on April 6, 1830. But there was no mention of any angels or resurrected men stepping in and giving them the authority!

Again, LISTEN to the truth!

In being called to baptize one another, and then in baptizing one another, and in being authorized to ordain each other "elders" so as to "give the gift of the Holy Ghost," *no angelic ministrations are mentioned anywhere, at all*, until years later.

In the LDS *Book of Commandments*, chapter 24:1-12 – which was a precursor book to the *Doctrine and Covenants* – an outline is given for what qualified Joseph Smith to have the authority to found the Church. It says his qualifications are that:

1. He had received a remission of his sins;
2. He had received a call to this holy work by the angel who had given him the means to translate the *Book of Mormon*;
3. Angels had showed the book to others "confirming" it to them;
4. The Church of Christ was organized on April 6, 1830;
5. On that same day, Joseph Smith and Oliver Cowdery ordained each other "elders," having been called of God to do so; and
6. By these great witnesses (the "elders" of the Church) all will be judged.

There is no mention of angelic visitors named John the Baptist or Peter, James, and John stepping in and transferring any supposed authority by the laying on of hands. One of the witnesses to the Book of Mormon, David Whitmer, when interviewed in

1885, said there was never anything about any visits of John the Baptist or Peter James and John – at first.

One time member of the faith, William E. McLellin, recorded ("Notebook of William E. McLellin," page 10, as cited in Palmer, *An Insider's View of Mormon Origins*, page 224):

> I joined the church in 1831. For years I never heard of John the Baptist ordaining Joseph and Oliver. I heard not of James, Peter, and John doing so.

He later continued (Palmer, page 224):

> I heard Joseph tell his experience of his ordination [by Cowdery] and the organization of the church, probably, more than twenty-times, to persons who, near the rise of the church, wished to know and hear about it. I never heard of Moroni, John [the Baptist] or Peter, James, and John.

It wasn't until 1834, four years after the establishing the Church, that Joseph Smith mentions that the "*priesthood 'office' had 'been conferred upon me by the ministering* [sic] *of the Angel of God* (Palmer, page 226) ..."

It wasn't until September of 1834 that Oliver Cowdery made his official announcement about these heavenly ordinations. Why? Because, like so many other very important issues in Mormonism, they too were added to the script later!

For more information on this go the 2007 archives at www.hotm.tv and watch program number 21.

Under the tutelage of Joseph Smith's fraudulent and mesmerizing ways, the church grew, fueled by extreme millennial fervor. What many people do not realize is that the early Mormons were convinced that the end was near and that it was their sacred duty to prepare the world for Jesus to come and reign. In a very short order everything Joseph Smith did, directed, or demanded was couched in the theme that *Jesus is coming and we have to prepare the world through our righteousness for His arrival.* This was the fuel that energized everything early Mormonism did.

When things got tough, Joseph had a fantastic knack for introducing new revelations, new practices, and newly revealed doctrine which would serve to unsettle growing suspicions of charismatic fraud and re-direct early believers' efforts *toward* the cause instead of away from it. With a move to Kirkland Ohio and the trials that came with it, Joseph introduced a miraculous translation of some Egyptian scrolls – saying they were father Abraham's writings – and making them more new scripture.

Suffice it to say, between 1830 and his death, Joseph introduced a tremendous amount of "prophesying" and "official proclamations and promises of the Lord" many of which fell flat, leaving the Saints without a lot of faith in the man or His office of prophet, seer and revelator. John Corrill, a once-faithful LDS man, explained, at the end of his 1839 account of early Mormonism, why he had abandoned it all together (Bushman, page 379):

> When I retrace our track, and view the doings of the church for six years past, I can see nothing that convinces me that God has been our leader; calculation after calculation has failed, and plan after plan has been overthrown, and our prophet seemed not to know the event until too late. If he said go up and prosper, still we did not prosper; but have labored and toiled, and waded through trials, difficulties, and temptations, of various kinds, in hope of deliverance. But no deliverance came.

LDS historian and author Richard Bushman confirms matter-of-factly, *"Everything Corrill said was true."*

With a final move to Nauvoo, Illinois, the early LDS church entered into what I call, Joseph Smith's unrestrained years. Here, temples took on new and more Masonic meaning. Here, Joseph added unto himself dozens and dozens of wives – all secretly kept from the knowledge of his devoted wife, Emma, and some as young as 15.

It was in Nauvoo that Mormonism first began to foster and embrace temporal prosperity and political muscle. Few things pleased Joseph more. It was his kingdom of power, which, in my opinion, became far more important to Mormonism than truly preparing for the Kingdom of God. A letter written by Joseph and littered with this new "prosperity and power" hyperbole was sent abroad which said, in part (*History of the Church* 4:271):

> … [L]et the brethren who love the **prosperity** of Zion, who are anxious that her stakes should be **strengthened**, and her cords **lengthened**, and who prefer her **prosperity** to their chief joy, come and cast in their lots with us, and cheerfully engage in **a work so glorious and sublime**, and say with Nehemiah, "We, His servants will arise and build."

If you close your eyes and listen, you can literally hear these same sentiments echoed through the ages by subsequent LDS prophets like Gordon B. Hinckley.

No longer was Joseph pointing to the immediate return of Jesus as the answer to the wanting and troubled Saints; he had now entered into the newest and final phase of his life by offering the instant gratification of temporal success to anyone who sought to serve both God and mammon. Listen, for instance, to a segment from the Doctrine and Covenants section 124. Here, Joseph seems to make an attempt to command the Saints in Nauvoo to build a hotel – with God as voice. Speaking of the Nauvoo hotel investment scheme, Joseph has God say (just listen to this garbage):

> D&C 124:64, 65, 71. And they shall not receive less than fifty dollars for a share of stock in that house, and they shall be permitted to receive fifteen thousand dollars from any one man for stock in that house. But they shall not be permitted to receive over fifteen thousand dollars from any one man ... And if they do appropriate any portion of that stock anywhere else, only in that house, without the consent of the stockholder, and do not repay fourfold for the stock which they appropriate anywhere else, only in that house, *THEY SHALL BE ACCURSED*, and shall be moved out of their place, *SAITH THE LORD GOD; FOR I THE LORD*, am *GOD*, and cannot be mocked in any of these things [all emphases Shawn's]

This man had NO FEAR in speaking for God. None.

It is really interesting to watch as one phase of Joseph's methods sort of dies (Jesus, redemption, doctrine) as another phase begins to take hold (money, multiple wives, and him being President of the United States).

Even the Book of Mormon, in the Nauvoo years, seemed to take a back seat. After Oliver Cowdery apostatized, he took one of the two manuscripts of the Book of Mormon with him. The other manuscript Joseph decided to bury in the cornerstone of the Nauvoo house, and interrupted the ceremony of laying the stone to run and get the last remaining manuscript. Ebenezer Robinson, a faithful Latter-day Saint and printer in Nauvoo was shocked to hear Joseph say, as he scanned through the manuscript to ensure it was intact (Ernest H. Taves, *Trouble Enough: Joseph Smith and the Book of Mormon*, page 160):

I have had enough trouble with this thing.

Imagine an ancient scribe saying this about the book of Isaiah or a Christian saying that about the New Testament? But Joseph, like the Mormon Church today, was at this point only using the Book of Mormon as bait to his truest ambition which was total, uninhibited power.

By 1842, Nauvoo became the home to one of the most impressive military presences in America at the time. Just stop and think about this for a moment. This military presence was *established* by the founder of the Mormon religion. Why? With the increased growth and power of Nauvoo, Joseph's ambitions for power became more and more vocal. He began to see Nauvoo as the capital of international religion, a world power, as so stated in Doctrine and Covenants 133:7-9. This is the drive of Mormonism today: world power, world control, and the complete infiltration of the earth.

Back in Nauvoo, Joseph reminded the members at their October conference that "Zion" (our topic for this section) was to "*become the praise, the joy, and the glory of* ***the whole earth*** (Bushman, page 407; emphasis Shawn's)."

Funny, but the Bible tends to apply such appellations of praise and joy and glory to Jesus.

Joseph dictated Doctrine and Covenants 124, a revealing proclamation to "*all the KINGS of the world* (verse 3; emphasis Shawn's)," in the spring of 1841, which said, in part, that the powers of the earth were to "*give heed to the light and glory of Zion for the set time has come to favor her* (verse 6)." He also wrote that Nauvoo's temple would "*undoubtedly attract the attention of the great men of the earth (Times & Seasons,* June 1, 1841, 424-425, as cited in Bushman, page 413)."

Joseph proclaimed:

> D&C 124:11. Awake, O kings of the earth! Come ye, O! Come ye with your gold and your silver to the help of my people, to the house of the daughters of Zion.

This arrogance, this *lust of the flesh, lust of the eyes, and pride of life* which John tells us is "*not of the Father but is of the world* (1 John 2:16)" had set in Joseph's heart completely and become the foundation of Mormonism today. Don't believe me? Just look at the general attitude of its most prominent members.

After escaping from the long arm of the law in Missouri, he returned to Nauvoo and called the Saints to gather at a grove. There, in a speech, he said (*History of the Church* 5:466-467),

> I feel as strong as a giant … Relative to our city charter, courts, right of habeas corpus, etc… . I wish you to know and publish that we have all power; and if any man from this time forth says anything to the contrary, cast it into his teeth … All the power there was in Illinois she gave to Nauvoo; and any man that says to the contrary is a fool … This city has all the power that the state courts have … the time has come when forbearance is no longer a virtue; and if you or I are again taken unlawfully, you are at liberty to give loose to blood and thunder … But before I will bear this unhallowed persecution any longer—before I will be dragged away again among my enemies for trial, I will spill the last drop of blood in my veins, and will see all my enemies in hell! ... I wish the lawyer who says we have no powers in Nauvoo may be choked to death with his own words. Don't employ lawyers, or pay them money for their knowledge, for I have learned that they don't know anything. I know more than they all.

This stuff is certainly *NOT* the gospel of Jesus Christ! It is from the imaginations, the ego, and the flesh of man.

In the last years of Joseph Smith's life, he came to prefer the title of "General" to that of "prophet" or President of the Church. Oozing with military might the LDS prophet pranced about in a blue and gold braided uniform, high military boots, and a chapeau topped with flowing ostrich feathers. In 1844, a United States artillery officer witnessed a full-dress parade of the Mormon militia (which was nearly 3000 strong) and wrote an article on it in the *New York Herald*. He described them as (June 17, 1842):

> a fearful host, filled with religious enthusiasm, and led by ambitious and talented officers ... the time will come when this gathering host of religious fanatics will make this country shake to its center. A western empire is certain.

To be sure, Mormonism – almost from its beginning – has sought, fought, strived, and worked to become the world political power. Joseph Smith's ultimate intentions were to establish what he called the "Kingdom of God" here on earth. Understand that, to Mormons back then, and to Mormons today, the Kingdom of God is *MORMONISM*. It is not a mixture of believers. It is not a body of believers. It is not an interfaith or non-denominational approach. It is Mormonism. And it has been the intentions of Mormon leaders since 1840 for MORMONISM to take over the world.

On March 11, 1844, Joseph began to organize what he hoped would eventually become a sovereign Mormon state – Missouri – and he secretly formed a council of fifty "princes" to become "the highest court on earth (Fawn Brodie, *No Man Knows My History*, page 356)." One of the first actions of the council was to "ordain" Joseph Smith as *"King of the Kingdom of God* (Bushman, page 523)." In light of this ordination, Joseph Smith said of himself (Bushman, page 521):

> I calculate to be one of the Instruments of setting up the Kingdom of Daniel by the word of the Lord, and I intend to lay a foundation that will revolutionize the whole world...it will not be by the Sword or Gun that this Kingdom will roll on—the power of truth is such that—all nations will be under the *NECESSITY* of OBEYING the Gospel (emphasis Shawn's).

The political ambitions and rhetoric of Mormonism's founder went on and on, culminating in his running for president of the United States. "*Well,*" you may be saying to yourself, "*Joseph Smith was a long time ago, and Mormonism has moved well beyond the days of militias, political motives, and the goal of world theocratic domination.*"

I could not differ more.

In fact, we will be spending much time in the near future analyzing early and present day attempts by the LDS church to establish what they call "Zion" here on earth, with its Kingdom headquarters, what they call the *New Jerusalem*, located right here in the United States of America.

Hang on to your hats, folks.

If you want to know more about
Mormonism or biblical Christianity, you can
contact us in the following ways:

phone: 1-888-868-4686
email: shawn @alatheamedia.com
mail: 4760 Highland Drive #515
Salt Lake City, Utah 84117

website: www.hotm.tv
www.bornagainmormon.com
www.alatheaministries.com
www.campus.com

www.youtube.com/shawnmccraney